:::Forbes
TRAVEL GUIDE
Formerly Mobil Travel Guide

NEW ENGLAND
2011

ACKNOWLEDGMENTS

We gratefully acknowledge the help of our representatives for their efficient and perceptive inspections of the lodgings listed. Forbes Travel Guide is also grateful to the talented writers who contributed to this book.

Front Cover image: ©iStockphoto.com
All maps: Mapping Specialists

ISBN: 9781936010875
Manufactured in the USA
10 9 8 7 6 5 4 3 2 1

CONTENTS

STAR ATTRACTIONS

If you've been a reader of Mobil Travel Guide, you will have heard that this historic brand partnered in 2009 with another storied media name, Forbes, to create a new entity, Forbes Travel Guide. For more than 50 years, Mobil Travel Guide assisted travelers in making smart decisions about where to stay and dine when traveling. With this new partnership, our mission has not changed: We're committed to the same rigorous inspections of hotels, restaurants and spas—the most comprehensive in the industry with more than 500 standards tested at each property we visit—to help you cut through the clutter and make easy and informed decisions on where to spend your time and travel budget. Our team of anonymous inspectors are constantly on the road, sleeping in hotels, eating in restaurants and making spa appointments, evaluating those exacting standards to determine a property's rating.

What kinds of standards are we looking for when we visit a property? We're looking for more than just high-thread count sheets, pristine spa treatment rooms and white linen-topped tables. We look for service that's attentive, individualized and unforgettable. We note how long it takes to be greeted when you sit down at your table, or to be served when you order room service, or whether the hotel staff can confidently help you when you've forgotten that one essential item that will make or break your trip. Unlike any other travel ratings entity, we visit each place we rate, testing hundreds of attributes to compile our ratings, and our ratings cannot be bought or influenced. The Forbes Five Star rating is the most prestigious achievement in hospitality—while we rate more than 5,000 properties in the U.S., Canada, Hong Kong, Macau and Beijing, for 2011, we have awarded Five Star designations to only 54 hotels, 23 restaurants and 20 spas. When you travel with Forbes, you can travel with confidence, knowing that you'll get the very best experience, no matter who you are.

We understand the importance of making the most of your time. That's why the most trusted name in travel is now Forbes Travel Guide.

STAR RATED HOTELS

Whether you're looking for the ultimate in luxury or the best value for your travel budget, we have a hotel recommendation for you. To help you pinpoint properties that meet your needs, Forbes Travel Guide classifies each lodging by type according to the following characteristics:

★★★★★These exceptional properties provide a memorable experience through virtually flawless service and the finest of amenities. Staff are intuitive, engaging and passionate, and eagerly deliver service above and beyond the guests' expectations. The hotel was designed with the guest's comfort in mind, with particular attention paid to craftsmanship and quality of product. A Five-Star property is a destination unto itself.

★★★★These properties provide a distinctive setting, and a guest will find many interesting and inviting elements to enjoy throughout the property. Attention to detail is prominent throughout the property, from design concept to quality of products provided. Staff are accommodating and take pride in catering to the guest's specific needs throughout their stay.

★★★These well-appointed establishments have enhanced amenities that provide travelers with a strong sense of location, whether for style or function. They may have a distinguishing style and ambience in both the public spaces and guest rooms; or they may be more focused on functionality, providing guests with easy access to local events, meetings or tourism highlights.

Recommended: These hotels are considered clean, comfortable and reliable establishments that have expanded amenities, such as full-service restaurants.

For every property, we also provide pricing information. All prices quoted are accurate at the time of publication; however, prices cannot be guaranteed. Because rates can fluctuate, we list a pricing range rather than specific prices.

STAR RATED RESTAURANTS

Every restaurant in this book has been visited by Forbes Travel Guide's team of experts and comes highly recommended as an outstanding dining experience.

★★★★★Forbes Five-Star restaurants deliver a truly unique and distinctive dining experience. A Five-Star restaurant consistently provides exceptional food, superlative service and elegant décor. An emphasis is placed on originality and personalized, attentive and discreet service. Every detail that surrounds the experience is attended to by a warm and gracious dining room team.

★★★★These are exciting restaurants with often well-known chefs that feature creative and complex foods and emphasize various culinary techniques and a focus on seasonality. A highly-trained dining room staff provides refined personal service and attention.

★★★Three Star restaurants offer skillfully prepared food with a focus on a specific style or cuisine. The dining room staff provides warm and professional service in a comfortable atmosphere. The décor is well-coordinated with quality fixtures and decorative items, and promotes a comfortable ambience.

Recommended: These restaurants serve fresh food in a clean setting with efficient service. Value is considered in this category, as is family friendliness.

Because menu prices can fluctuate, we list a pricing range rather than specific prices. The pricing ranges are per diner, and assume that you order an appetizer or dessert, an entrée and one drink.

STAR RATED SPAS

Forbes Travel Guide's spa ratings are based on objective evaluations of more than 450 attributes. About half of these criteria assess basic expectations, such as staff courtesy, the technical proficiency and skill of the employees and whether the facility is clean and maintained properly. Several standards address issues that impact a guest's physical comfort and convenience, as well as the staff's ability to impart a sense of personalized service. Additional criteria measure the spa's ability to create a completely calming ambience.

★★★★★ Stepping foot in a Five Star Spa will result in an exceptional experience with no detail overlooked. These properties wow their guests with extraordinary design and facilities, and uncompromising service. Expert staff cater to your every whim and pamper you with the most advanced treatments and skin care lines available. These spas often offer exclusive treatments and may emphasize local elements.

★★★★ Four Star spas provide a wonderful experience in an inviting and serene environment. A sense of personalized service is evident from the moment you check in and receive your robe and slippers. The guest's comfort is always of utmost concern to the well-trained staff.

★★★ These spas offer well-appointed facilities with a full complement of staff to ensure that guests' needs are met. The spa facil ties include clean and appealing treatment rooms, changing areas and a welcoming reception desk.

TOP HOTELS, RESTAURANTS AND SPAS

HOTELS

★★★★★FIVE STAR

Blantyre *(Lenox, Massachusetts)*

Boston Harbor Hotel
(Boston, Massachusetts)

Four Seasons Hotel Boston
(Boston, Massachusetts)

Mayflower Inn & Spa
(Washington, Connecticut)

Twin Farms *(Barnard, Vermont)*

★★★★FOUR STAR

Charlotte Inn
(Edgartown, Massachusetts)

Hotel Le St. James
(Montreal, Quebec)

Mandarin Oriental, Boston
(Boston, Massachusetts)

The Ritz-Carlton, Boston Common
(Boston, Massachusetts)

Taj Boston *(Boston, Massachusetts)*

The Wauwinet
(Nantucket, Massachusetts)

Wequassett Resort and Golf Club
(Chatham, Massachusetts)

The White Barn Inn
(Kennebunkport, Maine)

XV Beacon, Boston
(Boston, Massachusetts)

RESTAURANTS

★★★★★FIVE STAR

The White Barn Inn Restaurant
(Kennebunkport, Maine)

★★★★FOUR STAR

Asana *(Boston, Massachusetts)*

Clio *(Boston, Massachusetts)*

L'Eau à la Bouche
(Sainte-Adele, Quebec)

L'Espalier *(Boston, Massachusetts)*

Menton *(Boston, Massachusetts)*

Meritage *(Boston, Massachusetts)*

Mill's Tavern
(Providence, Rhode Island)

No. 9 Park *(Boston, Massachusetts)*

Restaurant Initiale
(Quebec City, Quebec)

Rialto *(Cambridge, Massachusetts)*

Toppers *(Nantucket, Massachusetts)*

Toque! *(Montreal, Quebec)*

Twenty-Eight Atlantic
(Chatham, Massachusetts)

SPAS

★★★★★FIVE STAR

Spa at Mandarin Oriental *(Boston, Massachusetts)*
Mayflower Spa *(Washington, Connecticut)*

★★★★FOUR STAR

The White Barn Inn Spa *(Kennebunkport, Maine)*

WELCOME TO CONNECTICUT

WHEN SOME PEOPLE THINK OF CONNECTICUT, THEY

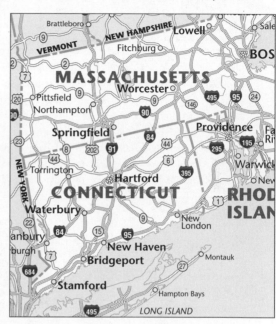

envision khaki-clad millionaires sipping martinis on manicured Greenwich lawns. Others call to mind the state's capital city, Hartford, home to insurance companies and the country's first newspaper. Still others think of charming Mystic and the southeastern coastal area that has been wildly popular ever since Julia Roberts' performance in the film *Mystic Pizza* (1988). Some will picture the state's quiet northwestern and northeastern corners, full of rambling old farmhouses and hilly country roads. All would be correct.

Located in the Northeastern United States, Connecticut is part of the six-state New England region, though it's also counted among the tri-state New York area. This small but densely populated state packs 3 ½ million residents into just 4,844 square miles of land. Connecticut's Fairfield County, a tendril of the New York City metro area, is the most populous area of the states with over 900,000 residents. Hartford was long regarded as the home-state metropolis, but lately it's being eclipsed by New Haven—as of the 2000 census, New Haven (123,626) edged out Hartford (121,578) by about 2,000 residents. The Connecticut economy is famous for its high productivity and wealth of resources, two things that enabled manufacturing and financial industries to flourish. Today, the state's industry revolves around agriculture, manufacturing and insurance. But most travelers will continue to remember it fondly as a beautiful state full of grand old summer homes, endless green pastures, soft sand beaches and the occasional fleet of mega yachts.

HIGHLIGHTS

CONNECTICUT'S BEST ATTRACTIONS

GREENWICH
One of the wealthiest towns in the country, Greenwich boasts a broad spectrum of upscale shopping. World-famous designers and ritzy boutiques grace the community's well-manicured streets, which makes window-shopping just as pleasurable.

MYSTIC SEAPORT
Pique your aquatic curiosity at the nation's largest maritime museum. You can tour ships from the 1800s, explore a working shipyard or play at the children's museum. Don't forget to grab a slab of Italian pie at the film-famed Mystic Pizza parlor on Main Street.

YALE REPERTORY THEATER
This award-winning stage features a diverse collection of fare, everything from Shakespeare to avant-garde contemporary plays. And who knows, maybe you'll catch a rising star. Jodie Foster and Dan Aykroyd are just two of the theater's famous alums.

MAYFLOWER INN AND SPA
Conduct your morning asanas in the outdoor yoga and meditation garden, then relax with a steeprock stone massage or hydrating facial at the New England country-style retreat.

MYSTIC COUNTRY

Connecticut's nautical capital, Mystic Country offers a counterpoint to the big spenders and big brains found westerly along the state's coast. The town of Mystic, in fact, was a shipbuilding and whaling center from the 17th and 19th centuries. Today, the town is more famous for its world-class aquarium and maritime museum, not to mention its status as the setting for *Mystic Pizza*, a film that persists to lure visitors despite its more than 20-year vintage.

New London is another of those classic New England seafaring towns. Located at the mouth of the Thames River, just ten miles from Mystic, it boasts one of the finest deep-water ports on the Atlantic coast, something that once enabled whalers to amass fortunes here. Today, the town still welcomes submarines, yachts and ship of all sorts, though the economy has moved onshore with steel, pharmaceuticals and high-tech manufacturing dominating the scene. For more industrial sights, travel 13 miles upriver to the colorful port and manufacturing center of Norwich. Here in 1766 was the nation's first paper mill, which set the cornerstone for a primary industry. Norwich is also a great place to explore Native American history.

WHAT TO SEE

MYSTIC

DENISON HOMESTEAD
120 Pequotsepos Road, Mystic, 860-536-9248; www.denisonsociety.org

Continuously owned by the Denison family, this 1717 colonial farmhouse is full of heirlooms from 11 generations of a single family—each room reflects a different period in the family's history. The home is surrounded by 200 acres of woodlands, meadows and nature trails. Guided tours are available.

Late May-mid-October, Friday-Monday afternoons, closed Tuesday-Thursday; all other times, by appointment.

MYSTIC AQUARIUM
55 Coogan Blvd., Mystic, 860-572-5955; www.mysticaquarium.org

The exhibits here feature more than 6,000 live specimens from around the world, including dolphins, sea lions and the only captive whales in New England. Young and old alike are delighted by Seal Island, an outdoor exhibit featuring seals and sea lions in natural settings, as well as the bustling penguin pavilion. The facility also includes Dr. Robert Ballard's Institute for Exploration, dedicated to searching the deep seas for lost ships. The museum's Challenge of the Deep exhibit allows visitors to use state-of-the-art technology to re-create the search for the Titanic or explore the biology of undersea ocean vents.

Admission: adults $26, seniors $23, children 3-17 $19, children 2 and under free. Combination ticket with Seaport: adults $55, seniors $50, children 6-17 $40, children 3-5 $22, children 2 and under free. Daily; hours vary by season.

HIGHLIGHT

WHAT'S THE NEWEST ATTRACTION IN MYSTIC COUNTRY?

In the verdant countryside of eastern Connecticut, a pair of glittering, Vegas-style casino-resorts are seen towering above the treeline. While the Foxwoods Resort Casino has been an unlikely fixture of this landscape since the late 1990s, the gargantuan MGM Grand at Foxwoods is a new development. Inside these developments, a visitor finds endless shopping, plenty of restaurants, big-ticket concerts and, yes, gambling galore. Garish as the sprawling casino campus may seem, however, it's not without New England-style class. Luxury hotel accommodations and topnotch spa services are also part of the package.

MYSTIC SEAPORT
75 Greenmanville Ave., Mystic, 860-572-5315; www.mysticseaport.org

This 17-acre complex is the nation's largest maritime museum, dedicated to the preservation of 19th-century oceanic history. Visitors can board the 1841 wooden whale ship Charles W. Morgan, the square-rigged ship Joseph Conrad or the fishing schooner L.A. Dunton. The collections also include some 400 smaller vessels; a representative seaport community with historic homes and waterfront industries; and a working shipyard, children's museum and planetarium.

Admission: adults $24, seniors $22, children 6-17 $15, children 5 and under free. Combination ticket with Aquarium: adults $55, seniors $50, children 6-17 $40, children 3-5 $22, children 2 and under free. May-October, daily 9 a.m.-5 p.m., November-November 25, daily 10 a.m.-4 p.m.; November 26-late March, Thursday-Sunday 10 a.m.-4 p.m.

NORWICH

INDIAN LEAP
Yantic and Sachem streets, Norwich, 860-886-4683

These falls were once a favorite resort and outpost of the Mohegans (more popularly known as the Mohicans). Legend has it that a band of Narragansetts, unfamiliar with the area, reached this treacherous point while fleeing the Mohegans during the 1643 Battle of Great Plain. Many Narragansetts chose to leap to their deaths rather than surrender. Today, newcomers can enjoy this natural wonder without threat of being chased.

ROYAL MOHEGAN BURIAL GROUNDS
Sachem and Washington streets, Norwich, 860-862-6390; www.mohegan.nsn.us

Located on a hillside above the falls, these are the scraps of an old burial ground. A few graves remain, however, including a prominent memorial to Samuel Uncas, descendent of Chief Uncas of the Mohicans.

TANTAQUIDGEON INDIAN MUSEUM
1819 Norwich-New London Turnpike, Uncasville, 860-848-0594; www.mohegan.nsn.us

This one-room, fieldstone museum was founded in 1930 by father and son, Mohegans who sought to preserve important tribal artifacts and the Mohegan way of life.

May-November, Wednesday-Saturday 10 a.m.-4 p.m.

NEW LONDON

EUGENE O'NEILL THEATER CENTER

305 Great Neck Road, Waterford, 860-443-5378; www.oneilltheatercenter.org

The complex includes the O'Neill Playwrights Conference, the O'Neill Critics Institute, the O'Neill Music Theater Conference, the O'Neill Puppetry Conference and the National Theater Institute. Come summertime, the center presents a series of staged readings of new plays and musicals.

Center open year-round; theater performances run June-August.

JOSHUA HEMPSTEAD HOUSE

11 Hempstead Court, New London, 860-443-7949; www.ctlandmarks.org

The oldest house in the city and one of few remaining 17th century houses in the state, the Hempstead House captures colonial life, thanks in part to the diary Hempstead kept for more than 50 years.

May-June, Saturday-Sunday noon-4 p.m.; July-August, Friday-Sunday noon-4 p.m.; September-October, Saturday-Sunday noon-4 p.m.

LYMAN ALLYN ART MUSEUM

625 Williams St., New London, 860-443-2545; www.lymanallyn.org

Housed in a stately neo-classical building, the museum features more than 10,000 paintings, drawings, prints, sculptures and decorative art created by Americans between the 18th and 20th centuries.

Tuesday-Saturday 10 a.m.-5 p.m., Sunday 1-5 p.m.

MONTE CRISTO COTTAGE

325 Pequot Ave., New London, 860-443-5378; www.oneilltheatercenter.org

The restored boyhood home of Nobel Prize-winning playwright Eugene O'Neill features artifacts and memorabilia, including an O'Neill portrait and poster gallery.

Late May-August, Sunday 1-3 p.m. and Thursday-Saturday noon-4p.m.

NATHANIEL HEMPSTEAD HOUSE

11 Hempstead Court, New London, 860-443-7949; www.ctlandmarks.org

The son of Joshua Hempstead created a comparatively modern home. Today, the structure survives as one of the state's two remaining examples of mid-18th-century cut-stone architecture.

May-June, Saturday-Sunday noon-4 p.m.; July-August, Friday-Sunday noon-4 p.m.; September-October, Saturday-Sunday noon-4 p.m.

OCEAN BEACH PARK

1225 Ocean Ave., New London, 800-510-7263; www.ocean-beach-park.com

Walk the sandy beach or boardwalk, then cool off with a swim in the ocean or in an Olympic-sized pool (complete with waterslide). If that fails to entertain, the park also boasts an amusement arcade and mini-golf.

Late May-August, daily.

SHAW PERKINS MANSION

11 Blinman St., New London, 860-443-1209; www.newlondonhistory.org

Once the state's Naval headquarters during the Revolutionary War, the granite mansion is now a genealogical and historical library, not to mention the

SPECIAL EVENTS

CONNECTICUT STORYTELLING FESTIVAL

Connecticut College, 270 Mohegan Ave., New London, 860-439-2764; www.connstorycenter.org
Designed for people of all ages who want to experience storytelling, the 30th annual festival features nationally acclaimed dancers, musicians and writers leading readings, workshops and concerts.
Late April.

SAILFEST

New London City Pier, Bank St., New London, 860-443-1879; www.sailfest.org
Arts, crafts and food vendors line the streets of downtown New London, while hundreds of people browse, eat and enjoy a weekend of free concerts and other entertainment. The grand finale is the Saturday night fireworks display, the largest on the East Coast.
Early July.

headquarters of the New London County Historical Society.
Wednesday-Friday 1-4 p.m. and Saturday (Mid-May-mid-October) 10 a.m.-4 p.m.

US COAST GUARD ACADEMY
31 Mohegan Ave., New London, 860-444-8444; www.cga.edu
The halls of this federal service academy school buzz with 800 active cadets. Visitors can get a feel for life inside the academy through a multimedia show in the Visitors' Pavilion (May-October daily) and the onsite museum, which includes a 295-foot-long ship called the *Eagle*.
Friday-Sunday, when in port; limited hours.

WHERE TO STAY

MYSTIC
★★★HILTON MYSTIC
20 Coogan Blvd., Mystic, 860-572-0731, 800-774-1500; www.hilton.com
Located on a quiet side street near the noisy Olde Mystic Village, just one block from Interstate 95, this business-oriented hotel is all about location—shopping outlets, the Seaport Museum and the aquarium are all nearby. Avoiding the tourist hoards is easy, so long as you stay inside to mellow out next to the pool.
183 rooms. Restaurant, bar. $151-250

★★★INN AT MYSTIC
3 Williams Ave., Mystic, 860-536-9604, 800-237-2415; www.innatmystic.com
This five-building property is the only inn to overlook both Mystic Harbor and Long Island Sound. Outside, you'll find romantic structures spread over 15 manicured acres, in the center of which sits the 1904 Classical Revival mansion where Lauren Bacall and Humphrey Bogart once honeymooned. Inside, the

rooms come with period furnishings, whirlpools and orchard views.

68 rooms. Restaurant, bar. $151-250

★★★WHALER'S INN

20 E. Main St., Mystic, 860-536-1506, 800-243-2588;
www.whalersinnmystic.com

Homey, comfortable and located in the heart of historic Mystic, the Whaler's Inn is ideal for those seeking an upscale New England bed and breakfast experience. Outside, the 1865 Colonial clapboard oozes charm with its wide front porch and rocking chairs. Inside, rooms are outfitted with Waverly wall coverings, four-poster beds, wingback chairs, and large bathrooms with pedestal sinks and whirlpool tubs. Each guest room comes with a view of the scenic Mystic River—the luckiest guests snag ones with private verandas.

49 rooms. Complimentary breakfast. Restaurant, bar. $151-250

NORWICH

★★★THE SPA AT NORWICH INN

607 W. Thames St., Norwich, 860-886-2401, 800-275-4772;
www.thespaatnorwichinn.com

From the outside, this 42-acre property looks like any other New England country inn. Step across the Norwich Inn's threshold, though, and you're transported to pampering paradise: The 32-room treatment spa offers massages, facials and cutting-edge treatments like hydrotherapy and energy work.

65 rooms. Restaurant, bar. Golf. Fitness center. Pool. $151-250

WHERE TO EAT

MYSTIC

★★★BRAVO BRAVO

20 E. Main St., Mystic, 860-536-3228;
www.ckrestaurantgroup.com

Located at the seaside Whaler's Inn, this local favorite serves creative gourmet dishes like shrimp bruschetta and champagne risotto. Thanks to floor-to-ceiling windows, the spacious dining room is bright and inviting.

Italian. Lunch, dinner. Bar. Reservations recommended. $16-35

WHICH HOTEL HAS THE BEST VIEW?

Inn at Mystic:
With views of Mystic Harbor and Long Island Sound, the inn is a dream whenever you're longing for yachts, sailboats or blue-green vistas. Here, a visitor can start the day with the sun rising over the harbor. Later in the day, you can take a sailboat tour, or spend a lazy evening with the crashing waves and fresh, salty air.

★★★FLOOD TIDE

Inn at Mystic, 3 Williams Avenue, Mystic, 860-536-8140, 800-237-2415; www.mysticinns.com

Complimentary hors d'oeuvres are served in the piano lounge at this water-front restaurant. Comforting dishes such as lobster ravioli, a terrific Sunday brunch and harbor views make this restaurant well worth the trip.

American, Continental. Breakfast, lunch, dinner, Sunday brunch. Bar. Children's menu. Reservations recommended. Outdoor seating. $36-85

RECOMMENDED

MYSTIC

MYSTIC PIZZA

56 W. Main St., Mystic, 860-536-3700; www.mysticpizza.com

Situated in a prime Main Street location, this family-style pizzeria was in business long before it caught the eye of a vacationing screenwriter, who borrowed its name for the 1988 film starring Julia Roberts. The pies persist to be simple and satisfying, with a thin, doughy crust and choice of toppings.

Pizza. Lunch, dinner. $15 and under

NORWICH

KENSINGTON

607 W Thames St., Norwich, 860-886-2401, 866-410-5942; www.thespaatnorwichinn.com

Located at the Spa at Norwich Inn, this upscale restaurant serves contemporary cuisine with a focus on health-conscious choices. Everything from the vegetable cannoli to the ossobuco comes with its nutritional value listed, with most falling firmly in the waistline-friendly range.

American. Breakfast, lunch, dinner, Sunday brunch. Bar. Outdoor seating. $36-85

CENTRAL CONNECTICUT

From the tree-lined streets of New Haven to the river valley that slices Hartford and its surrounding metro, Central Connecticut is so diverse it's hard to encapsulate. One thing's certain, however—the region offers a concentrated lesson in state history, especially where business and politics are concerned. Settled in 1633 on the state's eponymous river, Hartford has a rich history of intellectual and industrial innovation. Here, in one of the nation's earliest cities, visitors can explore the nation's oldest art museum (Wadsworth Atheneum Museum of Art) and public park (Bushnell Park). In the morning, they can take their coffee with the nation's oldest newspaper (Hartford Courant). But Hartford is more than the sum of its artifacts. The city kept evolving over the years, and is now famous for a robust business community—in fact, the concentration of insurance company headquarters earned it the nickname "insurance capital of the world."

As travelers venture south along the Connecticut River, they encounter all manner of classic New England villages: With its idyllic main street, Essex is often described as the "best small town in America." The peaceful hamlet of 6,000 exudes storybook charm in the form of its brick post office, antique shops and 1700s-era mansions, many of which were once owned by successful ship captains. In a similar vein, Old Lyme is an affluent, albeit sleepy, little village with a gorgeously preserved main street and a cache of restored manors. Home to a burgeoning design scene and historic art colony, it's also a great place to get inspired. Meanwhile, in the larger town of Old Saybrook, the original site of Yale College, visitors find a plenty of magnificent summer homes and pristine beaches.

Forty miles south of Hartford, where the river empties into Long Island Sound, is the present home of Yale University—the growing metropolis of New Haven. No doubt every Yale University student knows the historic importance of his or her adopted city: This is where Eli Whitney worked out the principles of mass production, and where Revolutionary War hero Nathan Hale once studied. Today, pilgrims flock to see the country's first planned downtown, the tree-lined New Haven green and its procession of glorious old buildings. Whatever you do, don't let the scenery distract you from the city's other big attraction—the world-class arts organizations affiliated with Yale University, especially the Peabody Museum of Natural History and the Yale Repertory Theater.

WHAT TO SEE

AVON

FARMINGTON VALLEY ARTS CENTER
25 Arts Center Lane, Avon, 860-678-1867; www.artsfvac.org

Located in a historic stone explosives plant, the center features twenty studios occupied by resident artists. Visitors can meet these artists and spy their living quarters during open studio events, or they can simply shop for unique gifts onsite at the Fisher Gallery.

January-October, Wednesday Saturday, Sunday afternoons; November-December daily 9 a.m.-5 p.m.

ESSEX

CONNECTICUT RIVER MUSEUM
67 Main St., Essex, 860-767-8269; www.ctrivermuseum.org

Housed in the last remaining steamboat dock building on the Connecticut River, the museum features exhibits that celebrate the rich cultural heritage and natural resources of the River Valley. The marquee attraction is a full-size operating replica of the *Turtle*, America's first successful submarine.

Tuesday-Sunday 10 a.m.-5 p.m.

ESSEX STEAM TRAM AND RIVERBOAT
1 Railroad Ave., Essex, 860-767-0103, 800-377-3987; www.essexsteamtrain.com

A restored 1930s railcar plows 20 miles through the Connecticut River Valley, from Essex to Chester, with an optional one-hour Connecticut River cruise.

Early May-late October.

FARMINGTON

HILL-STEAD MUSEUM
35 Mountain Road, Farmington, 860-677-4787; www.hillstead.org

A Colonial Revival-style country house, once owned by the prominent Pope family, contains an impressive art collection. Browse 250 photographs

HIGHLIGHTS

WHAT ARE THE BEST PLACES FOR FAMILY FUN IN CENTRAL CONNECTICUT?

ESSEX STEAM TRAIN AND RIVERBOAT

Even if they're past their Thomas the Tank Engine phase, children are sure to be fascinated when you treat them to a scenic trip through the Connecticut River Valley aboard an old-fashioned, coal-fired locomotive.

WADSWORTH ATHENEUM MUSEUM OF ART

Sure, kids like art, but they love the Wadsmorth's "To Catch a Thief" program, an initiative that directs pint-sized detectives to make scavenger hunts through the nation's oldest museum.

YALE UNIVERSITY PEABODY MUSEUM OF NATURAL HISTORY

Here, your little ones can gape at dinosaur skeletons, skulls and other frightening fossils of the Mesozoic Era.

and prints, 290 ceramics and an outstanding cache of French Impressionist paintings by no less than Degas and Monet.

May-October, Tuesday-Sunday 10 a.m.-5 p.m; November-April, Tuesday-Sunday 11 a.m.-4 p.m.

STANLEY-WHITMAN HOUSE

37 High St., Farmington, 860-677-9222; www.stanleywhitman.org

This 1720 home is one of the finest, best-preserved 18th-century houses in the United States. Today, it functions as a heritage museum, with period antiques and history actors that work to recreate the daily realities of colonial life.

May-October, Wednesday-Sunday noon-4 p.m.; November-April, Saturday-Sunday afternoons, also by appointment.

HARTFORD

BUTLER-McCOOK HOMESTEAD AND MAIN STREET HISTORY CENTER

396 Main St., Hartford, 860-522-1806; www.ctlandmarks.org

This preserved 1782 house, occupied by four generations of one family between 1782 and 1971, is the perfect destination for antiques lovers and history buffs: it showcases possessions dating back 200 years, including a collection of Victorian toys and paintings, Japanese armor and a Victorian garden.

Tours: Wednesday, Friday, Saturday and Sunday 11 a.m.-4 p.m. Closed November-April.

HARRIET BEECHER STOWE CENTER

77 Forest St., Hartford, 860-522-9258; www.harrietbeecherstowecenter.org

A fitting tribute to the author of *Uncle Tom's Cabin*, Stowe's Victorian cottage holds more than a cache of well-preserved furniture and personal memorabilia. It also serves as an educational outpost with an emphasis on civil rights and social justice issues.

Tours: Monday-Saturday 9:30 a.m.-4:30 p.m., Sunday noon-4:30 p.m.

MARK TWAIN HOUSE

351 Farmington Ave., Hartford, 860-247-0998; www.marktwainhouse.org

Mark Twain wrote his masterpieces, including *Adventures of Huckleberry Finn*, while living here, a three-story Victorian mansion designed and built in 1874 especially for the writer and his wife. In 2003, the original house received the addition of a sleek museum where visitors can learn even more about this great American author.

Monday-Saturday 9:30 a.m.-5:30 p.m., Sunday noon-5:30 p.m. Closed Tuesday January-March.

MUSEUM OF CONNECTICUT HISTORY

Connecticut State Library, 231 Capitol Ave., Hartford, 860-757-6335; www.museumofcthistory.org

Dedicated to preserving the state's political, industrial and military history, this museum houses everything from contemporary to colonial artifacts, including the original 1662 Royal Charter and portraits of every Connecticut governor. The state's importance to weapons manufacturing is especially well represented by a collection of Colt firearms from the 19th and 20th centuries.

Monday-Friday 9 a.m.-4 p.m., Saturday 9 a.m.-3p.m.

NOAH WEBSTER FOUNDATION AND HISTORICAL SOCIETY

227 S. Main St., West Hartford, 860-521-5362; www.noahwebsterhouse.org

This 18th-century homestead was the birthplace of America's first lexicographer, writer of the Blue-Backed Speller and creator of the first American Dictionary. Today, it serves as a charming history museum and educational center with interpretive displays and literary artifacts.

Thursday-Monday 1-4 p.m.

OLD STATE HOUSE

800 Main St., Hartford, 860-522-6766; www.ctoldstatehouse.org

Completed in 1796, the nation's oldest state house was designed by Charles Bulfinch in the Federal style. Although the state's capitol was moved to its current location in the late nineteenth century, the old state house is packed with historic attractions, including a Victorian-style museum of curiosities and a Gilbert Stuart portrait of George Washington.

October-June, Monday-Friday 10 a.m.-5 p.m.; July-September, Tuesday-Saturday 10 a.m.-5 p.m.

STATE CAPITOL

210 Capitol Ave., Hartford, 860-240-0222; www.cga.ct.gov

Take one-hour guided tours of the restored gold-domed capitol, completed in 1878 in an ornate Victorian style with French and Gothic revival elements.

SPECIAL EVENTS

ARTS AND CRAFTS SHOW

Town Green, Main St., Old Saybrook, 860-388-3266; www.oldsaybrookct.com
Have your pick of jewelry, handbags, handmade confections and other gifts.
More than 200 artisans are represented at this annual craft show.
Late July.

CHRISTMAS TORCHLIGHT PARADE

Main Street, Old Saybrook, 860-388-3266; www.connecticutblues.com
Forty fife-and-drum corps, bagpipe bands and a dozen or so Christmas-themed
floats march together down Main Street as part of this charming nighttime
tradition.
Mid-December.

*Monday-Friday 9:15 a.m.-1:15 p.m.; July-August, Monday-Friday 9:15 a.m.-2:15 p.m.;
April-October, also on Saturday 10:15 a.m.-2:15 p.m.*

UNIVERSITY OF HARTFORD

200 Bloomfield Ave., West Hartford, 860-768-4100; www.hartford.edu
This private institution has 6,844 students spread over a 320-acre, suburban-
style campus. For visitors, the university's numerous arts events are a big
draw—check out a free concert, opera, lecture or art exhibit, many starring
students from The Hartt School, a top-tier conservatory and school of the
performing arts.

WADSWORTH ATHENEUM MUSEUM OF ART

600 Main St., Hartford, 860-278-2670; www.wadsworthatheneum.org
The nation's oldest continuously operating public art museums has more
than 40,000 works of art spanning 5,000 years, everything from 15th century
paintings to modern art, American decorative art and furniture, sculpture and
the Amistad Collection of African-American art.
*Admission: free. Wednesday-Friday 11 a.m.-5 p.m., Saturday-Sunday 10 a.m.-5 p.m.; first
Thursday of each month until 8 p.m.*

OLD LYME
FLORENCE GRISWOLD MUSEUM

96 Lyme St., Old Lyme, 860-434-5542; www.flogris.org
This stately late-Georgian mansion was America's most celebrated art colony
at the turn of the 20th century. It became known as the center of American
impressionism, a.k.a. "the American Giverny," a history handily reflected by the
collections of paintings by Willard Metcalf, Childe Hassam and Edward Rook.

Krieble Gallery: Tuesday-Saturday 10 a.m.-5 p.m., Sunday 1-5 p.m. Chadwick Studio: mid-May-October.

OLD SAYBROOK

FORT SAYBROOK MONUMENT PARK
Highway 154, Saybrook Point, Old Saybrook, 860-395-3152; www.oldsaybrookct.org

This 18-acre park is peppered with the remains of Fort Saybrook, the state's first military fortification. It also includes storyboards depicting the history of the Saybrook Colony, as well as bird watching, a boardwalk and lovely views of mouth of the Connecticut River.

Daily.

GENERAL WILLIAM HART HOUSE
350 Main St., Old Saybrook, 860-388-2622; www.oldsaybrookct.com

The 1767 Georgian-style residence of prosperous New England merchant and politician William Hart is as lavish as they come with eight corner fireplaces, one of which is decorated with Sadler and Green transfer-print tiles illustrating *Aesop's Fables*. Other well-preserved flourishes include decorative clapboards, Dutch tiling and period-style gardens.

June-August, Saturday-Sunday 1-4 p.m. or by appointment.

NEW HAVEN

AMISTAD MEMORIAL
165 Church St., New Haven; www.edhamiltonworks.com

Created by Ed Hamilton, this 14-foot bronze relief sculpture is a unique three-sided form that depicts a trio of significant episodes in the life of Joseph Cinque, one of 50 Africans kidnapped from Sierra Leone and slated for sale in Cuba in 1839. His ship was secretly rerouted to Long Island Sound, after which a fierce battle for the would-be slaves' freedom ensued in New Haven. Two years later, victory was won and their liberty ensured.

EAST ROCK PARK
Orange and Cold Spring Streets, New Haven, 203-946-6086; www.cityofnewhaven.com

Situated atop a dramatic ridge with 300-foot cliffs, this park is the best place to catch a look at downtown New Haven. Other attractions include the Pardee Rose Gardens, a bird sanctuary, hiking trails and the towering Soldiers and Sailors monument, an 1887 structure that honors locals who died at war.

April-November daily; December-May, Saturday-Sunday and holidays.

FORT NATHAN HALE PARK AND BLACK ROCK FORT
36 Woodward Ave., New Haven, 203-946-8790; www.fort-nathan-hale.org

Federal gunners kept British warships out of New Haven Harbor in 1812. Today, this battlefront is home to Black Rock Fort, a reconstructed Revolutionary fort, and Fort Nathan Hale, a partially restored Civil War facility. Both offer spectacular—and unobstructed—views of the harbor.

June-August, daily 10 a.m.-4 p.m.

GROVE STREET CEMETERY
227 Grove St., New Haven, 203-787-1443; www.grovestreetcemetery.org

Located next to the Yale campus, these 18 acres served as the nation's first planned cemetery with family sub-plots. Surrounded by a stone wall, with an imposing Egyptian Revival gateway at the entrance, it serves as a majestic resting place for notables like Noah Webster, Charles Goodyear and Eli Whitney.

Daily.

LIGHTHOUSE POINT PARK

2 Lighthouse Point Road, New Haven, 203-946-8005; www.cityofnewhaven.com

The 82-acre park on Long Island Sound is home to a shingled wooden lighthouse. Though its beacon is no longer used, the lighthouse's namesake park packs plenty of alternate attractions, including a restored antique carousel, bird sanctuary, bathhouse and beach.

Daily.

NEW HAVEN GREEN

Church and Elm Streets, New Haven; www.pps.org

In 1638, these 16 acres were laid out, making New Haven the first planned city in America. Talk a stroll along the nation's oldest, prettiest green. You'll pass all manner of public buildings, from City Hall and the library to the outskirts of Yale University and a trio of historic churches: United, Trinity Episcopal and Center Congregational. Throughout the year, the green is the setting for an array of free concerts and events, including the New Haven Jazz Festival and the International Festival of Arts and Ideas.

PEABODY MUSEUM OF NATURAL HISTORY

170 Whitney Ave., New Haven, 203-432-5050; www.peabody.yale.edu

Permanent exhibitions feature meteorites, minerals, birds of Connecticut and several life-size dinosaur dioramas, though the showstopper is the collection of pristine stegosaurus and apatosaurus skeletons reconstructed from original fossil material.

Monday-Saturday 10 a.m.-5 p.m., Sunday noon-5 p.m.

YALE REPERTORY THEATER

1120 Chapel St., New Haven, 203-432-1234, 800-833-8134; www.yalerep.org

From Edward Albee and August Wilson to brand-new works by emerging playwrights, some of the best theater in the country is staged right here. Founded in 1966, this regional playhouse has put on more than 100 premieres, including two Pulitzer Prize-winners, eight Tony Award-winners and many productions that advance to Broadway.

Early October-mid-May.

YALE UNIVERSITY

149 Elm St., New Haven, 203-432-2300; www.yale.edu

Founded by 10 Connecticut ministers and named for Elihu Yale, an early donor to the school, Yale is widely recognized as one of the best universities in the country. Take a walking tour to absorb the brainy vibe and see the gorgeous architecture. The campus is dominated by gothic buildings, though there's an occasional modern gem by the likes of Louis Kahn and Eero Saarinen.

Monday-Friday 10:30 a.m., 2 p.m., Saturday-Sunday 1:30 p.m.

HIGHLIGHTS

WHAT ARE SOME EXAMPLES OF GREAT ARCHITECTURE AT YALE UNIVERSITY?

INGALLS RINK

Yale University has one of the most architecturally distinct campuses in the world, with a cluster of gothic buildings that strike fear into the hearts of undergrads. The campus has a smattering of modern structures, too. Designed by Eero Saarinen and completed in 1958, the hockey rink features an undulating roof—that's why people call it the "Yale Whale."

PAUL RUDLOPH HALL

Formerly known as the Arts and Architecture building, this 1963 structure (now named for its architect) was one of the earliest examples of Brutalist-style architecture in the United States. Since the beginning, this stoic, seven-story building has been wildly popular and widely praised.

STOECKEL HALL

Opened in 1897, Stoeckel Hall is home to the college's music school and the only example of Venetian-Gothic style on campus.

WINDSOR LOCKS

NEW ENGLAND AIR MUSEUM
36 Perimeter Road, Windsor Locks, 860-623-3305; www.neam.org

One of the largest and most comprehensive collections of aircraft and aeronautical memorabilia in the world is located right next to Bradley International Airport. More than 80 aircraft, including bombers, fighters, helicopters and gliders, are on display, some of which date as far back as 1909. There's even a jet fighter cockpit simulator.

Daily 10 a.m.-5 p.m.

NODEN-REED HOUSE & BARN
58 West St., Windsor Locks, 860-627-9212

This Victorian farmhouse and 1826 brick barn hold an array of historic treasures: period room displays, an antique sleigh bed, antique quilts, kitchen utensils, newspapers and other periodicals from the 1800s and myriad farming tools. It's situated on a 22-acre park and surrounded by nature trails.

May-October, Sunday 1-4 p.m.

OLD NEWGATE PRISON

115 Newgate Road, East Granby, 860-653-3563; www.eastgranby.com

This 1707 copper mine found new life as a prison during the Revolutionary War. It was used to hold Tories and other British loyalists. It later became a state prison, the first in the nation. Today, visitors come of their own free will to take self-guided tours of the dark, underground caverns where inmates once lived.

Mid-May-October, Wednesday-Sunday 10 a.m.-4:30 p.m.

WHERE TO STAY

AVON

★★★AVON OLD FARMS HOTEL

279 Avon Mountain, Avon, 860-677-1651, 800-836-4000; www.avonoldfarmshotel.com

Avon has many "authentic," albeit rusty (yes, that's rusty, not rustic), bed and breakfasts. So if you're looking for quaint yet comfortable, try the Avon Old Farms Hotel instead. The 160-room property is low on kitsch and high on service. The hotel features twenty landscaped acres, brass chandeliers and white-canopied beds. A lively outdoor pool scene adds even more life to this mountainside retreat.

160 rooms. Complimentary breakfast. Restaurant. Fitness center. Pool. $151-250

ESSEX

★★★COPPER BEECH INN

46 Main St., Ivoryton, 860-767-0330, 888-809-2056; www.copperbeechinn.com

The ultimate romantic getaway, this 1889 Victorian-style inn features carved mahogany four-poster beds, plush linens and Parisian-style extras, including an onsite French restaurant. Once the residence of a prominent ivory importer, the inn is set on intimate wooded grounds with plenty of luxuries, including oriental rugs, thick tapestries and a 3,500-bottle wine cellar.

22 rooms. No children under 16. Complimentary breakfast. Restaurant. Closed one week in January. $61-150

★★★GRISWOLD INN

36 Main St., Essex, 860-767-1776; www.griswoldinn.com

Known to locals as "The Gris," this 1776 inn is one of the oldest continuously operated inns in the country. Today, it's best known for a lavish English-style Sunday buffet breakfast complete with mimosas. The rooms and suites are filled with fresh flowers and antiques, but also feature updates such as wireless Internet access.

31 rooms. Complimentary breakfast. Restaurant. $61-150

FARMINGTON

★★★THE FARMINGTON INN OF GREATER HARTFORD

827 Farmington Ave., Farmington, 860-677-2821, 800-648-9804;
www.farmingtoninn.com

With its Colonial décor and small touches like complimentary tea and cookies, this hotel has all the charms you'd expect from a quaint country inn. The rooms, however, feature a little something unexpected: original works by local artists.

72 rooms. Complimentary breakfast. Restaurant, bar. Business center. $61-150

★★★HARTFORD MARRIOTT FARMINGTON
15 Farm Springs Road, Farmington, 860-678-1000, 800-228-9190; www.marriott.com

Close enough to downtown to be convenient (10 miles, to be exact), yet far enough away from the city center to be serene, this Marriott pampers business travelers and vacationers alike with a full range of amenities, including two swimming pools and a tennis court. Rooms feature plush beds, high-speed Internet access and flat-screen TVs.

374 rooms. Restaurant, bar. Business center. Fitness center. Pool. $151-250

HARTFORD

★★★SHERATON HARTFORD HOTEL
100 E. River Drive, East Hartford, 860-528-9703, 888-530-9703; www.sheraton.com

Located outside downtown Hartford in a corporate office park, this outpost of the national hotel chain caters to business travelers. Rooms feature large desks, separate working and dining areas and comfortable beds. Come quitting time, guests can unwind at the newly expanded fitness center and lap pool.

215 rooms. Restaurant, bar. Business center. Fitness center. Pool. $151-250

RECOMMENDED

HARTFORD MARRIOTT DOWNTOWN
200 Columbus Boulevard, Hartford, 860-249-8000; www.marriott.com

Connected to the Connecticut Convention Center, this large chain hotel is ideal for business travelers, plus the onsite Starbucks offers an extra morning jolt. Rooms include high-speed Internet access, flat-screen TVs and work stations, and many come with gorgeous views of the Connecticut River.

409 rooms. Restaurant, bar. Business center. Fitness center. Pool. Spa. $151-250

HILTON HARTFORD
315 Trumbull St., Hartford, 860-728-5151; www.hilton.com

Spacious guest rooms offer cityscape views of the Connecticut State Capitol and Bushnell Park. Plus, the hotel is adjacent to the Hartford XL Center, so it's a great destination for UCONN basketball fans. Sporty types will appreciate the indoor pool and fitness center.

404 rooms. Restaurant, bar. Business center. Fitness center. Pool. $151-250

OLD LYME

★★★THE BEE AND THISTLE INN AND SPA
100 Lyme St., Old Lyme, 860-434-1667, 800-622-4946; www.beeandthistleinn.com

Known as one of the state's most romantic getaways, this 1756 inn features elegant antique-decorated rooms and a new onsite restaurant, the Chestnut Grille.

11 rooms. Closed two weeks in January. No children under 12. Restaurant, bar. Spa. $151-250

★★★OLD LYME INN
85 Lyme St., Old Lyme, 860-434-2600, 800-434-5352; www.oldlymeinn.com

Located in the town's historic district, this classic bed and breakfast is close to Essex, Mystic Seaport, Mystic Aquarium and several local art galleries. Most guests, however, keep put in their sumptuous rooms or watch the sunset from a deep Adirondack chair on the front lawn.

13 rooms. Complimentary breakfast. Restaurant, bar. $151-250

OLD SAYBROOK

★★★SAYBROOK POINT INN AND SPA

2 Bridge St., Old Saybrook, 860-395-2828, 800-243-0212;
www.saybrook.com

Views of Long Island Sound and the Connecticut River provide a postcard-perfect backdrop to this seaside getaway. Guest rooms are just as pretty, with 18th-century style furnishings and accessories. A recent renovation brought a touch of luxury to the resort, including Anichini linens, flat-screen TVs and a full-service onsite spa.

62 rooms. Restaurant, bar. Pool. Fitness center. Pets accepted. $151-250

★★★WATER'S EDGE RESORT AND CONFERENCE CENTER

1525 Boston Post Road, Westbrook, 860-399-5901, 800-222-5901;
www.watersedge-resort.com

Located on Long Island Sound, there's fun for the whole family at the Water's Edge Resort. Kids get their own activity center, though adults are free to partake in myriad activities, including softball, face painting, scavenger hunts, kite flying, football, horseshoes and volleyball. Rooms are decorated in a charming Colonial style.

32 rooms. Restaurant, bar. Beach. Spa. $151-250

NEW HAVEN

★★★OMNI NEW HAVEN HOTEL AT YALE

155 Temple St., New Haven, 203-772-6664, 800-843-6664;
www.omnihotels.com

Located close to the Yale campus, this hotel is a popular choice for unlucky parents who have the task of moving their kids to college. After all that heavy lifting, the hotel's comfy beds and feather pillows do the trick. The hotel houses a restaurant and bar for further decompressing.

305 rooms. Restaurant, bar. Fitness center. Pool. Spa. Pets accepted. $151-250

RECOMMENDED

THE STUDY AT YALE

1157 Chapel St., New Haven, 203-503-3900, 866-930-1157; www.studyhotels.com

Located just five minutes from the Yale campus, this boutique hotel is prime real estate for parents and collegiate visitors. Guest rooms are modern and chic, with large picture windows, beds topped with Frette linens, and grand marble bathrooms with glass showers. The Living Room (a.k.a. the lobby) is stocked with professorial leather lounge chairs, daily periodicals and an endless collection of coffee table books.

124 rooms. Restaurant. Fitness center. $151-250

WINDSOR LOCKS

★★★SHERATON BRADLEY AIRPORT HOTEL

1 Bradley International Airport, Windsor Locks, 860-627-5311, 877-422-5311;
www.sheraton.com

This hotel is conveniently situated between terminals A and B at Bradley Airport, just a 25-minute drive from Hartford. Guest rooms are eminently comfortable, with the Sheraton's signature Sweet Sleeper beds, flat-screen TVs and complimentary high-speed Internet access.

237 rooms. Restaurant, bar. Fitness center. Pool. Pets accepted. Business center. $61-150

WHERE TO EAT

AVON

★★★AVON OLD FARMS INN
1 Nod Road, Avon, 860-677-2818, 860-674-2434; www.avonoldfarmsinn.com

Set in a 1757 stagecoach stop, this eatery is themed accordingly. Old stirrups and bridles hang from the ceiling, and the floors and walls are built from smooth stone. Entrées range from hearty (filet mignon, short ribs) to healthy (spinach salad, tomato-basil linguine) with a few kosher options, to boot.

American. Lunch, dinner, Sunday brunch. Bar. Children's menu. $16-35

ESSEX

★★★BRASSERIE PIP AT COPPER BEECH INN
46 Main St., Ivoryton, 860-767-0330, 888-809-2056; www.copperbeechinn.com

Much like the inn, this restaurant is all soft elegance and warm romance. Patrons here dine on hearty, French country fare amidst fresh flowers, sparkling silver and soft candlelight.

American, French. Dinner. Bar. Jacket required. Closed Monday. Reservations recommended. $36-85

HARTFORD

★★★CARBONE'S
588 Franklin Ave., Hartford, 860-296-9646; www.carbonesct.com

Hearty Italian dishes and friendly service have kept Carbone's a longtime Hartford favorite. Need proof? Just look at the walls plastered with auto-graphed photos of local politicians, sports figures and other satisfied customers.

Italian. Lunch, dinner. Closed Sunday. Bar. Reservations recommended. $36-85

★★★MAX DOWNTOWN
185 Asylum St., Hartford, 860-522-2530; www.maxrestaurantgroup.com

Lively and centrally located, Max Downtown is a hit with staffers from the nearby Capitol Building. But

---

WHAT IS THE BEST PLACE TO SAMPLE CLAM PIZZA?

For a slice of culinary heaven, a.k.a. clam pizza with white sauce, go directly to the source of this regional dish: **Frank Pepe Pizzeria Napoletana** (*157 Wooster St., New Haven, 203-333-7373; www. pepespizzeria.com*). As legend has it, Mr. Pepe stumbled upon the idea sometime during the mid 1960s. The idea was likely born of pragmatism, since Pepe's was already serving raw clams on the half shell as an appetizer. Whatever the case, the newly turned pizza was a hit. Clam pizza quickly became a signature dish of Pepe's restaurant, and eventually, thanks to inspired copycats, the entire state.

the fan list doesn't stop there—all sorts of city-dwellers are eager to partake in the upscale atmosphere, extensive wine list and inventive New American cuisine.

American. Lunch, dinner, late-night. Bar. Reservations recommended. $36-85

OLD LYME

★★★THE CHESTNUT GRILLE

The Bee and Thistle Inn and Spa, 100 Lyme St., Old Lyme, 860-434-1667, 800-622-4046; www.beeandthistleinn.com

The white tablecloths and candlelit dining room look like something out of a Jane Austen novel, but the food is all 21st-century, with chef Kristofer Rowe blending fresh produce with first-rate seafood and steak to make hearty yet arty meals.

American. Breakfast, lunch, dinner, Sunday brunch. Bar. Closed two weeks in January. $36-85

★★★OLD LYME INN

85 Lyme St, Old Lyme, 860-434-2600, 800-434-5352; www.oldlymeinn.com

The meat-heavy menu and clubhouse-like decor of the inn's grill room gives way to the dining room's more elegant appeal. The real draw is the mouthwatering homemade desserts such as the triple chocolate silk tower.

American. Lunch, dinner. brunch. Bar. $36-85

RECOMMENDED

NEW HAVEN

PACIFICO

220 College St., New Haven, 203-772-4002; www.pacificorestaurants.com

Friendly service, an upbeat atmosphere and consistently good food make this one of New Haven's go-to restaurants. The two-story space is constantly abuzz thanks to the open kitchen and eclectic décor. The mojitos are perfectly tart and minty and the mini tuna tacos are exceptional. If you're extra hungry, the seafood paella is the best bang for your buck.

Latin. Dinner. Bar. $16-35

ZINC

964 Chapel St., New Haven, 203-624-0507; www.zincfood.com

The food at this bustling spot is eclectic and fun—think duck nachos with fried wonton skins and chipotle aioli, and Scottish salmon in a carrot butter sauce with spaghetti squash cake. There is a lively bar scene, too, so your meal can get noisy—especially on weekends.

Contemporary American. Lunch, dinner. Bar. $36-85

LITCHFIELD HILLS

Filled with lakes, farms, nature preserves and forests, the state's Northwestern corner is perfect for quiet getaways. This is Connecticut's least populous area, though travelers will encounter no shortage of quaint villages and posh small towns. With upward of 8,000 residents, Litchfield is virtually a metropolis, though its country bona fides are entirely uncompromised—for the most part, the industrial revolution bypassed this quiet hamlet, ensuring the survival of classic clapboard inns and primo antique shopping. That's not to say, however, that Litchfield is without an intellectual and political history. Famous citizens include the Reverend Henry Ward Beecher and his sister, Harriet Beecher Stowe, author of *Uncle Tom's Cabin*.

Just 13 miles from Litchfield, the town of Washington offers another high-class rural retreat. The tiny town has an enviable history of progressivism, covering everything from environmental conservation to active volunteerism. Visitors, though, are more interested to troll the antique shops, ogle the historic buildings and emulate the locals' slow, relaxed way of life.

WHAT IS THE BEST SPA IN THE AREA?

Mayflower Spa: This 20,000-square-foot, ultra-deluxe spa specializes in the full-service experience. After completing a pre-arrival consultation, visitors are treated to a custom-prepared schedule of pampering services, as well as fitness and nutrition classes.

WHAT TO SEE

LITCHFIELD

HAIGHT-BROWN VINEYARD AND WINERY
29 Chestnut Hill Road, Litchfield, 800-577-9463; www.haightvineyards.com
Opened in 1975, Haight is Connecticut's oldest winery. Drop by to sample the varietals, everything from merlot and riesling to apple and strawberry wines.
Tours, tastings. Daily.

LITCHFIELD HISTORY MUSEUM
7 South St., Litchfield, 860-567-4501; www.litchfieldhistoricalsociety.org
Seven galleries capture work and family life during the 50 years that immediately followed the American Revolution, a time when Litchfield was an important political, business and culture center. Collections include clothing, furniture, decorative objects, art and other artifacts.
Admission: adults $5, seniors and students $3, children 14 and under free. Mid-April-November, Tuesday-Saturday 11 a.m.-5 p.m., Sunday 1-5 p.m.

TAPPING REEVE HOUSE
82 South St., Litchfield, 860-567-4501; www.litchfieldhistoricalsociety.org
Through interpretive exhibits, hands-on learning exercises and role-playing, visitors experience this

retrospective of 19th-century Litchfield through the lives of the students who attended the Litchfield Law School, American's first formal law school.
Admission: adults $5, seniors and students $3, children 14 and under free. Mid-April-November, Tuesday-Saturday 11 a.m.-5 p.m., Sunday 1-5 p.m.

TOPSMEAD STATE FOREST
46 Chase Road, Litchfield, 860-567-5694; www.ct.gov
The highlight of this 511-acre forest and picnic grounds is a 1923 English Tudor mansion. Once the summer home of a nature-loving heiress, it overlooks 40 acres wildlife preserve and beautifully manicured gardens.
Second and fourth weekends of June-October.

WASHINGTON
HISTORICAL MUSEUM OF GUNN MEMORIAL LIBRARY
5 Wykeham Road, Washington, 860-868-7756;
www.gunnlibrary.org
This gorgeous building, dating to 1908, is rich with architectural detail—pilasters, moldings and a spectacular ceiling mural. The library also contains troves of the town's historic paintings, furnishings, gowns, dolls, dollhouses and tools.
Library: Monday-Tuesday, Thursday-Sunday, hours vary. Museum: Thursday-Saturday 10 a.m.-4p.m., Sunday noon-4 p.m.

INSTITUTE FOR AMERICAN INDIAN STUDIES
38 Curtis Road, Washington, 860-868-0518; www.birdstone.org
Artifacts and interpretive exhibits preserve the history of the region's Native Americans. Special exhibits include art displays, a replicated indoor longhouse, an outdoor replicated Algonkian village and a simulated archaeological site.
Monday-Saturday 10 a.m.-5 p.m., Sunday noon-5 p.m.

WHERE TO STAY

LITCHFIELD
★★★LITCHFIELD INN
7 Village Green Drive, Litchfield, 860-567-4503, 800-499-3444; www.litchfieldinnct.com
Rooms are wrapped in colonial style, with antique furnishings and thick tapestry wallpapers. You'll find plenty of modern conveniences, too, such as complimentary wireless Internet and family-style dining at the onsite restaurant.
32 rooms. Complimentary breakfast. Restaurant, bar. $61-150

WASHINGTON

★★★★★MAYFLOWER INN & SPA

118 Woodbury Road, Washington, 860-868-9466; www.mayflowerinn.com

This country inn, located less than two hours from New York City, evokes the feeling and quiet elegance of an English countryside hotel. Set on 28 acres of rolling hills, streams and lush gardens, guest rooms and suites are swathed in luxurious fabrics and feature four-poster, canopied beds, 18th and 19th-century art and modern touches like flat-screen TVs. The dining room's seasonal menu makes good use of fresh, local ingredients with dishes such as organic Atlantic salmon with fresh vegetables. Meanwhile, the Tap Room features a more casual menu of Vermont cheddar-topped burgers and lemon-rosemary chicken. The sprawling Mayflower Spa is superlative.

24 rooms. No children under 12. Restaurant, bar. Spa. $351 and up

SPA

★★★★★MAYFLOWER SPA

The Mayflower Inn & Spa, 118 Woodbury Road, Washington, 860-868-9466; www.mayflowerinn.com

The 20,000-square-foot Mayflower Spa, opened in 2006, features the same classic design, elegant furnishing and quiet luxury of its namesake inn. Those who come for the full spa experience receive a pre-arrival consultation to create a schedule of pampering services and fitness and nutrition classes. The spa has an indoor heated pool and mosaic-domed whirlpool. A wide variety of classes range from kickboxing to ballet. Private yoga classes and Pilates studios are also available. Guests are even provided with goodies including yoga mats, MP3 players, loungewear and even rain boots.

FAIRFIELD COUNTY

One of the richest counties in the United States, Fairfield goes a long way to bolster Connecticut's status as a wealthy state. This is the land of plenty, with tree-lined streets and high-density populations. It goes to figure, then, that there's also plenty to keep a visitor occupied. Kickoff your sojourn in the county's most talked about town, Greenwich, the long-time home to hedge fund barons, ladies who lunch and other moneyed folk. It's close to the ocean, with mega-mansions dotting the so-called Gold Coast, a parade of seaside palaces that stretches all the way to Fairfax. It's also close to New York City—just 28 miles from Times Square. Visitors can readily enjoy the leafy, photo-friendly 18th-century streets and Manhattan-style shopping boutiques.

Neighboring Westport also boasts its share of corporate warriors, but the town gets additional nourishment from its cluster of thriving small businesses and its community of artists, especially actors and illustrators. What's more, the area is surrounded by wooded hills and lovely beaches, making it a pretty, if pricey, place to retreat.

It's not exactly Paris, but Ridgefield features the rare Champs Elysées-style shopping boulevard. Ninety-nine feet wide, the street is lined with trees and

HIGHLIGHT

WHAT IS THE TOP THING TO DO IN GREENWICH?

STROLL AROUND
The leafy town of Greenwich is full of charming restaurants and great boutiques. Plan to spend at least an afternoon taking in this beautiful town.

stately houses. It was here that, in 1777, a pre-traitorous Benedict Arnold set up barricades and fought the Battle of Ridgefield. Nowadays, it's a better place to spy a modern variety of conspirator—namely, Wall Street tycoons who can't help but blow through their bonuses.

Then again, not everyone in Fairfield County commutes to New York City. More than 20 Fortune 500 companies are headquartered right here in Stamford, a Fairfield County business haven that one-ups Gotham with its plentiful marinas and sandy beaches.

WHAT TO SEE

GREENWICH
AUDUBON CENTER
613 Riversville Road, Greenwich, 203-869-5272; greenwich.audubon.org
This 295-acre sanctuary is populated by hardwood forests, old fields, lakes, streams, ponds and seven miles of nature trails. The property is sprinkled with historic buildings, too—one holds the Kimberlin Nature Education Center, where families find hands-on nature activities and interpretive natural history displays.
Daily.

BRUCE MUSEUM
1 Museum Drive, Greenwich, 203-869-0376; www.brucemuseum.org
This century-old museum highlights arts, sciences and natural history with ever-changing exhibits, lectures, concerts and educational programs. Highlights of the permanent exhibition include a beautiful display of rare butterflies.
Tuesday-Saturday 10 a.m.-5 p.m., Sunday 1-5 p.m.

BUSH-HOLLEY HOUSE
39 Strickland Road, Cos Cob, 203-869-6899; www.hstg.org
This 18th-century Georgian-style home was once the site of the prominent Cos Cob art colony. Today, the house's history is captured by an impressive art collection of paintings by Childe Hassam, Elmer Livingston MacRae and John Henry Twachtman, as well as sculptures by John Rogers and pottery by Leon Volkmar.
March-December, Wednesday-Sunday noon-4 p.m.; January-February, Friday-Sunday noon-4 p.m.

PUTNAM COTTAGE/KNAPP TAVERN
243 E. Putnam Ave., Greenwich, 203-869-9697; www.putnamcottage.org

More mansion than cottage, this structure is popularly associated with its one-time owner, General Israel Putnam, and his heroic escape from the redcoats. Today, the red-shingled house is filled with colonial and revolutionary artifacts.

April-November, Sunday 1-4 p.m.; also by appointment December-March.

RIDGEFIELD
ALDRICH CONTEMPORARY ART MUSEUM
258 Main St., Ridgefield, 203-438-4519; www.aldrichart.org

How is the Aldrich different from other contemporary art museums? It hasn't bothered to build a permanent collection. Rather, it specializes in ever-changing exhibitions featuring today's best emerging and mid-career artists.

Admission: adults $7, seniors and college students $4, children 18 and under free. Tuesday-Sunday noon-5 p.m. Free Tuesday.

KEELER TAVERN MUSEUM
132 Main St., Ridgefield, 203-438-5485; www.keelertavernmuseum.org

This restored 18th-century tavern, stagecoach stop and home once served as the revolutionary patriot headquarters. Today, it lives on as a colonial history museum. Don't leave without examining the British cannonball still embedded in the wall.

February-December, Wednesday, Saturday-Sunday 1-4 p.m. Closed January.

STAMFORD
BARTLETT ARBORETUM AND GARDENS
151 Brookdale Road, Stamford, 203-322-6971; www.bartlettarboretum.org

Collections of dwarf conifers, rhododendrons, azaleas, wildflowers, perennials and witches brooms are open to the public, as are ecology trails and the natural woodlands surrounding the gardens.

Daily 8:30 a.m.-dusk. Visitor center: Monday-Friday 8:30 a.m.-4:30 p.m.

WESTPORT
LEVITT PAVILION FOR THE PERFORMING ARTS
Jesup Green, 260 Compo Road South, Westport, 203-226-7600; www.levittpavilion.com

A magnet for picnicking couples and families, this pavilion hosts more than 50 nights of free outdoor entertainment, from jazz, pop and rock concerts to theater and dance.

Mid-June-early August.

WHERE TO STAY

GREENWICH
★★★THE DELAMAR
500 Steamboat Road, Greenwich, 203-661-9800; www.thedelamar.com

The Delamar looks more like a Lake Como mansion than an old Connecticut retreat. Its sprawling cream-colored façade hides an interior rich with original artwork, sparkling chandeliers, ornate sconces and marble surfaces. Overlooking the Greenwich Marina, the property has 82 rooms filled with up-to-date electronics, luxe Italian linens and cast-iron tubs. Even dogs are pampered here with the resort's "Sophisticated Pet" program.

82 rooms. No children under 12. Restaurant, bar. Spa. $251-350

★★★HOMESTEAD INN
420 Field Point Road, Greenwich, 203-869-7500; www.homesteadinn.com

Owned by Greenwich hoteliers Thomas and Theresa Henkelmann, the inn—and its accompanying restaurant—is a study in old-school extravagance. The rooms here are not called rooms—they're "chambers." And the lodging at this renovated 1799 inn is anything but average: second and third-floor suites boast imported furniture, Frette linens and original artwork, plus heated bathroom floors.

18 rooms. Closed two weeks in March. No children under 12. Restaurant, bar. $351 and up

★★★HYATT REGENCY GREENWICH
1800 E. Putnam Ave., Old Greenwich, 203-637-1234, 800-633-7313; www.greenwich.hyatt.com

Before magazine giant Condé Nast moved to Manhattan, the Vogue and Glamour publisher was headquartered here, at 1800 E. Putnam. Now owned by the Hyatt, the building has retained much of its early glamour with an elegant atrium-style lobby with ponds, stone walls and an impressive array of trees, plants and flowers. Guest rooms are spacious and feature Internet access, bathrobes and plush pillows. Refresh and renew with a spa treatment at the onsite Enzo Riccobene Salon & Spa.

373 rooms. Restaurant, bar. Business center. Fitness center. Pool. Spa. $251-350

RIDGEFIELD

★★★THE ELMS INN
500 Main St., Ridgefield, 203-438-2541; www.elmsinn.com

Established in 1799, this is the oldest continuously run inn in the state. A recent restoration only bolstered the historic appeal, with antique furnishings peacefully coexisting beside modern conveniences like wireless Internet access and dry-cleaning services.

23 rooms. Complimentary breakfast. Restaurant, bar. $251-350

★★★STONEHENGE INN
35 Stonehenge Road, Ridgefield, 203-438-6511; www.stonehengeinn-ct.com

Set on a swan-filled lake, Stonehenge has plenty of country charm. Rooms are elegant with English country style furningings and service is attentive. The restaurant is also top-notch.

16 rooms. Complimentary breakfast. Restaurant, bar. $151-250

STAMFORD

★★★SHERATON STAMFORD HOTEL
2701 Summer St., Stamford, 203-359-1300, 800-325-3535; www.sheraton.com

This Sheraton is 45 minutes from Manhattan, though most guests never make it into the city—instead they opt to ogle the mansions along Connecticut's Gold Coast. Cream-colored walls, blue and white furnishings and lots of plants lend the hotel a coastal theme. Pets are welcome here, thanks to the resort's "Love that Dog" program.

448 rooms. Restaurant, bar. Fitness center. Business center. $251-350

★★★STAMFORD MARRIOTT HOTEL & SPA

243 Tresser Blvd., Stamford, 203-357-9555, 800-732-9689; www.marriott.com

The biggest draw is this hotel's prime location, across the street from the Stamford Town Center Mall. If you can't find something you like in those 130 stores, don't worry—the Marriott is also close to the Palace Theater, Playland Amusement Park and the Whitney Museum.

508 rooms. Restaurant, bar. Business center. Fitness center. Pool. Spa. $251-350

WHERE TO EAT

GREENWICH

★★★JEAN-LOUIS

61 Lewis St., Greenwich, 203-622-8450; www.restaurantjeanlouis.com

Sophisticated and elegant with professional service to match, this cozy restaurant has a classic French menu. The décor, too, is decidedly Parisian, as the serving china and candle lamps were all custom-made in France. The food, however, is of an American provenance. Chef Jean-Louis works directly with local farmers to buy the freshest ingredients. In addition to the standard à la carte menu, he also offers Yankee favorites like tastings, petit tastings, plus vegetarian and vegan menus.

French. Lunch, dinner. Closed Sunday; also first two weeks of August. Reservations recommended. $36-85

★★★L'ESCALE

500 Steamboat Road, Greenwich, 203-661-4600; www.lescalerestaurant.com

This French-Mediterranean restaurant earned its stars by re-creating the Mediterranean on the North Atlantic shore. Diners are greeted to the warm dining room by a stone fireplace and terra-cotta floors, whereas light-filtering thatched bamboo shades the sophisticated patio. The menu by Francois Kwaku-Dongo includes a salad of caramelized leeks and chanterelles; apple and prune-paired foie gras; and crispy duck breast. The eatery has become a gathering place for locals and travelers alike, and it's no wonder why: L'Escale lets guests sail in and tie up their yachts at its waterfront dock.

French, Mediterranean. Breakfast, lunch, dinner, Sunday brunch. Bar. Reservations recommended. Outdoor seating. $36-85

★★★THOMAS HENKELMANN

420 Field Point Road, Greenwich, 203-869-7500; www.thomashenkelmann.com

German-born, French-trained chef Thomas Henkelmann goes for a clever take on traditional French fare. His eatery is especially famous for its lobster bisque—a rich, creamy concoction full of sweet and savory flavors. After a meal like that, you'll need time to digest; try taking a stroll through the surrounding gardens.

French. Breakfast, lunch, dinner. Closed Sunday; also two weeks in March. Bar. Jacket required. Reservations recommended. $86 and up

WESTPORT
★★★COBB'S MILL INN
12 Old Mill Road, Weston, 203-227-7221, 800-640-9365; www.cobbsmillinn.com

At the Cobb's Mill Inn, excellent quality merges with the historic ambience of a rustic, old barn. No matter what you order, whether it's the olive oil poached halibut or sake-glazed sea bass, it's sure to be tasty and beautifully presented.
Seafood, steak. Lunch, dinner. Bar. Brunch. $36-85

RIDGEFIELD
★★★THE ELMS
500 Main St., Ridgefield, 203-438-9206; www.elmsinn.com

A warm, cozy fireplace sets the tone at the Elms, where award-wining chef Brendan Walsh creates standout Yankee cuisine. Signature dishes include pulled wild boar and lobster Shepherd's pie.
American. Lunch, dinner. Closed Monday-Tuesday. Reservations recommended. Outdoor seating. $16-35

WHERE TO SHOP

FAIRFIELD
CARGO BAY
1561 Post Road, Fairfield, 203-254-8387

This Fairfield boutique specializes in casual separates that are eminently comfortable, but no less fashionable. Think leggings, designer jeans and super-soft, super-stylish sweaters. Best of all, prices are within striking range.
Monday-Saturday 10 a.m.-6 p.m., Thursday until 8 p.m, Sunday 10 a.m.-5 p.m.

WESTPORT
DOVECOTE
56 Post Road East, Westport, 203-222-7500; www.dovecote-westport.com

From the antique to the unique, this sliver of a Westport shop features a carefully curated selection of beautiful furnishings, jewelry and more. In fact, the shop is a favorite of New York fashion editors.
Monday-Saturday 10 a.m.-6 p.m., Sunday noon-5 p.m.

TINA DRAGONE
1687 Post Road East, Westport, 203-259-1184

Do you want to look like a Fairfield denizen? Or a Hollywood starlet? Take your pick at this Westport boutique, because it stocks everything from casual classics to eveningwear with edge.
Monday-Saturday 10 a.m.-5:30 p.m., Sunday noon-5 p.m.

WELCOME TO MASSACHUSETTS

TO SOME, NEW ENGLAND MEANS ONE THING: MASSACHUSETTS.

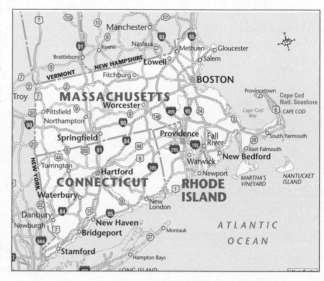

For more than five centuries, the Bay State has served as the region's poster child, one that's rich with history and character. Talk to the locals and you'll soon see—the past is very important here. Many local families still trace their roots to John Cabot, an Italian explorer who landed on these shores in 1497, just five years after Columbus' trans-Atlantic trip. The legendary Mayflower followed shortly thereafter, establishing a settlement that would later sprout political and literary innovators. A group of Massachusetts men were responsible for jump-starting the American Revolution. Paul Revere, John Hancock, Sam Adams and, of course, the Kennedys all hailed from Massachusetts. So did literary giants like Ralph Waldo Emerson, Henry David Thoreau and Emily Dickinson.

But for all its historic heft, the Bay doesn't live entirely in the past. The biggest city in New England, Boston is a lively metropolis with booming businesses, a gorgeous promenade along the Charles River and thousands of fiercely devoted Red Sox fans. What's more, the city boasts a series of distinct neighborhoods—the North End, the city's Little Italy, bursts with gelaterias and traditional trattorias, whereas the South End features chic clothing boutiques and avant-garde eateries. To the west, north and south of the city there are verdant, upscale suburbs and quiet, laid-back beach towns. From Boston, drive west along the Massachusetts Pike to find the Berkshires, a hilly county hugging New York state that's so rich with arts, culture and culinary experiences, it has become a go-to destination for people the world over.

Then there's Cape Cod and the Islands—Nantucket and Martha's Vine-

HIGHLIGHTS

MASSACHUSETTS' BEST ATTRACTIONS

BERKSHIRES ROAD TRIP

The Berkshire Mountains sit just 120 miles west of Boston, but they infuse the area with a sense of rural tranquility. Listen to a classical concert at Tanglewood, tour the Norman Rockwell Museum in Stockbridge or simply spend the night luxuriating at Blantyre's Tudor-style mansion.

FOURTH OF JULY WITH THE BOSTON POPS

How fitting that the American cradle of liberty has one of the best Fourth of July celebrations in the country. Check out the Charles River Esplanade to catch a free Boston Pops concert and a riveting fireworks display.

CAPE COD AND THE ISLANDS

Come summertime, Cape Cod and the Islands of Martha's Vineyard and Nantucket become the quintessential New England playground. This is when locals and visitors alike spend their days visiting farmers' markets and hosting sunset clambakes on the area beaches.

FREEDOM TRAIL

This self-guided walking tour takes you past Boston's major historical sights—from Paul Revere's house, to the Old North Church, the Bunker Hill Monument and more. Best of all, you don't even need a map—just follow the distinctly painted red line through the city.

RED SOX GAME AT FENWAY PARK

Sure, tickets are hard to come by. But watching Big Papi hit a homer over the wall of the Green Monster is one for the bucket list.

yard—a few of America's most sought-after summer spots. The area's hundreds of miles of coastline and soft sandy beaches are a vacationer's dream. Here, the locals live in gray-shingled houses along oceanfront and postcard-perfect main streets.

A statewide trip takes travelers from Plymouth Rock, where the May-flower landed, to the battle of Bunker Hill, to the philosophers' favorite Walden Pond, to the academic powerhouses in Cambridge, and to the constantly innovating Boston. Indeed, the state is a melting pot of old tra-ditions and new ideas, lived out along a breathtaking coastline and within myriad tiny villages.

BOSTON, CAMBRIDGE AND BROOKLINE

Boston, the so-called "Athens of America," serves as the social, financial, educa-tional, historical, culinary and sports capital of New England. It's no surprise, then, that the city goes by such a lofty nickname—"the Hub," shortened from "the Hub of the Universe". After all, Paul Revere's fabled ride—and indeed the Revolution itself—started in Boston, thereby giving the city's 600,000 residents bragging rights over every other American city.

Early settlers started moving to the Boston area in the mid 1600s. Their legacies are still alive in the old towhouses of nearby Charlestown and the narrow, winding streets of the city's European-looking North End neighborhood. Visitors can retrace Revere's and other early patriots' steps along the city's famous Freedom Trail, a three-hour self-guided walking tour that delivers all the major historic sites.

Current citizens, though, leave the past to tourists and instead obsess over the Boston Red Sox and New England Patriots, two championship teams known as much for their die-hard fans as for their athletic prowess. After taking in a game at the legendary Fenway Park, the locals scatter (mostly on foot) to the city's distinct neighborhoods—the upscale Beacon Hill area, the heavily Italian North End, the attractive South End with its young professionals and hip eateries, and the rapidly gentrifying Irish enclave of South Boston. No matter where they travel, they're assured an easy commute. This is the nation's preeminent walking city, thanks to the compact layout and easy-to-understand subway system. From Fenway, it's a short, 10-minute walk to Brookline, a first-ring suburb with an urban feel of shops, pubs and restaurants.

The Boston area is also known for its top-tier universities. Some of the most famous are Harvard, M.I.T., Boston University and the Berklee School of Music, though there are more than 100 schools in all. Check out "the People's Republic of Cambridge," just across the river from Boston proper, to explore the rich neigh-borhoods that ring the Harvard and M.I.T. campuses. Harvard Square, in particu-lar, is an excellent area to shop, dine, people-watch or even initiate an impassioned discussion with perfect strangers. You'll find more youth culture over in Boston's Back Bay neighborhood, especially on Commonwealth Avenue and Newbury Street. On a perfect spring evening, this is where the air fills with the sounds of Berklee students practicing their instruments.

At the end of the day, Boston's robust culinary scene awaits its hungry guests. With an ever-expanding circle of talented chefs, many of whom grew up and learned to cook right here in New England, the town offers everything from traditional seafood fare to nouveau French tasting menus.

WHAT TO SEE

BOSTON AFRICAN AMERICAN NATIONAL HISTORIC SITE AND BLACK HERITAGE TRAIL

14 Beacon St., Boston, 617-742-5415; www.nps.gov/boaf

Yes, plenty of Bostonians claim to trace their heritage to the Mayflower. But here's the thing—Boston is, and always has been, a diverse city. See for yourself by exploring the Boston African American National Historic Site and the Black Heritage Trail, which winds through the elegant and small streets of Boston's chic Beacon Hill neighborhood. Important stops include the memorial to the Massachusetts 54th Volunteer Infantry, the first documented African American regiment for the North in the Civil War and the John J. Smith House, the former home of a Bostonian who allowed abolitionists to meet in his barbershop. With 14 sites along the way, this self-guided tour allows you to explore a few stops or devote the whole day.

Monday-Saturday 10 a.m.-4 p.m.

BOSTON CHILDREN'S MUSEUM

300 Congress St., Boston, 617-426-6500; www.bostonkids.org

You won't find any "do not touch" signs here. This museum prides itself on providing kids with tactile play experiences, though a few lessons are imparted in the process. Check out learning exhibits like the popular recycling display, or fun stations such as Airplay—where kids get to play with Blue Man Group PVC instruments. Don't miss the real, 100-year-old Japanese house, complete with a futon bed, tatami floors and (kids love this) an old-fashioned toilet.

Admission: adults $10, seniors and children over 2 $8. Daily 10 a.m.-5 p.m., Friday until 9 p.m.

BOSTON COMMON

Bound by Tremont, Beacon, Charles and Boylston streets, Boston; www.cityofboston.gov

From British barracks to cow pastures, to visits by Judy Garland, Martin Luther King, Jr. and Pope John Paul II—America's oldest city park has seen it all. Today, the 50-acre Common is the starting point for the Freedom Trail and the anchor for Boston's "Emerald Necklace" string of urban parks. A large underground parking garage makes the Common a great jumping off point for exploring this eminently walkable city. If you're visiting during the summer, don't miss the free Shakespeare on the Common performances at the Parkman Bandstand, which generally runs from mid-July to early August.

HIGHLIGHTS

WHAT ARE THE CAN'T-MISS FIRST VISIT TO BOSTON SIGHTS?

BOSTON COMMON

Located at the southern edge of ultra-Brahmin Beacon Hill neighborhood, America's oldest city park is a pastoral destination for street performances, ice skating, picnics, running and people-watching. It's also a great place to glimpse the golden cupola of the Massachusetts State House.

BOSTON PUBLIC GARDEN

Though it's attached to Boston Common, the Public Garden strikes a very different mood. Covered with formal gardens, the Public Garden has a lovely pond, memorials, monuments and the famous pedal-powered swan boats.

THE FREEDOM TRAIL

Fifty years ago, Bostonians painted a line through the city in order to help visitors find all the important historic sites. To this day, the popular trail links historic sites like Paul Revere's house and the Old North Church, the oldest church in Boston.

BOSTON HARBOR ISLANDS NATIONAL RECREATION AREA

617-223-8666; www.bostonislands.org

You don't have to drive all the way to Cape Cod for sandy beaches. The Boston Harbor Islands National Park is an urban wilderness that juxtaposes sea breezes with city views. A set of 34 islands just off the Boston shoreline, the isles are a treasure trove of family fun with beaches, ocean tide pools, a lighthouse, a Civil War fort, salt marshes, camping, hiking, fishing and swimming. Make sure to explore the dark, earthen tunnels of Fort Warren, supposedly haunted by the ghostly wife of a Confederate prisoner who tried to help her husband escape. Ferries run from Long Wharf at Christopher Columbus Park, making it an easy day trip from downtown.

Check the website for specific island ferry schedules.

THE BOSTON OPERA HOUSE

539 Washington St., Boston, 617-259-4300; www.bostonoperahouse.com

Boston's theater district, which was a thriving center for performing arts during the first half of the 20th century, went into a steep decline over the last 50 years. In fact, after dark, you'll still be happier wandering this area in a group, with your wallet firmly in hand. But even so, lately the neighborhood has started to emerge from that state of blight. The newly renovated Opera House, which has hosted everything from vaudeville to film screenings, was built in 1928 and features flamboyant Rococo detailing and extensive gold leaf accents. It's the central jewel of the neighborhood, and provides an extravagant stage for elaborate musical productions like *A Chorus Line* and *Legally Blonde*. During the holiday season, the Boston Ballet's production of *The Nutcracker*, is a requisite outing for Boston-area families.

BOSTON PUBLIC GARDEN
Bound by Charles, Boylston, Arlington and Beacon streets, Boston

An elegant park with flowers and swans, rather than concerts and basketball courts, the public garden offers a refined respite. Make sure to leave time for a short trip around this gorgeous park's pond and island on one of the garden's famous pedal-powered swan boats, or take a stroll over its picturesque bridge. The park is at its best in the spring, but it's attractive year-round.

BOSTON PUBLIC LIBRARY
700 Boylston St., Boston, 617-536-5400; www.bpl.org

The nation's first public library is centrally located in Boston's Copley Square. The library's main building, constructed in 1895 by famed architects McKim, Mead, and White, is a Beaux Arts masterpiece, while the nearby addition, designed by Philip Johnson and opened in 1972, is a modernist nod to the original and constructed of the same pink granite. Together, they form the third largest library in the U.S. Check out impressive Bates Hall with its decorative vaulted ceiling and special historical collections. If you were a fan of HBO's *John Adams* or read the best-selling book on which the mini-series was based, be sure to check out his library in the rare books and manuscripts department. An afternoon attending one of the library's varied workshops or lectures is well worth your while—topics range from Shakespeare to opera to haiku poetry.
Monday-Thursday 9 a.m.-9 p.m., Friday-Saturday 9 a.m.-5 p.m.

BOSTON TEA PARTY SHIPS & MUSEUM
Congress Street Bridge, Boston, 800-868-7482; www.bostonteapartyship.com

Every American schoolchild thinks he knows the story behind the Boston Tea Party, but the real history is fairly complex: American settlers and tea smugglers (like John Hancock) stood to lose money when the British East India Tea Company was allowed to sell its tea at below-market prices, hitting entrepreneurial merchants in their pocketbooks. On December 16, 1773, tanked up on free-flowing liquor and anti-British rhetoric, a group of colonists swarmed the recently docked British ships and dumped the fated tea into the harbor. The Boston Tea Party Ships and Museum have been undergoing renovation (due to an extensive fire in 2007), but by summer 2011 you will once again be able to tour the ships.

CHARLES RIVER ESPLANADE
Storrow Drive, Boston; www.esplanadeassociation.org

Running along the western edge of Boston, the Charles River and its three-mile Esplanade Park offer a pleasant escape. The Esplanade is especially popular on the Fourth of July, when crowds gather to hear the Boston Pops Orchestra and watch the fireworks over the river. Throughout the rest of the summer, catch free concerts and movies at the Hatch Shell. No matter what time of year, look for the multi-layer sculpture of legendary Boston Pops conductor Arthur Fiedler, who led the orchestra for a half-century.

CITI PERFORMING ARTS CENTER/THE WANG THEATRE/THE SHUBERT THEATRE

270 Tremont St., Boston, 617-482-9393; www.citicenter.org

Boston's performing arts community would be at a loss without the Wang and Shubert theaters, an impressive pair that operates under the rubric of the Citi Performing Arts Center. The 3,600-seat Wang Theatre hosts large Broadway productions such as *Rent, Annie, Riverdance* and the Alvin Ailey American Dance Theater, whereas the Shubert Theatre hosts smaller engagements. The theaters are open only for performances—no individual tours are available currently. Ticket availability varies by specific show.

COMMUNITY BOATING

21 David Mugar Way, Boston, 617-523-1038; www.community-boating.org

From its docks near the Museum of Science, the non-profit Community Boating has been teaching novice sailors since 1946. After some basic instruction and passing the appropriate tests, you, too, can glide across the river toward Cambridge in a rented boat. The program is relatively cheap—a 30-day intro to sailing and kayaking membership costs a mere $89, while a 60-day boating pass is $159. The junior program for kids ages 10 through 18 is only $1. For experienced sailors on holiday in Boston, Community Boating offers sailboat rental for just $100 for two days.

COPLEY PLACE

2 Copley Place, Boston, 617-369-5000; www.shopcopleyplace.com

Sure, it's a mall—but it's the city's most upscale mall. Retailers include Tiffany & Co., Jimmy Choo, Barneys New York and Louis Vuitton. Copley Place is especially great when the unpredictable New England turns windy and cool. Even though the shops, restaurants and bars are spread across multiple downtown blocks, each building is linked via skybridge. The Boston Marriott Copley Place, the Westin Hotel and the Shops at Prudential Center are also connected.
Monday-Saturday 10 a.m.-9 p.m., Sunday 11 a.m.-6 p.m.

COPP'S HILL BURYING GROUND

Hull Street, Boston, 617-635-4505; www.cityofboston.gov

Another stop on the Freedom Trail, Copp's Hill Burying Ground is the final resting place of thousands of early Boston settlers—including the Mather family of ministers and the man who hung the lanterns in the Old North Church on the night of Paul Revere's ride. While you're there, why not take a moment to imagine life in the "skinny house" across the street. The remarkably narrow four-story house is only 10.4 feet wide at its broadest point.
Daily 9 a.m.-5 p.m. (hours may vary slightly).

DUCK TOURS

Back Bay, 617-267-3825; www.bostonducktours.com

Duck Tours are everywhere these days, from Austin to Albany. But Boston Duck Tours were one of the first city tours to use original World War II amphibious vehicles. Code-named DUKWs, these boat-bus hybrids were originally designed to unload men and supplies in places without docks or traditional landings. Today, these amphibious adventures will take a bite out of your wallet, though the view of downtown from the Charles River is well worth the price of admission.

Tickets: adults $29, seniors and students $25, children 3-11 $19, children under 3 $5. March-November, daily 9 a.m.-sunset on the half-hour or hour (depending on the season). Tours depart from the Prudential Center and the Museum of Science.

FANEUIL HALL MARKETPLACE

75 State St., Boston, 617-523-1300; www.faneuilhallmarketplace.com

Want to blend in with the locals? First, learn to properly announce the name of this landmark. Hint: it rhymes with "Daniel." The original Faneuil Hall was constructed in 1742 as a marketplace and meeting hall. The area long lingered in a state of disrepair until it was redeveloped in the 1970s. Today, the eating and shopping options are no longer unique, due to the proliferation of chains over the past 10 years, but Faneuil Hall is still a great place to wander around and soak up the scene of roving entertainers and partying tourists.

Monday-Saturday 10 a.m.-9 p.m., Sunday noon-6 p.m.

FENWAY PARK TOURS

4 Yawkey Way, Boston, 877-733-7699; www.redsox.com

If you pay attention, you'll notice that the Boston Red Sox are more than a bunch of guys in matching uniforms and cleats. The Boston Red Sox are a way of life. While it's hard to get tickets to the perpetually sold-out games, it's easy to get a feel by taking a tour of Fenway Park. Explore the dugout, look at one of the last hand-operated scoreboards in the major leagues and see the infield and outfield up close. If your trip feels incomplete without a stub in hand, try for the limited number of game-day tickets made available at Gate E on Lansdowne Street two hours before the first pitch. Alternatively, try the Red Sox official online ticket agency, Ace Ticket (www.aceticket.com), for ticket resales.

Tour tickets: adults $12, seniors $11, children over 3 $10. Tours: in season, on the hour from 9 a.m.-4 p.m. (or 3.5 hours before game time); off-season, 9 a.m.-3 p.m.

THE FIRST CHURCH OF CHRIST, SCIENTIST

210 Massachusetts Ave., Boston, 617-450-2000; www.tfccs.com

The First Church of Christ, Scientist makes a thoughtful pause on any sightseeing tour through Boston. The church (also known as the Mother Church) is the world headquarters for the Christian Science Church, which was founded by Mary Baker Eddy in 1866. The structure itself is a huge Romanesque church built in 1894, with elaborate stained windows and a small seating area. An expansive plaza, pristine reflecting pool and pretty fountains round out the property. While tours of the church are available, what's really worth the time is a stop at the Mapparium in the Mary Baker Eddy library. There, a huge, walk-through globe boasts perfect acoustics and a map of the world circa 1935.

Along with the interactive exhibit, this provides for a fascinating way to experience geography.

Admission: adults $6, seniors, students and children 6 and over $4. Mapparium and exhibits: Tuesday-Sunday 10 a.m.-4 p.m.

THE FREEDOM TRAIL

Boston Common Visitor Information Center, 148 Tremont St., Boston, 617-357-8300; www.thefreedomtrail.org

The original self-guided city walking tour, this trail follows a distinct line that was painted on the ground 50 years ago and links historical sites like Paul Revere's house and the Old North Church. Start at the Boston Common Visitor Center (148 Tremont St.), where you can arm yourself with a map that allows you to jump on and off the trail as you please.

Daily 9 a.m.-5 p.m.

GRANARY BURYING GROUND

Park and Tremont streets, near the eastern edge of Boston Common, Boston, 617-635-4505; www.cityofboston.gov

The third oldest cemetery in the city, the Granary Burying Ground claims to hold the remains of Revolutionary favorites such as Paul Revere, John Hancock, Crispus Attucks and Benjamin Franklin's parents. If it's not too morbid, bring the kids to the supposed final resting place of Mother Goose. Wondering what this has to do with a granary? Nearby Park Street Church occupies land that was formerly a main grain storage facility.

Daily 9 a.m.-5 p.m.; hours may vary slightly.

HAYMARKET

Blackstone Street, Boston

Before there was Whole Foods, there was Boston's Haymarket. Located around the corner from touristy Quincy Market and Faneuil Hall, Haymarket is an open-air produce market held on Friday afternoons and all day Saturdays. Originally, Haymarket was dominated by vendors from the nearby North End, Boston's Little Italy neighborhood. Today, it gathers a healthy mix of locals and tourists. While the best deals are found later in the day, the quality of the selection decreases as the clock ticks. Before you go, prepare yourself for rude behavior, loud vendors, cash-only transactions and a generally competitive atmosphere. But if you're in the right mood, Haymarket makes for a bargain-hunting blast.

Friday-Saturday during daylight hours.

INSTITUTE OF CONTEMPORARY ART

100 Northern Ave., Boston, 617-478-3100; www.icaboston.org

Opened in 2006, the glass and steel contemporary art museum is as much a sight as the galleries inside. After years of displaying works in a former fire station, the founders of the ICA finally found a permanent home with this Diller Scofidio + Renfro-designed four-story structure. Today, the museum hosts exhibitions, performance art, film and video screenings as well as special family programs. The museum's opening kicked off a renaissance for its waterfront neighborhood and now the area is filled with sleek, new condo developments

and even Louis Boston, the city's most iconic upscale department store.
Admission: adults $15, seniors $13, students $10, children 17 and under free. Tuesday, Wednesday, Saturday, Sunday 10 a.m.-5 p.m., Thursday-Friday 10 a.m.-9 p.m.,

ISABELLA STEWART GARDNER MUSEUM
280 The Fenway, Boston, 617-566-1401; www.gardnermuseum.org

Isabella Stewart Gardner never walked her lion along Commonwealth Avenue, as local lore has it, but she was a lioness herself when it came to amassing a world-class art collection. Gardner wanted to share her treasures with the city of Boston, so she simply built a museum. Today, her legacy stands like a Venetian palazzo on the Fenway, filled with Titians and Matisses as well as a few reminders of the famous 1990 art heist. There's no denying that the place used to feel far more mausoleum than museum. Director Anne Hawley and her creative staff have found ways to circumnavigate the rigid restrictions of Gardner's will, which stated, among other things, that not one work of art be moved or rearranged from it's general position. Today, the museum offers imaginative programs and exhibitions that combine the works of old masters with contemporary art forms. The flower-filled central courtyard is a delight, as are the concerts that are held from September to May in the Tapestry Room.
Admission: $12 (all those named "Isabella" are admitted free). Tuesday-Sunday 11 a.m.-5 p.m.

KING'S CHAPEL AND BURYING GROUND
Tremont and School streets, Boston, 617-635-4505; www.kings-chapel.org

When the king wants something, he gets it. However, since none of the colonists were interested in selling England's King James II the necessary land on which to build a sizeable Anglican Church, he ordered then-Governor Andros to hand over a portion of the burying ground. Today, the large stone Unitarian Church you see along the Freedom Trail includes a bell that was recast by Paul Revere in 1814.
Burying ground: daily 9 a.m.-5 p.m; hours may vary slightly. King's chapel: Tuesday-Saturday 10 a.m.-4 p.m.; Sunday hours vary depending on church services.

HATCH SHELL
Esplanade, Boston; www.hatchshell.com

In the summer, one of the best seats in Boston isn't a seat at all, but a grassy swatch of lawn on the Esplanade in front of the Hatch Shell. Home to the Boston Pops' famous Fourth of July concert, the Hatch Shell is also Boston's epicenter for large outdoor performances and events, including free Friday flicks, oldies concerts, classical orchestra performances and more.
Check the website for a list of current events.

MAKE WAY FOR DUCKLINGS AT THE BOSTON PUBLIC GARDEN
Public Garden, Boston; www.cityofboston.gov

A lot has changed since Robert McCloskey first published *Make Way For Ducklings* in 1941, but some things haven't—the story of a pair of mallard ducks raising their offspring on an island in Boston's Public Garden remains a perennial favorite. To commemorate the book and its story, Boston erected a bronze statue of Mrs. Mallard and her eight ducklings (Jack, Kack, Lack, Mack,

Nack, Ouack, Pack and Quack) in the Public Garden. Get a closer look at Mrs. Mallard's homeland by taking a pedal-powered Swan boat ride in the Public Garden's picturesque lagoon.

MUSEUM AT THE JOHN FITZGERALD KENNEDY LIBRARY
Columbia Point, Boston, 866-535-1960; www.jfklibrary.org

It's hard to visit Boston without being reminded of President John F. Kennedy. Camelot is seemingly everywhere. Nowhere is that presence stronger than at the John F. Kennedy Library, located just south of downtown on a magnificent 10-acre park overlooking the harbor. Come for the elaborate and well-displayed exhibits. Stay for the view, as it provides a unique, southern perspective of the city skyline. Inside, continuously running clips of Kennedy's speeches help convey his magnetism and appeal. Other popular sights include the partial replica of the Oval Office and the coconut on which JFK wrote a message after his PT-109 boat crashed in World War II.

Admission: adults $12, seniors and students $10, children 13-17 $9. Daily 9 a.m.-5 p.m.

MUSEUM OF FINE ARTS
465 Huntington Ave., Boston, 617-267-9300; www.mfa.org

The grande dame of Boston's cultural fleet, the Museum of Fine Arts just underwent a $500 million renovation, which brought soaring new galleries to the Beaux Arts museum. The MFA boasts beautiful impressionist paintings and one of the world's preeminent collections of Asiatic art. Once in danger of being considered a cherished, if somewhat dusty, relic, the MFA is back where it belongs, in the center of Boston's museum scene.

Admission: $17. Daily 10 a.m.-4:45 p.m., Wednesday-Friday until 9:45 p.m. Free Wednesday from 4-9:45 p.m.

MUSEUM OF SCIENCE
1 Science Park, Boston, 617-723-2500; www.mos.org

Always a good bet on winter weekends or rainy days, Boston's Museum of Science provides tons of hands-on exploration opportunities for kids of all ages. A few of the vintage exhibits show their age, but the museum works hard to continually reinvent and update with the times. The biggest oohs and ahhs come from the world's largest Van de Graaff generators, designed by Dr. Robert J. Van de Graaff himself. Other crowd-pleasers include the IMAX Theater and weekly stargazing program at the Gilliland Observatory on the museum's roof (weather permitting).

Admission: adults $19, seniors and students $17, children 3-11 $16. Daily 9 a.m.-5 p.m., Friday until 9 p.m.

NEW ENGLAND AQUARIUM
One Central Wharf, Boston, 617-973-5206; www.neaq.org

Picture New York's Guggenheim Museum. Now picture it under water. That's the experience you find at one of America's first modern aquariums, situated on Boston's waterfront. With its Giant Ocean Tank in the center of the building and a spiral pathway running along the sides, the well-designed museum allows you to spy a huge variety of sea life at all different depths. Don't miss the aquarium's huge penguin exhibit featuring multiple breeds of the birds swimming, lounging and frolicking around their 150,000-gallon habitat.

Admission: adults $20, seniors $18, children 3-11 $12. July-August, Sunday-Thursday 9 a.m.-6 p.m., Friday-Saturday 9 a.m.-7 p.m.; September-June, Monday-Friday 9 a.m.-5 p.m., Saturday-Sunday 9 a.m.-6 p.m.

NEW ENGLAND AQUARIUM WHALE WATCHES

New England Aquarium Dock, Boston, 617-973-5206; www.neaq.org

It's one thing to visit an aquarium and watch the fish swim around a tank. It's another to climb aboard a fast-moving boat and head out to the ocean. The New England Aquarium's high-speed *Voyager III* catamaran brings you 30 miles off the coast of Boston to the Stellwagen Bank whale feeding grounds, a playground for whales of all kinds. Humpbacks, finback whales, minky whales all gather here. They can't guarantee a glimpse of these gentle giants, though each of these well-timed trips is famous for producing a sighting or two.

Admission: adults $40, children under 11 $34. April-October. Reservations recommended.

NICHOLS HOUSE MUSEUM

55 Mount Vernon St., Boston, 617-227-6993; www.nicholshousemuseum.org

Small but impressive, the Nichols House Museum doesn't try to overwhelm with eye-popping video or flashy interactives. It can't, because this museum is all about bringing visitors back to an age where computers didn't exist. The 1804 townhouse was the home of Rose Standish Nichols from 1885 until her death in 1960. Today, it is filled with the possessions she gathered on her trips around the world—the collection includes Asian art, Flemish tapestries and works by Augustus Saint Gaudens.

Admission: adults $7. April-October, Tuesday-Saturday noon-4 p.m.; November-March, Thursday-Saturday noon-4 p.m.

OLD NORTH CHURCH

193 Salem St., Boston, 617-523-6676; www.oldnorth.com

While everyone knows the phrase "one if by land, two if by sea" from Longfellow's famous poem about the midnight ride of Paul Revere, they probably don't know the Old North Church, where the signals were hung. This Freedom Trail highlight remains a marvel of its historic time— built in 1723, it remains the oldest church in Boston. Today, you can also see the original chandeliers installed in time for the church's first Christmas in 1724. Episcopalian services, open to the public, are still held in the church twice a week on Wednesday and Sunday.

Admission: adults $8, students and seniors $6, children 3-16 $5. January-February, Tuesday-Sunday 10 a.m.-4 p.m., closed Monday; March-May, daily 9 a.m.-5 p.m. June-October, daily 9 a.m.-6 p.m.; November-December, daily 10 a.m.-5 p.m. Tours: July-October, daily on the hour. Sunday services: 9 a.m., 11 a.m.

OLD SOUTH CHURCH

645 Boylston St., Boston, 617-536-1970; www.oldsouth.org

A stunning building near Copley Square and across from the Boston Public Library, the Old South Church is an unusually ornate structure and example of Northern Italian Gothic architecture. The church's bell tower soars above Copley Square, while the pink, brown and gray stonework adds a colorful flourish. Original members of the congregation include luminaries such as Benjamin Franklin, Samuel Adams and even Elizabeth Vergoose, a.k.a. "Mother Goose."

Worship services: Sunday 9 a.m., 11 a.m.

OLD SOUTH MEETING HOUSE

310 Washington St., Boston, 617-482-6439;
www.oldsouthmeetinghouse.org

If the slew of cemeteries along the Freedom Trail brings you down, head to the Old South Meeting House for a bit of rabble-rousing. The largest structure in colonial Boston, the building was the rallying point for the Boston Tea Party in 1773. A Congregationalist church whose members included Samuel Adams and Benjamin Franklin, the Old South Meeting House is now a museum dedicated to the free expression of ideas. Its "Voices of Protest" interactive exhibit is a fun and interesting way to explore the history of the building as well as the people who spoke there.

April-October, daily 9:30 a.m.-5 p.m.; November-March, Monday-Friday 10 a.m.-4 p.m.

OLD STATE HOUSE/SITE OF THE BOSTON MASSACRE

206 Washington St., Boston, 617-720-1713; www.bostonhistory.org

Now isolated by busy streets and dwarfed by nearby commercial buildings, the Old State House serves as portal to pre-United States history. Early American patriots debated their futures in this structure, and the Declaration of Independence was first read in Boston from its balcony. With two floors of hands-on exhibits and galleries, the Old State House makes colonial history interesting. Nearby is the site of the Boston Massacre, where five protesting colonists were killed by British soldiers in March 1770.

Daily 9:30 a.m. 5 p.m.

THE PAUL REVERE HOUSE

19 North Square, Boston, 617-523-2338;
www.paulreverehouse.org

Unlike many historical sites that have been rebuilt, replaced or reconstructed, the Paul Revere House is the real deal. All but the windows are original to this 1680 structure, which served as Revere's home from 1770 to 1800. Self-guided tours along with museum interpreters give a feel for Revere's upscale colonial living. Cobblestones, greenery and the small colonial garden in the courtyard are endearing. While you're at it, check out the 900-pound bell and other artifacts made by Paul Revere & Sons for the *USS Constitution* warship.

Admission: Adults $3, seniors and students $2.50, children 5-7 years $1. April 15-October 31, daily 9:30 a.m.-5:15 p.m.; November 1-April 14, daily 9:30 a.m.-4:15 p.m. Closed Monday January-March.

PARK STREET CHURCH

1 Park St., Boston, 617-523-3383; www.parkstreet.org

A church of firsts, Park Street Church is home to a long tradition of social and theological movements—the first Protestant missionaries to visit Hawaii, the United States' first humane society, one of the nation's first Sunday school programs. It also served as the musical home of Lowell Mason, the church's first organist. Mason composed well-known hymns such as "Joy to the World" and "Nearer My God to Thee." Though it's not as well known as other stops on the Freedom Trail, the church is still worth a visit.

Tuesday-Saturday 9:30 a.m.-3:30 p.m.; closed Monday. Worship services: Sunday, 8:30 a.m., 11 a.m., 4 p.m., 6 p.m.

SAMUEL ADAMS BREWERY

30 Germania St., Boston, 617-368-5080; www.samueladams.com

A close reading of Revolutionary history proves it—drinking and patriotic speeches went hand in hand. And the founding of Boston's own Samuel Adams lager in 1984 proved there's still a call for good grog in Beantown. Located just south of downtown, Samuel Adams brewery offers first-come, first-served 45-minute tours of the small but impressive facility. Visitors are free to sample the brew, though it's worth noting, there's no restaurant onsite.

Admission: $2, which goes to a local charity. Tuesday-Thursday 10 a.m.-3 p.m., Friday 10 a.m.-5:30 p.m., Saturday 10 a.m.-3 p.m.

STATE HOUSE

Beacon Street at Park Street, Boston 617-727-3676; www.cityofboston.gov

The State House sits atop ritzy Beacon Hill, with its gilded dome a shiny focal point amidst a sea of old-fashioned brick buildings. If time allows, explore the statues inside the building and around its grounds, including ones dedicated to Major General Joseph Hooker from the Civil War, Mary Dyer (who was executed for being a Quaker) and Daniel Webster.

Monday-Friday 10 a.m.-4 p.m.

SYMPHONY HALL

301 Massachusetts Ave., Boston, 617-266-1492; www.bso.org

An architectural and acoustical masterpiece built by McKim, Mead and White in 1900, Symphony Hall houses both the Boston Symphony Orchestra and the Boston Pops. Classical music fans swoon at the programs these world-class organizations offer every season. In the summer, the BSO, under the visionary leadership of James Levine, moves to Tanglewood in the Berkshires (an easy two-hour drive down the Massachusetts Turnpike). Led by the char-ismatic director Keith Lockhart, the Pops fill the sizable gap with enthusiastic aplomb—not only at Symphony Hall, but also at the Hatch Shell along the banks of the Charles River.

TD BANKNORTH

100 Legends Way, Boston, 617-624-1050; www.tdbanknorthgarden.com

Home to the Celtics and the Bruins, TD Banknorth Garden is a modern and noisy arena. It lacks the gritty charm of the old Boston Garden, where the legendary teams of the past played, but there's still magic in the air. You can usually get tickets to Celtics games at the box office (and Bruins games are easier). Avoid the rafters by checking Internet ticket sites like StubHub, where season ticket holders who, in the case of the Celtics, bought tickets low, when the team was in the cellar, and are now selling them sky-high.

SPECIAL EVENTS

BOSTON MARATHON

Hopkinton to Boston; www.bostonmarathon.org
If you happen to find yourself in Boston on the third Monday in April, don't be surprised if it feels like a holiday, because it is. It's Patriots' Day, to be exact, but locals are quicker to associate the day with the famed Boston Marathon. This is the world's oldest annual marathon, and one of few 26.2-mile races to require a qualifying time. Every year, it draws about 25,000 runners and roughly 500,000 spectators. To add to the festive atmosphere, the Red Sox usually play a home game that day, with fans emptying onto nearby Kenmore Square just as the race nears completion over on Boylston Street.

FIRST NIGHT BOSTON

617-542-1399; www.firstnight.org
There's no ball drop, and it's usually below freezing. But that doesn't stop Bostonians from spending New Year's Eve outdoors with dancers, musicians, comedy acts, ice sculptors and a blowout fireworks display. Boston held the first organized First Night in the nation in 1976, and the tradition seems to have caught on with cities like Auckland, New Zealand and Whistler, British Columbia. If you're looking for a New Year's Eve filled with tubs of champagne, this isn't for you—First Night is a strictly non-alcoholic affair. If you've got kids in tow, or if you're aiming for a fun evening you'll remember the next morning, by all means—bundle up and head out.
Tickets: $15, children under 4 free.

TRINITY CHURCH
206 Clarendon St., Boston, 617-536-0944; www.trinitychurchboston.org
Trinity Church is one of the landmarks that give Boston's Copley Square such an impressive and historic feel. With its balanced spires, pleasant pinkish-brown coloring and wonderful façade, the church serves as a cheerful backstop to the openness of Copley Square. This church and parish house were designed by Henry Hobson Richardson and served as the archetype of his Richardson Romanesque style that proliferated across the United States and other countries in the late 1800s. Today, its active Episcopal congregation hosts a variety of religious and community services.
Worship services: Sunday 7:45 a.m., 9 a.m., 11:15 a.m., 6 p.m.

BROOKLINE
JOHN F. KENNEDY NATIONAL HISTORIC SITE
83 Beals St., Brookline, 617-566-7937; www.nps.gov
The 35th President spent his boyhood years in this modest clapboard house on a quiet, leafy Brookline street. Open for tours seasonally, the site includes mementos, photographs and furniture detailing Kennedy family history, all

HIGHLIGHT

WHAT IS THE BEST WAY TO SEE HARVARD SQUARE?

Harvard has more than a great reputation. It also has one of the country's coolest neighborhoods: Harvard Square. Thanks to its hefty student population, the area maintains a casual, independent vibe enhanced by local boutiques, night-spots and emerging restaurants. Then there are the historic sites, from Harvard Yard to narrow lanes like the circa 1630s Church Street. An avid walker could spend an entire day (or an entire weekend) exploring these environs. For those tight on time, though, here's where to go:

Start with a cup of coffee at the spot where hipster coeds and bemused professors power up for the day: **Crema Café** (*27 Brattle St., Cambridge, 617-876-2700; www.cremacambridge.com*). Here, the baristas serve a sinfully creamy cappuccino and the café's cozy seats make a great perch for people watching. Once you're amply caffeinated, walk four blocks southeast on Massachusetts Avenue to **Harvard Book Store** (*1256 Massachusetts Ave., Cambridge, 617-661-1515; www.harvard.com*), an independently-owned and family-run shop that acts as the neighborhood's nucleus. Selling everything from Harvard paraphernalia to Harry Potter books, it's also a worthy browsing point. Book-lovers will also want to check out the **Globe Corner Bookstore** (*90 Mt. Auburn St., Cambridge, 617-497-6277; www.globecorner.com*), a shop dedicated to maps and travel literature. Four blocks east on Mass. Ave., **Mr. Bartley's Gourmet Burgers** (*1246 Massachusetts Ave., Cambridge, 617-354-6559; www.mrbartley.co*) is a must-stop for lunch. The kitchsy, cash-only spot serves more than two-dozen varieties of burger, from the "The Yuppie Burger" (Boursin and bacon) to the "The People's Republic of Cambridge" (cole slaw and Russian dressing). The square has no shortage of cultural offerings, either. The aesthetically minded can visit the art trifecta of the **Fogg Art Museum** on nearby Quincy Street, the **Arthur M. Sackler Museum** half a block north of the Fogg, and the **Harvard Museum of Natural History**, a five-minute stroll north on Quincy, west on Kirkland Street and north on Oxford. All are within walking distance of one another and showcase revolving exhibits.

No visit to Harvard Square is complete without a stroll through Harvard Yard. Bordered by freshmen dormitories and some of the oldest college buildings in America, this 22-acre campus green dates back to the 17th century and is now a National Historic Landmark.

Finally, why not cap off the afternoon with a screening at the non-profit **Brattle Theatre** (*40 Brattle St., Cambridge, 617-876-6837; www.brattlefilm.org*), located just a quick walk southwest on Church Street? Brattle is independent cinema at its best. Stop in for a black-and-white or foreign film, then head three blocks southeast to indulge your sweet tooth at upscale local sweet shop **Finale** (*30 Dunster St., Cambridge, 617-441-9797; www.finaledesserts.com*).

donated to the National Park Service in 1967 by Kennedy's mother, Rose Fitzgerald Kennedy.

Admission: adults $3. May-October, 10 a.m.-4:30 p.m.

CAMBRIDGE

CHRIST CHURCH

0 Garden St., Cambridge, 617-876-0200; www.cccambridge.org

Dating back to 1759, this Episcopal Church building is the oldest church in Cambridge. The fine Georgian colonial designed by Peter Harrison, who also designed King's Chapel in Boston, was also used as a barracks during the Revolution. Services are still held on Wednesday and Sunday, and are open to the public.

Daily.

HARVARD UNIVERSITY

24 Quincy St., Cambridge, www.harvard.edu; Information center: 1350 Massachusetts Ave., Cambridge, 617-495-1573

Harvard has been accepting students since 1636, making it the country's oldest institute of higher learning. Originally called New College, America's most prestigious university was renamed in 1638 after local minister John Harvard bequeathed half his estate to the school. The prototypical brick and quad-filled campus spans Harvard and Radcliffe colleges, as well as 10 graduate and professional schools, encompassing about 7,000 undergraduate students and 14,000 post-graduates. The university's rich history and endowments make the campus a great place to catch a lecture by visiting notables, an arts performance or an exhibition at one of the many university-owned museums.

AMERICAN REPERTORY THEATRE

64 Brattle St., Cambridge, 617-547-8300; www.amrep.org

A.R.T. presents some of the most cutting-edge theater around, including the world premiere of Marsha Norman's Pulitzer Prize-winning play *Night, Mother*. Theatrical purists may occasionally find fault with the relentlessly innovative spirit that prevails in A.R.T. productions, but the scene is always lively and provocative. Watching the funky Cantabrigian audience—a blend of self-consciously iconoclastic students, academics and local luminaries—is diverting and amusing entertainment that, on some nights, actually steals the show.

Check website for schedule and prices.

HARVARD UNIVERSITY ART MUSEUMS

32 Quincy St., Cambridge, 617-495-9400; www.artmuseums.harvard.edu

Visit three museums in one: the Fogg Art Museum (which includes wide-ranging collections of paintings and sculpture), the Busch-Reisinger Museum (features mostly German art) and the Arthur M. Sackler Museum (showcases ancient art, plus Asian and Islamic collections). Admission to one museum covers all three; allow a half-day for all.

Admission: adults $9, seniors $7, students $6, children under 18 free. Monday-Saturday 10 a.m.-5 p.m., Sunday 1-5 p.m.

HARVARD MUSEUM OF NATURAL HISTORY
26 Oxford St., Cambridge, 617-495-3045; www.hmnh.harvard.edu

Most people think of flowers as soft and delicate. At least Harvard's Museum of Natural History got the delicate part right. The museum boasts a collection of more than 3,000 flowers made of glass—that's right, delicate hand-blown glass flowers representing over 800 plant species. Some of these flowers date to the 1880s. The museum also offers everything you'd expect from a Natural History museum, including a zoological gallery and a study on "Arthropods: Creatures that Rule."

Admission: adults $9, seniors and students $7, children 3-18 $6. Daily 9 a.m.-5 p.m.

HARVARD SQUARE
Cambridge, 617-491-3434; www.harvardsquare.com

More than a nexus of higher education, Harvard Square teems with international students, travelers and local legends as well as bohemian shops and cafés. Get a glimpse of the university when you pass through the wrought-iron gates into Harvard Yard. Stop by Charlie's Kitchen (*10 Eliot St., Cambridge, 617-492-9646*) for a famous double cheeseburger.

JOHN ADAMS MINUTEMAN COMMUTER BIKEWAY
Alewife Station, Cambridge to Depot Park, Bedford; www.minutemanbikeway.org

What better way to celebrate the American Revolution and its opening battles at Lexington and Concord than by starting a revolution of your own—a revolution of your bike wheels, that is. By winding from Cambridge and Arlington through Lexington to Bedford, this commuter bikeway approximates the famous path taken by Paul Revere in 1775. For a break from the cycling, pull over at Spy Pond in Arlington or Great Meadows in East Lexington, with its miles of trails for hiking, bird watching or just relaxing.

LIST VISUAL ARTS CENTER AT MIT
Wiesner Building, 20 Ames St., Cambridge, 617-253-4680; listart.mit.edu

Here, the contemporary art exhibits are every bit as riveting as the scientific research that takes place at this storied university. The MIT campus boasts an outstanding permanent collection of outdoor sculpture, including works by Calder, Moore and Picasso. Check out the school's architecture, too—featuring buildings by Aalto, Pei and Saarinen.

Admisson: free. Tuesday-Wednesday, Friday-Sunday noon-6 p.m., Thursday noon-6 p.m.

LONGFELLOW NATIONAL HISTORIC SITE
105 Brattle St., Cambridge, 617-876-4491; www.nps.gov

After assuming command of the Continental Army, General George Washington used this large, yellow colonial-style house as his base of operations. The house was also home to the great American poet and writer Henry Wadsworth Longfellow. Today, it boasts an array of portraits and busts depicting many of Longfellow's famous contemporaries, including Nathaniel Hawthorne and Ralph Waldo Emerson.

Admission: adults $3. Tours: May 1-June 3, Thursday-Saturday 10:30 a.m., 11:30 a.m., 1 p.m., 2 p.m., 3 p.m., 4 p.m.; June 4-September, Wednesday-Sunday 10:30 a.m., 11:30 a.m., 1 p.m., 2 p.m., 3 p.m., 4 p.m.

MASSACHUSETTS INSTITUTE OF TECHNOLOGY
77 Massachusetts Ave., Cambridge, 617-253-1000; www.mit.edu

Some of the world's most brilliant minds convene here, at this 150-year-old institute of higher learning. With strengths in science, medicine, engineering, medicine, mathematics and economics, M.I.T. educates about 10,000 under-graduate and post-graduate students each year. Located on the Charles River across from Boston's Back Bay neighborhood, the campus features an impres-sive combination of neoclassic structures and modern buildings by famous architects like Eero Saarinen, Frank Gehry and I.M. Pei.

MOUNT AUBURN CEMETERY
580 Mount Auburn St., Cambridge, 617-547-7105; www.mountauburn.org

Founded in 1831, this cemetery is lauded as one of the first large-scale public landscapes in the U.S. It has an impressive roster of residents, to boot—Oliver Wendell Homes, Winslow Homer, Isabella Stewart Gardner and Henry Wadsworth Longfellow, among 80,000 others. Gravestones aside, the 175-acre grounds are spectacular on their own, with natural woodlands, ornamental gardens and ponds.

Daily 8 a.m.-5 p.m.

CHARLESTOWN
BUNKER HILL MONUMENT
Monument Square, Charlestown, 617-242-5641; www.cityofboston.gov

Don't look to Bunker Hill for the Bunker Hill Monument—look to nearby Breed's Hill instead. This Freedom Trail stop marks the first major conflict between the British and the rag-tag colonial militia. A statue of Colonel William "don't fire until you see the whites of their eyes" Prescott stands in front of the landmark. Erected between 1827 and 1843, the Bunker Hill Monument recently received updated facilities and a new museum directly across the street.

Daily 9 a.m.-4:30 p.m.

USS CONSTITUTION
1 Constitution Road, Charlestown, 617-242–7511; www.ussconstitution.navy.mil

Christened "Old Ironsides" during the War of 1812, the *USS Constitution* is famous for the British cannonballs that simply bounced off her thick oak sides. Now stationed at the Charlestown Navy Shipyard, the *USS Constitution* has been an active navy vessel for more than 210 years, and is the oldest commis-sioned ship still afloat in the world. As a "ship of state," she traditionally makes a voyage every Independence Day.

April-October, Tuesday-Sunday 10 a.m.-6 p.m.; November-March, Thursday-Sunday 10 a.m.-4 p.m.

WHERE TO STAY

★★★THE BACK BAY HOTEL
350 Stuart St., Boston, 617-266-7200; www.doylecollection.com

When friends ask how you passed the time in Boston, tell them you spent the night at the police station. If you stayed at The Back Bay Hotel, you won't be lying. Formerly the Boston Police headquarters, the historic building now provides visitors with a surprisingly luxurious place to stay, with high-end amenities like down comforters and multi-head showers in the bathrooms. Don't miss Cuffs, the onsite Irish bar on the ground floor, for an unforgettable night of revelry.

225 rooms. Restaurant, bar. Fitness center. Business center. $251-350

★★★BEACON HILL HOTEL
25 Charles St., Boston, 617-723-7575; www.beaconhillhotel.com

This petite boutique hotel is tucked between the shops and cafés of Charles Street, the Beacon Hill neighborhood's main thoroughfare. The twelve guest rooms and one suite are delightful though tiny, with special touches like plantation shutters and local photography. But it's the surroundings that make this hotel special. Spend a warm afternoon on the sunny roof deck, or stop in for modern French fare in the busy Beacon Hill Bistro downstairs. You might have to fight the well-heeled locals who come here for dinner, but after tasting the seasonally inspired cuisine, you'll understand why they do. Breakfast at the Bistro is included in your stay.

13 rooms. Restaurant. $251-350

★★★★★BOSTON HARBOR HOTEL
70 Rowes Wharf, Boston, 617-439-7000; www.bhh.com

If you're going to have a celebrity sighting somewhere in this city, chances are good it'll be at the Boston Harbor Hotel. Why is it such a favorite place for the famous to catch some z's? Probably because the brocade-bedecked rooms feature skyline or water views and down-to-the-details provisions like collar stays and stain-removal wipes. Every service imaginable is available, from same-day dry cleaning to auto detailing, and all are delivered by an affable, professional staff that make you feel like a celebrity yourself. The dining options are also excellent—from the impressive wine list at Meritage to the indulgent service at Rowes Wharf Sea Grille. The water taxi from Logan airport to the hotel's own marina is the savviest way to get from touchdown to cocktail hour without delay.

230 rooms. Restaurant, bar. Fitness center. Pool. Spa. Business center. $351 and up

★★★BOSTON MARRIOTT COPLEY PLACE
110 Huntington Ave., Boston, 617-236-5800; www.copleymarriott.com

A fashionista's paradise, the 1,000-plus room Back Bay Marriott lies adjacent to some of the city's best high-end shopping. Think Barneys, Dior, Gucci and Jimmy Choo. Thanks to indoor walkways that connect the hotel with Copley Place, the Prudential Center and the Back Bay train station, guests can access some of Boston's sights without setting foot outside—that's a lifesaver when a Nor'Easter blows through. Rooms aren't exceptional, but they do feature 300 thread-count sheets and 24-hour room service. Try to snag a room on the concierge level, which has a private lounge, or on one of the higher floors for views of Copley Square or the Charles River.

1,148 rooms. Restaurant, bar. Fitness center. Pool. Business center. $251-350

★★★BOSTON MARRIOTT LONG WHARF
296 State St., Boston, 617-227-0800; www.marriottlongwharf.com

If you're traveling with children, there's no better place than Long Wharf. The historic waterfront location is surrounded by kid-friendly activities, from the street performers of nearby Quincy Market to the New England Aquarium and, just a short taxi ride away, the Children's Museum. Add to that the Marriott's indoor pool and the hotel's resemblance to a docked ship, and you've got a recipe for smiles. Parents get some perks too, including 300-thread-count linens and tons of local dining options. Here's some advice: hire a babysitter and make a break for the North End.

412 rooms. Restaurant, bar. Fitness center. Pool. Business center. $351 and up

★★★BOSTON PARK PLAZA HOTEL
50 Park Plaza, Boston, 617-426-2000; www.bostonparkplaza.com

From the bright red awnings to the always-busy restaurants to the hotel's dominating presence near the Public Garden, there's nothing subtle about the Park Plaza. In fact, every U.S. President since the hotel's 1927 opening has stayed here. Multiple renovations mean some guest rooms are oddly proportioned, though a few larger rooms have been created. The rooms received a $5 million update in 2008 that added new carpeting, pillow-top mattresses and furniture, whereas the property's common areas saw another $2.5 million upgrade in 2009.

941 rooms. Restaurant, bar. Fitness center. Business center. $351 and up

★★★CHARLESMARK HOTEL
655 Boylston St., Boston, 617-247-1212; www.charlesmarkhotel.com

Walking down Boylston Street, it's easy to mistake the Charlesmark for just another swanky retail store. It features a minimalist exterior and a busy ground-floor bar. In other words, it hardly looks like a place for tourists to hole up. This 1892 Back Bay townhouse contains a surprising number of cozy guest suites. Though small, all rooms are decked out in modern, minimalist style by local designer Dennis Duffy, giving it a fun, updated feel. Best of all, the service feels pleasantly personal compared to most Back Bay mega-hotels.

33 rooms. Bar. Business center. $151-250

★★★COPLEY SQUARE HOTEL
47 Huntington Ave., Boston, 617-536-9000; www.copleysquarehotel.com

One of Boston's most recognizable, landmark hotels (the signature red sign can be seen from almost anywhere in Back Bay) just got a major makeover. In business for more than 115 years, the 143-room hotel became increasingly rundown during the last decade. Upgrades restored its historic charm and lent a modern boutique-hotel feel to the space. New features include contemporary light fixtures, fabrics and glossy details in the lobby. New restaurants are also on the docket.

143 rooms. Restaurant, bar. Fitness center. $251-350

★★★THE COLONNADE HOTEL
120 Huntington Ave., Boston, 617-424-7000; www.colonnadehotel.com

One of the last independent hotels in Boston, the Colonnade Hotel recently poured $25 million into a gut renovation of its rooms and public spaces, giving

HIGHLIGHT

WHICH BOSTON HOTELS ARE THE MOST HISTORIC?

FAIRMONT COPLEY PLACE:

With one of the city's most recognizable facades, this 1912 hotel is newly fashionable thanks to a recent $34 million makeover. Today, the historic guest rooms feature period-style furnishings as well as minibars, marble bathrooms and windows that open.

OMNI PARKER HOUSE

The history of this 1855 hotel is the richest in all of the city: It once served as the stomping grounds of presidents Franklin D. Roosevelt and Ulysses S. Grant and authors Ralph Waldo Emerson and Henry David Thoreau. The in-house restaurant, Parker's, was the birthplace of Boston cream pie and Parker House dinner rolls, as well as the venue for John F. Kennedy's bachelor party.

LENOX HOTEL

Built in 1900, the historic Lenox still features traditional interiors with wood detailing, a chandelier-filled lobby and guest rooms with private wood-burning fireplaces. Notably, the Lenox hotel overlooks the finish line of the Boston Marathon, the nation's oldest 26.2-mile race.

TAJ BOSTON

Perched at the top of Newbury Street across from the Public Garden, this venerable hotel hasn't changed much since it opened in the 1920s. Check out the bar with its original fireplace, dark wood paneling and cushy club chairs—this is where Boston power deals are made.

its once-tired interior a glossy new look. Nowadays the lobby is done up with black woods, gleaming tile and detailed molding, while the guest rooms are dressed in soothing neutrals. Guests might not notice new touches like extra outlets for charging up iPods and laptops, or the air conditioning that automatically activates when you enter the room. But they're there, and they make a stay here very comfortable. For all the flashy upgrades, the hotel's greatest asset has remained untouched: on hot summer days, the glistening rooftop pool teems with sun worshippers.

285 rooms. Restaurant, bar. Fitness center. Pool. Business center. $251-350

★★★THE ELIOT HOTEL
370 Commonwealth Ave., Boston, 617-267-1607; www.eliothotel.com

Situated amid Commonwealth Avenue's multi-million dollar townhouses, private clubs and tree-lined mall, the Eliot Hotel allows guests to take luxury for granted. Each guest room is outfitted with a marble bathroom, down comforter and plush robes. Meanwhile, the heavy toile drapery, dramatic valances and upholstered furniture set a classically stylish tone. Other perks include 24-hour room service, clothes pressing and complimentary shoe-shines. For guests with pets, dog-sitting is even available. Traveling foodies shouldn't miss dining at Clio for French-Asian cuisine. Check out sushi bar Uni for light bites.

95 rooms. Restaurant. Business center. $251-350

★★★THE FAIRMONT BATTERY WHARF BOSTON
Three Battery Wharf, Boston, 617-994-9000, 800-257-7544; www.fairmont.com

Located on the waterfront, this new hotel stands where shipyards and ware-houses used to be. The location has its pros and cons. On the one hand, you're near the North End with all its excellent restaurants. On the other, the area is still developing, so you don't get much of a neighborhood feel. Still, guests enjoy glorious water views and even water-taxi service to and from the airport. Plus, the restaurant and outdoor patio are excellent summer destinations. Guest rooms are modern and comfortable with large desks and marble bathtubs.

150 rooms. Restaurant, bar. Fitness center. Spa. Business center. $251-350

★★★THE FAIRMONT COPLEY PLAZA BOSTON
138 St. James Ave., Boston, 617-267-5300; www.fairmont.com

Don't be fooled by the imposing columned exterior, the glittering chandeliers and opulent trompe l'oeil ceilings. This hotel is far from stuffy. Take it from black lab Catie, the Copley Plaza's "canine ambassador," who greets guests from the concierge desk. Following $34 million in upgrades to this circa-1912 hotel, guest rooms include minibars, windows that open and marble bathrooms. The traditional styling—striped wallpaper, flowery bedding, mahogany furniture—has stayed put. If you're feeling flush, reserve a Fairmont Gold room, which comes with upgraded room amenities and access to a private lounge with free refreshments.

383 rooms. Restaurant. Fitness center. Business center. $251-350

★★★★★FOUR SEASONS HOTEL BOSTON
200 Boylston St., Boston, 617-338-4400; www.fourseasons.com

When it comes to superlative service, no one does it like the Four Seasons. So guests can expect to be spoiled at this parkside hotel. Guest rooms feature tradi-tional styling, though they're best equipped for comfort with down pillows and luxury linens. After check-in, go for an afternoon tea at the hotel's Bristol Lounge. With all the fixings of traditional English high tea service, including finger sandwiches and buttery scones, it's the definition of Old Boston refine-ment. Be sure to take a dip in the indoor pool, which overlooks the Public Garden and State House. And don't miss all the upscale boutiques nearby—Escada, La Perla and Hermès.

273 rooms. Restaurant, bar. Fitness center. Pool. Spa. Business center. $351 and up

★★★HILTON BOSTON BACK BAY

40 Dalton St., Boston, 617-236-1100;
www.hiltonfamilyboston.com

This massive hotel fills with tourists and conventioneers year-round, and for good reason—a plethora of sights, including Fenway Park, Newbury Street and Copley Square are nearby. That's not to say you need to leave the property to sightsee. If you're lucky enough to get a room on one of the tower's upper floors, you can glimpse sailboats on the Charles River or the lights of Fenway Park. Guest rooms are decked out in dark woods and modern neutrals. Bathrooms come stocked with Crabtree & Evelyn products.

385 rooms. Restaurant, bar. Fitness center. Pool. Business center. $151-250

★★★HILTON BOSTON LOGAN AIRPORT

1 Hotel Drive, Boston, 617-568-6700; www.hiltonfamilyboston.com

A round-the-clock shuttle to the terminals means you'll never miss a flight when you stay at this hotel. If you would rather walk, there's also a covered skybridge connecting the property to the airport. Inside, guest rooms come equipped with Serta mattresses and Crabtree & Evelyn toiletries. A 6,000-square-foot pool, spa, fitness complex makes your stay even cushier—you'll forget you're practically sleeping on the tarmac.

599 rooms. Restaurant, bar. Fitness center. Pool. Spa. Business center. $251-350

★★★HOTEL COMMONWEALTH

500 Commonwealth Ave., Boston, 617-933-5000; www.hotelcommonwealth.com

It's hard to believe that the Hotel Commonwealth hasn't been there forever. The stately hotel that rises over Kenmore Square just opened in 2003, though it features an architectural style that's pure, traditional Boston. More than a place to lay your head, the complex includes the always-hopping brasserie Eastern Standard. But it's the oversized guest rooms that impress with their luxe Italian linens and L'Occitane bath products. Check out the hotel's menu of superb services, like in-room spa treatments and free shoe shines.

148 rooms. Restaurant, bar. Fitness center. Business center. $351 and up

★★★HYATT HARBORSIDE

101 Harborside Drive, Boston, 617-568-1234; www.harborside.hyatt.com

Airport hotels aren't known for being luxurious, but this one is. Here, the loft-like guest rooms feature cushy beds and soundproofed windows, so you're sure to be well rested for that morning flight. A 24-hour business center lets you work till the wee hours. And no joke, there's hardly a better view of Boston than the one you'll enjoy from the fitness center. It's the perfect place to say goodbye to the city before takeoff.

270 rooms. Restaurant, bar. Fitness center. Pool. Business center. $151-250

★★★HYATT REGENCY BOSTON FINANCIAL DISTRICT

1 Avenue de Lafayette, Boston, 617-912-1234; www.regencyboston.hyatt.com

For business travelers coming to the Financial District, simple and reliable trumps buzz-worthy anytime. You won't find any crazy design features here—just 500 centrally located, well-equipped guest rooms at the ready. An indoor pool and eucalyptus steam room help you wind down after a long day of meetings, while Sealy mattresses and Neutrogena products ensure you're comfortable, too. Don't forget the Nintendo 64 in every room—perfect when you can't sleep.

500 rooms. Restaurant, bar. Fitness center. Pool. Business center. $251-350

★★★INTERCONTINENTAL BOSTON

510 Atlantic Ave., Boston, 617-747-1000; www.intercontinentalboston.com

If most Boston hotels seem cramped, then the recently opened InterContinental Hotel is an oasis of space. As soon as you enter the giant marble-covered lobby, the soaring ceilings send the signal—you're not in compact Boston anymore. Adding to the sense of openness are a giant outdoor patio and two acres of waterfront gardens, where you can dine outside and get some sun. Meanwhile, the sizeable guest rooms feature contemporary décor and deluxe bathrooms with separate soaking tubs.

424 rooms. Restaurant, bar. Fitness center. Pool. Spa. Business center. $251-$350

★★★THE LANGHAM BOSTON

250 Franklin St., Boston, 617-451-1900; www.langhamhotels.com

Convenient to Faneuil Hall, the Freedom Trail and the North End, the Langham makes a great base for those who want to retrace the patriots' steps. Housed in the former Federal Reserve building, the Langham features colorful guest rooms and the Asian-inspired Chuan Spa, a perfect place for massage and other pampering services. While you're there, check out the power-lunch set at the Julien Bar. And don't miss the long-standing weekend chocolate bar brunch, featuring a dizzying array of chocolate-based desserts and treats

325 rooms. Restaurant, bar. Spa. Fitness center. Business center. Pool. $151-250

★★★LENOX HOTEL

61 Exeter St., Boston, 617-536-5300; www.lenoxhotel.com

You'd be hard-pressed to find a more action-packed location than the Lenox Hotel. Located in the heart of the bustling Back Bay neighborhood, the Lenox sits on a corner that overlooks the Boston Marathon finish line, Copley Square and Boylston Street. While all the other hotels chase the Mid-Century modern trend, the Lenox maintains elegantly traditional interiors. Wood detailing and brass chandeliers fill the lobby, while the guest rooms have satin damask bedding and floral upholstery. If you're in town during the winter months, request a room with a wood-burning fireplace. Aveda toiletries and access to the nearby Bella Sante spa are other frill factors.

214 rooms. Restaurant, bar. Fitness center. Business center. $351 and up

★★★LIBERTY HOTEL

215 Charles St., Boston, 617-224-4000; www.libertyhotel.com

In 2007, Boston scenesters were blessed with the arrival of the Liberty Hotel, a unique statement piece set in the previously vacant Charles Street Jail. Many of the 1851 building's historical details were preserved, including swinging iron cell doors, an impressive rotunda and exposed brick walls. Guests get a thrill from walking past a row of barred windows as they make way for the lavishly appointed cells, now stocked with Molton Brown bath products, sleek neutral linens and cozy knit blankets. Everywhere you wander on this property, you encounter the hotelier's sense of humor. The lobby bar and restaurant is called

Clink. Celebrity mug shots grace the walls of another bar, called Alibi. Local star chef Lydia Shire's serves up inventive Italian cuisine at Scampo, the hotel's contemporary but cozy restaurant.

298 rooms. Restaurant, bar. Fitness center. $351 and up

★★★★MANDARIN ORIENTAL, BOSTON

800 Boylston St., Boston, 617-535-8888; www.mandarinoriental.com

One of the most hotly anticipated real estate projects to hit Boston in decades, the Mandarin Oriental opened in October 2008 to great fanfare. In addition to some of the city's chicest hotel accommodations, the property also includes a 16,000-square-foot spa, a vitality pool, a state-of-the-art Kinesis wall, condominiums and three gourmet dining options, including the upscale French restaurant L'Espalier. Best of all, you're right on Boylton Street where all the great shopping is, and just minutes from the Charles River.

148 rooms. Restaurant, bar. Fitness center. Spa. Pool. Business center. $351 and up

★★★MILLENNIUM BOSTONIAN HOTEL

26 North St., Boston, 617-523-3600; www.millenniumhotels.com

It's hard to get any closer to the action than the Millennium Bostonian—it sits at the edge of Boston's bustling Quincy Market. A full renovation, completed in fall 2008, brought a much-needed touch of modern comfort to the hotel's formerly uninspiring interior spaces. Today, the guest rooms are decked out with Frette linens and pillow-top mattresses. During the summer, book a room with a private balcony; in winter months, the rooms with fireplaces are the coziest for those cold Boston nights.

201 rooms. Restaurant, bar. Fitness center. Business center. $151-250

★★★NINE ZERO HOTEL

90 Tremont St., Boston, 617-772-5800; www.ninezero.com

With its glossy interior of glass, stone, polished nickel, chrome and steel, Nine Zero adds a touch of glamour to your hotel stay. Don't be surprised if you spot a familiar face in the lobby, since this hotel is a favorite of visiting celebrities. Meanwhile, a stylish crowd is always eating up Chef Ken Oringer's upscale offerings at the onsite steakhouse KO Prime.

190 rooms. Restaurant. Fitness center. Business center. Pets accepted. $351 and up

★★★OMNI PARKER HOUSE

60 School St., Boston, 617-227-8600; www.omniparkerhouse.com

Despite the recent $30 million renovation, the appeal of this 1855 hotel is pure history—it was once the stomping ground of famed authors like Emerson and Thoreau as well as presidents Franklin D. Roosevelt and Ulysses S. Grant. Its in-house restaurant, Parker's, was the birthplace of Boston cream pie and Parker House dinner rolls, as well as the spot where JFK held his bachelor party. History buffs also love its location on the Freedom Trail. The rooms, however, have everything a 21st-century traveler needs, including work desks and flat-screen TVs.

551 rooms. Restaurant, bar. Fitness center. $251-350

★★★ONYX HOTEL

155 Portland St., Boston, 617-557-9955; www.onyxhotel.com

Positioned near the North End, this boutique hotel has a decidedly downtown feel, enhanced by bold, contemporary décor. Guest rooms feature a palette of red, taupe and black with comfy accoutrements like down pillows, ultra-thick mattresses and suede furniture. The downstairs restaurant, The Ruby Room, provides 24-hour room service. Pets are particularly welcome here—they're even greeted with treats and amenities like water bowls and beds.

112 rooms. Restaurant, bar. Fitness center. $251-350

★★★SHERATON BOSTON HOTEL

39 Dalton St., Boston, 617-236-2000; www.sheraton.com

Size may not matter, but in the case of this Back Bay hotel, it can't be ignored. The largest hotel in the city, it contains a whopping 1,200-plus rooms and suites. But these rooms are no cookie-cutters. While the standard lodgings are small and not particularly outstanding—decent linens, inoffensive décor, an ergonomic desk chair—the hotel's towering size guarantees excellent views from any perch. If you're here in summer, the 18-meter indoor/outdoor pool on the fifth floor is reason enough to book a room. It boasts a retractable roof and a deck—so on warm, clear days you can take in some sun or, in the evening, the starry night sky.

1,216 rooms. Restaurant. Fitness center. Business center. $151-250

★★★RENAISSANCE BOSTON WATERFRONT HOTEL

606 Congress St., Boston, 617-338-4111; www.marriott.com

One of the city's newest additions, the Renaissance hotel is bright, airy and right on the harbor. Guest rooms feel fresh and fun with bold splashes of colorful patterns. Conveniently close to South Boston's new Convention & Exhibition Center, the hotel hosts a large number of business travelers in its straightforward but eminently comfortable rooms. While staying there, be sure to check out chef Michael Schlow's newest venture, the seafood-heavy eatery 606 Congress, located on the first floor.

450 rooms. Restaurant. Fitness center. Pool. $251-350

★★★★THE RITZ-CARLTON, BOSTON COMMON

10 Avery St., Boston, 617-574-7100; www.ritzcarlton.com

This hotel's deep-pocketed patrons get perks like

WHAT ARE BOSTON'S BEST BOUTIQUE HOTELS?

Ames Hotel:
A stylish newcomer in a town where traditional reigns, this new boutique hotel makes good use of the historic building's original fixtures—from fireplaces to Romanesque arched windows, with a smattering of new Federalist-style accents to temper the cutting-edge redesign.

The Eliot Hotel:
Here, guest rooms are stylish though classic, but the greatest virtue is the in-house dining. Traveling foodies shouldn't miss dining at Clio for an unforgettable fusion of French and Asian cuisines.

XV Beacon:
The service here is suitably extravagant, with amenities like Lexus sedan service to shuttle you around town. Architecture- and design-lovers will be especially smitten with this 1903 Beaux Art landmark, which features an old-fashioned cage elevator and brass details throughout.

access to the luxe SportsClub/LA fitness center, Bulgari toiletries, Bose radios and Bang & Olufsen stereos, all of which come standard with a stay here. Then there are the accommodations. Even the most basic, pastel-toned guestrooms are nicely appointed with impossibly crisp bed linens, extra-fluffy pillows and three telephones (one in the bathroom). Still not impressed? Ask for a bath butler to come prepare an evening soak in the marble tub, then order room service at any hour you please. On weekdays, guests can call for complimentary limo rides to their morning meeting. Or reserve a room on the club level, which has its own lounge and concierge.

193 rooms. Restaurant, bar. Fitness center. Pool. Spa. Business center. $351 and up

★★★SEAPORT HOTEL

1 Seaport Lane, Boston, 877-732-7678; www.seaportboston.com

Catering largely to convention-goers and visitors to Boston's World Trade Center, the Seaport Hotel provides everything your satellite office needs—two business centers, 24-hour business services, computer stations and private offices, even ample meeting spaces. Rest up for your morning presentation on the 300-thread count, triple-sheeted beds and luxuriate in bathrooms stocked with oversized robes and towels. When the day is done, savor chef Rachel Klein's local, seasonal cuisine at Aura, or sip a martini at the Tamo bar.

426 rooms. Restaurant, bar. Fitness center. Pool. Spa. Business center. $351 and up

★★★★TAJ BOSTON

15 Arlington St., Boston, 617-536-5700; www.tajhotels.com

This venerable hotel hasn't changed much since it opened in the 1920s. Where else in town can you call for a bath butler (to fill your tub), a fireplace butler (to light your in-room hearth) or a technology butler (to ensure you don't miss a single email)? In true blueblood fashion, the hotel is decorated with richly textured wall fabrics and tasseled drapes in a palette of beige, gold, rose and blue. Shoe-shines, turndown service and high-end European toiletries are included, of course, as are the fantastic views of Newbury Street and the Public Garden. With its original fireplace, dark wood paneling and cushy club chairs, the hotel's bar is where Boston power deals are brokered.

273 rooms. Restaurant, bar. Fitness center. Business center. $351 and up

★★★W HOTEL

100 Stuart St., Boston, 617-261-8700; www.starwoodhotels.com

The city's first W hotel opened in 2010 along with its new glass tower in the city's Theater District. It's a look that fits nicely with the area's fashion-forward nightclubs. Meanwhile, the W gave the neighborhood two additional night-spots—a new outpost of star chef Jean-Georges Vongerichten's Market draws stylish eaters, while the W Lounge has become a popular after-work cocktail spot. Don't miss the only Boston location of Bliss Spa. All in all, the hotel's complex contains 235 upscale guest rooms and more than 100 high-priced luxury condos, further helping to speed along the neighborhood's long-awaited redevelopment.

235 rooms. Restaurant, bar. Spa. Fitness center. $251-350

★★★WESTIN COPLEY PLACE
10 Huntington Ave., Boston, 617-262-9600; www.westin.com

Westin hasn't forgotten why people book hotels—for comfortable places to sleep. Like the chain's other properties, every room in the Back Bay location has a Heavenly Bed with pillow-top mattress, plus a Heavenly Bath with dual showerheads. Even pets get the plush treatment with their own Heavenly dog beds. All this blissful snoozing is sure to leave you relaxed, well rested and ready to explore the nearby attractions, including the steakhouse The Palm, the local seafood spot Turner Fisheries and the indulgent Grettacole Spa.

803 rooms. Restaurant, bar. Fitness center. Spa. Pool. Business center. $251-350

★★★WESTIN BOSTON WATERFRONT
425 Summer St., Boston, 617-532-4600; www.westin.com/boston

What's the first sign that the Westin isn't the typical Boston hotel? The lobby bar—it features faux birch trees, wood-and-stone walls and ambient lighting for a spa-like feel. Once you ascend to your hotel room, you find all the comforts you expect—the chain's trademark Heavenly Bed, Heavenly Bath slippers and robes, ergonomic desk chairs, turndown service and 24-hour room service. If you want to catch your flight without the hassle of downtown traffic, catch the hotel's convenient water taxi.

793 rooms. Restaurant, bar. Fitness center. Pool. Business center. $251-350

★★★★XV BEACON, BOSTON
15 Beacon St., Boston, 617-670-1500; www.xvbeacon.com

There's no such thing as a second-tier guest at XV Beacon—everyone is treated like a VIP. The service is suitably extravagant, with over-the-top amenities such as complimentary Lexus sedan service. Featuring an old-fashioned cage elevator and brass details, the interior oozes Old Boston style. Every guest room has a four-poster bed, a private fireplace and toiletries from Fresh. Plus, an arrangement of flowers greets you as you enter your room. Come mealtime, head downstairs to Mooo, one of the city's top steakhouses. Its wine cellar is one of the most coveted private dining spaces in town. If you'd rather venture elsewhere for dinner, check with the hotel's stylishly dressed doormen—they're some of the city's friendliest and most knowledgeable.

60 rooms. Restaurant, bar. Fitness center. $351 and up

RECOMMENDED

AMES HOTEL
1 Court St., Boston, 617-979-8100; www.ameshotel.com

A stylish newcomer in a town where tradition reigns, this boutique hotel is the latest installment in the Morgans Hotel Group collection—think South Beach's Delano and London's Sanderson. Opened in 2010 in the 1889 Ames Building, the hotel features a design that incorporates the building's history, including original fixtures from fireplaces and Romanesque arched windows. But with muted colors, sleek furnishings and luxury linens, the hotelier didn't compromise on style. Rooms are loaded with upscale touches such as marble rain showers and luxury linens. Check out the onsite Woodward restaurant for a cozy vibe and craft cocktails. Meanwhile, the main dining room serves updated takes on fresh New England fare.

114 rooms. Restaurant, bar. Fitness center. $351 and up

COURTYARD BOSTON COPLEY SQUARE
88 Exeter St., Boston, 617-437-9300; www.courtyardboston.com

If you're looking for an economical bed in Back Bay, the Courtyard in Copley is a great place to stay. Plopped right in the thick of the neighborhood, between the Prudential Center and Copley Square, it's a quick walk to Newbury Street shopping, the Boston Public Library and the Charles River Esplanade. If you're in town for the Boston Marathon, you won't get any closer to the action—or the finish line, for that matter, which is just steps from the hotel's entrance.

81 rooms. Restaurant. Fitness center. Business center. $151-250

DOUBLETREE HOTEL BOSTON DOWNTOWN
821 Washington St., Boston, 617-956-7900; www.hiltonfamilyboston.com

Situated at the crossroads of the three neighborhoods—downtown, the Theatre District and Chinatown—this Doubletree is prime real estate for nightlife-lovers. The hotel's beige-and-white décor isn't much to speak of, though you won't require further stimulation after experiencing the area's sensory overload. Guest rooms provide further refuge from the urban jungle with comfortable beds. Guests get access to the adjoining YMCA for workouts and swimming.

267 Rooms. Restaurant, bar. Business center. $251-350

HAMPTON INN & SUITES BOSTON CROSSTOWN CENTER
811 Massachusetts Ave., Boston, 617-445-6400; www.bostonhamptoninn.com

Picturesque surroundings are not this hotel's selling point—it overlooks a busy intersection and a blighted area of town. Its virtue, however, is the proximity to Boston University Medical Center and one of Boston's hottest restaurant neighborhoods, the historic South End. Here, the guest rooms are basic but well maintained and feature the chain's standard "Cloud Nine" bed. The hotel offers a generous and free breakfast and a complimentary shuttle to destinations around Boston.

175 rooms. Restaurant, bar. Fitness center. Pool. Business center. $151-250

HOTEL 140
140 Clarendon St., Boston, 617-585-5600; www.hotel140.com

Business travelers who frequent Boston keep Hotel 140's number on speed dial. It's a wallet-friendly choice that's close to the John Hancock and Prudential towers, as well as the Back Bay train station. The historic building served as the YWCA's first U.S. headquarters, but it underwent a $30 million renovation in 2005. Today, the guest rooms are small and simply appointed with the very basics. The rooms with single twin beds, for that matter, are downright YMCA-like, but if you're staying in Boston long-term, there's no better deal and few more convenient options.

54 rooms. Restaurant. Fitness center. Business center. $151-250

HOLIDAY INN BOSTON AT BEACON HILL

5 Blossom St., Boston, 617-742-7630; www.hisboston.com

This pleasantly utilitarian option is located in the most posh neighborhood possible—Beacon Hill, an area packed with over-the-top, trend-conscious shops and restaurants. You won't find anything fancy back in your room, but you will enjoy friendly service, clean rooms and a prime location. Not only are the quaint shops of the Hill just around the corner, the hotel is also convenient to Government Center, Quincy Market and the TD Banknorth Garden, where the Bruins and Celtics play. If you're in town to see a top doctor, its proximity to Massachusetts General Hospital also makes it a convenient choice.

303 rooms. Restaurant. Fitness center. Pool. Business center. $251-350

BROOKLINE
RECOMMENDED
HOLIDAY INN BOSTON-BROOKLINE

1200 Beacon St., Brookline, 617-277-1200; www.ichotelsgroup.com

A good alternative to staying in downtown Boston, this efficient hotel offers a quick commute to downtown, Longwood Medical area hospitals and Fenway Park. Nothing too fancy here can be found here, just basic, well-kept rooms with special features like an indoor pool and whirlpool, room service and shuttle service to select destinations in the city.

225 rooms. Fitness center. Pool. $151-250

CAMBRIDGE

★★★BOSTON MARRIOTT CAMBRIDGE

2 Cambridge Center, Cambridge, 617-494-6600; www.marriott.com

Busy Kendall Square provides the backdrop for this 26-story hotel. In fact, the Kendall/MIT subway stop is just downstairs, making the five-minute ride to downtown Boston fast as well as easy. Here, the best rooms are on the higher floors, where guests enjoy an impressive view of the Boston skyline across the Charles River. All of the usual accoutrements are found in the comfortable rooms, but given the hotel's proximity to the best Cambridge and Boston neighborhoods, few guests spend their time holed up in their rooms.

433 rooms. Restaurant, bar. Fitness center. Pool. $151-250

★★★CHARLES HOTEL

1 Bennett St., Cambridge, 617-864-1200; www.charleshotel.com

If you're sick of chain hotels, the Charles is the perfect antidote. It has all of the amenities you'd need—down comforters, Origins bath products, Bose radios—but it also has distinctive touches like homemade checkered quilts, Shaker furniture and a 500-volume book collection. The dining options are no afterthought, either—inside the hotel, guests find Jody Adams' lauded Rialto and the rustic-themed Henrietta's Table. World-famous jazz acts perform regularly at the hotel's Regattabar. If it's Cambridge flavor you seek, the quirky shops, theaters and nightlife of Harvard Square are just steps away.

294 rooms. Restaurant, bar. $251-350

★★★HOTEL MARLOWE
25 Edwin H. Land Blvd., Cambridge, 617-868-8000; www.hotelmarlowe.com

The Hotel Marlowe is close to Harvard and MIT, but it's neither stuffy nor geeky. In fact, the property is practically bursting with style, thanks to leopard-print carpeting, rich velvet fabrics and eclectic patterns throughout. The Marlowe goes all out with services, too, including a daily complimentary wine hour, round-the-clock room service from Bambara restaurant, complimentary bike and kayak rentals for exploring the nearby Charles River and treats for four-legged guests. If you forget your pair of sunglasses or some other essential, the hotel is connected to the sprawling CambridgeSide Galleria mall.

236 rooms. Restaurant, bar. Fitness center. Business center. Pets accepted. $151-250

★★★HYATT REGENCY CAMBRIDGE
575 Memorial Drive, Cambridge, 617-492-1234; www.hyatt.com

With a ziggurat-shaped exterior rising grandly beside the Charles, the Cambridge Hyatt is one of the chain's most distinctive Boston-area properties. Inside it's mostly frills-free, but guests get their choice between rooms that face the interior atrium or ones with exterior views. Opt for the latter, especially if you can land a river-facing room with a balcony. The hotel's upper floors afford excellent views of the Boston skyline.

469 rooms. Restaurant. Fitness center. Pool. Business center. $151-250

★★★INN AT HARVARD
1201 Massachusetts Ave., Cambridge, 617-491-2222; www.theinnatharvard.com

Owned by Harvard University, this boutique inn frequently hosts visiting dignitaries and academics. Its design exemplifies Georgian architecture and boasts classic New England elegance. An enclosed atrium lends a sense of airiness, even during the winter months, and the quiet dining room provides a pleasant place for a bite. Wherever you wander, you're sure to be met by artwork and photography that depicts Harvard architecture and landmarks.

111 rooms. Restaurant, bar. Fitness center. Business center. $151-250

★★★KENDALL HOTEL
350 Main St., Cambridge, 617-577-1300; www.kendallhotel.com

Once a Victorian firehouse, the Kendall Hotel maintains timeworn charm despite all the thorough updates. Each guest room is individually decorated with homey quilts and antique furniture. Recently, the addition of a seven-story tower added eight guest rooms and four one-bedroom suites, all featuring more modern décor, but the ambience remains cozy and casual. Don't miss the free breakfast buffet of homemade pastries and other sugary treats. Dinner in the Black Sheep restaurant is surprisingly upscale, with an ever-changing menu featuring local and organic cuisine.

77 rooms. Restaurant, bar. Complimentary breakfast. $151-250

★★★LE MERIDIEN CAMBRIDGE
20 Sidney St., Cambridge, 617-577-0200; www.starwoodhotels.com

Formerly the HOTEL@MIT, this hotel is situated near Cambridge's Central Square and University Park, a complex of office buildings, biotech labs and green space. Consequently, it's often filled with visiting executives, researchers and families of students, though the updated, clean-lined design reflects its tech-savvy surroundings. It's not the most atmospheric hotel you'll find, but it's well equipped with pillow-top mattresses and computer-friendly work desks. If you're pulling a pre-meeting all-nighter, the 24-hour fitness center and business center come in handy.

210 rooms. Restaurant, bar. Fitness center. Business center. $151-250

★★★ROYAL SONESTA HOTEL

40 Edwin H. Land Blvd., Cambridge, 617-806-4200; www.sonesta.com

Set on perhaps the most picturesque stretch of the Charles River, the Royal Sonesta provides guests with spectacular views (think sailboats silhouetted by the city skyline). It also contains one of the area's best Italian eateries, Dante, which has earned countless accolades since opening in 2006. Hypoallergenic down blankets and complimentary shuttle service make up for the out-of-the-way location. Solo travelers looking for value should check out the hotel's single rooms, designed for one person with a double bed, stall shower and rock-bottom rates.

400 rooms. Restaurant. Fitness center. Pool. Spa. Business center. $151-250

★★★SHERATON COMMANDER HOTEL

16 Garden St., Cambridge, 617-547-4800; www.sheraton.com

This landmark 1927 hotel is the best home base for those exploring Harvard. It's located smack in the middle of the sprawling campus, alongside the Cambridge Common Park. The suites, of course, are lovely and spacious, with Colonial-style furniture and down duvets. But the best value is the Club rooms—located on "preferred" floors, these guest rooms include upgrades like a free fitness center access and a private lounge serving complimentary breakfast, hors d'oeuvres and cocktails.

175 rooms. Restaurant, bar. Business center. $151-250

WHERE TO EAT

★★★AQUITAINE

569 Tremont St., Boston, 617-424-8577; www.aquitaineboston.com

Aquitaine feels a bit like a Parisian café parked in the middle of the South End. There's a chic clientele, the energizing hum of close-knit conversation, cozy banquettes and, of course, a menu of comfortable French classics like steak frites and roast chicken. Sunday brunch is a must—the line will be long if the weather is nice, but the omelette Basquaise with ham and gruyère is worth it.

French bistro. Lunch, dinner, Saturday-Sunday brunch. $36-85

★★★★ASANA

Mandarin Oriental Boston, 776 Boylston St., Boston, 617-535-8888; www.mandarinoriental.com

This upscale dining room housed on the ground level of the recently opened Mandarin Oriental Boston has two key things going for it: an unbeatable location in the heart of Back Bay with views of the action outside on Boylston Street through floor-to-cciling windows, and a streamlined, Asian-influenced menu loaded with flavorful, lightly sauced seafood that fills a gap in a dining scene heavy on steak and Italian fare. The space is cocooned in rich, dark woods, cozy, upholstered banquets and spacious tables, and an affable waitstaff keeps the service as polished as its surroundings. Chef Nathan Rich sources local seafood for memorable dishes such as classic John Dory, served with Atlantic Clams, mushrooms and herb fumet, or steamed Maine lobster with cognac meringue and coral foam. For a unique experience, reserve the 10-seat chef's table, a glass enclosed space that lets you view the action in the kitchen without feeling as if you're in the thick of things.

New England. Breakfast, lunch, dinner, Saturday-Sunday brunch. $36-85

★★★★CLIO

The Eliot Hotel, 370 Commonwealth Ave., Boston, 617-536-7200; www.cliorestaurant.com

With its leopard-print carpet and creamy walls, the dining room is as playful as the food at Clio. For example, you might find chef-owner Ken Oringer showing off eel, if that particular fish happens to be in season. Seafood plays a big role on the menu—and for those who prefer theirs raw, Clio has a separate sashimi bar, Uni, where for a hefty price you can nibble on bite-sized spoons of sea urchin or fresh scallops. Together, Clio and Uni attract a loyal following of both suited folks with expense accounts and serious gourmands, but it also draws a fair number of couples who want nothing more than a darkened corner for cuddling.

French, Pan-Asian. Breakfast, dinner. Closed Sunday. $36-85

★★★EASTERN STANDARD

528 Commonwealth Ave., Boston, 617-532-9100; www.easternstandardboston.com

This Kenmore Square spot attracts a true smorgasbord of patrons, from students to financial power players. Join them at the bar as they suck down classic cocktails and nibble on hanger steak frites. While you're at it, don't miss the bar menu's superb Reuben made from Guinness-braised corn beef. Or skip to the vintage-inspired, red-accented dining room for classics like meatloaf and mashed potatoes or beef short-rib bourguignon. The "Standard" burger is anything but, perched on a brioche bun with cheddar slathered on top, and you can't go wrong with the salt cod fritters (ask for an extra dollop of the spicy ketchup). The outdoor patio is a prime people-watching perch, though it gets mobbed when the Red Sox are playing at nearby Fenway.

Classic American. Breakfast, lunch, dinner, Sunday brunch. $16-35

★★★GRILL 23 & BAR

161 Berkeley St., Boston, 617-542-2255; www.grill23.com

Grill 23 fits all the major steakhouse stereotypes—it features massive cuts of prime, aged beef and a huge wine list focusing on full-bodied reds, not to mention a sizeable corporate clientele that swills martinis at the bar. But there's more to this ornately outfitted, wood-paneled club than its oriental rugs and polished marble floors. Executive chef Jay Murray insists upon all-natural Brandt beef, and he's fanatical about how it's prepared. The results are outstanding—savory steak au poivre with fingerling potatoes, dry-aged prime ribeye with asparagus and duck fat fries. Murray also offers a selection of dayboat seafood and raw bar choices, as well as a few inventive lamb and poultry dishes, too. Don't miss the restaurant's most famed side dish—truffle tater tots.

Seafood, steak. Dinner. $36-85

★★★HAMERSLEY'S BISTRO

553 Tremont St., Boston, 617-423-2700; www.hamersleysbistro.com

Chef Gordon Hamersley has the perfect formula: Put simple ingredients into no-fuss dishes and serve them without a hint of pretension. It's worked for more than 20 years, with diners still packing this bright bistro-style dining room every night. Remarkably, Hamersley still spends most of his time at the stove. When he's not perfecting the house specialty of chicken roasted with garlic, lemon and parsley, he's drawing new fans by cooking up his crispy polenta smothered in wild mushrooms. Hamersley's also features an eclectic, though pricey, wine list and plenty of vegan options, too.

French bistro. Dinner, Sunday brunch. $36-85

★★★KO PRIME

Nine Zero Hotel, 90 Tremont St., Boston, 617-772-0202; www.koprimeboston.com

Accented by leather and cowhides, KO Prime is a trendy spot where diners can dig into achingly tender braised Korubuta pork shoulder and Kobe iron steaks (as well as a few seafood options). Chef Jamie Bissonnette helms the kitchen, putting his charcuterie skills to good use and acquiring many ingredients from the hotel's rooftop garden. Inventive side dishes like short-rib mac and cheese and spaetzle with herbs and parmesan round out the decadent experience. As for the cocktail list, it veers into the outrageous with a few liquid nitrogen-based creations.

Steak. Breakfast, lunch, dinner, Saturday-Sunday brunch. $86 and up

★★★★L'ESPALIER

774 Boylston St., Boston, 617-262-3023; www.lespalier.com

Despite its recent relocation from a 19th-century townhouse to this tony spot adjacent to the Mandarin Oriental, this stalwart managed to keep its intimate charm. The dishes here are a mix of French-influenced, traditional New England recipes such as roasted Vermont rabbit with potato gnocchi and peas, and butter-poached Maine lobster with braised pork belly and sweet corn. Chef-owner Frank McClelland's over-the-top prix-fixe menu

---

WHERE IS THE BEST CLAM CHOWDER IN BOSTON?

Legal Sea Foods: Boston's venerable chain restaurant, Legal Seafood serves a bowl so good it earned the loyalty of the Kennedy family—in fact, this clam chowder has been served at dozens of Presidential inaugurations.

Union Oyster House: Plump clams, potatoes, herbs, bacon, heavy cream—this version is thicker than the usual brew, and is best enjoyed with a crown of crispy oyster crackers.

O Ya: What to expect from Boston's best sushi restaurant? An unusual take on the Boston classic, this bowl of chowder is rich and savory with flakes of tempura batter and a drizzle of pork fat.

is the ultimate in lavish, and can be amped up even more with caviar courses and an overflowing fromage cart. Meanwhile, the monster-sized wine list puts plenty of stellar bottles alongside a few choices under $50.

French, contemporary American. Dinner, lunch, Saturday-Sunday tea. $86 and up

★★★LOCKE-OBER

3 Winter Place, Boston, 617-542-1340; www.lockeober.com

Chef Lydia Shire took the helm of this icon in 2001 and has managed to breathe new life into the aging space without losing any of the old-world charm. Locke-Ober has long been the stomping ground of foodies, financiers and politicians. You can practically hear the echoes of 19th-century Boston in the front-room bar. Today's diners are treated to chef Shire's updated takes on traditional American fare, including old Yankee classics like clams casino and tiny pots of garlicky escargot. Passé dishes such as beef Stroganoff even get an edge— they're made with hand-cut egg noodles and onion soup gratinée.

American. Dinner. Closed Sunday. $36-85

★★★MAMMA MARIA

3 North Square, Boston, 617-523-0077; www.mammamaria.com

The North End has a trattoria in nearly every storefront, though picking a good one can be a chore. Packed into a 19th-century townhouse, Mamma Maria, strives to avoid cheesy pastas and generic meat sauces. Winter brings a menu filled with slowly braised sauces and meats, whereas spring and summer find locally sourced asparagus, ramps and mushrooms tossed into a number of pastas and salads. If you're a sucker for classics, order the pasta Bolognese with homemade porcini pasta.

Italian. Dinner. $36-85

★★★★MENTON

354 Congress Street, Boston, 617-737-0099; www.mentonboston.com

From famed Boston chef Barbara Lynch comes her seventh venue in the city. Capitalizing on previous successes running the gamut from a casual oyster to a cocktail bar, Lynch returns to the fine dining roots she perfected at No 9 Park with the opening of Menton. Located in the up and coming Fort Point neighborhood, Menton is at once absolutely glamorous as well as comfortable. The updated French food is modern and refined, including such recent dishes as torchon of foie gras de canard with ginger, monbazillac gelée, and candied quince. An à la carte or a chef's tasting menu is available. The well-edited wine list is certain to compliment the cuisine.

French, Contemporary American. Dinner. $86 and up.

★★★★MERITAGE

Boston Harbor Hotel, 70 Rowes Wharf, Boston, 617-439-3995;
www.meritagetherestaurant.com

If the custom-made wine cases are any indication, this hot spot takes its vino seriously. With more than 850 options, visitors are sure to find one that suits their mood and menu selections. A key player at the Boston Wine Festival, chef Daniel Bruce incorporates local ingredients into his menu whenever possible, exemplified by dishes like maple-smoked salmon croustades with caramelized fennel and French bean salad, and wood-grilled filet mignon with soft whipped potatoes and horseradish onion cream. Every menu item can be ordered as a small or large plate, so feel free to share and taste more than a few. The restaurant also features one of the best views of Boston Harbor. Good food, exceptional wine, romantic vistas—Meritage is a solid date-night destination.

International. Dinner. Closed Sunday-Monday. $36-85

★★★MASA

439 Tremont St., Boston, 617-338-8884;
www.masarestaurant.com

Masa inhabits a cozy, little spot near the edge of the South End neighborhood. Check out the bar for killer margaritas and one of the city's most expansive tequila lists. Meanwhile, the dining room is decorated with exposed brick walls, large mirrors and chandeliers. Settle into an oversized booth for the tapas combo platter of shredded chicken taquitos and a spicy ahi tuna ceviche. You'll find more tapas-sized portions on the brunch menu. If you come late on a Thursday evening, you won't find a place to sit—the tables get pushed aside to make way for salsa dancing. (Better have another drink.)

Southwestern. Dinner. $16-35

★★★METROPOLIS CAFÉ

584 Tremont St., Boston, 617-247-2931

South Enders rely on Metropolis Café for approachable comfort fare with inspired touches. The tiny space is situated in an old ice-cream parlor, so it feels cramped and comfortable all at once. Tables are nudged closely together and servers can have a hard time maneuvering the crowded space, but that's hardly an issue when you bite into a dinner of horseradish-crusted salmon or rigatoni sprinkled with sausage. For lunch, you can't beat the bowl of warm roasted-carrot soup with a touch of cilantro-jalapeño salsa. You'll encounter long lines if you appear for the acclaimed weekend brunch, though your reward is the perfectly realized huevos rancheros.

American. Lunch, dinner, Saturday-Sunday brunch. $16-35

★★★MIEL

InterContinental Boston, 510 Atlantic Ave., Boston, 617-747-1000,
www.intercontinentalboston.com

Miel is French for honey, so the restaurant acts as a fun waterfront gathering spot for hotel guests and local condo-dwellers alike. Miel's outdoor patio features big, comfortable couches, whereas its indoor space goes heavy on country-yellow, blond wood and wispy cream-colored curtains. The menu is classically French with Pistou soup and bouillabaisse, but there's also a daily raw bar. Few things taste better than a dinner of the Parisian crepe filled with ham and Swiss and topped with roquette, but a breakfast of the banana-nut French toast comes close.

French. Breakfast, lunch, dinner. $36-85

★★★MISTRAL

223 Columbus Ave., Boston, 617-867-9300; www.mistralbistro.com

Mistral makes no apologies for its overdone décor and pricey food. It is, after all, the favorite spot for Boston's playboy set. Vaulted ceilings create a lofty effect, along with the towering arched windows that flood the space with natural light. Chef-owner Jamie Mammano specializes in approachable dishes, but throws in a few fussy ones, too, like a decadent foie gras and Dover sole. Mostly, guests come for his grilled thin-crust pizzas, the spicy tuna tartare and the colorful cocktails. The outstanding wine list fuels a cacophonous singles scene on weekends.

French, Mediterranean. Dinner, Sunday brunch. $36-85

★★★MOOO RESTAURANT

XV Beacon Hotel, 15 Beacon St., Boston, 617-670-2515; www.mooorestaurant.com

Take your conventional idea of a steakhouse, turn it on its head, and you get the irreverent Mooo. After an extensive facelift in 2007, this formerly formal restaurant now feels akin to an urban French boîte. Though the dishes are refined, they adhere to the steakhouse norms of massive portions and à la carte offerings. Classics like filet and ribeye now have the company of playful options like soy-glazed short-ribs and skillet-roasted Cornish game hen. If you're on an expense account, live large with the $120 Kobe beef sirloin. If you're not, the Kobe dumpling for $19 still satisfies. The former restaurant's wine cellar escaped the renovation mostly intact (you can still order ancient bottles that cost well into the thousands), though the list now includes more affordable options.

Steakhouse. Lunch, dinner, breakfast, Saturday-Sunday brunch. $86 and up

★★★★NO. 9 PARK

9 Park St., Boston, 617-742-9991; www.no9park.com

The dark wooden floors and cream-colored booths inside this Beacon Hill townhouse don't scream excitement. That reaction is reserved for the food. Chef Barbara Lynch is the brains behind a bevy of Boston eateries like B&G Oysters, Sportello and The Butcher Shop. Here, she uses local produce to create some of the city's most celebrated fare. Playing with both Italian and French techniques, Lynch gives herself the freedom to constantly reinvent the menu, though a few favorites never stray—prune-stuffed gnocchi topped with seared foie gras, crispy pork belly with braised Belgian endive and jalapeño aioli. The whole staff is trained under wine director Cat Silirie, so every server is ready with the story behind every bottle on the list. The bar staff, meanwhile, leads a revival of the city's cocktail scene. The smooth vodka-lime Palmyra is a local favorite.

French, Italian. Lunch, dinner. Closed Sunday. $36-85

★★★O YA

9 East St., Boston, 617-654-9900;
www.oyarestaurantboston.com

After opening O Ya, a modern den of Japanese treasures, chef/owner Tim Cushman quickly became the darling of local and national food writers. It's easy to see why—his fanciful take on Japanese cuisine, and sushi in particular, can be downright mind-blowing. Here, the bite-sized dishes involve complex ingredient pairings—foie gras with balsamic chocolate Kabayaki, Santa Barbara sea urchin with blood orange and fresh wasabi. The presentation, meanwhile, is as precise as the food is fresh, with dishes looking nearly too pretty to touch. Cushman's wife Nancy has crafted a sensational sake list.

Be prepared, though—you'll reach deep into your pockets for such an extreme gustatory experience.
Japanese. Dinner. Closed Sunday-Monday. Bar. $86 and up

★★★THE OAK ROOM
The Fairmont Copley Plaza Hotel, 138 St. James Ave., Boston, 617-267-5300;
www.theoakroom.com

The Oak Room is a steakhouse so richly elaborate and over the top it feels like you're entering a staged murder-mystery dinner theater. Think baroque woodwork, intricately carved plaster ceiling and heavy burgundy drapes. Against that distinguished décor, though, the food holds its own. Try the Châteaubriand with asparagus and a béarnaise sauce, or the wild boar chops atop a cranberry-and-goat cheese tart. Hearty grilled fish, oysters Rockefeller and clams casino constitute the menu's lighter side. The bar and lounge are usually flush with cocktail-swillers. Settle in like James Bond and order yourself a classic martini—it's served in a carafe that's chilled in a bucket of ice.
American. Breakfast, lunch, dinner, Sunday brunch. $86 and up

★★★PIGALLE
75 Charles St. South, Boston, 617-423-4944;
www.pigalleboston.com

Named for the red light district in Paris, this restaurant trades in the exotic. Though the menu reads like a traditional French bistro's with duck liver terrine and halibut en croûte, a closer look reveals the chef's flair for Asian and Italian touches—for example, wasabi oil and Chinese greens are served alongside that halibut. The atmosphere is intimate and personal with tiny tables and low lighting, whereas the waitstaff is as attentive as they come at a French bistro. Check out the bar for snack-sized plates of Arancini and Malaysian street food.
French. Dinner. Closed Monday. $36-85

★★★RADIUS
8 High St., Boston, 617-426-1234; www.radiusrestaurant.com

Radius feels as moneyed and elitist as the power brokers and financial analysts who eat there. The space is slick, modern and, appropriate to the name, round with silver and red accents, minimalist wall décor and a relaxed downstairs lounge. Clearly, the handsome servers in pristine suits take their jobs very seriously—they act more like hosts than

WHERE ARE BOSTON'S BEST OYSTERS?

Neptune Oyster: When it opened four years ago, this slip of a North End restaurant earned huge acclaim. Decorated to look like a French brasserie, Neptune features a boisterous environment and a daily menu of the freshest East Coast and West Coast bivalves.

B&G Oysters: Noted local chef Barbara Lynch packs her subterranean South End spot with fashionable diners thanks to a topnotch menu of raw oysters, not to mention the best lobster BLT in Boston.

Union Oysters: Though it claims to be America's oldest eatery, there's nothing passé about the Union Oyster House. The old-school restaurant serves fresh oysters for lunch and dinner, seven days a week, and prepares its oysters in many different ways.

food-and-drink caddies. Meanwhile, chef-owner Michael Schlow keeps the restaurant on the gourmand's short list. His take on French cooking is spare—no heavy sauces, just bright, clean flavors and fresh, seasonal ingredients. He flirts with techniques like foams and emulsions. Mostly, though, he sticks to what he knows best, like preparing simple fish dishes. Check out the bar for Schlow's signature burger—it gets loads of press for its juicy, pure beef flavor. While you're there, order up a raspberry beret cocktail to go with your burger. It features a devilishly good and seriously addictive blend of Bombay gin, lime, raspberry purée and fresh ginger beer.

French. Lunch, dinner. Closed Sunday. $36-85

★★★RISTORANTE TOSCANO

47 Charles St., Boston, 617-723-4090; www.toscanoboston.com

After a much-needed makeover, Ristorante Toscano has been revived into a sophisticated Italian café. Massive antique doors now decorate the Beacon Hill institution, but the glassed-encased wine cave hasn't changed a bit—it still houses more than 1,000 bottles of Tuscan wine. At lunch, the floor-to-ceiling windows open to the street, sending a breeze through the room. At dinner, join the cardigan-wearing couples who munch on quattro formaggi pizzas and hearty antipasti platters. Or try the Caprese pie with its imported buffalo mozzarella and beefsteak tomatoes.

Italian. Lunch, dinner. $16-35

★★★ROCCA KITCHEN & BAR

500 Harrison Ave., Boston, 617-451-5151; www.roccaboston.com

Inspired by her own Ligurian heritage, restaurateur Michela Larson built this space with the palette of her homeland in mind. One of the few places to offer free parking in the South End, Rocca provides a convenient dinner stop to this growing neighborhood. On warm afternoons, local schmoozers clamor to the spacious outdoor patio with yellow shade umbrellas and comfy chairs. Parties of one, on the other hand, are right at home at the restaurant's horseshoe-shaped bar. Also inspired by Liguria, the cuisine features artisan ingredients like a warm ricotta and handmade pesto. Check out the housemade pastas—especially the hand-rolled trofie. Other favorites include the whole-roasted fish and the pork chop Milanese. Be sure to order the gelati for dessert.

Italian. Dinner. $36-85

★★★SCAMPO

The Liberty Hotel, 215 Charles St., Boston, 617-224-4000; www.libertyhotel.com

Chef Lydia Shire made waves over the years with her playful ingredients and presentations at now-shuttered restaurants like Biba and Excelsior. She now oversees the kitchen at Scampo (that's Italian for "escape"), set inside the Liberty Hotel. Every night, an eclectic bunch of patrons turns out for fare that manages to be whimsical yet firmly rooted in the Italian tradition of rustic. Crispy brick-oven pizzas are layered with mounds of ingredients. Spaghetti is tossed with everything from tomatoes to lobster. Mozzarella is made onsite. The restaurant features an open configuration that makes it easy to see and be seen, even from the kitchen.

Italian, American. Lunch, dinner. $36-85

★★★SORELLINA

1 Huntington Ave., Boston, 617-412-4600; www.sorellinaboston.com

Sexy. Low-lit. Packed with well-dressed patrons. Sorellina is hardly demure. But then, in conservative Boston, it's also a refreshing change of pace. The low banquettes, cork floors and gleaming white bar lend the look of an exciting nightspot. Sorellina just happens to serve big, sophisticated plates of pasta, roasted meats and seafood, too. Chef-owner Jamie Mammano dresses up these usual suspects with gulf shrimp, chiles and scoops of saffron risotto. Finding a decent bottle of American or French wine isn't a problem, though paying less than $100 is more difficult. One splurge you won't regret is the Ciambelle, a sugar-and-cinnamon spiced doughnut served on a bed of vanilla cream.

Italian. Dinner. $36-85

★★★TROQUET

140 Boylston St., Boston, 617-695-9463; www.troquetboston.com

Troquet owners Chris and Diane Campbell take their wine and food-pairing skills seriously. So it's no surprise that this bistro wine bar boasts one of the most comprehensive lists in the city. Here, the atmosphere is sophisticated yet understated, with impressive views of Boston Common and the State House. In contrast with the exhaustive wine list, chef Scott Hebert's menu is pleasantly edited, offering a few light dishes like East Coast halibut with lobster succotash and more substantial entrées like pan-roasted rib steak with root vegetables and potato purée. A newly installed desserterie on the lower level is a relaxing spot to sample a smattering of creative sweet plates including the delicately crunchy milk chocolate mille feuille drizzled with a rum-and-honey reduction sauce. And, of course, there's a nice selection of dessert wines to match.

Contemporary American, French. Dinner. Closed Sunday-Monday. $36-85

★★★UNION BAR AND GRILLE

1357 Washington St., Boston, 617-423-0555; www.unionrestaurant.com

Union Bar and Grille's funky, fruit juice-filled martinis satisfy the South End's insatiable appetite for fun. Meanwhile, the swanky bar and black leather banquettes appeal to the neighborhood's stylish inclinations. Here, the kitchen churns out trendy dishes like short-rib laced burgers and rack of lamb drizzled with fig sauce. Another local favorite is Union's 10K Tuna, appropriately named after the chef's spice rub that won a $10,000 contest. Brunch here is as much a scene as dinner, with Bellinis and Pimosas (champagne with pomegranate purée) on just about every table loaded with huge stacks of fluffy pancakes.

American. Dinner, Saturday-Sunday brunch. $36-85

★★★VIA MATTA

79 Park Plaza, Boston, 617-422-0008; www.viamattarestaurant.com

Via Matta may be the closest Boston will ever get to a celebrity hangout. Chef-owner Michael Schlow attracts a lineup of big names like Billy Joel, Mick Jagger and Steven Tyler when they're in town. But the place buzzes on celeb-less days, too. Schlow's take on simple Italian food includes big portions of chicken Milanese and tangy Sicilian tuna salad layered with white beans and caper berries. For dessert, order the chocolate and hazelnut cheesecake with coconut gelato. If the weather's nice, ask about the shaded outdoor patio that's hidden behind the tall walls of climbing vines. For late-night eats, stick to the Enoteca/ Caffe, a small candlelit bar at the front of the restaurant that dishes out pizzas and other small plates.

Italian. Lunch, dinner. Closed Sunday. $36-85

RECOMMENDED

B&G OYSTERS LTD

550 Tremont St., Boston, 617-423-0550; www.bandgoysters.com

This intimate eatery specializes in fresh-off-the-boat oysters, a no-brainer in Boston. Cool blue hues and sleek steel tables make the tiny dining room seem bigger than it is, while an open kitchen and oyster bar lets you watch the shucking team in action. Boasting a dozen bivalve varieties daily, it's one of the best spots to sit and learn about oyster "terroir". The restaurant also features a plump, meat-filled lobster roll (served with or without bacon), fried clams, charcuterie boards and entrées like Portuguese-style seafood stew. Check out the backyard patio on warmer evenings. As with Chef Barbara Lynch's other spots (The Butcher Shop, Sportello, Drink and No. 9 Park), wine director Cat Silirie puts together a solid line-up of pairings. Just be prepared to wait if you're in a party bigger than, say, one.

Seafood. Lunch, dinner. $36-85

THE BUTCHER SHOP

552 Tremont St., Boston, 617-423-4800; www.thebutchershopboston.com

Inside Barbara Lynch's European-style butcher shop and wine bar, you can snack on the daily salumi or simply shop for it. Check out the selection of cured meats, cuts of beef and pâtés, perfect for lunch or dinner. For a mid-afternoon snack, try the hot dog à la maison with zucchini relish and housemade rosemary potato chips. Limited seating is available at the bar and along the restaurant's bank of windows (reservations are accepted for parties of six or more), but some folks choose to stand beside the butcher block and graze on platters of cheese and charcuterie while drinking a robust red off the wine list. In the end, the Butcher Shop doesn't feel like a restaurant—it's more like a wine tasting at a friend's house.

International. Lunch, dinner, Saturday-Sunday brunch. $36-85

CASA ROMERO

30 Gloucester St., Boston, 617-536-4341; www.casaromero.com

Chef-owner Leo Romero brings a taste of Mexico to chilly New England in this cozy dining room filled with imported artifacts. Casa Romero focuses on traditional Mexican dishes while incorporating local herbs and vegetables picked from the restaurant's own community-garden plot. The results are flavor-packed and authentic, especially the beef tips simmered in chile guajillo sauce and anything doused in Romero's famous mole sauce. A secluded, plant-lined patio fills up quickly on summer nights, so go early—or be prepared to wait.

Mexican. Dinner, Sunday brunch. $36-85

DURGIN PARK

340 Faneuil Hall Marketplace, Boston, 617-227-2038; www.durgin-park.com

This family-style stop sits inside the same Faneuil Hall market building it has since 1827, so act impressed. It draws visitors from every part of the world who settle in for the checkered tablecloths and down-and-dirty lobster bakes. Where else can you rub elbows (literally) with a family from Texas while digging into a plate of fried clams and a pot of baked beans? The menu carries everything from chicken fingers to New England corned beef and cabbage. Keep it simple and be sure to save room for the homemade Indian pudding. In the main dining room upstairs, mealtime can be loud and messy, while downstairs in the bar, there's always a game on the TV and plenty of Sam Adams Lager on tap.

American. Lunch, dinner. $16-35

FIGS

42 Charles St., Boston, 617-742-3447; 67 Main St., Charlestown, 617-242-2229; www.toddenglish.com

Figs introduced gourmet pizza to Boston in the early 1990s, and the locals have been clamoring for the pies ever since. Here, the inspired creations are all served on extra-crispy, super-thin crusts weighted down with palate-pleasing combinations like Gulf shrimp and caramelized leeks or crispy eggplant with dollops of whipped ricotta. If the pizzas aren't filling enough, try the dinner-sized salads, fried asparagus spears and rich, flavorful pastas.

Pizza menu. Lunch, dinner. $16-35

FLOUR BAKERY

1595 Washington St., Boston, 617-267-4300; 12 Farnsworth St., Boston, 617-338-4333; 190 Massachusetts Ave., Cambridge, 617-225-2525; www.flourbakery.com

This beloved sandwich shop and bakery seems to have a perpetual line snaking out its door. No matter which location you choose, the atmosphere promises to be comfortable and cozy with stacks of alt-weekly newspapers for afternoon browsing and a chalkboard listing daily specials. So grab a seat at one of the communal tables and get to know your neighbors. Together, you'll enjoy addictive sandwiches like the roast chicken sandwich with avocado and jicama or the curried tuna mixed with apples, carrots and golden raisins. The endless spread of sweets includes delicious sticky buns and cookies, with not a bad choice among them.

Bakery. Breakfast, lunch, dinner (Monday-Friday). $15 and under

GINZA

16 Hudson St., Boston, 617-338-2261

Those who believe Chinatown is best left to Chinese food haven't discovered Ginza. Lauded as one of the top sushi restaurants in the city, Ginza puts out inventive rolls and pristine slivers of sashimi. Though the cooked dishes are popular, they're not nearly so addictive. Fan favorites include the gleaming sashimi appetizer and fashion maki (eel, avocado, cream cheese, cucumber and mountain burdock root). Never mind the chintzy floral chair coverings and casual atmosphere. Here, the scene still manages to be hip thanks to kimono-clad servers and a kitchen that stays open late—very late, as in 4 a.m. on weekends.

Japanese. Lunch, dinner, late-night. $16-35

JASPER WHITE'S SUMMER SHACK

50 Dalton St., Boston, 617-867-9955; www.summershackrestaurant.com

An outpost of his larger restaurant in Cambridge, Jasper White's Summer Shack is just as fun as it is delicious. The front room is filled with a spacious, circular bar flanked by flat-screen TVs and affable bartenders. Meanwhile, the sound of cracking shells dominates the bustling dining room as hungry patrons dig into clam bakes and crab legs. Also, the brown-paper tablecloths make for handy backup napkins when you're in a pinch. On a cold Boston day, nothing beats a bowl of Bermuda fish and crab chowder. And if you're going for lobster, Jasper's pan-roasted preparation is a worthy splurge. Don't miss the oyster shooter— you'll get a whole oyster, cocktail sauce and vodka in one quick swallow. While a fierce debate rages in Boston as to who makes the best lobster roll, White's version is both a worthy and economical contender.

Seafood. Lunch, dinner. $16-35

LA VERDAD

1 Lansdowne St., Boston, 617-421-9595; www.laverdadtaqueria.com

If the Mexican wrestling masks that adorn the tiled dining room don't give it away, the enormous bar and wall of tequila bottles will—this place is built for fun and frivolity. Best of all, this hopping Mexican taqueria turns out authentic street food made with fresh, local ingredients—including turkey, housemade sausage, fish and tongue. The tortillas are handmade, and the tacos are served with traditional salsas and toppings. The bar whips up a killer margarita along with a range of other tequila-laced cocktails. If you're thinking of grabbing a post-game taco or two, you won't be alone—the line gets surprisingly long at the takeout counter. On these occasions, you're better off waiting for a seat inside.

Mexican. Lunch (Saturday), dinner. Closed Sunday-Monday $16-35

LALA ROKH

97 Mount Vernon St., Boston, 617-720-5511; www.lalarokh.com

It's impossible to separate cuisine from culture at this romantic, Persian-themed dining spot. The interior is dotted with old maps and artifacts from Iran, making it seem somewhat out of place along the cobblestone streets of Beacon Hill. Nevertheless, owners (and siblings) Babak Bina and Azita Bina-Seibel have created a homey spot to serve Azerbaijan-style cuisine from the northwest corner of Iran. Bina-Seibel loves to dish out slow-roasted meats, smoky spices and pickled accompaniments. Decadent cream sauces bring inventive flavors to heart-warming native dishes such as Addas Pollo, a fork-tender veal sitting atop Basmati rice sweetened by dates, currants and caramelized onion. Don't leave without sampling the bite-sized Baklavettes, which result in sticky fingers and a thoroughly sated sweet tooth.

Persian. Lunch (Monday-Friday), dinner. $16-35

LES ZYGOMATES

129 South St., Boston, 617-542-5108; www.winebar.com

Named for the facial muscles you use when smiling, this restaurant is sure to keep you grinning. The French-inspired wine bar boasts a split personality— one room offers a quiet retreat in which to grab a glass of wine and a light snack,

while the other delivers a livelier environment via jazz music. Signature dishes include steak frites and oysters on the half shell. The enormous wine list is par excellence, with an extensive by-the-glass section and even three-ounce pours.
French. Lunch, dinner. Closed Sunday. $36-85

MARKET BY JEAN GEORGES

W Boston,100 Stuart St., Boston, 617-310-6790; www.marketbyjgboston.com

Star chef Jean-Georges Vongerichten brings his simple farm-to-table concept to the city where he first honed his cooking chops 25 years ago. This restaurant is a casual, contemporary space with plenty of warm woods and streamlined furnishings. In other words, the focus is on the food. And here Vongerichten is focused on the clean, Asian-influenced flavors he's famous for. The menu changes seasonally, though it often includes black truffle pizza with fontina cheese and prime rib-eye with parmesan crusted squash and scotch bonnet pepper sauce. Desserts are classic with a twist: the salted caramel ice cream sundae, garnished with peanuts, popcorn and chocolate sauce, is a welcome update to an old favorite.
American. Breakfast, dinner, Saturday-Sunday brunch. Bar. $36-85

MYERS + CHANG

1145 Washington St., Boston, 617-542-5200; www.myersandchang.com

Bright, funky and colorful, Myers + Change is a contemporary Chinese diner that focuses on simple, home-style Asian cuisine. The names of some menu items are identical to those you find at a traditional takeout joint, but the similarities stop there. The scallion pancakes are grease-free. The pork stir-fry is served with crispy sweetbreads. Best of all, the well-priced dishes are great for sharing, so you'll often find large groups passing platters of food. At lunchtime, Myers + Change feels like a quiet café, but when the lights dim, the music goes up and it becomes something of a party scene.
Asian. Lunch, dinner, Saturday-Sunday brunch. Bar. $16-35

NEPTUNE OYSTER

63 Salem St., Boston, 617-742-3474; www.neptuneoyster.com

An oyster bar amidst the North End's sea of Italian eateries, Neptune Oyster has fewer than 30 tables and lives in a dining room the size of a postage stamp. It feels bigger than that, thanks to mirrored walls that are covered in the daily specials. Behind the bar, bartenders pour frosty beers and chilled white wines while sharing space with the shucker, who rips through shells at amazing speed. Oyster varieties change daily, though the menu has a few staples like the hot and buttery lobster roll and the Cioppino, a tomato-based seafood stew. If you're a beef lover with an adventurous streak, don't miss the Neptune Burger, a juicy beef patty topped with flash-fried oysters.
Seafood. Lunch, dinner. $16-35

POST 390

406 Stuart St., Boston, 617-399-0015; www.post390restaurant.com

Located in a two-story space inside a newly constructed tower with views of Trinity Church and the Hancock Tower, this restaurant delivers a dressed up tavern experience in a contemporary setting. Classic comfort foods like mac 'n' cheese are amplified by the addition of unexpected ingredients—in this case, beer and bacon. The brunch menu is equally inventive, with eggs benedict served with Irish bacon and doused in house-made hollandaise, or cinnamon French toast served with banana crème brulée.

American. Lunch, dinner, brunch. Bar. $36-85

THE RED FEZ

1222 Washington St., Boston, 617-338-6060; www.theredfez.com

Housed inside a cavernous warehouse, this Moroccan-tiled gem was reborn in 2002 (it had been shuttered for many years after its heyday as a '70s hot spot). Today, the space looks surprisingly intimate with Persian rugs, exposed brick walls and arched windows. Laid-back diners fill up on Middle Eastern mezzes like spinach pie and falafel. There's also a romantic outdoor patio that gets fairly festive on weekend nights. Jazz fans swarm to the Fez's Sunday brunch, where a sip of the strong Turkish coffee will have you amped all afternoon.

Middle Eastern. Lunch, dinner, late-night. $16-35

SEL DE LA TERRE

774 Boylston St., Boston, 617-266-8800; 255 State St., Boston, 617-720-1300; www.seldelaterre.com

This restaurant has been around for ten years at its Long Wharf location. But chefs and co-owners Frank McClelland and Geoff Gardiner just expanded their French country fare concept by opening two new branches of Sel de la Terre—one lives inside the same building as Mandarin Oriental Boston, the other is a suburban outpost near the city in Natick. The menu remains as focused as ever on rustic recipes—a juicy, satisfying steak frites with red wine reduction; hand-made gnocchi with mushrooms, peas and ricotta; and house-made charcuterie. The boulangerie is popular with locals for its fresh, crusty baguettes, hearty loafs, and, at breakfast, muffins, scones and brioche crowns. The wine list is tops for its well-edited selection of French and American pours.

French. Lunch, dinner, Saturday-Sunday brunch. Bar. $36-85

SONSIE

327 Newbury St., Boston, 617-351-2500; www.sonsieboston.com

Despite its location on the scruffy lower end of Newbury Street, Sonsie lures scores of highbrow Euro sophisticates and preppies. It also attracts celebrities like Matt Damon and Ben Affleck, who stop by while they're in town. The food isn't bad, but make no mistake—people come for the scene. Shoppers crowd the window-front café tables to nosh on crispy focaccia pizzas and spicy Cubano sandwiches. The dinner menu offers something for everyone, including wok-seared salmon with coconut green curry and purple sticky rice. A swanky little wine bar with a dozen tables is open downstairs—it's a quieter, low-lit option for scenesters who need time off.

International u. Breakfast, lunch, dinner, Saturday-Sunday brunch. $16-35

SPORTELLO

348 Congress St., Boston, 617-737-1234; www.sportelloboston.com

Another Barbara Lynch restaurant, Sportello takes the concept of simple Italian counter service and makes it slightly more sophisticated. Here, diners gather around one of two u-shaped white marble counters to dig into bowls of handmade pastas made of fresh, local ingredients. The humble menu features an edited selection of appetizers (try the spicy tomato soup with grilled cheese), entrées (half roasted chicken with farro) and desserts (housemade ice cream). A well-curated selection of reasonably priced Italian wines completes the experience.

Italian. Lunch, dinner, brunch. $16-35

STELLA

1525 Washington St., Boston, 617-247-7747; www.bostonstella.com

The South End was already swimming in stylish restaurants when chef-owner Evan Deluty opened this hip Italian café, but the locals still arrived in droves to sample dishes like handmade linguine tossed with asparagus and a plain poached egg on top. Deluty's simply prepared pastas, pizzas and salads are brimming with local produce and heaps of flavor. The indoor dining room is ultra-cool with all white interiors. Meanwhile, the patio carries a more casual vibe with its lemon-yellow umbrellas. The bar consistently buzzes from early evening until well past midnight, with a kitchen that stays open till 1:30 a.m. For sandwiches and take-out salads, try the café next door. Perhaps the best part of the experience is the bill, because few items cost more than $20. So go ahead and order that second glass of grappa.

Italian. Dinner, late-night, Sunday brunch. $16-35

TAPEO

266 Newbury St., Boston, 617-267-4799; www.tapeo.com

Sure, the Boston dining scene is having a tapas movement, but one of the most authentic (and original) places to find these eats is Tapeo. The tile-lined space captures the spirited atmosphere of a Madrid tapas bar, while the food is bona fide Spanish. Your first decision should be your easiest—start by ordering a pitcher of sangria. From there, the enormous list of hot and cold plates can be overwhelming, but you can't go wrong here. Cold plates of jamón Serrano (sliced, cured ham) and anchovy fillets are tempting starters. Meanwhile, the heaping hot plates of sizzling gambas al ajillo (garlic shrimp), patatas bravas (spicy potatoes) and platters of paella Valenciana are great for large groups. You might find large, loud crowds hoarding all the big tables. For something quieter, simply request a corner table in the upstairs dining room. On a warm afternoon, the outdoor patio is aflutter with sangria-sipping people-watchers. If the wait is long, throw your name on the list and pass the time window-shopping at all the nearby boutiques.

Spanish, tapas. Dinner, lunch (Friday-Sunday). $16-35

TARANTA

210 Hanover St., Boston, 617-720-0052; www.tarantarist.com

Peruvian and Italian cuisines collide, oddly enough, in Venezuela, which is where Taranta chef-owner José Duarte learned to prepare both. Leaning heavily on Italian basics, Duarte plays with Peruvian ingredients in dishes like cassava root gnocchi served with slow-braised lamb ragout, and espresso-crusted filet mignon over parsnip purée and sautéed escarole. Rare in the North End, this tri-level space feels expansive and open with exposed brick walls and windows overlooking Hanover Street. Duarte has made strides to become one of the city's first eco-friendly restauranteurs—he even features a number of organic and biodynamic wines on his well-priced list.

Peruvian, Italian. Dinner. $36-85

TERRAMIA RISTORANTE

98 Salem St., Boston, 617-523-3112; www.terramiaristorante.com

Set on the corner of a tucked-away street in the North End, this perpetually crowded, 39-seat spot is as authentic as it gets—white tablecloths, modern Italian fare and a long waiting list. The menu features updated classics enhanced with regional ingredients, such as creamy risotto peppered with chunks of Maine lobster and open-faced, seafood-filled ravioli. Don't be deterred by the cramped seating and gradually rising noise levels. Prepare yourself for a jostling, lean in close and dive into three or four courses of well-prepared plates. Just don't plan on sticking around for dessert—they don't serve it.

Italian. Dinner. $36-85

TORO

1704 Washington St., Boston, 617-536-4300; www.toro-restaurant.com

After running the kitchen at Clio for ten years, chef Ken Oringer got antsy and decided to open a Spanish tapas bar. Inspired by his many travels to that country, Oringer crafted a menu filled with Spanish favorites like Iberian jamón and salt-crusted sea bass, as well as Kobe beef sliders and grilled corn smothered in aged Cotija cheese. The sangria is good, but the mojitos are better, and a nice selection of Spanish wines is listed on a chalkboard and served in standard juice glasses. Here, you'll see the neighborhood's hipsters settling beside the suburbanites who travel far for the well-priced food. Come summertime, snagging a seat on the patio is challenging but worth it.

Spanish Lunch, dinner, Sunday brunch. $36-85

TOWNE STOVE AND SPIRITS

900 Boylston St., Boston, 617-247-0400; www.towneboston.com

If ever there were a grandfather or grand dame of New England cuisine, Jasper White and Lydia Shire are it. The two star chefs have helmed dozens of local restaurants over the years. Convenient to the Hynes Convention Center, Towne Stove and Spirits features an eclectic menu—foie gras with white pepper and roasted grape risotto; wood-grilled pizza with lobster, corn and honeyed ricotta; Peking chicken and pot pie. It's difficult to craft a multi-course meal of complementary dishes, though it's easy to enjoy the varied flavors. Meanwhile, the bar is an excellent spot to sample unique concoctions you won't find anywhere else.

International. Lunch, dinner. Bar. $36-85

UNION OYSTER HOUSE

41 Union St., Boston, 617-227-2750; www.unionoysterhouse.com

Boston's oldest restaurant is also one of America's longest running—the 1826 Union Oyster House has the weathered hardwood floors to prove it. Still located in its original building, the restaurant near Faneuil Hall has been frequented by many notables, including John F. Kennedy, whose favorite booth is labeled with a plaque. Today, Union Oyster sees more tourists than locals, but it's still a fine bet for creamy bowls of New England clam chowder or oysters on the half shell. The Lazy Man's Lobster is a popular dish for anyone who doesn't feel like donning a plastic bib, and the old-school raw bar is never short on oysters (or clams).

Seafood. Lunch, dinner. $16-35

BROOKLINE

★★★THE FIREPLACE

1634 Beacon St., Brookline, 617-975-1900; www.fireplacerest.com

Thanks to its gentrified neighborhood, the Fireplace can seem like a cross between *Friends* and *Cheers*, where everyone knows everyone else, and half the diners are just stopping by to chat and sip a glass of sancerre. Hungry patrons are devoted to the hearty fare, including braised brisket, grilled halibut and gingerbread pudding, much of it made from scratch in the smoke box or wood-fired oven, which lends the space extra coziness during the winter.

American. Lunch, dinner, brunch. Children's menu. $16-35

★★★FUGAKYU

1280 Beacon St., Brookline, 617-734-1268; www.fugakyu.net

It's considered one of the best sushi restaurants in Boston, despite the location just outside the city limits. Mostly, a visit to Fugakyu is an experience. The sprawling space houses a huge, wrap-around sushi bar (replete with a moat rotating sushi-stocked wooden boats) and two floors of dining alcoves, including a few shoji-screen-enclosed sunken tables for private groups. Kimono-clad waitresses wear headsets to keep things flowing smoothly between the kitchen and the sushi bar, while the front-of-the-house staff has a knack for keeping peace in the face of eager crowds. As for the sushi, it's spectacularly presented in massive bamboo boats and inside martini glasses. Don't miss the torched uni and spicy duck. Skip the mints on the way out, opting instead for a soothing serving of lightly battered green tea ice cream with red-bean paste.

Japanese, sushi. Lunch, dinner. $36-85

CAMBRIDGE

★★★CRAIGIE ON MAIN

853 Main St., Cambridge, 617-497-5511; www.craigieonmain.com

Chef Tony Maws gives his full attention to every dish that leaves the kitchen, and he's fanatical about crafting dishes from scratch and using organic ingredients to create his flavorful bistro-style dishes. The duck is confit-ed onsite, vegetables are pickled in house, and consommés are strained and re-strained for just the right clarity and flavor. The chef often hits nearby farmer's markets to create "market menus" on the day items become available. Craigie on Main's original space on Harvard Square was intimate and dark, thanks to its basement locale, but a move in fall 2008 brightened things considerably. A decent-sized wine list is filled almost completely with organic and biodynamic producers, and the plethora of house wines are unique—because they happen to be very good.

French. Dinner, Sunday brunch. $86 and up

★★★DANTE
Royal Sonesta Hotel, 40 Edwin H. Land Blvd., Cambridge, 617-497-4200;
www.restaurantdante.com

Though this terraced restaurant is hidden at the back of a Cambridge hotel, it boasts one of the best views of the cityscape and the Charles River. The patio is the perfect spot to devour chef Dante de Magistris' precisely prepared Italian-inspired menu. In the dining room, cream-colored walls, warm lighting and lounge-like chairs keep diners relaxed for hours. With its symphony of Mediterranean ingredients, the menu jumps from region to region, offering duck, oysters, sweetbreads and a number of cheeses. Try the chef's tasting menu for a multi-course sampling. The small bar fills up on weekends as revelers imbibe on flashy cocktails such as sparkling sangria and delectable cosmos.

Italian. Breakfast, lunch, dinner, Saturday-Sunday brunch. $36-85

★★★HARVEST
44 Brattle St., Cambridge, 617-868-2255; www.harvestcambridge.com

Harvest's rustic ambiance—pewter tableware, dried flowers, dark wood—is at odds with its locale, a modern office building off Harvard Square. Even so, the cozy American restaurant boasts one of the area's best outdoor patios for warm weather dining. Inside, diners are treated to classic New England cuisine, an open kitchen and a family-friendly dining room. Don't miss the nightly risotto.

American. Lunch, dinner, Sunday brunch. Children's menu. $36-85

★★★OLEANA
134 Hampshire St., Cambridge, 617-661-0505; www.oleanarestaurant.com

Mediterranean menus are a dime a dozen in Boston, but few chefs expose the cuisine's diverse influences as well as Oleana chef-owner Ana Sortun. To do so, she mixes Middle Eastern almonds with herbs from Provence to create a delectable chicken dish. She even endeavors a Basque-influenced venison with caramelized turnip. Regulars enjoy the outdoor patio and fireplace-lit interior just as much as they do the scallops with basmati-pistachio pilaf.

Mediterranean. Dinner. Bar. Reservations recommended. Outdoor seating. $36-85

★★★★RIALTO
The Charles Hotel, 1 Bennett St., Cambridge, 617-661-5050; www.rialto-restaurant.com

After nearly 12 years inside the Charles Hotel, Rialto got a makeover, reopening in 2007 as a posh, more-polished version of itself with plantation shutters and crisp white table linens. As always, chef Jody Adams shines in the kitchen, letting her Italian cuisine take center stage. A few of her signature dishes (grilled Wolfe's Neck sirloin and slow-roasted Long Island duck breast, to name a few) can't be taken off the menu because they're so popular. Instead, she's added a handful of modern Italian specialties like gnocchi with rabbit bolognese and spaghetti with lobster. The wine list is easy to dip in and out of with a few 4-ounce offerings (though the price may have you thinking you deserve a bottle), and the lounge is now a happening spot to grab drinks and appetizers from the bar.

Italian. Lunch, dinner. $36-85

★★★SALTS

798 Main St., Cambridge, 617-876-8444; www.saltsrestaurant.com

With just 40 seats, the dining room at Salts has the feel of a private dinner party. In fact, the tables are situated so tightly you can often hear your neighbor's conversation—so the setting is intimate, if not private. Fans of fromage should request a seat next to the cheese table that holds court in the center of the dining room. Meanwhile, chef Gabriel Bremer will be putting his finishing touches on French-inspired dishes. The lavender-honey whole-roasted boneless duck feeds two, which makes it the most romantic dish on the menu. Bremer also has a light touch with seafood, allowing the dayboat halibut or sea trout flavors to shine. His wife, Analia Verolo, runs the dining room with precision and grace, which makes you feel like a part of the family.

French, American. Dinner. Closed Sunday-Monday. $36-85

★★★UPSTAIRS ON THE SQUARE

91 Winthrop St., Cambridge, 617-864-1933; www.upstairsonthesquare.com

As if plucked from a scene in *Alice In Wonderland,* this fluffy dining room has whimsical splashes throughout—jewel tones, pinks and purples. It's a celebratory space and the food complements the atmosphere, with sweet peas, fava beans and pickled accompaniments sprinkled throughout. The bacon-wrapped beef tenderloin with ramp spaetzle, heirloom carrots and cilantro is a local favorite, so is the sweet watermelon gazpacho with poached shrimp. The first-floor Monday Club Bar and Zebra Room offers a more casual option, with affordable salads and pizzas on the menu. When weather allows, the restaurant sets up pink umbrellas on its tiny outdoor patio. If you're looking for a spot to clink china and stretch your pinkies, afternoon tea is a Saturday dream with savory sandwiches and a slew of sweet treats such as butterscotch pudding and zebra cakes.

French, American. Lunch, dinner, Sunday brunch. $36-85

RECOMMENDED

CHEZ HENRI

1 Shepard St., Cambridge, 617-354-8980; www.chezhenri.com

This cozy bistro delivers a reliable sampling of French and Cuban fare, including a sublime classic Cuban sandwich piled high with pork and spicy mustard. Entrées include sautéed rainbow trout with parsnip purée and paella made with fresh local seafood. The cocktail menu is the highlight of any visit, with craft takes on the classics—including caipirinhas and mojitos made from fresh muddled fruit.

Cuban, French. Dinner. Bar. $36-85

EAST COAST GRILL AND RAW BAR

1271 Cambridge St., Cambridge, 617-491-6568; www.eastcoastgrill.net

Chef Chris Schlessinger's ode to barbecue and seafood has been serving hungry locals for 25 years. The menu runs the gamut from oak-smoked pit barbecue in the form of ribs, brisket and shredded beef, to pork sandwiches, grilled spiced mahi mahi and grilled white pepper crusted tuna. Locals line up for the Sunday brunch, which includes a make-your-own Bloody Mary bar.

Seafood. Dinner, Sunday brunch. Bar. $16-35

CHARLESTOWN
★★★OLIVES
10 City Square, Charlestown, 617-242-1999; www.toddenglish.com

Twenty years later, the original restaurant in chef Todd English's empire still delivers wows. Today, a team of devoted chefs churns out Mediterranean cuisine from an open kitchen). The high ceilings and pack-em-in mentality in don't help the noise factor, but when food tastes this good, who cares? Dishes are spiked with regional ingredients like anchovies, feta and, of course, olives, whereas the wood-grilled meats carry a pleasant fire-roasted flavor. Don't miss the classic-cut French fries, perfectly paired with any of the numerous (and slightly overpriced) wines by the glass.

Mediterranean. Dinner. $36-85

SPAS

BOSTON
★★★★★SPA AT MANDARIN ORIENTAL
Mandarin Oriental, 776 Boylston St., Back Bay, 617-535-8820;
www.mandarinoriental.com

Sure, this 16,000-squarefoot space has all of the bells and whistles you expect—full-body massages, salt scrubs, anti-aging facials, spa pedicures. But this spa ups the ante with full-day location-specific programs like the Boston Breather, which aims to counteract the stress of East Coast urban living with several treatments—a welcoming foot ritual; coffee and frankincense scrub; aroma stone massage; facial of your choice and luxury mani-pedi (plus lunch at the healthful Spa Café). For an above-and-beyond experience, request a treatment in one of the Mandarin Oriental's spa suites, like the Mandarin Suite, which includes 700 square feet of ultimate privacy, a personal stone sauna, a soaking tub, two treatment tables (in case you want to invite a friend) and an enormous daybed for those who need yet another surface to recline on.

WHERE TO SHOP

BOSTON
ALAN BILZERIAN
34 Newbury St., Boston, 617-536-1001; www.alanbilzerian.com

This two-floor boutique in a four-story building sits on Newbury Street's first block, the one that's considered to be the most high-end. Drawing an upscale, often European clientele, the shop features a men's and women's floor filled by major labels such as Issey Miyake, Lanvin, Alexander McQueen and a few items by the owner's daughter Lana Bilzerian. It's a stunning spread (with jaw-dropping price tags to boot) but it's a one-stop shop for designer fashions. The place had deep roots in the music biz, too—Steven Tyler and Mick Jagger call on Bilzerian when they're in town.

Monday-Saturday 10 a.m.-6 p.m.

BLISS HOME
225 Newbury St., Boston, 617-421-5544; www.blisshome.com

Bliss Home is a petite store with a tightly edited collection of home accessories, ranging from tableware to furniture. The store-front's bay window displays softer home goods like pillows, vases, umbrellas, tablecloths, napkins and lamps, whereas the back of the shop has neatly arranged stacks of dishware and china collections. Boston brides choose to register here because of the vast selection of Wedgwood china and Waterford crystal, but you'll also find hand-painted pieces from Denmark and stylized collections from Seychelles and Swedish maker Boda.

Monday-Saturday 10:30 a.m.-6:30 p.m., Sunday noon-6 p.m.

BODEGA

6 Clearway St., Boston; www.bdgastore.com

Pay close attention or you might miss this sneaker-freak haunt. The shop's entrance is disguised as a bodega, complete with a vending machine and displays of toilet paper rolls. Once you're inside, though, the loft-like space opens up to reveal a few rows of neatly arranged, rarely found, limited-edition sneakers by Reebok, New Balance and Converse. An in-house DJ provides the hip-hop accompaniment as you shop for Adidas track jackets and clothing by Vans. Don't bother to call the store for directions—it doesn't have a phone number. The owner strives to keep his business under wraps, but the secret is out.

Monday-Thursday 11 a.m.-6 p.m., Friday-Saturday 11 a.m.-7 p.m., Sunday noon-5 p.m.

DRESS

221 Newbury St., Boston, 617-424-7125; www.dressboston.com

The most fashionable ladies of Back Bay shop here for little black dresses and casual wear by the likes of 3.1 Phillip Lim, Vanessa Bruno and Shipley & Halmos. Don't miss the trendy boutique's table of feather-light T-shirts by T Luxury. Designer handbags are scattered throughout the store, while the jewelry case, which usually has a solid selection of local lines of the delicate and dainty variety, anchors the room.

Monday-Thursday 11 a.m.-7 p.m., Friday-Saturday 11 a.m.-6 p.m., Sunday noon-5 p.m.

FRESH

121 Newbury St., Boston, 617-421-1212; www.fresh.com

Thanks to low-hanging modular lamps and Lucite trim, this beauty boutique has a space-age feel. Fresh is a national line of bath and body products, though

---

WHICH BOSTON STORE HAS THE MOST UNIQUE ITEMS?

Formerly known as Louis Boston—and now, simply, **Louis**—Boston's most celebrated depart-ment store pushes all kinds of boundaries in fashion, thanks to propri-etor Debi Greenberg and her excellent taste in couture. Here, you'll find unusual luxury lines like Marni, Dries van Noten and Joseph Abboud. Meanwhile, the home goods section is packed with everything from vintage lamps and china pieces to organic soaps and luxury sunglass lines—an excellent place to pick-up an inspired wedding or housewarming gift.

HIGHLIGHT

WHAT IS BOSTON'S BEST SHOPPING AREA?

Boston's version of Rodeo Drive is found along a stretch of Newbury Street, located in the city's Back Bay neighborhood. Here, the independent boutiques mix with international brands; the historic brownstones peacefully coexist with newer constructions and mega-retailers. Blocks are named alphabetically according to their cross-streets, from Arlington to Massachusetts Avenue, each with its own personality and sense of style. For the best experience, start your shopping trip on the high-end side—located across from the Public Garden, the Arlington block features tony shops like Chanel, Alan Bilzerian and Valentino, but it also has a few polished-up flagships from national retailers like Banana Republic and Brooks Brothers. The stretch of Newbury between Berkeley and Dartmouth is packed with coffee shops, day spas and boutiques—from cosmetics brand Fresh, to international candle maker Diptyque to the beach-ready fashion label Calypso St. Barth. Moving toward Dartmouth and Exeter, the upscale retailers continue to dissipate in favor of smaller, local boutiques like denim retailer Riccardi. Around here, you'll also find upscale consignment shops like The Closet and Second Time Around, where careful shoppers can unearth the occasional Stella McCartney handbag or Chanel jacket. At Exeter Street and beyond, you'll start seeing restaurants and cafes with sidewalk patios. You'll also get an edgier attitude from the stores—Stel's favors a bohemian, punk and rocker vibe, whereas Dress specializes in pretty party dresses. Further down Newbury Street, on the corner of Gloucester, you'll see the massive, four-story Emerge by Giuliano Spa & Salon. By the time you hit Massachusetts Avenue, you will have sampled the range of Boston's fashion sensibilities.

the label got its start in Boston. Today, the flagship shop stocks an indulgent selection of Fresh brand hand lotions, soaps, body butters and candles as well as other manufacturers' makeup and skin care lines. Fresh's Sugar-Acai Age Delay Body Cream is a treat, as is the Sugar Lip Treatment, a wax balm that protects and plumps the lips—and just happens to be the company's best product. *Monday-Saturday 10 a.m.-7 p.m., Sunday noon-6 p.m.*

FLAT OF THE HILL
60 Charles St., Boston, 617-619-9977; www.flatofthehill.com
This ultra-preppy home goods and accessories store appeals to the conservative sensibilities of its Beacon Hill neighborhood. Think of it as a tribute to Lilly Pulitzer. The boutique is filled to the gills with pinks, apple greens and plaids, not to mention the hand-painted wooden signs hanging all over the place. Pick up embroidered pillows, scented candles, hand-painted coasters and fragrant sachets for the closet, plus punchy greeting cards and terrific gifts. Ribbon-wrapped beauty items like lipglosses and body lotions are sprinkled throughout the store, and there's a decent assortment of evening bags and clutches from designer Lauren Merkin. *Tuesday-Friday 11 a.m.-6 p.m., Saturday 10 a.m.-5 p.m., Sunday noon-5 p.m.*

GRETTA LUXE

Copley Place, 10 Huntington Ave., Boston, 617-536-1959; www.grettastyle.com

Gretchen Monahan is Boston's most famous fashionista, and her high-fashion boutique is a direct expression of her style—confident, sexy and always ahead of the curve. The shelves of this bright, sophisticated store are arranged with shoes by Jimmy Choo, bags by Stella McCartney and Balenciaga, signature pieces of clothing from Rachel Roy, Michael Kors and Zac Posen, and denim from J Brand and Earnest Sewn. Exclusive labels like these come at a price, though you might find a deal—say, a pair of Jimmy Choos for $100 or less— during one of the stellar seasonal sales.

Monday-Saturday 10 a.m.-8 p.m., Sunday noon-6 p.m.

KOO DE KIR

65 Chestnut St., Boston, 617-723-8111; www.koodekir.com

Claustrophobics, take note—this tightly packed home store is as small as the Beacon Hill apartments it's wedged between. The clutter won't matter so much once you behold the merchandise—delicate stemware and pitchers for entertaining, colorful Teema dishware, linen tablecloths, even writing desks and decorative mirrors. An assortment of glamorous and modern lamps are positioned throughout the store, along with a few well-placed handbags.

Tuesday-Friday 10 a.m.-7 p.m., Saturday 10 a.m.-6 p.m., Sunday noon-6 p.m.

LEKKER

1317 Washington St., Boston, 617-542-6464; www.lekkerhome.com

Specializing in minimalist and out-of-the-ordinary housewares, this boutique features a highly edited selection of singular, high-priced pieces. Shoppers will find a few deals, though, mostly on small kitchen gadgets and decorative items. Here, you'll see no-fuss wooden furniture from Palau sitting beside oblong vases and stacks of dishes from Royal Delft and Kahla. Tables are set with pretty runners and place settings by obscure European companies like Arzberg. Don't miss the selection of tabletop trinkets and handy kitchen organizing tools. The store runs a gift registry and continually updates its online shop.

Monday-Friday 10 a.m.-7 p.m., Saturday 11 a.m.-6 p.m., Sunday noon-5 p.m.

LEOKADIA

667 Tremont St., Boston, 617-247-7463; www.leokadiaboutique.com

Leokadia became the South End neighborhood's first dedicated shoe boutique when it arrived in spring 2008. Owner Jessica Lynn had been the manager of another shoe shop before launching this endeavor, which is named for Lynn's mother. The selection emphasizes pricey heels by the likes of Badgley Mischka and Pucci, but a limited selection of denim and accessories fall into the affordable range. The tiny, chandeliered space makes for a sparkly backdrop for the gorgeous shoes, including stilettos, flip-flops, rain boots and strappy sandals. A few handbags by Botkier and a slew of luxury sunglasses sit prettily beside glittering lines of jewelry.

Tuesday-Friday 11 a.m.-7 p.m., Saturday 10 a.m.-6 p.m., Sunday noon-5 p.m.

WHAT ARE BOSTON'S BEST UPSCALE BOUTIQUES?

Alan Bilzerian:
A haute boutique with a rock 'n' roll aesthetic, Alan Bilzeraian specializes in funky, high-end labels like Alexander McQueen, Lanvin and more.

Gretta Luxe:
The city's sweetheart fashionista stocks her flagship boutique with confident and sexy styles from the likes of Chloe, Zac Posen, Stella McCartney and more.

LOUIS BOSTON

60 Northern Ave., Boston, 617-262-6100; www.louisboston.com

In 2010, this iconic department store vacated its former home inside a stately, historic manse on Newbury Street. Now it lives inside an open, new contemporary space in the Fort Point Channel neighborhood on Boston's waterfront. Owner Debi Greenberg pushes all kinds of boundaries when it comes to fashion—she sells couture and ready-to-wear from a number of luxury lines like Marni, Dries van Noten and Joseph Abboud. The home goods section is packed with everything from vintage lamps and china pieces to organic soaps and luxury sunglass lines. Best of all, the department store features an onsite restaurant, Sam's, which serves a casual menu of New England fare for lunch, brunch and dinner.

Monday 11 a.m.-6 p.m., Tuesday, Friday-Saturday 10 a.m.-6 p.m., Wednesday-Thursday 10 a.m.-7 p.m.

MATSU

259 Newbury St., Boston, 617-266-9707; www.matsuboston.com

Filled with quirky, whimsical wardrobe embellishments, this sun-soaked shop gets props for being one of the more eclectic stops on Newbury Street. The selection is a patchwork of flowing skirts from Rozae Nichols, distressed jackets, lacey gloves and vintage, chunky pieces of jewelry, along with odds-and-ends housewares, scarves and clutches. Owner Dava Muramatsu likes to keep lines like Jamin Puech and Commes des Garçons stocked on the shelves. Muramatsu also gives styling consultations and, for a fee, she'll use her artist's eye to personalize a complete outfit for you.

Monday-Saturday 11 a.m.-6 p.m., Sunday 1-5 p.m.

POLKA DOG BAKERY

256 Shawmut Ave., Boston, 617-338-5155; www.polkadog.com

A bona-fide bakeshop for the four-legged set, the Polka Dog Bakery also features gleaming displays of cookies for humans in the shapes of bones and cupcakes. Everything is made onsite, everything is dog-friendly. The South End boutique also features canine fashion items like fur-rimmed jackets and velvet beds.

Monday-Friday 10 a.m.-7:30 p.m., Saturday 10 a.m.-7 p.m., Sunday 11 a.m.-6 p.m.

SHREVE, CRUMP & LOW

440 Boylston St., Boston, 800-225-7088; www.shrevecrumpandlow.com

Cloaked in mahogany paneling and glass, this first-floor jewelry store is glamorous, to say the least. The selection features owner David Walker's collection of gem stones, purchased in every corner of the world, as well as restored antique pieces, stunning watches and a hefty assortment of glittering diamonds. If you ask for a peek at rare, exclusive pieces, you'll be guided to a showroom in the downstairs vault. Or simply pick up the store's famed "gurgling cod" pitcher—it's the preferred wedding gift for every Brahmin bride.

Monday-Wednesday 10 a.m.-6 p.m., Thursday 10 a.m.-7 p.m., Friday 10 a.m.-6 p.m., Saturday 10 a.m.-5 p.m., Sunday noon-5 p.m.

STEL'S
334 Newbury St., Boston, 617-262-3348; www.shopstels.com

This spacious, industrial room looks like a funky downtown bachelor pad with its exposed brick and steel beams, but all that hardware is offset by plush curtains and comfy furnishings, not to mention the owner's amiable dog. Shop here to uncover youthful, urban men's and women's lines like Gary Graham, United Bamboo and Alexander Wang. Looks can veer from punk to prep, sort of like owner Tina Burgo's personal style (she's constantly picking up new lines in New York and L.A.). Scroll through the racks for a peek at Brazilian cult label Coven, statement jackets, limited-edition T-shirts by Rogan and funky shoes by local designer Kristina Kozak.

Monday-Saturday 11 a.m.-7 p.m., Sunday noon-6 p.m.

TURTLE
619 Tremont St., Boston, 617-266-2610; www.turtleboston.com

South End shoppers go to Turtle to learn about the best emerging designers, artisans and jewelers. It's a tiny, overflowing spot filled with lines that are still on the rise like Aimee G., Chulo Pony and shoe designer Farylrobin. But don't let these newbies fool you—owner Storey Hieronymus Hauck proudly culls a unique range of quality one-of-a-kind items. Here, you'll find everything from a floppy-collared dress by a small Icelandic label to simple, organic handbags from a young Rhode Island designer. Meanwhile, the jewelry case shows off First Lady-inspired necklaces by Audrey Jacks alongside delicate, nature-influenced bracelets and earrings by Twigs & Heather.

Tuesday-Saturday 10 a.m.-6 p.m., Sunday noon-5 p.m.

VESSEL
125 Kingston St., Boston, 617-292-0982; www.vesselinc.com

This shop is somewhat messily organized to display the product design firm's playful, modern housewares. The inexpensive lamps can be modular and offbeat, but they cast a lovely glow, while rounded dishes and drinking vessels look like they come from the future. A few decently priced benches and chairs are placed strategically throughout the Kingston Street store.

Tuesday-Saturday 11 a.m.-6 p.m., Sunday noon-5 p.m.

CAMBRIDGE

CAMBRIDGE CONCEPTS
37 Brattle St., Cambridge, 617-868-2001; www.cncpts.com

Originally, Concepts was a store within a store inside The Tannery, a sportswear shop now located down the street. In 2008, Cambridge Concepts found its own space, which resembles the belly of a ship with blonde-wood arches down the length of its ceiling. Inside, you'll find limited-edition Nike Airs, urban wear by Pumas and Adidas, and wildly colored hats and hoodies. The hipster staff is slow when it comes to customer service, but their vibe only reflects the laid-back sneaker culture that has invaded Boston. If you express enough interest, you might be led downstairs to a clubby private room where they show off small-release editions of top brands like the Nike SB Dunk.

Daily 10 a.m.-7 p.m.

FORMAGGIO KITCHEN

244 Huron Ave., Cambridge, 617-354-4750; 268 Shawmut Ave., South End, 617-350-6996; www.formaggiokitchen.com

Home to the city's best selection of artisanal cheeses, Formaggio has been a culinary hot spot for more than 20 years. The cheese department is loaded with imported goats' and cows' milk cheeses that are usually brought in and aged in the store's basement-level cave before showing up in the dairy case. The staff knows every cheese backward and forward. Don't be bashful about asking for samples—they're happy to share. Also available are pantry staples like olive oil from Greece and Morocco, and a small selection of organic wines and pastas. Meanwhile, the fresh market features local vegetables, fruits, sauces and breads that are brought in daily. The South End location, called South End Formaggio, is smaller, but locals stop in often for pre-made salads, sandwiches and light entrées.

Cambridge: Monday-Friday 9 a.m.-7 p.m., Saturday 9 a.m.-6 p.m., Sunday 10 a.m.-4 p.m. South End: Monday-Friday 9 a.m.-8 p.m., Saturday 9 a.m.-7 p.m., Sunday 11 a.m.-5 p.m.

HARVARD BOOK STORE

1256 Massachusetts Ave., Harvard Square, Cambridge, 617-661-1515; www.harvard.com

Holding court in Harvard Square for decades, this independent book shop boasts an impressive philosophy section as well as a basement stacked to the ceiling with discount used paperbacks and hardcovers. But the staff is the thing that sets this bibliophile paradise apart—here, the booksellers are a helpful crew whose adoration for the written word is pleasantly contagious.

Monday-Saturday 9 a.m.-11 p.m., Sunday 10 a.m.-10 p.m.

MINT JULEP

6 Church St., Cambridge, 617-576-6468; 1302 Beacon St., Brookline, 617-232-3600; www.shopmintjulep.com

Just like the sassy cocktail it's named for, this hip women's shop is full of refreshing lines. Here, the atmosphere and the price tags are all about comfort. You'll find a few dress-up pieces thrown into the mix, but mostly you'll see piles of denim by Joe's Jeans and Raven along with adorable tops from LA Made, Rachel Palley and Ella Moss. Both the Cambridge and Brookline locations are tiny—they fill up quickly on weekends, so the owners simply throw open the front doors to make it feel like a party.

Cambridge: Monday-Wednesday 10 a.m.-7 p.m., Thursday-Saturday 10 a.m.-8 p.m., Sunday 11 a.m.-6 p.m. Brookline: Monday-Saturday 10 a.m.-7 p.m., Sunday 11 a.m.-6 p.m.

GREATER BOSTON

Boston's suburbs are more than bedroom communities. Cities such as Concord and Lexington, for example, boast histories so impressive as to rival their big-city neighbor. Lexington is often called "the birthplace of American liberty," since the town green saw the first battle of the American Revolution. Concord, on the other hand, is "the birthplace of the republic", thanks to the peaceful "concord" that established the city, not to mention the literary titans who once lived there— Ralph Waldo Emerson, Henry David Thoreau, Nathanial Hawthorne, Louisa May Alcott.

Despite its picturesque streets, the nearby town of Salem will forever be known for the brutal blip in its history. In 1692, at the peak of the town's infamous witch trials, 19 people were hanged on Gallows Hill, another was "pressed" to death and at least two others died in jail. A museum now memorializes the terrible events and much of the town's tourist trade revolves around the old trials.

Still, Boston's suburbs offer more than history lessons. The region's North Shore, in particular, is rich with relaxing resorts and classic country inns. Gloucester is a blue-collar enclave and fishermen's town-turned-summer resort. Newburyport is a picture-perfect New England town lined with Federalist-style mansions and a bustling downtown shopping center, filled with unusual boutiques, galleries and seafood restaurants. Meanwhile, in the verdant hills of Metro West, visitors uncover all matter of treasure: Wellesley is home to the deeply forested Wellesley College, not to mention a quaint downtown with surprisingly stylish businesses. Foxborough to the south is home to Gillette Stadium and Boston's second-most-beloved sports team, the New England Patriots.

WHAT TO SEE

ANDOVER
PEABODY MUSEUM
175 Main St., Andover, 978-749-4490; www.andover.edu

This Native American archaeological museum features exhibits on the physical and cultural evolution of man as well as the prehistoric archaeology of New England, the Southwest, Mexico and the Arctic.
Monday-Friday 8 a.m.-5 p.m., by appointment only.

PHILLIPS ANDOVER ACADEMY
180 Main St., Andover, 978-749-4000; www.andover.edu

Nearly 1,100 students attend this co-ed boarding school for grades 9 through 12. Notable alumni include photographer Walker Evans, poet Oliver Wendell Holmes, child-rearing expert Benjamin Spock and actor Humphrey Bogart. The pretty campus consists of 170 buildings and 450 acres. Don't miss the Cochran Sanctuary, a 65-acre landscaped area consisting of walking trails, a brook and two ponds.

BRAINTREE

ABIGAIL ADAMS HOUSE

180 Norton St., Weymouth, 781-335-4205; www.abigailadamsbirthplace.org

This site is the birthplace of Abigail Smith Adams, daughter of a local clergyman, wife of President John Adams, mother of President John Quincy Adams and also a smart, innovative thinker in her own right. Today, the house contains personal artifacts and antiques.

July-early September, Tuesday-Sunday.

ADAMS NATIONAL HISTORICAL PARK

135 Adams St., Quincy, 617-770-1175; www.nps.gov

This park includes the birthplace of the second U.S. President John Adams, as well as Peacefield, his home following his retirement from Washington. The fireproof Stone Library was built in 1870 on the order of John Quincy Adams for the storage of the family's books and papers. Today, it houses more than 14,000 volumes.

Daily, April-November, 9 a.m.-5 p.m.

GILBERT BEAN MUSEUM

786 Washington St., Braintree, 781-848-1640; www.braintreehistorical.org

Home to the Braintree Historical Society, this house contains 17th and 18th-century furnishings, military and other historical exhibits and an extensive research library.

Thursday-Saturday 10 a.m.-4 p.m. or by appointment.

CONCORD

CONCORD MUSEUM

200 Lexington Road, Concord, 978-369-9763; www.concordmuseum.org

On display are period rooms, galleries of domestic artifacts and decorative arts chronicling the history of Concord, from its days as a Native American habitation to the present. Exhibits include Ralph Waldo Emerson's study, Henry David Thoreau's belongings used at Walden Pond and Paul Revere's signal lantern.

January-March, Monday-Saturday 11 a.m.-4 p.m., Sunday 1-4 p.m.; April-December, Monday-Saturday 9 a.m.-5 p.m., Sunday noon-5 p.m.; extended Sundays during June-August, 9 a.m.-5 p.m.

LOUISA MAY ALCOTT'S ORCHARD HOUSE

399 Lexington Rd., Concord, 978-369-4118; www.louisamayalcott.org

The two-story house where *Little Women* author Louisa May Alcott penned her famous novel has been preserved much as it was during the Alcott family's stay during the mid-1800s. Located in the leafy upscale Boston suburb of Concord, visitors can tour the house and see Alcott's writing desk, the family's collection of books and heirloom china.

Admission: Adults $9, seniors, students $8, children 6-17 $5, children 5 and under free. November 1-March 31, Monday-Friday 11 a.m.- 3 p.m., Saturday 10 a.m.-4:30 p.m., Sunday 1 p.m.-4:30 p.m.; April 1-October 31, Monday-Saturday 10 a.m.-4:30 p.m., Sunday 1 p.m.-4:30 p.m.

HIGHLIGHTS

WHAT ARE THE BEST HISTORIC SITES IN GREATER BOSTON?

BATTLE GREEN
The shot heard 'round the world still echoes here, the site of the first battle of the American Revolution. Check out Lexington's town green to see the handsome Minuteman monument and Buckman Tavern, the place where rabble-rousers once plotted against the British.

SALEM WITCH MUSEUM
Relive the Salem witch trials of 1692 in this eerie museum. Thankfully, old Salem has since come to embrace witches of all sorts—especially on Halloween, when the museum hosts a fun festival with haunted houses and other performances.

WALDEN POND
What inspired Henry David Thoreau's opus? See for yourself by visiting this gorgeous nature preserve and swimming pond, complete with a recreation of the hand-built cabin where Thoreau once lived.

MINUTE MAN NATIONAL HISTORICAL PARK
174 Liberty St., Concord, 978-369-6993; www.nps.gov
The park consists of 900 acres along the Battle Road between Lexington and Concord. Walk the 5½-mile Battle Road Trail, stop at Hartwell Tavern to see reenactments of colonial life and continue to North Bridge, the site of the first battle of the Revolutionary War (a.k.a., the shot heard round the world).
March-November, daily; December-February, Saturday-Sunday.

OLD MANSE
269 Monument St., Concord, 978-369-3909; www.thetrustees.org
This was the parsonage of Concord's early ministers, including Reverend William Emerson, Ralph Waldo Emerson's grandfather. Nathaniel Hawthorne lived here for a time and made it the setting for the short story *Mosses from an Old Manse*.
Mid-April-October, Monday-Saturday 10 a.m.-5 p.m.

RALPH WALDO EMERSON HOUSE
28 Cambridge Turnpike, Concord, 978-369-2236; www.rwe.org
Ralph Waldo Emerson lived most of his life here, from 1835 to 1882. Today, the house museum contains personal items, furniture, photographs and books original to the famous writer.
Mid-April-late October, Thursday-Saturday 10 a.m.-4:30 p.m., Sunday 1-4:30 p.m.

HIGHLIGHT

WHAT IS THERE TO SEE AT WALDEN POND?

In the mid-19th century, the eminent naturalist and philosopher Henry David Thoreau lived for two years in voluntary seclusion in an austere cabin at Walden Pond. During his two-year sojourn at the peaceful Concord spot, he kept a journal of his thoughts and experiences with nature and society. Later, his notes would become one of the most famous works in American literature—*Walden*, the book that inspired the nation's environmental movement. Today, the pond remains as calm as it was during Thoreau's fabled residency, save for a few modern improvements. Where Thoreau once hiked through dense berry bushes, paved walking trails now run. The water that once swam with pickerel is now stocked with various fishes for amateur anglers. Now a National Historic Landmark, the site features miles of paved and dirt trails, a 102-foot-deep pond, a facsimile of Thoreau's hand-built cabin and myriad opportunities for outdoor action. Water enthusiasts kayak or canoe, swimmers bathe in a specified area and families picnic on a small beach. Come wintertime, cross-country skiers take advantage of the ideal snow trails.

If the pond has one constant, it's this—not everyone can get in at once. The nature preserve welcomes just 1,000 people at a time. When the $5-per-car parking lot is full, visitors are turned away or told to wait. If your day is too tightly scheduled to take the risk, try going early or call ahead to check availability.

SLEEPY HOLLOW CEMETERY
Bedford Street, Concord; www.concordma.gov

This legendary cemetery is the final resting place of the Alcott family, Ralph Waldo Emerson, Nathaniel Hawthorne, Margaret Sidney, Daniel Chester French and Henry David Thoreau.

WALDEN POND STATE RESERVATION
915 Walden St., Concord, 978-369-3254; www.mass.gov

Henry David Thoreau, the American writer and naturalist, made Walden Pond famous when he wrote about his experiences living in a nearby rustic cabin. Today, the structure still stands as part of the park. The reservation offers a 1 ½-mile walking trail that circles the pond, which is an excellent place for open-water swimming. Visitors are advised to arrive early—before 11 a.m. Park officials close the park once the lot is full.
Daily.

WAYSIDE
455 Lexington Road, Concord; www.nps.gov

This remarkable house traded hands among Concord's famous 19th-century authors. Louisa May Alcott lived here as a teenager. Later, Nathaniel Hawthorne and Margaret Sidney, author of the *Five Little Peppers* books, also lived here. Today, the house features an audiovisual tour and several exhibits on its famous residents.
May-October.

DORCHESTER

FRANKLIN PARK GOLF COURSE (WILLIAM J. DEVINE GOLF COURSE)
Franklin Park, Dorchester, 617-265-4084; www.sterlinggolf.com

The second-oldest public golf course in America, the William J. Devine Golf Course combines gently rolling hills, open fairways and a break from the city. Located just south of downtown, the course is part of Frederick Law Olmsted's famous "Emerald Necklace" string of parks that ring Boston. Today, the course includes an updated clubhouse, pro shop and even some history—golf great Bobby Jones used to practice here while attending Harvard.

FOXBOROUGH

GILLETTE STADIUM
60 Washington St., Foxborough, 800-543-1776; www.gillettestadium.com

Home to the New England Patriots, this sleek and modern stadium is located 30 miles outside of Boston. What's less known, though, is that the stadium also houses the New England Revolution, Boston's professional soccer team. It's a new sports arena made even more destination-friendly by the adjacent Patriot Place, a recently completed stadium of commerce with a hotel, restaurants and a live-entertainment venue. Try to be nonchalant, in a very Boston sort of way, if you see heartthrob Patriot quarterback Tom Brady and his Brazilian super-model wife, Gisele Bündchen, in the crowd.

GLOUCESTER

BEAUPORT, THE SLEEPER-MCCANN HOUSE
75 Eastern Point Blvd., Gloucester, 978-283-0800; www.spnea.org

Early 20th-century interior designer Henry Davis Sleeper built a 26-room house here in 1907. With the help of local architect Halfdan Hanson, Sleeper kept adding rooms until, decades later, there were 40. Twenty-five are now on view and contain collections of antique furniture, rugs, wallpaper, ceramics and glass.
June-mid-October, Tuesday-Saturday. Tours: on the hour 10 a.m.-4 p.m. Open until 7 p.m. on Thursdays July-August.

CAPE ANN HISTORICAL MUSEUM
27 Pleasant St., Gloucester, 978-283-0455; www.capeannhistoricalmuseum.org

This history museum has an extensive collection of maritime paintings and landscapes by Fitz Hugh Lane as well as decorative arts, furnishings, and plenty of exhibitions on the Cape Ann area's history.
Tuesday-Saturday 10 a.m-5 p.m., Sunday 1-4 p.m.

HAMMOND CASTLE MUSEUM
80 Hesperus Ave., Gloucester, 978-283-2080; www.hammondcastle.org

Built by inventor Dr. John Hays Hammond, Jr. to resemble a medieval castle, this house museum contains a rare collection of Roman, medieval and Renaissance art objects, including an 8,200-pipe organ.
June-August, daily; September-mid-October, Thursday-Sunday; rest of year, Saturday-Sunday.

SARGENT HOUSE MUSEUM
49 Middle St., Gloucester, 978-281-2432; www.sargenthouse.org

This late 18th-century Georgian residence was built for Judith Sargent, an early feminist writer and sister of Governor Winthrop Sargent. Today, its displays feature period furniture, china, glass, silver, needlework, Early American portraits and paintings by John Singer Sargent.

June-mid-October, Friday-Monday noon-4 p.m.

HARVARD
FRUITLANDS MUSEUMS
102 Prospect Hill Road, Harvard, 978-456-3924; www.fruitlands.org

This cluster of historic farmhouses sits on the site of Fruitlands, an unsuccessful utopian community from the 19th century. Today, the collections include furniture, books, and memorabilia from the Alcott family, especially Fruitlands founder Amos Bronson Alcott (father of Louisa May) and his association with the Transcendentalists. The Shaker Museum features furniture and handicrafts, while the Picture Gallery houses American primitive portraits and paintings by Hudson River School artists. The Native American Museum shows prehistoric artifacts and Native American art.

Mid-May-October, Monday-Friday 11 a.m.-4 p.m., Saturday-Sunday 11 a.m.-5 p.m.

IPSWICH
CRANE BEACH
290 Argilla Road, Ipswich, 978-356-4354; www.ipswichma.com

Among the best beaches on the Atlantic coast, Crane features five miles of sand, lifeguards, bathhouses, a refreshment stand and plenty of walking trails.

Daily 8 a.m.-dusk.

JOHN HEARD HOUSE
54 S. Main St., Ipswich, 978-356-2811; www.ipswichmuseum.net

Built by prominent citizen Thomas F. Waters in 1795, this colonial-style house features Chinese furnishings—even a gilded Buddha—to commemorate Waters' work in the China sea trade.

May-mid-October, Wednesday-Saturday 10 a.m.-4 p.m., Sunday from 1-4 p.m.

THE JOHN WHIPPLE HOUSE
1 S. Village Green, Ipswich, 978-356-2811; www.ipswichmuseum.net

Built in 1640 and later sold to Ipswich resident John Whipple, this house features 17th and 18th-century furniture and a lovely garden.

May-mid-October, Wednesday-Saturday 10 a.m.-4 p.m., Sunday 1-4 p.m.

LEXINGTON
BATTLE GREEN
Lexington, center of town

Site of the opening shots of the American Revolution, Lexington's town green features Buckman Tavern and a statue depicting a common Lexington Minuteman. Seven Minutemen soldiers are also buried here.

BUCKMAN TAVERN
1 Bedford St., Lexington, 781-862-1703; www.lexingtonhistory.org

Located on the Battle Green, this tavern served as an important gathering place for the minutemen, who assembled here before the Battle of Lexington and Concord.

Mid-April-May: weekends only; June-October: daily 10 a.m.-4 p.m.

SPECIAL EVENT

PATRIOT'S DAY PARADE

Concord, 978-369-3120, 888-733-2678; www.concordnet.org

Patriot's Day commemorates the Battle of Lexington and Concord, which marked the beginning of the Revolutionary War on April 18, 1775. In this town, schools and many businesses close so the entire city can celebrate with parades and reenactments of Paul Revere's famous ride.

Third Monday in April.

HANCOCK-CLARKE HOUSE

36 Hancock St., Lexington, 781-862-1703; www.lexingtonhistory.org

Here, John Hancock and Samuel Adams were awakened by Paul Revere's alarm on April 18, 1775. Today, the modest house is open for tours and serves as headquarters of the Lexington Historical Society.

Mid-April-May, Saturday-Sunday; June-October, daily. Tours: hourly 11 a.m.-2 p.m.

MUNROE TAVERN

1332 Massachusetts Ave., Lexington, 781-862-1703; www.lexingtonhistory.org

This tavern served as a British field hospital during the Battle of Lexington and Concord. In fact, visitors can still see a single bullet hole in the taproom ceiling. The museum also features an 18th century tavern sign and other historic artifacts.

Mid-April-October. Tours: Daily 3 p.m.

NATIONAL HERITAGE MUSEUM

33 Marrett Road, Lexington, 781-861-6559, 781-457-4142; www.monh.org

The museum features exhibits on American history, with an emphasis on the Revolutionary War—especially the Battle of Lexington and Concord.

Tuesday-Saturday 10 a.m.-4:30 p.m., Sunday noon-4:30 p.m.

LINCOLN

CODMAN HOUSE

Codman Road, Lincoln, 781-259-8843

Originally a two-story, L-shaped Georgian mansion, this 1740 house was more than doubled in size by Federal merchant John Codman to imitate an English-country residence. Today, it features period-style gardens and antique furnishings.

Tours: June-mid-October, first Saturday of each month 11 a.m.-4 p.m.

DECORDOVA MUSEUM & SCULPTURE PARK

51 Sandy Pond Road, Lincoln, 781-259-8355; www.decordova.org

Best known as a sculpture park, the DeCordova grounds feature large contemporary works sprinkled across 35 wooded acres. The museum also has an eclectic collection of paintings, posters, photography and media, as well as rotating exhibitions and occasional artists-in-residence programs. In early June, rain or shine, the museum sponsors the Annual Art in the Park Festival and Art Sale.

Tuesday-Sunday 11 a.m.-5 p.m.

DRUMLIN FARM EDUCATION CENTER
208 S. Great Road, Lincoln, 781-259-2200; www.massaudubon.org

This demonstration farm features domestic and native creatures, gardens and even hayrides.

March-October, Tuesday-Sunday 9 a.m.-5 p.m.; November-February, Tuesday-Sunday 9 a.m.-4 p.m.

GROPIUS HOUSE
68 Baker Bridge Road, Lincoln, 781-259-8098; www.spnea.org

This remarkable structure served as the family home of Bauhaus architect Walter Gropius, one of the pioneering masters of modern architecture. In fact, the house was the first building he designed after arriving in the United States in 1937.

June-October, first Saturday of the month. Tours: 11 a.m.-4 p.m.

LOWELL

AMERICAN TEXTILE HISTORY MUSEUM
491 Dutton St., Lowell, 978-441-0400; www.athm.org

The site's permanent exhibit, "Textiles in America," uses displays of 18th- to 20th-century textiles, artifacts and machinery to demonstrate the impact of the Industrial Revolution on labor.

Admission: adults $8, seniors $6. Wednesday-Sunday 10 a.m.-5 p.m.

LOWELL HERITAGE STATE PARK
160 Pawtucket Blvd., Lowell, 978-458-8750; www.mass.gov

The park consists of six miles of canals and two miles of green space along the banks of the Merrimack River. It also offers a boathouse, boat rentals, a concert pavilion and interpretive programs.

Schedule varies; call for details. Free parking is available to visitors.

LOWELL NATIONAL HISTORICAL PARK
246 Market St., Lowell, 978-970-5000; www.nps.gov

The nation's first large-scale center for the mechanized production of cotton cloth, Lowell became a model for 19th-century industrial development. This park was established to commemorate Lowell's unique legacy as the most important planned industrial city in America. It includes mill buildings and a five-and-a-half-mile canal system.

May-mid-October.

NEW ENGLAND QUILT MUSEUM
18 Shattuck St., Lowell, 978-452-4207; www.nequiltmuseum.org

This unusual museum features changing exhibits of antique, traditional and contemporary quilts.

Admission: adults $5, seniors and students $4. Tuesday-Saturday 10 a.m.-4 p.m.; May-December, Sunday noon-4 p.m.

WHISTLER HOUSE MUSEUM OF ART
243 Worthen St., Lowell, 978-452-7641; www.whistlerhouse.org

The birthplace of painter James Abbott McNeill Whistler, this Federal- and Greek Revival-style house is now a house museum featuring several of his etchings.

Admission: adults $5, seniors and students $4. Wednesday-Saturday 11 a.m.-4 p.m.

MARBLEHEAD

ABBOT HALL
188 Washington St., Marblehead, 781-631-0000; www.abbothall.org

In addition to Marblehead city hall, this building houses the famous *Spirit of '76* painting by Archibald MacNeal Willard as well as the town's original 1684 deed from the Nanapashemet tribe.

Memorial Day-October, daily; rest of year, Monday-Friday.

JEREMIAH LEE MANSION
170 Washington St., Marblehead, 781-631-1768; www.marbleheadmuseum.org

Built by local craftsmen in 1768, this colonial Georgian house is now run by the Marblehead Historical Society and feature original decorative elements like hand-painted wallpapers, ceramics, early American furniture and period-style gardens.

June-October, Tuesday-Saturday 10 a.m.-4 p.m.

KING HOOPER MANSION
8 Hooper St., Marblehead, 781-631-2608; www.marbleheadarts.org

Home to the Marblehead Arts Association, this restored mansion features a period-style garden, colonial-style furnishings and monthly art exhibits in three in-house galleries.

Tuesday-Saturday 10 a.m.-4 p.m., Sunday 1-5 p.m.

NEWBURYPORT

COFFIN HOUSE
14 High Road, Newburyport, 978-462-2634; www.historicnewengland.org

This old house was occupied by the three generations of the coffin family. Today, it provides visitors with a peek of domestic rural life via 17th and 18th-century kitchens, in addition to a buttery and parlor with early 19th-century wallpaper.

June-mid-October, first Saturday of the month 11 a.m.-5 p.m.

CUSHING HOUSE MUSEUM
98 High St., Newburyport, 978-462-2681; www.newburyhist.com

This Federalist-style mansion was once the home of Caleb Cushing, the first U.S. envoy to China. Today, it features lovely collections of silver, needlework, antique fans, toys, hat boxes and more.

May-November, Tuesday-Friday 10 a.m.-4 p.m., Saturday noon-4 p.m.

CUSTOM HOUSE MARITIME MUSEUM
25 Water St., Newburyport, 978-462-8681;
www.customhousemaritimemuseum.org

Committed to maritime history, this museum features collections of ship models, navigational instruments, shipwreck artifacts, U.S. Coast Guard memorabilia and more.

Mid-May-mid-December, Tuesday-Saturday 10 a.m.-4 p.m., Sunday noon-4 p.m.

PARKER RIVER NATIONAL WILDLIFE REFUGE
6 Plum Island Turnpike, Newburyport, 978-465-5753; www.fws.gov

This breathtaking natural barrier beach is six-and-a-half miles long and the home to many species of birds, mammals, reptiles, amphibians and plants.

Visitors are free to go hiking, bicycling or waterfowl hunting on the park's nature trail.
Daily.

NEWTON
CHARLES RIVER CANOE & KAYAK CENTER
2401 Commonwealth Ave., Newton, 617-965-5110; www.paddleboston.com
If you're not afraid of getting wet, you'll love this Charles River entry point. Kayaks and canoes are available for rent.
April-October, daily.

JACKSON HOMESTEAD MUSEUM
527 Washington St., Newton, 617-552-7238; www.ci.newton.ma.us
Once a station on the Underground Railroad, the 1809 home of the Newton Historical Society features changing interpretive and historical exhibits as well as a children's gallery.
Tuesday-Friday 11 a.m.-5 p.m., Sunday noon-5 p.m.

QUINCY
ADAMS NATIONAL HISTORICAL PARK
135 Adams St., Quincy, 617-770-1175; www.nps.gov/adam
This national historic park preserves the birthplaces of the second and sixth U.S. presidents as well as Peacefield, the home to which John Adams retired after leaving Washington, D.C. The buildings are accessible via guided tour during the summer months, and provide a fascinating look into the history of America's first political family. The Stone Library, situated on the grounds of Peacefield, was built in 1870 on the order of John Quincy Adams. It provides storage for the family's books and papers in a fireproof structure, and houses more than 14,000 volumes.
Admission: adults $5, children under 16 free. April-November, daily 9 a.m.-5 p.m.

ROCKPORT
OLD CASTLE
Granite and Curtis Streets, Rockport, 978-546-9533; www.sandybayhistorical.org
This 1715 structure offers a fine example of early 18th-century "saltbox" architecture, a quintessential New England style made with one story in the back and two in the front.
July-August, Saturday; rest of year, by appointment.

THE PAPER HOUSE
52 Pigeon Hill St., Rockport, 978-546-2629; www.paperhouserockport.com
The pet project of an engineer, this house is made almost entirely of newspaper. Later, that very engineer outfitted his paper cottage with furniture made of paper, too.
April-October, daily.

SALEM
CROWNINSHIELD-BENTLEY HOUSE
126 Essex St., Salem, 978-745-9500
Reverend William Bentley, an important minister, thinker and diarist, was a

border in this colonial-style house between 1791 and 1819.
June-October, daily; rest of year, Saturday-Sunday.

DERBY HOUSE
174 Derby St., Salem, 978-740-1660; www.nps.gov

This was the home of maritime merchant Elias Hasket Derby, one of the country's first millionaires. The garden features roses, herbs and 19th-century flowers. Visits are by tour only; call to make an appointment.

GARDNER-PINGREE HOUSE
128 Essex St., Salem, 978-745-9500

Designed by Samuel McIntire for a wealthy merchant, this 1804 house has been restored and handsomely furnished with period-style furniture.
June-October, daily; rest of year, Saturday-Sunday.

HOUSE OF SEVEN GABLES
115 Derby St., Salem, 978-744-0991; www.7gables.org

Nathaniel Hawthorne's 1851 novel of the same name is said to have been inspired by this 1668 house. Today, the structure features Colonial Revival gardens, a secret staircase and thousands of historic artifacts.
Admission: adults $12.50, seniors $11.50, children 5-12 $7.50. July-October, daily 10 a.m.-7 p.m.; November-December, daily 10 a.m.-5 p.m.; January 15-June, daily 10 a.m.-5 p.m.

JOHN WARD HOUSE
161 Essex St., Salem, 978-745-9500

The 1684 house was built by John Ward, a Brit who fled the plague in 1680. Today, it provides a glimpse of 17th-century furniture and domestic life.
June-October, daily; rest of year, Saturday Sunday

PEABODY MUSEUM & ESSEX INSTITUTE
East India Square, Salem, 978-745-9500, 866-745-1876; www.pem.org

Founded by sea captains in 1799, the Peabody Museum & Essex Institute features artwork created from 1700 to today, much it originating from Africa, Native American, Asian and Oceanic cultures.
Tuesday-Sunday 10 a.m.-5 p.m.

PEIRCE-NICHOLS HOUSE
80 Federal St., Salem, 978-745-9500

One of the earliest examples of Samuel McIntire's architectural genius, this 1782 Colonial has been lovingly preserved and authentically furnished.
By appointment only.

PIONEER VILLAGE: SALEM IN 1630
Forest River Park off W. St., Salem, 978-740-9636; www.essexheritage.org

A reproduction of an early Puritan settlement, the village features dugouts, wigwams and thatched cottages now peopled by costumed interpreters.

ROPES MANSION AND GARDEN
318 Essex St., Salem, 978-745-9500; www.salemmass.com

This is a restored, gambrel-roofed Georgian and Colonial mansion furnished

with period pieces. The 1912 garden is known for its beauty and variety.
June-October daily; limited hours Sunday.

SALEM WITCH MUSEUM

19½ Washington Square, Salem, 978-744-1692; www.salemwitchmuseum.com

The Salem witch trials of 1692 are recreated here with a 30-minute narrated presentation that uses special lighting and life-size figures. Be warned, however—this exhibit may be frightening to young children. Slightly less gruesome is the town's October Salem's Haunted Happenings, a Halloween festival that features street merchants, performances, witch-themed games and haunted houses.

Daily; extended hours in July and August.

WITCH DUNGEON MUSEUM

16 Lynde St., Salem, 978-741-3570; www.witchdungeon.com

Catch the reenactment of the 1692 witch trial of Sarah Good and a tour a recreation of the dungeon where accused witches once awaited trial.

April-November, daily.

WITCH HOUSE

310 Essex St., Salem, 978-744-8815; www.salemweb.com

The only remaining structure with direct ties to the 1692 witch trials, this house was once home to witchcraft trial judge Jonathan Corwin. Some of the accused witches may have been interrogated here.

May-early November, daily 10 a.m.-5 p.m.; extended hours in October.

SUNDBURY CENTER

GREAT MEADOWS NATIONAL WILDLIFE REFUGE

Lincoln St., and 73 Weir Hill Road, Sudbury Center, 978-443-4661; www.fws.gov

A network of terrific dirt walking trails winds through this wildlife refuge for more than 200 species of birds, including the magnificent great blue heron.

Daily dawn-dusk.

WHERE TO STAY

ANDOVER

★★★ANDOVER INN

4 Chapel Ave., Andover, 978-475-5903, 800-242-5903; www.andoverinn.com

Located on the campus of Phillips Andover Academy, this neo-Georgian country inn was built in 1930 to accommodate visiting parents and alumni. Today, the rooms are decorated with period-style furnishings and the inn features a mahogany bar and an impressive wine selection. The in-house restaurant, Samuel's, features sophisticated fare with international influences.

23 rooms. Restaurant, bar. Complimentary breakfast. $61-150

BRAINTREE

★★★SHERATON BRAINTREE HOTEL

37 Forbes Road, Braintree, 781-848-0600, 800-325-3535; www.sheraton.com

Located just 12 miles from Logan International Airport, near the JFK library and Bayside Exposition Center, the Sheraton Braintree is a good choice for those who want to visit Boston without paying the city's sky-high hotel rates. Relax in the indoor or outdoor pool, the sauna or the steam room. Or go for an invigorating workout at the extensive onsite health club that has racquetball, aerobics and Nautilus machines.

396 rooms. Restaurant, bar. Fitness center. $61-150

CONCORD

★★★COLONIAL INN

48 Monument Square, Concord, 978-369-9200, 800-370-9200; www.concordscolonialinn.com

Henry David Thoreau's family once owned this property, which has been an inn since 1889. Anchoring the western edge of Monument Square in historic Concord, the Colonial Inn is a short walk from the town's shops and cafés. Guest rooms are individually decorated and feature four-poster beds. The inn features a variety of dining venues—the main restaurant for breakfast, lunch, dinner and Sunday brunch; the outdoor porch for High Tea; and the rustic, colonial tavern for beer and live jazz.

56 rooms. Restaurant, bar. $151-250

★★★HAWTHORNE INN

462 Lexington Road, Concord, 978-369-5610; www.concordmass.com

Built in 1870, the Hawthorne Inn is located less than a mile east of the village center. The pink house is surrounded by gardens and its neighbors include Minuteman National Historic Park as well as the historic Wayside and Orchard houses. Nineteenth-century antiques, original artwork, Japanese woodcuts, pre-Columbian pottery, a kitschy collection of salt and pepper shakers, books and old maps are tastefully displayed throughout the hotel.

7 rooms. Complimentary breakfast. $151-250

GLOUCESTER
RECOMMENDED

BASS ROCKS OCEAN INN

107 Atlantic Road, Gloucester, 978-283-7600, 800-780-7234; www.bassrocksoceaninn.com

Spread over three buildings, this sprawling seaside inn features rooms with glorious views of the ocean. The inn's elegance is epitomized by the afternoon tea and cookies, served daily. But there's plenty of activity, too, including croquet, darts and billiards.

51 rooms. Complimentary breakfast. Closed December-March. $151-250

NEWTON

★★★BOSTON MARRIOTT NEWTON

2345 Commonwealth Ave., Newton, 617-969-1000, 800-228-9290; www.marriott.com

Ideal for business travelers, the Newton Marriott has a 24-hour, self-serve business center and more than 16,000 square feet of meeting space. The prime location along the Charles River offers great views.

430 rooms. Restaurant, bar. Fitness center. $61-150

★★★HOTEL INDIGO RIVERSIDE

399 Grove St., Newton, 617-969-5300; www.newtonboutiquehotel.com

Who would guess you'd find a little bit of Vegas-meets-South Beach in unassuming Newton? Formerly a tired-looking Holiday Inn, this space reopened in 2008 with platform beds, all-marble bathrooms and Aveda bath products. The best reasons to shack up here, though, are found on the ground floor—Bokx109 is a "concept" steakhouse with occasional celebrity guest chefs and the Bokx Pool is an oddly appealing oasis replete with cabanas and cocktail service. Seasonal décor shifts mean the hotel gets a mini-facelift every couple months.

193 rooms. Restaurant, bar. Fitness center. Pool. Business center. $151-250

★★★SHERATON NEWTON HOTEL

320 Washington St., Newton, 617-969-3010, 800-325-3535; www.sheraton.com

All rooms and suites at this recently renovated property feature contemporary décor with sleek white bedding, well-designed work areas and warm, mustard-colored walls. Those not wanting to shell out for Boston rates can stay here and hop the downtown express, which departs for Faneuil Hall every 20 minutes.

270 rooms. Restaurant, bar. Pool. Fitness center. $61-150

ROCKPORT

★★★EMERSON INN BY THE SEA

1 Cathedral Ave., Rockport, 978-546-6321, 800-964-5550; www.emersoninnbythesea.com

This traditional country inn has hosted guests at its Pigeon Cove location since 1846. From March to the end of December, visitors can partake in the glorious ocean views from the inn's pool, porch, restaurant and most of the floral-bedecked guestrooms.

36 rooms. Restaurant. Spa. $61-150

TYNGSBORO

★★★STONEHEDGE INN AND SPA

160 Pawtucket Blvd., Tyngsboro, 978-649-4400, 888-649-2474; www.stonehedgeinn.com

Inspired by an English country manor, this luxurious inn features spacious guest rooms, private balconies, enclosed porches and in-suite fireplaces. Set on the grounds of a horse farm, it also makes a private retreat for a romantic rendezvous or corporate retreat. The inn boasts the largest wine cellar in New England. Check out Left Bank Restaurant for a few tastes, then head for the in-house spa to indulge in some vinotherapy, a.k.a. soaking in Chardonnay grapes.

30 rooms. Restaurant, bar. $151-250

RECOMMENDED

MARBLEHEAD

HARBOR LIGHT INN

58 Washington St., Marblehead, 781-631-2186; www.harborlightinn.com

Each room at this 1729 inn comes with a fireplace, a canopy bed and a Jacuzzi. What's more, guests can help themselves to continental breakfast and fresh-baked cookies in the colonial dining room.

21 rooms. No children under 8. Complimentary breakfast. $61-150

NEWBURYPORT
GARRISON INN
11 Brown Square, Newburyport, 978-499-8500; www.garrisoninn.com

This historic hotel offers basic guest rooms, though they do come with comfortable featherbeds. The location in central Newburyport can't be beat.
24 rooms. Restaurant, bar. Pool. Fitness center. Spa. $61-150

CLARK CURRIER INN
45 Green St., Newburyport, 978-465-8363; www.clarkcurrierinn.com

Guest rooms at this traditional, New England-style inn are individually decorated with antiques and period-style reproductions. Though the Federal-style building has been fully updated, it offers plenty of classics: don't miss the parlor with its elegant Samuel McIntyre-designed fireplace.
7 rooms. Complimentary breakfast. $61-150

ROCKPORT
ADDISON CHOATE INN
49 Broadway, Rockport, 978-546-7543, 800-245-7543; www.addisonchoateinn.com

This Cape Ann bed and breakfast is less than an hour's drive from Boston. Here, visitors will find English country-style rooms with antiques, period-style reproductions and four-poster beds. Breakfast includes homemade granola and fresh-baked scones, and in the afternoons, the innkeepers are quick to offer homemade cookies, lemon bread and iced coffees.
8 rooms. No children under 11. Complimentary breakfast. $61-150

THE INN ON COVE HILL
37 Mount Pleasant St., Rockport, 978-546-2701, 888-546-2701; www.innoncovehill.com

Built in 1791 after the soon-to-be innkeepers found pirates' gold nearby, this inn is rich with period detail—a spiral staircase, crown molding, white picket fence. Guest rooms share in that spirit with antiques, period furnishings and canopied beds.
8 rooms. Complimentary breakfast. Closed mid-October-mid-April. $61-150

WHERE TO EAT

IPSWICH
★★★1640 HART HOUSE
51 Linebrook Road, Ipswich, 978-356-1640; www.1640harthouse.com

Just 20 years after landing in the town of Ipswich, the Pilgrims built this now-restored house. Today, the building features upscale tavern dining at its best, with wood-beamed ceilings, rich, leather wingback chairs and a working fireplace. The menu features comfort food favorites, from hangar steak to corn chowder.
American. Lunch, dinner. Bar. Children's menu. Reservations recommended. $16-35

LOWELL
★★★LA BONICHE
143 Merrimack St., Lowell, 978-458-9473; www.laboniche.com

Though the food is upscale, the dress code is easygoing. So get cozy and enjoy the menu's eclectic dishes with French accents, from grilled garlic chicken to

duck with cranberry and orange.
International. Lunch, dinner. Closed Sunday-Monday, first week of July. Bar. $16-35

NEWBURYPORT

★★★DAVID'S
11 Brown Square, Newburyport, 978-462-8077; www.davidstavern.com

A favorite of locals and visitors alike, this restaurant serves a wide variety of global fare—caprese salads, pizzas, bouillabaisse stews, even wasabi sea scallops. Enjoy a casual atmosphere in the downstairs pub, or more formal dining upstairs.
International. Dinner. Bar. Children's menu. $36-85

NEWTON

★★★LUMIERE
1293 Washington St., West Newton, 617-244-9199; www.lumiererestaurant.com

Warm and whimsical, this French spot features all manner of playful flourish—the handle on the front door is spaced like a repurposed spoon, Scrabble tiles adorn the restroom floors. The chef doesn't fool around in the kitchen, where he turns out French-inspired seafood, soups and meat dishes—the best bistro fare for miles around.
French. Dinner. $36-785

SALEM

★★★LYCEUM
43 Church St., Salem, 978-745-7665; www.lyceumsalem.com

One of the area's top restaurants, this comfortable dining room is located in the building where Alexander Graham Bell made his first call in 1877. An emphasis on seasonal, local ingredients shines in dishes like pan-seared scallops with chorizo sausage and shitake risotto.
American. Lunch, dinner, Sunday brunch. Bar. $16-35

TYNGSBORO

★★★LEFT BANK RESTAURANT
160 Pawtucket Blvd., Tyngsboro, 978-649-4400, 888-649-2474; www.stonehedgeinnandspa.com

Home to one of the world's most impressive wine caves, this out-of-the-way restaurant is an oenophile's delight. Choose from nearly 2,000 wines—the cellar allegedly holds more than 90,000 bottles. Pair your pour with an equally impressive serving of French-style pork, chicken, veal, salmon and more.
French. Breakfast, lunch, dinner, Sunday brunch. Closed Monday. Outdoor seating. $36-85

RECOMMENDED

CONCORD

COLONIAL INN
48 Monument Square, Concord, 978-369-2373, 800-370-9200; www.concordscolonialinn.com

Choose between the inn's two excellent eateries: The Liberty Restaurant & Village Forge Tavern specializes in classic tavern fare like fish and chips, lobster rolls and juicy hamburgers. Meanwhile, the entrées at Merchant's Row Restaurant tend toward the formal—think brown sugar- and apple cider-brined salmon and brick-roasted chicken.

American. Breakfast, lunch, dinner, Sunday brunch. Bar. Children's menu. Reservations recommended. Outdoor seating. $151-250

NEWBURYPORT

TEN CENTER STREET

10 Center St., Newburyport, 978-462-6652; www.tencenterstreet.com

This building was first occupied by an 18th century bakery, but now it's inhabited by a chic contemporary bistro. Standout dishes include truffled mac 'n' cheese and lobster chowder. Enjoy them in the formal upstairs dining room, or take your supper in a cozy booth downstairs.

American. Lunch, dinner, Sunday brunch. Bar. Outdoor seating. Closed Monday. $16-35

CAPE COD AND THE ISLANDS

From quiet seaside respites to beachy social scenes, Cape Cod and its nearby islands feature everything a vacationer could possibly want. When it's time to decompress, frazzled travelers head for the resorts and inns in laid-back towns like Brewster and Dennis, while sun-worshippers and beach bums head for Falmouth and Harwich with their long stretches of coastline. If they can't stomach the traffic (of which the Cape has plenty), they simply stop over in Hyannis, a quaint town with plentiful boutiques, antiques and of course, a beach.

The Cape has its share of arts and culture, too. Sandwich is known for its glass art and glass industry. Wellfleet is a summer resort town with a helping of tasteful art galleries, and Provincetown is the rowdy one with its theaters and active arts association, not to mention the pervading party scene that washes ashore every summer. As for the history-lovers, they stop in Eastham, site of the first encounter between the pilgrims and the Nauset Native Americans. Or these history-lovers drive a few miles north of Cape Cod to Plymouth, site of the famous rock and the 1620 landing of the Mayflower.

Just ten miles long and 20 miles wide, the island of Martha's Vineyard has an outsized reputation. What began as a whaling center has now morphed into an offshore resort for the rich and famous. Its acres of sandy beaches, grassy dunes, craggy cliffs and cultivated farmland are all but perfect. Not as ideal, though, are the island's lofty prices—housing, shopping and dining here come at a steep price. Nevertheless, tourists persist to pack the streets of Edgartown, Oak Bluffs and Vineyard Haven in the summer.

As for Nantucket, it's regarded as even more exclusive than the Vineyard. This, too, was once a whaling center—Nantucket still has the seaman's houses to prove it. Today, it's a small island full of fancy cottages, prime beachfront and first-rate restaurants. In the peak summer season, the population nearly doubles with day-trippers and weekenders arriving by way of the Steamship Authority ferries. Somehow, the island retains its charm and its flush residents take the tourists in stride. A plethora of outdoor activity can be explored here, from biking to swimming to sailing to tennis and golf. Siasconset ("Sconset" to the natives) and Nantucket Town are the isle's shopping and dining hubs, though you'll find small shops and eateries are sprinkled throughout the land's 48 square miles.

WHAT TO SEE

BARNSTABLE

CAPE COD PATHWAYS

3225 Highway 6A, Barnstable, 508-362-3828; www.capecodcommission.org

The Cape Cod Commission oversees a network of dirt walking and hiking trails that links together most Cape towns. Check out the Commission's detailed map of the trail system or drop by one of the pathways' many events. In early June, hearty souls hike from one end of the cape to the other on the Cape Walk. During the October Walking Weekend, guides lead groups on short and long hikes.

Daily.

HYANNIS WHALE WATCHER CRUISES

Barnstable Harbor, 269 Mill Way, Barnstable, 508-362-6088, 888-942-5392; www.whales.net

Try your luck aboard the *Whale Watcher*, a 297-passenger super-cruiser, custom designed and built specifically for whale watching. Each tour features live narration by an onboard naturalist.

Admission: adults $45, seniors $40, children 4-12 $26, children 3 and under free. April-October, daily.

WEST PARISH MEETINGHOUSE

2049 Meetinghouse Road, West Barnstable, 508-362-4445; www.westparish.org

Built in 1719 and continually renovated and expanded over the years, this building is said to be the oldest Congregational church in the country. Guests are free to attend regular Sunday services.

Sunday 10 a.m.

BREWSTER

CAPE COD MUSEUM OF NATURAL HISTORY

869 Main Street/Route 6A, Brewster, 508-896-3867; www.ccmnh.org

Dedicated to the Cape's wildlife and ecology, this history museum offers everything from lectures, exhibits and field walks to trips to nearby Monomoy Island.

February-March, Thursday-Sunday 11 a.m.-3 p.m.; April-May, Wednesday-Sunday 11 a.m.-3 p.m.; June-September, Daily 9:30 a.m.-4 p.m.; October-December, Wednesday-Sunday 11 a.m.-3 p.m.; open only for special programs in January.

CAPE COD REPERTORY THEATER COMPANY

3299 Highway, 6A, Brewster, 508-896-1888; www.caperep.org

With both an indoor and outdoor theater, this troupe offers children's performances on Tuesday and Friday mornings in July and August. In addition, you'll find productions for the whole family in the outdoor theater in the woods near Nickerson State Park.

NEW ENGLAND FIRE & HISTORY MUSEUM

1439 Main St., Brewster, 508-896-5711

This six-building complex houses an extensive collection of firefighting equipment. Check out a diorama of Chicago's 1871 fire, several antique

HIGHLIGHTS

WHAT ARE THE BEST BEACHES ON CAPE COD AND THE ISLANDS?

AQUINNAH CLIFFS
Swim in the shadows of glacier-formed cliffs at this dramatic beach on Martha's Vineyard. This was once a popular place to sunbathe in the nude, though the local police have worked to bust this trend over the past five years.

JETTIES BEACH
A family-friendly beach at its finest, this Nantucket beach has all manner of amenities—showers, a snack bar, changing rooms, a playground. It offers plenty of activity, too, like kayak and sailboat rentals.

NAUSET BEACH
This Cape Cod beach is a magnet for Atlantic surfers, thanks to the comparatively big waves it attracts. Even better, the beach is prime real estate for sandcastles and sunrises.

engines, the world's only 1929 Mercedes-Benz fire engine, a life-size reproduction of Ben Franklin's firehouse, a 19th-century blacksmith shop and the largest apothecary in the country (that's 664 gold-leaf bottles of medicine).
June-August, Monday-Saturday 10 a.m.-4 p.m., Sunday noon-4 p.m.; September-mid-October, weekends.

NICKERSON STATE PARK
3488 Highway, 6A, Brewster, 508-896-3491; www.mass.gov
Nickerson State Park offers an unusual experience on Cape Cod—its densely wooded areas show no sign of the typically marshy Cape region. The park features campsites, challenging hiking trails, an eight-mile bike path, fishing, swimming, canoeing and bird-watching.

OCEAN EDGE GOLF COURSE
2660 Highway, 6A, Brewster, 508-896-9000; www.oceanedge.com
Just a stone's throw from the ocean, this beautiful golf course offers 6,665 yards of manicured greens, plus five ponds for challenging play. Green fees drop considerably in the off-season; the course offers lessons from PGA pros.
Daily.

CATAMET

CAPE COD KAYAK

1270 Highway 28A, Cataumet, 508-563-9377; www.capecodkayak.com

This outdoor outfitter also runs guided kayak tours on area lakes, rivers and harbors. Experienced kayakers are free to rent boats and head out on their own for as long as a week.

March-November.

CHATHAM

CHATHAM LIGHT

Bridge and Main Streets, Chatham, 508-430-0628;

This quintessential Cape lighthouse has been through many incarnations and restorations, but has always offered a superb view of the Atlantic and the seals on the beach below. The lighthouse still serves as an active Coast Guard station, with public tours available on select, pre-determined days.

Daily.

MONOMOY NATIONAL WILDLIFE REFUGE

Monomoy Island, Chatham, 508-945-0594; www.monomoy.fws.gov

The refuge is 2,750 acres of a bird-lover's paradise. The spectacle is greatest in spring, when the inhabitants exhibit bright plumage while breeding.

DENNIS

JOSIAH DENNIS MANSE

77 Nobscusset Road, Dennis, 508-385-3528; www.dennishistsoc.org

The town of Dennis was named for Minister Josiah Dennis. Today, his 1736 saltbox home is filled with antiques, a Pilgrim chest, a children's room, a spinning and weaving exhibit and a maritime wing.

July-August, Tuesday, Thursday.

EASTHAM

EASTHAM HISTORICAL SOCIETY

190 Samoset Road, Eastham, 508-255-0558;
www.easthamhistorical.org

Housed in an 1869 one-room schoolhouse, this history museum features Native American artifacts, farming equipment, nautical implements, shipwreck remnants and antique school furniture.

July-August, Tuesday-Wednesday 1-4 p.m., Thursday-Friday 10 a.m.-4 p.m.

EASTHAM WINDMILL

Windmill Green, Eastham, 508-240-7211; www.easthamhistorical.org

Originally built in Plymouth in 1680, this is the oldest gristmill on the Cape. Moved to its present site in 1808, it was restored to its original grandeur in 1936.

Late June-early September, daily.

VINCENT HOUSE

Pease's Point Way, Edgartown, 508-627-4440

Built in 1672, the oldest known house on the island has been carefully restored to allow visitors to see how buildings were constructed 300 years ago. Take a

SPECIAL EVENT

CAPE PLAYHOUSE

820 Main St., Dennis, 508-385-3911, 877-385-3911; www.capeplayhouse.com

All summer long, the oldest summer stock theater in the nation hosts both established Broadway stars and emerging actors for two-week runs of musicals, comedies and dramatic plays. On summer Friday mornings, the Cape Playhouse has special children's performances like puppetry, storytelling and musicals. The complex also houses the Cape Museum of Fine Arts, the Playhouse Bistro and the Cape Cinema.

Late June-early September.

tour through the five-bedroom cedar home, which is furnished to depict life on the island centuries ago.

May-early October, daily 10:30 a.m.-3 p.m.; rest of year, by appointment.

FALMOUTH
ASHUMET HOLLY & WILDLIFE SANCTUARY

Ashumet and Currier Roads, Falmouth, 508-362-1426; www.massaudubon.org

Run by the Massachusetts Audubon Society, this 45-acre wildlife preserve features a holly trail, a herb garden and an observation beehive.

Daily dawn-dusk.

HARWICH
CAPE COD BASEBALL LEAGUE

11 North Road, Harwich, 508-432-3878; www.capecodbaseball.org

This is baseball as it should be—local, passionate, affordable and played with wooden bats. The league's ten teams are made up of college players from around the country who live with host families during the summer. Each season consists of 44 games. Meanwhile, spectators pack picnics and sit on wooden benches to cheer for their favorite players.

Mid-June-mid-August.

HARWICH HISTORICAL SOCIETY

80 Parallel St., Harwich, 508-432-8089; www.harwichhistoricalsociety.org

This history center features Native American artifacts, a marine exhibit, historic items from the local cranberry industry and early newspapers and photographs from the area. It's also the site of one of the first schools of navigation in the United States.

Mid-June-mid-October, Wednesday-Friday; schedule may vary.

HYANNIS
CAPE COD POTATO CHIP COMPANY

100 Breed's Hill Road, Hyannis, 508-775-3358; www.capecodchips.com

Cape Cod chips, now sold all over the world, are probably the area's most recognizable food product. Perhaps the best part about the factory's self-guided tours is

SPECIAL EVENTS

CAPE COD OYSTER FESTIVAL

20 Independence Drive, Hyannis, 508-775-4746; www.capecodclash.org

It's all you can eat at the Cape Cod Oyster fest and, thanks to local vineyards, all you can drink, too. Held at the Naked Oyster restaurant under a big tent, the event draws locals and tourists alike.

Late September.

FIGAWI SAILBOAT RACE AND CHARITY BALL

486 W. Hyannisport, 508-737-2987; www.figawi.com

The largest regatta on the East Coast, Figawi features 200 sailboats racing from Hyannis to Nantucket on Saturday, then back again in a Return Race on Monday. A black-tie charity ball precedes the event by one week. Held in Hyannis, but also celebrated on Nantucket, the important social event features live bands, dancing and a big feast.

Memorial Day weekend.

POPS BY THE SEA

Town Green, Hyannis, 508-362-0066; www.artsfoundationcapecod.org

In early August, the Boston Pops visits the Cape for a concert on the Hyannis Town Green. Each year brings a new celebrity guest conductor, not the usual types, though—they're usually famous actors, poets or celebrity chefs. The performance serves as a fundraiser that supports the Arts Foundation of Cape Cod.

WILLOWBEND CHILDREN'S CHARITY PRO-AM

100 Willowbend Drive, Mashpee, 508-539-5030

The biggest names in professional golf pair up with celebrities for this annual charity golf event on the Willowbend course. The $20 fee is among the lowest you can pay to watch professional golf. Best of all, the event's proceeds benefit a variety of worthy children's charities.

Early July.

the free samples, though seeing the chips cook in huge kettles is also pretty cool.
Admission: free. Monday-Friday 9 a.m.-5 p.m.

JOHN F. KENNEDY HYANNIS MUSEUM
397 Main St., Hyannis, 508-790-3077; www.jfkhyannismuseum.org

Here, visitors can peruse photography exhibits and view a seven-minute video narrated by Walter Cronkite that focus on Kennedy's relationship with Cape Cod, a favorite vacation spot for the president and his family.

Admission: adults $5, children 10-17 $2.50, children 9 and under free. Mid-April-October, Monday-Saturday 9 a.m.-5 p.m., Sunday noon-5 p.m.; rest of year, Thursday-Saturday 10 a.m.-4 p.m., Sunday noon-4 p.m. Closed in January.

STEAMSHIP AUTHORITY
Ocean Street, Hyannis, 508-477-8600, 508-693-9130; www.steamshipauthority.com

Catch ferries to Woods Hole, Martha's Vineyard and Nantucket from the South Street dock. See website for schedule and ticket pricing.

MARTHA'S VINEYARD
AQUINNAH CLIFFS
230 Jones Road, Aquinnah, 508-540-0448, 508-444-0173; www.aquinnahcliffs.com

The most photographed attraction on Martha's Vineyard, these glacier-formed cliffs are more than 150 feet tall and brilliantly colored. Today, the cliffs are owned by the Wampanoag Indians, who hold them sacred. At their peak sits the Aquinnah Light lighthouse, commissioned by President John Adams in 1798. At the bottom of the cliffs is a gorgeous beach.

April-November.

BLACK DOG BAKERY
3 Water St., Vineyard Haven, 508-693-4786; www.theblackdog.com

More than a bakery, the Black Dog is a local cultural phenomenon. Watch for the bakery's logo—a black Labrador retriever—on T-shirts, hats, mugs and belts throughout the area. The company's General Store has four Vineyard locations. All sell souvenirs and even dog treats. The bakery serves coffee, pastries, torts, truffles and other treats. Not to be outdone, the nearby Black Dog Tavern has tasty seafood and other island-appropriate dishes.

June-August, daily 5:30 a.m.-9 p.m.; rest of year, daily 5:30 a.m.-5 p.m.

FEATHERSTONE MEETING HOUSE FOR THE ARTS
Barnes Road, Oak Bluffs, 508-693-1850; www.featherstonearts.org

This arts center offers tourists the hourly use of studios, as well as classes on photography, woodworking, pottery, weaving and stained-glass. The Meeting House also includes a gallery of works from local artists and a camp for kids. Featherstone plays host to various gallery shows throughout the year. Past exhibits have included "The Art of Glass" and "The Art of Black & White Photography." People of all ages can attend art camp.

Daily; call for studio availability.

FELIX NECK SANCTUARY
Edgartown-Vineyard Haven Road, Vineyard Haven, 508-627-4850; www.massaudubon.org

This 350-acre wildlife preserve is a haven for kids and bird-lovers alike. Four miles of trails (guided or self-guided) meander through meadows, woods, salt marshes and beaches. The visitor center has exhibits and a gift shop. In the summer, kids enroll in the site's Fern & Feather Day Camp.

Admission: adult $4, seniors and children 2-12 $3. Nature Center: Monday-Saturday 9 a.m.-4 p.m., Sunday 10 a.m.-3 p.m.; closed Monday in September-May. Trails: Daily dawn-dusk.

FLYING HORSE CAROUSEL

33 Oak Bluffs Ave., Oak Bluffs, 508-693-9481; www.mvpreservation.org

This carousel is the oldest in the country and a national historic landmark. Its flying horses are gorgeous, hand-carved and lifelike. Anyone who grasps the center brass ring has earned his next ride for free. Just one of two known carousels built by Charles W.F. Dare, the renowned carousel maker, in 1876, the Flying Horse Carousel came to the Vineyard from Coney Island in 1884.

Admission: $1.50 per ride.

MENEMSHA FISHING VILLAGE

North Street, Menemsha

Full of cedar-sided clam shacks, fishermen in waterproof gear and lobster traps strewn about, Menemsha is a picturesque fishing village on Martha's Vineyard. The movie *Jaws* was filmed here and the main street has a few shops. Sitting on Menemsha Pond and the Vineyard Sound, this 300-year-old fishing village will send you back to the time when fishing was all they did. In fact, these days fishing is still a huge part of life in this quaint township.

MYTOI

Dike Road, Chappaquiddick, 508-693-7662; www.thetrustees.org

Martha's Vineyard isn't the logical location for a Japanese garden, though Mytoi wins praises for its mix of azaleas, irises, dogwood, daffodils, rhododendron and Japanese maple. The 50-year-old garden's centerpiece is a pond filled with goldfish and koi. Watch ospreys swoop down for lunch as you make your way over the footbridge to Poucha Pond.

Daily dawn-dusk.

OAK BLUFFS

www.ci.oak-bluffs.ma.us

In 1835, this Methodist community on Martha's Vineyard served as the site of annual summer camps for church groups. Over the years, the communal tents gave way to family tents, which in turn became wooden cottages designed to look like tents. Today, visitors to this marina and resort community can view the resulting "gingerbread cottages."

OLD WHALING CHURCH

89 Main St., Edgartown, 508-627-4442; www.mvpreservation.org

Built in 1843 by whaling captains, this church is a fine example of Greek Revival architecture. It is now owned by Martha's Vineyard Preservation Trust and is used for events such as weddings. Located in the heart of Edgartown, this picturesque building accommodates 500 people.

THE YARD

Middle Road, Chilmark, 508-645-9662; www.dancetheyard.org

For 30 years, the Yard has played host to summertime performances by international choreographers and dance troupes as well as classes for children and seniors. The 100-seat theater is housed in a renovated Chilmark barn, surrounded by gorgeous hills and beautiful views.

Admission: premium seating $50, general seating $25, seniors and under 30 $15. June-September.

VINEYARD MUSEUM

59 School St., Edgartown, 508-627-4441; www.marthasvineyardhistory.org

Four buildings, dating back to pre-Revolutionary War times, form the Vineyard Museum. The Thomas Cooke House, a historic Colonial home, specializes in antiques and folk art. The Foster Gallery displays exhibits from the whaling industry. The Pease Galleries specialize in Native American exhibits. The Gale Huntington Library, meanwhile, is a useful tool for those researching their genealogy.

NANTUCKET

1800 HOUSE

8 Mill St., Nantucket, 508-228-1894; www.nha.org

This early 19th-century house has period furnishings, a large, round cellar and a kitchen garden. The Nantucket Historical Association renovated this structure in 2004, creating a place for people to go to celebrate early American arts and crafts. Before the renovation, this house was just another old home in this historic whaling community. It now features a variety of art classes taught by New England artisans. Discover techniques that have been used for centuries.

Check website for schedule.

ALTAR ROCK

Off Polpis Road, Nantucket

It was once thought that this was Nantucket's highest point, but it has since been discovered that it is just a foot shorter than Folger Hill. Altar Rock rises 108 feet above sea level and affords stunning views of Nantucket and the surrounding Cape. Go at dawn or dusk for the best views.

BARTLETT'S FARM

33 Bartlett Farm Road, Nantucket, 508-228-9403; www.bartlettsfarm.com

The Bartlett family has tilled the land of Nantucket's largest farm for nearly 200 years. Stop by for fresh vegetables, milk, eggs, cheese, freshly baked bread and cut flowers. A handful of prepared foods such as salads, pies, snacks, jams and chutneys are also available.

Daily 8 a.m.-6 p.m.

CISCO BREWERS

5 Bartlett Farm Road, Nantucket, 508-325-5929; www.ciscobrewers.com

Local beer-makers Cisco Brewers concoct dozens of micro-specialties such as Whale's Tale Pale Ale, Baileys Ale, Moor Porter, Captain Swains Extra Stout, Summer of Lager and Baggywrinkle Barleywine. The Triple Eight Distillery and Nantucket Vineyards also have tasting rooms at the site, where you can sample everything from vodka to chardonnay. Guided tours are also available at the brewery, vineyard and distillery.

June-August, Monday-Saturday 10 a.m.-6 p.m., Sunday until 5 p.m.; tours by appointment.

ENDEAVOR SAILING ADVENTURES

Straight Wharf, Nantucket, 508-228-5585; www.endeavorsailing.com

U.S. Coast Guard Captain James Genthner built his sloop, the *Endeavor*, and has been sailing it for more than 20 years. Step aboard for a 90-minute tour of Nantucket Sound and let Genthner and his wife, Sue, introduce you to Nantucket's sights, sounds and history.

May-October.

FIRST CONGREGATIONAL CHURCH

62 Centre St., Nantucket, 508-228-0950; www.nantucketfcc.org

Also known as the Old North Church, this spot features Nantucket's best view of the island and surrounding ocean. Before you can enjoy it, you'll first have to climb 94 steps to the top of the 120-foot-tall steeple.

Mid-June-mid-October, Monday-Saturday.

FOLGER-FRANKLIN MEMORIAL FOUNTAIN

Madaket Road, Nantucket, 508-228-1894

Built in 1900, this memorial fountain marks the birthplace of Abiah Folger, mother of Benjamin Franklin.

HADWEN HOUSE

96 Main St., Nantucket, 508-228-1894; www.nha.org

Built in 1845 by a wealthy merchant, this Greek Revival mansion was once the most opulent on the island. Today, it features antique furnishings from the whaling period as well as Victorian-style gardens.

Monday-Saturday 10 a.m.-5 p.m., Sunday noon-5 p.m.

JETHRO COFFIN HOUSE (OLDEST HOUSE)

16 Sunset Hill Lane, Nantucket, 508-228-1894

Built in 1686, Oldest House is, true to its name, one of the oldest houses in the United States. The building was a wedding present given to the children of two feuding families (the Gardners and the Coffins) by their in-laws, who reconciled after the happy event. The Jethro Coffin House is the sole survivor of the island's original English settlement of the 1600s. The Nantucket Historical Association acquired the home in 1923 to reconstruct the original settlement. After being struck by lightning in 1987, the house was restored again and is now a monument to the English settlers.

Admission: adults $6, children 6-17 $3. Thursday-Monday, 11 a.m.-4 p.m. Closed December 1-4.

JETTIES BEACH

Bathing Beach Road, Nantucket, 508-228-2279; www.thejetties.com

Kid-friendly Jetties is the best bet for beach-going families. The sand is rough, but that's how it is on the shores of Nantucket. There are restrooms, showers, changing rooms, a snack bar, lifeguards, rental chairs, a playground, volleyball and tennis courts, and a skateboarding park. Enjoy lunch on the patio at the beachfront restaurant or sit at the bar for a drink while the kids play in the sand. You can also rent kayaks, sailboards and sailboats through Nantucket Community Sailing (*508-228-5358*).

LOINES OBSERVATORY
59 Milk St., Nantucket, 508-228-9273; www.mmo.org

Named for the first professional female astronomer, the 1968 observatory lets guests peek through an antique telescope to view star-filled skies.

Monday, Wednesday, Friday evenings in summer, Saturday evenings year-round; closed Tuesday, Thursday, Sunday in summer, Sunday-Friday year-round.

MIACOMET GOLF COURSE
12 W. Miacomet Road, Nantucket, 508-228-9764, 508-325-0333; www.miacometgolf.com

Nantucket's only public golf course offers nine holes (two are par-fives). Reserve a tee time at least one week in advance, since it's safe to say, the chances of playing in the summertime without a reservation are zero.

MURRAY'S TOGGERY
62 Main St., Nantucket, 508-228-0437, 800-368-2134; www.nantucketreds.com

Murray's Toggery was the first store on the island to sell Nantucket Reds, the casual pink khaki pants that became a local fashion staple and, later, a symbol of preppiness across America.

March-October, Monday-Saturday 9 a.m.-7 p.m., Sunday 10 a.m.-6 p.m.; November-February, Monday-Saturday 9 a.m.-5 p.m.

NANTUCKET HISTORICAL ASSOCIATION WHALING MUSEUM
15 Broad St., Nantucket, 508-228-1894; www.nha.org

Redesigned and reopened in 2005, this museum is the premier institution devoted to the history of the whaling industry. Check out the 46-foot-long preserved sperm whale skeleton, which washed ashore in 1998. Other artifacts recall the island's heyday as a center for whale oil production.

Mid-May-mid-October, daily 10 a.m.-5 p.m.; mid-October-mid-December, Thursday-Monday 11 a.m.-4 p.m.; closed mid-December-April.

NANTUCKET MARIA MITCHELL ASSOCIATION
4 Vestal St., Nantucket, 508-228-9198; www.mmo.org

The scientific library has historical documents, science journals and family memorabilia from the early astronomer. There's also a natural science museum featuring local wildlife, as well as an aquarium at nearby 28 Washington Street.

Mid-June-August, Tuesday-Saturday; library also open rest of year, Wednesday-Saturday.

NANTUCKET TOWN
Nantucket, 508-228-1700; www.nantucketchamber.org

Nantucket Town is a shopper's dream. As you walk the cobblestone main street, you will encounter a variety of upscale boutiques—home, clothing, culinary, boat, jewelry, art and antiques, most of which are tasteful and well-edited.

OLD MILL
50 Prospect St., Nantucket, 508-228-1894; www.nha.org

Believed to be the oldest windmill in the United States, this Dutch-style structure is impressive for its beauty and height, a whopping 50 feet. It was built

SPECIAL EVENTS

NANTUCKET ARTS FESTIVAL

508-325-8588; www.nantucketartscouncil.org
This weeklong festival celebrates a full range of arts—film, poetry, fiction, acting, dance, paintings, photography and many other forms. Look for the wet-paint sale to bid on works completed that very day.
Early October.

NANTUCKET FILM FESTIVAL

508-228-6648; www.nantucketfilmfestival.org
Like other film fests, this one screens new independent movies that would otherwise fall under the radar. It's attended by screenwriters, actors, film connoisseurs and, occasionally, big-name celebrities. A daily event called Morning Coffee features film-industry types participating in Q&As.
Mid-June.

NANTUCKET WINE FESTIVAL

508-228-1128; www.nantucketwinefestival.com
This weekend event includes tastings, educational seminars and several wine dinners. The Great Wines in Grand Houses event allows you to visit one of the island's private mansions while sipping fine vintages—you'll get to choose from nearly 100 wineries and dine on food prepared by some of the area's finest chefs. Reservations are required.
Mid-May.

in 1746 with salvaged oak that washed ashore from shipwrecks. Don't miss the research center and whaling museum inside.
June-August: daily; call for off-season hours.

RAFAEL OSONA AUCTIONS
21 Washington St., Nantucket, 508-228-3942; www.rafaelosonaauction.com
This company hosts upscale estate auctions on select weekends, where shoppers will find rarities and valuables from both the United States and Europe. Call for exact dates and times.
Late May-early December.

SIASCONSET VILLAGE
East end of Nantucket Island
Located seven miles from Nantucket Town, Siasconset is best reached by bicycle or shuttle bus—driving often takes twice as long, thanks to heavy traffic. Today, this 18th-century fishing village is well preserved with quaint cottages, grand mansions, restaurants, a few gift shops, even a summer cinema.

THE STRAIGHT WHARF
Straight Wharf, Nantucket

Built in 1723, the wharf is Nantucket's launching area for sailboats, sloops and kayaks, but it's also a great destination for shopping, eating and entertainment. Loaded with restaurants and quaint, one-room cottage boutiques, the wharf also features an art gallery, museum and outdoor concert pavilion.

THEATRE WORKSHOP OF NANTUCKET
2 Centre St., Nantucket, 508-228-4305; www.theatreworkshop.com

Founded in 1985, this theater stages comedies, dramas, plays and concerts—everything from family-friendly shows like Peter Pan to American chestnuts like *On Golden Pond*. Both professionals and amateurs comprise the company, which offers up to 10 performances every summer.

WINDSWEPT CRANBERRY BOG
Polpis Road, Siasconset

To see how cranberries are grown and harvested, visit this 200-acre bog during the fall harvest—late September through October, to be precise. For the rest of the year, the bog serves as a peaceful place to walk and bike.
Daily dawn-dusk.

NEW BEDFORD

BUTTONWOOD PARK & ZOO
425 Hawthorn St., New Bedford, 508-991-6178; www.bpzoo.org

This 97-acre park features everything from forested walking trails to a greenhouse, ball fields, tennis courts, a playground, a picnic area and a fitness circuit. Meanwhile, the park's small zoo is home to elephants, lions, deer, bears, buffalo, seals and more.
Daily 10 a.m.-5 p.m.

NEW BEDFORD WHALING MUSEUM
18 Johnny Cake Hill, New Bedford, 508-997-0046; www.whalingmuseum.org

The most prominent feature of this museum is its 89-foot half-scale model of the 1916 whale ship *Lagoda*, the largest ship model in the world. Additionally, the museum features a variety of whaling-themed artifacts and art—everything from whale skeletons and ship logs to Japanese and Dutch whaling paintings.
June-December, daily 9 a.m.-5 p.m.; January-May, Monday-Saturday 9 a.m.-4 p.m., Sunday noon-4 p.m.; Second Thursday of the month, 9 a.m.-9 p.m.

ROTCH-JONES-DUFF HOUSE AND GARDEN MUSEUM
396 County St., New Bedford, 508-997-1401; www.rjdmuseum.org

Built by a wealthy whaling merchant in 1834, this Greek Revival mansion has been maintained to reflect the lives of three families that lived in the house. The house features period-style rooms, furnishings and decorative art.
Monday-Saturday 10 a.m.-4 p.m., Sunday noon-4 p.m.

SEAMEN'S BETHEL
15 Johnny Cake Hill, New Bedford, 508-992-3295;

Here lies the 1832 "Whaleman's Chapel" referred to by Melville in *Moby Dick*. Originally built in an effort to salvage the souls of area seaman, the church

houses dozens of monuments to men lost at sea, as well as a prow-shaped pulpit that was later built to match Melville's description.
Daily.

ORLEANS
FRENCH CABLE STATION MUSEUM
41 S. Orleans Road, Orleans, 508-240-1735; www.frenchcablestationmuseum.org

Built in 1890 as the American end of the transatlantic cable from Brest, France, the museum now serves as a tribute to that engineering feat. It features submarine cable equipment, vintage transmitters and stories about the messages that were once communicated via the wire—including the safe landing of Charles Lindbergh in Paris in the year of 1927.
July-August, Thursday-Sunday 1-4 p.m.; June, September, Friday-Sunday 1-4 p.m.

NAUSET BEACH
Beach Road, Orleans, 508-255-1386; www.capecod-orleans.com

One of the most spectacular ocean beaches on the Atlantic coast rests within the boundaries of Cape Cod National Seashore, where it attracts comparatively large waves. Swimming, surfing and fishing are allowed at the beach. Lifeguards keep watch over beachgoers. There is a nominal parking fee.

OSTERVILLE
OSTERVILLE HISTORICAL SOCIETY MUSEUM
155 W. Bay Road, Osterville, 508-428-5861; www.ostervillemuseum.org

Dedicated to preserving the history of Osterville, this museum is housed within a former sea captain's house with 18th- and 19th-century furnishings, ceramics, decorative arts and vintage boats. The site also includes an 18th-century herbal garden, a 19th-century ornamental garden and a boat-building museum.
Mid-June-September, Thursday-Sunday 1:30-4:30 p.m.; and by appointment.

PLYMOUTH
HARLOW OLD FORT HOUSE
119 Sandwich St., Plymouth, 508-746-0012; www.harlowfamily.com

Built by the prominent pilgrim William Harlow in 1677, this modest house features craft-making and candle-dipping demonstrations as well as a period-style herb garden.
July-August, Tuesday-Friday.

HEDGE HOUSE
126 Water St., Plymouth, 508-746-0012; www.visit-plymouth.com

Built by a wealthy merchant and ship-owner in 1809, this Federal-style house features 19th-century furnishings and special exhibits designed to illuminate the house's past.
June-August, Wednesday-Sunday 2-6 p.m.

HOWLAND HOUSE
33 Sandwich St., Plymouth, 508-746-9590; www.pilgrimjohnhowlandsociety.org

Built by the son of John Howland, a prominent passenger on the Mayflower (and to whom many New England families trace their roots), this modest 1666 pilgrim house features 17th and 18th-century furnishings as well as Howland

SPECIAL EVENT

AMERICA'S THANKSGIVING DINNER

137 Warren Ave., Plymouth, 508-746-1622; www.plimoth.org

Taking place at Plimoth Plantation's 1627 Pilgrim Village, this is a harvest celebration with Pilgrim role players and Native American interpreters re-creating a 17th-century event. There are onsite activities, coupled with feasting and games.

Thanksgiving Day.

---

family letters and documents.

June-mid-October, Monday-Saturday.

MAYFLOWER SOCIETY HOUSE MUSEUM

4 Winslow St., Plymouth, 508 746-3188; www.themayflowersociety.com

Housed in a stately 18th-century mansion, the national headquarters of the General Society of Mayflower Descendants overlooks a tiny harbor, where a scale-size replica of the Mayflower is moored. The grounds also feature Cole's Hill, the final resting place of many pilgrims.

July-August, daily; June, early September-October, Friday-Sunday.

MYLES STANDISH STATE FOREST

194 Cranberry Road, South Carver, 508-866-2526; www.mass.gov

The 15,000-acre park consists of 13 miles of hiking trails, 35 miles of equestrian trails and 16 ponds, as well as a sandy ocean beach for swimming, fishing, boating, picnicking and camping.

NATIONAL MONUMENT TO THE FOREFATHERS

Allerton St., and Highway 44, Plymouth, 508-746-1790

Built between 1859 and 1889 at a cost of $155,000, this colossal figure was designed to commemorate the Mayflower pilgrims and their many virtues. Standing 81 feet high, it is the tallest solid granite monument in the United States.

May-October, daily.

PILGRIM HALL MUSEUM

75 Court St., Plymouth, 508-746-1620; www.pilgrimhall.org

Built in 1824, this museum features the nation's largest collection of possessions—everything from decorative arts, handicrafts and furniture to myriad paintings, including the only known portrait of a Mayflower passenger.

Daily 9:30 a.m.-4:30 p.m.; closed January.

PLIMOTH PLANTATION/MAYFLOWER II

137 Warren Ave., Plymouth, 508-746-1622; www.plimoth.org

No, it's not a typo. The Plimoth Plantation, a re-creation of the 1627 Pilgrim village, uses the colony's old-fashioned spelling. Here, you'll find costumed actors with zero knowledge of the 21st—or even the 18th—century. They wear and use only the clothing, the equipment, the tools and the cookware of

the early settlers. Don't miss the *Mayflower II*, a full-scale reproduction of the original built by J.W. & A. Upham with oak timbers, hand-forged nails, linen canvas sails and hemp rope.
March-November, daily.

PROVINCETOWN FERRY
10 Town Wharf, Plymouth, 508-746-2643, 800-242-2469; www.provincetownferry.com
Here's a smart way to avoid the Cape's notorious traffic: A round-trip passenger ferry departs State Pier every morning and returns from Provincetown in the evening.
Mid-June-August, daily; May-mid-June, September-October, weekends.

RICHARD SPARROW HOUSE
42 Summer St., Plymouth, 508-747-1240; www.sparrowhouse.com
Dating to 1640, this is Plymouth's oldest restored home. Today, it serves as a history museum as well as an art gallery and pottery studio.
Daily 10 a.m.-5 p.m.; closed Wednesday.

SPOONER HOUSE
27 North St., Plymouth, 508-746-0012; www.visit-plymouth.com
Built in 1747, this gambrel-roofed house was occupied by the Spooner family for five generations. Today, it documents more than 200 years of the Spooners' accumulated furnishings, china, paintings and other heirlooms.
June-October, Thursday-Saturday.

PROVINCETOWN
COMMERCIAL STREET
Commercial Street, Provincetown
Stretching more than three miles in length, this narrow street is packed with art galleries, boutiques, nightclubs, restaurants and hotels. When the street was constructed in 1835, all the houses were built to face the harbor. By now, however, most homes have been turned 180 degrees to face the street—either that, or the homeowner has simply added a door on the house's opposite side.

EXPEDITION WHYDAH'S SEA LAB & LEARNING CENTER
16 MacMillan Wharf, Provincetown, 508-487-8899; www.whydah.com
Check out the archaeological site of the sunken pirate ship *Whydah*, which was struck by storms in 1717. Learn about the recovery of the ship's substantial treasures—which happened more than 200 years later, thanks to a team of underwater explorers. Today, this family-friendly museum features the world's only publicly displayed pirate treasure, a cache of jewelry, clothing and weapons. Visitors can also learn about the lives of the ship's passengers.
April-mid-October, daily; mid-October-December, Saturday-Sunday.

PILGRIM MONUMENT & MUSEUM
1 High Pole Hill, Provincetown, 508-487-1310; www.pilgrim-monument.org
This is a 252-foot granite tower that was built in 1910 to commemorate the Pilgrims' 1620 landing in the New World. Check out the affiliated museum for displays of whaling equipment, scrimshaw, ship models, artifacts from shipwrecks and a Pilgrim Room with a scale-model diorama of the *Mayflower*.
Summer, daily.

PROVINCETOWN ART ASSOCIATION & MUSEUM

460 Commercial St., Provincetown, 508-487-1750; www.paam.org

Established in 1914, the PAAM strives to preserve the artistic history of the Cape. Today, the organizations' galleries feature work by the region's living artists as well as pieces by artists of the past.

Late May-October, daily; rest of year, Saturday-Sunday.

WHALE WATCHING

306 Commercial St., Provincetown, 508-240-3636, 800-826-9300; www.whalewatch.com

Take a 3½ to 4-hour whale-watching tour, led by research scientists from the Provincetown Center for Coastal Studies—a remarkable source for biology and history lessons on the whales.

Mid-April-October, daily.

SANDWICH

HERITAGE MUSEUM AND GARDENS

67 Grove St., Sandwich, 508-888-3300; www.heritagemuseumsandgardens.org

Formerly known as the Heritage Plantation, Heritage Museum and Gardens features an eclectic mix of beautiful gardens, folk art, antique cars and military paraphernalia. Highlights include the 19th-century Old East Windmill and a restored 1912 carousel. Call ahead to inquire about unique exhibits, displays and concerts.

May-October, daily; November-April, Wednesday-Sunday.

HOXIE HOUSE & DEXTER GRIST MILL

Water St., Sandwich, 508-888-1173

The oldest house on the Cape, Hoxie has been restored to its original 1645 interior, thanks to items on loan from the Boston Museum of Fine Arts. Built in 1640, the Dexter Grist Mill is still in operation and features educational demonstrations on grinding corn into flour.

Mid-June-mid-October, daily.

SANDWICH GLASS MUSEUM

129 Main St., Sandwich, 508-888-0251; www.sandwichglassmuseum.org

Dedicated to preserving Sandwich town history, this museum features an array of historic items with a special emphasis on the local glass industry. Check out galleries of beautiful dinnerware glass, glass-blown art, glass lamps and more.

April-October, daily.

TRURO

HIGHLAND LIGHT/CAPE COD LIGHT

Highland Light Road, North Truro, 508-487-1121; www.lighthouse.cc

This was the first lighthouse on Cape Cod. Built in 1798 and fueled with whale oil, it was rebuilt in 1853 and switched to an automated facility in 1986. It now shines for 30 miles, the longest visible range of any lighthouse on the Cape. The museum next door, housed in a historic building, is open from June through September and highlights the area's fishing and whaling heritage.

May-late October, daily.

TRURO HISTORICAL SOCIETY MUSEUM

6 Highland Road, North Truro, 508-487-3397; www.trurohistorical.org

This collection of artifacts from the town's past includes shipwreck mementos, whaling gear, ship models, 17th-century firearms, a pirate chest, period-style furnishings, recreated rooms and more.

June-September, Monday-Saturday 10 a.m.-4:30 p.m., Sunday 1-4:30 p.m.

WELLFLEET

HISTORICAL SOCIETY MUSEUM

266 Main St., Wellfleet, 508-349-9157; www.wellfleethistoricalsociety.com

Dedicated to preserving Wellfleet history, this museum has collections of marine items, whaling tools, hand-painted china (with maritime scenes), needlecraft, photography, paintings and more.

Late June-early September, Tuesday-Saturday; schedule may vary.

WELLFLEET BAY WILDLIFE SANCTUARY

291 Highway 6, South Wellfleet, 508-349-2615; www.wellfleetbay.org

Operated by the Massachusetts Audubon Society, the 1,100-acre sanctuary features self-guiding nature trails that wind through marsh, beaches and woodlands. This is also the site of a natural history summer day camp for children.

June-mid-October, daily; rest of year, Tuesday-Sunday.

WELLFLEET DRIVE-IN THEATER

Highway 6, Wellfleet, 508-349-7176; www.wellfleetdrivein.com

The only outdoor theater on the Cape is an old-fashioned drive-in where family-oriented double features are projected every evening after dusk.

Mid-October-mid-April.

WOODS HOLE

BRADLEY HOUSE MUSEUM

573 Woods Hole Road, Woods Hole, 508-548-7270

Check out a scale model of the Woods Hole settlement circa 1895. The museum also features an audiovisual show of local history, restored ships and changing exhibitions on local history and culture.

July-August, Tuesday-Saturday; June, September, Wednesday, Saturday; schedule may vary.

YARMOUTH

CAPE SYMPHONY ORCHESTRA

712A Main St., Yarmouth Port, 508-362-1111; www.capesymphony.org

This 90-member professional orchestra performs 15 indoor concerts through-out the year, mostly at Barnstable High School's 1,400-seat auditorium. Selections range from classical to pops and special children's programs.

September-May; also two concerts in summer.

WHERE TO STAY

BREWSTER

★★★OCEAN EDGE RESORT

2907 Main St., Brewster, 508-896-9000, 800-343-6074; www.oceanedge.com

This sprawling 19th-century English country manor is an oasis of comfort and privacy on Cape Cod Bay. Resort activities include tennis, swimming, hiking and golf—in fact, the course is one of the finest in New England. Kids are welcome, but romantics shouldn't shy from here—the estate is big enough for everyone to enjoy a quiet vacation. With a private beach and four disparate dining options, the amenities also suit a variety of vacationers' needs.

406 rooms. Restaurant, bar. $151-250

CHATHAM

★★★THE BRADFORD OF CHATHAM
26 Cross St., Chatham, 508-945-1030, 888-242-8426; www.bradfordinn.com

Arranged in a series of nine white clapboard houses along a central, park-like yard, these guest rooms feature colonial style with fireplaces and four-poster beds. There are also ocean views and a heated outdoor pool. The inn is convenient to downtown Chatham with its myriad shopping and dining options.

38 rooms. No children under 12. Complimentary breakfast. $151-250

★★★CHATHAM BARS INN
297 Shore Road, Chatham, 508-945-0096, 800-527-4884; www.chathambarsinn.com

Built in 1814, this Cape Cod landmark has managed to maintain its historic charm—the polished foyer, the white-picket fencing. The luxury guest rooms feature 180-degree views of Pleasant Bay, with well-maintained gardens and a private beach also within sight. The resort recently added a large, state-of-the-art spa that offers plenty of pampering. The property also boasts four restaurants, offering everything from formal dining room to a cozy tavern.

205 rooms. Restaurant, bar. Beach. $351 and up

★★★CHATHAM WAYSIDE INN
512 Main St., Chatham, 508-945-5550, 800-242-8426; www.waysideinn.com

The lobby in this classic circa 1860s, village inn still has the original knotty pine flooring. The cozy property has 56 spacious guest rooms, some with private balconies and jetted bathtubs. Spend the evening dining at the inn's festive Wild Goose Tavern or walk to nearby Chatham to explore other restaurants.

56 rooms. Restaurant, bar. $251-350

★★★★WEQUASSETT RESORT AND GOLF CLUB
On Pleasant Bay, Chatham, 508-432-5400, 800-225-7125; www.wequassett.com

This country inn-resort hybrid appeals to antique lovers and sporty types alike. Located on 27 acres of gardens, salt marshes and woodlands, the full-service spot overlooks Pleasant Bay and the Atlantic Ocean. The polished staff oversees a variety of outdoor activities, from swimming on the nearby beaches to tennis on property and golf at the prestigious Cape Cod National Golf Club. Guests can stay in spacious suites or snug private cottages, all decorated with upscale country decor and plush bedding. For a special treat, book one of the new luxury suites, which come with gas fireplaces, marble bathrooms and plenty of room for relaxing.

104 rooms. Restaurant, bar. Beach. Closed December-March. $351 and up

FALMOUTH

★★★COONAMESSETT INN

311 Gifford St., Falmouth, 508-548-2300; www.capecodrestaurants.org

Just north of town, in a shady, wooded area, is the idyllic Coonamessett Inn. The property is convenient to sandy beaches, harbors and antique shops, though visitors won't want to leave once they spy these six landscaped acres with five guesthouses, a barn, a carriage house and a caretaker's cottage. Spacious guest rooms feature pine furniture, sitting areas, oversized closets, fresh flowers and in-suite refrigerators. In the morning, take advantage of the complimentary continental breakfast or try dinner at the inn's seasonal restaurant.

28 rooms. Complimentary breakfast. Restaurant, bar. $151-250

MARTHA'S VINEYARD

★★★BEACH PLUM INN

50 Beach Plum Lane, Menemsha, 508-645-9454, 877-645-7398; www.beachpluminn.com

Built in 1890 from the salvage of a shipwreck, this inn sits atop a dramatic hill, delivering dramatic views of the ocean. The seven-acre property is dotted with elegant cottages, each featuring antiques, balconies and French doors. A stone drive and garden-like path lead guests to the main house, where they can enjoy some of the finest cuisine on Martha's Vineyard.

11 rooms. Complimentary breakfast. Restaurant. $151-250

★★★★CHARLOTTE INN

27 S. Summer St., Edgartown, 508-627-4751; www.charlotteinn.net

This inn is an oasis of tranquility even though it's located in the middle of the busiest town on Martha's Vineyard. For the ultimate in relaxation, take a peaceful walk along the property's garden paths, passing under the linden and chestnut trees. Inside, guests are treated to elegant 19th-century art and original antiques. Guest rooms have flat-screen TVs, down pillows and comforters, and Bulgari toiletries.

25 rooms. Restaurant. $351 and up

★★★HARBOR VIEW HOTEL

131 N. Water St., Edgartown, 508-627-7000, 800-225-6005; www.harbor-view.com

The renovated Harbor View combines the island's heritage with modern hotel amenities. The 1891 hotel features bright, airy guest rooms with balconies and garden views. The hotel's lengthy veranda has many rocking chairs and overlooks Edgartown Harbor, making it the perfect perch for watching the ships roll in.

124 rooms. Restaurant, bar. Pool. Golf. Spa. $61-150

★★★KELLEY HOUSE

23 Kelley St., Edgartown, 508-627-7900, 800-225-6005; www.kelley-house.com

Located in central Edgartown, this 1792 hotel features several houses of guest rooms, each decorated with maritime artifacts and ocean-themed artwork. Check out the extensive kids' programs, which for some parents may really be babysitting disguised as adventure. The Kelley House's pub, Newes From America, is a popular spot for the locals to get burgers, sandwiches and lobster rolls.

53 rooms. Complimentary breakfast. Restaurant. Pool. Golf. $151-250

★★★THE WINNETU INN & RESORT
31 Dunes Road, Edgartown, 508-627-4747; www.winnetu.com

This family-friendly resort has a prime location on the beautiful, less crowded South Beach, found just outside of Edgartown. Here, the cheery guest rooms are decorated with beachy art prints and feature kitchens that can be stocked by the on-property grocery service. Activities include weekly clambakes, movie nights and fire-engine tours of the property.

52 rooms. Restaurant, bar. Pool. Tennis. $151-250

NANTUCKET

★★★JARED COFFIN HOUSE
29 Broad St., Nantucket, 508-228-2400; www.jaredcoffinhouse.com

Located in the center of Nantucket Town, location is the primary virtue of this 1845 property. The colonial-style inn features guest rooms in a variety of sizes, with a variety of price tags to match. The decor is traditional New England, and bathrooms are classically small but the inn offers complimentary wirelesss and daily coffee and pastries.

60 rooms. Restaurant, bar. $61-150

★★★★THE WAUWINET
120 Wauwinet Road, Nantucket, 508-228-0145, 800-426-8718; www.wauwinet.com

Staying at the Wauwinet is like being marooned on a remote island, but with impeccable service and amenities to make your stay all the more comfortable. Built in 1876 by ship captains, the Wauwinet is a secluded, grand resort with sophisticated, English, country-style guest rooms and suites. It has its own private beaches that front the harbor and Atlantic Ocean, and the clay tennis courts are exceptionally well maintained. The onsite restaurant, Toppers, boasts a 20,000-bottle wine cellar. A brand-new spa focuses on Nantucket's most relaxing elements: sand, sun, sea and sky.

36 rooms. Closed late October-early May. No children under 18. Complimentary breakfast. Restaurant. Tennis. Spa. $351 and up

★★★WHITE ELEPHANT RESORT
50 Easton St., Nantucket, 508-228-2500, 800-445-6574; www.whiteelephanthotel.com

This harbor-front hotel offers one of the most casual-chic places to stay on the island. Here, the guest rooms are comfortable with plush beds and luxurious bath amenities. A handful of cottages with equally deluxe furnishings are available, as are the newly opened White Elephant Hotel Residences. The Brant Point Grill serves updated takes on classic New England cuisine, whereas the full-service spa incorporates ingredients from the island's natural surroundings.

66 rooms. Restaurant, bar. Closed mid-December-March. Fitness center. $251-350

PROVINCETOWN

★★★CROWNE POINTE HISTORIC INN
82 Bradford St., Provincetown, 508-487-6767, 877-276-9631; www.crownepointe.com

Five of the buildings at this downtown P-town inn date to the 1600s. Today, the inn's peaceful grounds are populated by gardens, a fountain and a koi pond, whereas the stylish interiors feature hardwood floors, antiques, crown molding and vaulted ceilings. Spacious guest rooms come with deluxe amenities like fireplaces and whirlpool bathtubs. The innkeepers bookend the day with hearty breakfasts and evening cocktail receptions.

40 rooms. No children accepted. Complimentary breakfast. Restaurant, bar. Spa. $251-350

YARMOUTH
★★★LIBERTY HILL INN
77 Main St., Yarmouth Port, 508-362-3976, 800-821-3977; www.libertyhillinn.com

Built in 1825, this stately inn features lace canopy beds, oriental rugs, original claw-foot bathtubs, even a grand piano. Morning means home-cooked breakfast—quiche, warm muffins, fresh juices—in the formal dining room.

9 rooms. Complimentary breakfast. $61-150

RECOMMENDED

BARNSTABLE
ASHLEY MANOR
3660 Olde King's Highway, Barnstable, 508-362-8044, 888-535-2246; www.ashleymanor.net

Originally built in 1699, this romantic bed and breakfast features comfortable, modern suites bedecked with old-fashioned lace curtains and plush antiques. When it comes time to unwind, make way for the beautiful garden or gazebo, or enjoy afternoon tea in front of the fire.

6 rooms. No children under 14. Complimentary breakfast. $61-150

BREWSTER
BRAMBLE INN
2019 Main St., Brewster, 508-896-7644; www.brambleinn.com

Built in the 1860s, this inn features guest rooms with four-poster beds and private baths. At this bed and breakfast, the highlight of a stay is a cooked-to-order morning meal.

8 rooms. No children under 8. Restaurant. Closed January-April. $61-150

OLD SEA PINES INN
2553 Main St., Brewster, 508-896-6114; www.oldseapinesinn.com

Once the site of a girls' boarding school, this cedar-shingled bed and breakfast is big on wholesome delights. The property features family suites as well as kid-friendly cycling excursions. Couples are welcome, too—check out the romantic, antiques-filled appointments.

24 rooms. No children under 8 (except in family suites). Complimentary breakfast. $61-150

CHATHAM
CAPTAIN'S HOUSE INN
369-377 Old Harbor Road, Chatham, 508-945-0127, 800-315-0728; www.captainshouseinn.com

Once a sea captain's estate, this pretty bed and breakfast was built in 1839 and features period wallpapers, Williamsburg antiques and elegantly refined Queen Anne chairs. Many of the guestrooms are named for the ships that once sailed the nearby seas. In the morning, enjoy a gourmet meal of eggs benedict or raspberry and cream French toast.

16 rooms. No children under 12. Complimentary breakfast. Pool. Fitness center. $151-250

DENNIS

BY THE SEA GUESTS

57 Chase Ave., Dennisport, 508-398-8685, 800-447-9202; www.bytheseaguests.com

Situated on a beachfront road that faces Nantucket Sound, this inn has clean, bright guest rooms outfitted with chenille bedspreads and fine-art prints. The property's large veranda provides great scenery for alfresco morning meals of fresh-baked rolls and fresh-squeezed juices.

12 rooms. Complimentary breakfast. Beach. $151-250

EASTHAM

THE WHALEWALK INN

220 Bridge Road, Eastham, 508-255-0617, 800-440-1281; www.whalewalkinn.com

A stay at this stylish bed and breakfast is more like spending time at a friend's house—a particularly gracious, stylish friend, that is. Built in 1840, the inn features individually decorated guest rooms with private fireplaces and soaking tubs. The daily breakfast features fresh-baked breads and creative dishes such as frittata primavera and pecan waffles.

16 rooms. No children under 12. Complimentary breakfast. $251-350

FALMOUTH

CAPTAIN TOM LAWRENCE HOUSE

75 Locust St., Falmouth, 508-540-1445, 800-266-8139; www.captaintomlawrence.com

Vaulted ceilings, hardwood floors and a spiral staircase add to the romantic, old-world charm of this 1861 inn, housed in a former whaling captain's home. Located within walking distance of the town's main street, Captain Tom Lawrence House is convenient to plentiful shops and restaurants, though you'll want to stick around for the complimentary breakfast—home-cooked stratas, crepes, waffles and omelets served with fresh berries and seasonal fruit syrups.

7 rooms. Complimentary breakfast. Closed January. $151-250

INN ON THE SOUND

313 Grand Ave., Falmouth, 508-457-9666, 800-564-9668; www.innonthesound.com

Set on a bluff above a lovely beach, this waterfront inn features individually decorated guest rooms with fresh, modern interiors. Don't miss the full gourmet breakfast, served wherever you'd like—your room, the inn's waterfront patio or the formal dining room.

10 rooms. No children under 18. $151-250

THE PALMER HOUSE INN

81 Palmer Ave., Falmouth, 508-548-1230, 800-472-2632; www.palmerhouseinn.com

Convenient to the Shining Sea Bikeway, the ferries and plentiful beaches, this 1901 Queen Anne-style inn and guesthouse is open year-round. Here, the guest rooms are individually decorated with Victorian antiques but feature luxury linens and mattresses. The complimentary breakfast is outstanding—favorite dishes include baked pears and gingerbread pancakes.

16 rooms. No children under 10. Complimentary breakfast. $151-250

HARWICH
THE COMMODORE INN
30 Earle Road, West Harwich, 508-432-1180, 800-368-1180; www.commodoreinn.com

This budget-friendly inn is close to the beaches of Nantucket Sound. Some rooms feature Jacuzzi bathtubs and private fireplaces, though all are equipped with comfortable beds and modern décor. Be sure to visit the charming porch and the heated outdoor pool, but whatever you do, don't miss the innkeeper's delicious homemade Scottish-style scones.

27 rooms. Complimentary breakfast. Restaurant, bar. Pool. Closed November-April. $61-150

MARTHA'S VINEYARD
ASHLEY INN
129 Main St., Edgartown, 508-627-9655; www.ashleyinn.net

The owners of this bed and breakfast individually decorate their guest rooms with country chintzes and antiques. In addition to a delicious, home-cooked breakfast, they also provide daily servings of afternoon tea, cookies and lemonade. The inn is located in central Edgartown, so it's a terrific home base for those wanting to explore the island's most stylish town.

10 rooms. No children under 12. Complimentary breakfast. Restaurant. $61-150

THE HANOVER HOUSE
28 Edgartown Road, Vineyard Haven, 508-693-1066, 800-696-8633; www.hanoverhouseinn.com

Set on a half-acre of land on Martha's Vineyard, this cozy bed and breakfast is convenient to the ferry, shopping, restaurants and the library. The inn also offers shuttles to guests who want to travel to Edgartown and Oak Bluffs, as well as a homemade morning meal.

15 rooms. Complimentary breakfast. $151-250

HOB KNOB INN
128 Main St., Edgartown, 508-627-9510, 800-696-2723; www.hobknob.com

One of the most popular destinations on the island, this eco-friendly boutique hotel stocks its guest rooms with luxury linens, earth-friendly furniture and Aveda bath products. Other perks include gourmet breakfasts, pre-packed picnics and sunset wine and cheese tastings.

17 rooms. Complimentary breakfast. Spa. Fitness center. Business center. $151-250

OUTERMOST INN
171 Lighthouse Road, Chilmark, 508-645-3511; www.outermostinn.com

Trivia fans, take note—the innkeeper is the sibling of singer James Taylor. Fittingly, this Martha's Vineyard retreat provides guests with a bohemian home, complete with meals sourced from the property's own organic vegetable and herb garden. The inn's picture windows provide excellent views of Vineyard Sound and the Elizabeth Islands.

7 rooms. No children under 12. Complimentary breakfast. Restaurant, bar. $151-250

THORNCROFT INN
460 Main St., Vineyard Haven, 508-693-3333; www.thorncroft.com

Secluded on a tree-lined, three-acre peninsula, this charming inn is big on romantic charms—white window shutters, two-person hot tubs, private fireplaces, plush bedding. In the morning, head to the dining room for a country

breakfast or stay put and have a continental breakfast delivered to your room.
14 rooms. Complimentary breakfast. $251-350

NANTUCKET

CARLISLE HOUSE INN
26 N. Water St., Nantucket, 508-228-0720; www.carlislehouse.com

Located in Nantucket's historic district, this 1765 bed and breakfast features Oriental rugs, fine woodwork, fireplaces and four-poster beds. Despite those elegant touches, the ambience at this year-round property is extremely casual and relaxed.
17 rooms. Closed January-March. No children under 10. Complimentary breakfast. $61-150

CENTERBOARD GUEST HOUSE
8 Chester St., Nantucket, 508-228-9696; www.centerboardguesthouse.com

Housed in an 1886 whaling captain's mansion, this bed and breakfast was recently renovated, though the house's airy, late Victorian charms were retained. The inn includes plenty of common space for spreading out, including a large parlor and a hidden outdoor garden. It's also convenient to the bustle of the harbor and the downtown shops. Guest rooms feature down duvets, antiques and Caswell and Massey bath products.
8 rooms. Closed January-February, Complimentary breakfast. $61-150

CLIFFSIDE BEACH CLUB
46 Jefferson Ave., Nantucket, 508-228-0618; www.cliffsidebeach.com

Launched as a private beach club at the turn of the 20th century, this unique spot has a variety of sunny, simple rooms and suites, each of which is situated in a converted bathhouse. Access to the beach and beach umbrellas, an onsite organic restaurant and a new fitness facility and pool are included with each stay.
27 rooms. Closed November-April. Restaurant, bar. Beach. Spa. Pool. Complimentary breakfast. Fitness center. $151-250

COBBLESTONE INN
5 Ash St., Nantucket, 508-228-1987; www.nantucket.net

Cozy and centrally located, this 1725 inn features guest rooms with fireplaces, colorful quilts and other country-style furnishings. The innkeepers keep guests well supplied with snacks, sodas and a generous continental breakfast.
5 rooms. Closed January-March. Complimentary breakfast. $61-150

MARTIN HOUSE INN
61 Centre St., Nantucket, 508-228-0678; www.martinhouseinn.net

Built in 1803, this centrally-located inn features guest rooms with plush contemporary furnishings, fireplaces and four-poster or canopy beds. The inn provides afternoon snacks, wine and cheese and teas, best enjoyed in the garden or on the sun-soaked veranda.
13 rooms. Complimentary breakfast. Restaurant. $61-150

ROBERTS HOUSE INN
11 India St., Nantucket, 508-228-0600, 800-872-6830; www.robertshouseinn.com

This classic, colonial-style inn was restored in 2003. Rooms are decorated with antiques and period-style reproductions as well as plush beds. Some rooms include Jacuzzi bathtubs. Here, guests enjoy close proximity to the harbor and the shops of Nantucket.

45 rooms. Complimentary breakfast. $61-150

SEVEN SEA STREET INN

7 Sea St., Nantucket, 508-228-3577; www.sevenseastreetinn.com

Spread over three red oak post-and-beam houses, this inn features guest rooms with canopy beds, rain showers and Jacuzzi bathtubs. The bed and breakfast is convenient to the island's finest restaurants and the shops, with excellent views of Nantucket Harbor.

11 rooms. No children under 5. Complimentary breakfast. Closed January-mid April. Spa. $151-250

SHERBURNE INN

10 Gay St., Nantucket, 508-228-4425, 888-577-4425; www.sherburneinn.com

Built by whaling captain Obed Starbuck in 1835, this cheerful bed and breakfast features plush beds, fresh flowers and Aveda bath products. The inn is convenient to Main Street, with all its shops and restaurants, though guests will want to stick around for complimentary breakfast and afternoon tea.

8 rooms. No children under 6. Complimentary breakfast. $61-150

VANESSA NOEL HOTEL

5 Chestnut St., Nantucket, 508-228-5300; www.vanessanoelhotel.com

Opened by a New York-based designer in 2002, this boutique inn features minimalist style and convenience to the innkeeper's other business, the fashionable shoe shop downstairs. No nautical trinkets or antiques here—think sleek, mid-century modern décor, especially the lobby's leopard-trimmed carpeting by Phillipe Stark.

8 rooms. Complimentary breakfast. Bar. $351 and up

VERANDA HOUSE

3 Step Lane, Nantucket, 508-228-0695; www.theverandahouse.com

Renovations turned this classic inn into a retro-chic boutique hotel, complete with Frette linens and luxury bath products by Boston-based Fresh. Convenient to the area's beaches and the bustling main street, the inn also serves gourmet breakfast and warm chocolate chip cookies in the afternoon.

18 rooms. Complimentary breakfast. $351 and up

ORLEANS
SHIP'S KNEES INN

186 Beach Road, East Orleans, 508-255-1312; www.shipskneesinn.com

Location, location—housed in a restored sea captain's house, this inn is just steps from the sand dunes of Nauset Beach. Guest rooms are individually decorated in nautical themes and furnished with antiques and four-poster beds.

16 rooms. No children under 12. Complimentary breakfast. $61-150

PROVINCETOWN
FAIRBANKS INN
90 Bradford St., Provincetown, 508-487-0386, 800-324-7265; www.fairbanksinn.com

Dating to the 1770s, this inn has everything you want in a historic property—colonial-style décor, four-poster beds, original plank wooden floors and a courtyard garden. Come sunrise, make for the porch to enjoy a breakfast of muffins, granolas, fresh fruit and crumcakes.

14 rooms. No children under 15. Complimentary breakfast. $61-150

SNUG COTTAGE
178 Bradford St., Provincetown, 508-487-1616, 800-432-2334; www.snugcottage.com

This charming inn is surrounded by lush gardens and features individually decorated rooms, many with fireplaces. In the morning, sample the innkeeper's delicious fruit and nut granola, a favorite dish of past guests. The innkeeper also provides complimentary wine and snacks in the afternoon.

8 rooms. Complimentary breakfast. $151-250

SANDWICH
ISAIAH JONES HOMESTEAD
165 Main St., Sandwich, 508-888-9115, 800-526-1625; www.isaiahjones.com

An American flag and flower-lined porch adorn the exterior of this 1849 Victorian bed and breakfast. Decorated with antiques, country-patterned fabrics and ornate woodwork, the guest rooms are spacious and include private fireplaces.

7 rooms. No children under 16. Complimentary breakfast. $61-150

TRURO
CROW'S NEST RESORT
496 Shore Road, North Truro, 508-487-9031, 800-499-9799; www.caperesort.com

The suites couldn't be closer to the water—here, all the guest rooms are just steps from the water, with terrific water views. The décor is clean, crisp and beach-inspired with Jacuzzi bathtubs and private fireplaces.

33 rooms. Closed December-March. Beach. $61-150

YARMOUTH
CAPTAIN FARRIS HOUSE BED AND BREAKFAST
308 Old Main St., South Yarmouth, 508-760-2818, 800-350-9477; www.captainfarris.com

Built in 1849, this bed and breakfast has beautifully landscaped lawns and romantic décor. Some guest rooms feature Jacuzzi bathtubs, though all are individually decorated with sumptuous period-style furniture. In the morning, have breakfast on the charming glass-enclosed courtyard. Guests enjoy tea and homemade cookies in the afternoon, and at the end of the day, everyone relaxes in the parlor with gratis glasses of port wine and sherry.

10 rooms. No children under 10. Complimentary breakfast. Restaurant. $61-150

INN AT LEWIS BAY
57 Maine Ave., West Yarmouth, 508-771-3433, 800-962-6679; www.innatlewisbay.com

Located in a quiet seaside neighborhood just one block from Lewis Bay, this Dutch colonial bed and breakfast specializes in home-cooked meals of stuffed

French toast and fresh-squeezed juices. As for the guest rooms, they feature country-style décor with antique bathtubs, colorful quilts and fresh-cut flowers.
6 rooms. No children under 12. Complimentary breakfast. $61-150

WHERE TO EAT

BREWSTER
★★★BRAMBLE INN
2019 Main St., Brewster, 508-896-7644; www.brambleinn.com

Chef-owner Ruth Manchester delivers creative cuisine and heartwarming hospitality at this cozy eatery in Brewster's historic district. With four quaint dining rooms, including an enclosed porch, the restaurant offers a comfortable setting to sample Manchester's concoctions, including her standout espresso and spice rubbed filet mignon.

American. Dinner. Bar. Reservations recommended. Closed January-April. $36-85

★★★CHILLINGSWORTH
2449 Main St., Brewster, 508-896-3640, 800-430-3640; www.chillingsworth.com

The 300-year-old Chillingsworth Foster estate sprawls along the edge of the King's Highway, and for 30 years, the property's restaurant has been synonymous with epicurean eating on Cape Cod. The formal dining rooms, furnished with antiques, stretch across the central house. The seven-course dinner is a contemporary interpretation of classic French cuisine with seared veal steak with truffle risotto, for example, or lobster with sautéed spinach and fennel. If you go, get dressed up and plan for a long evening of tasting. If you're in the mood for lighter fare, try the more casual bistro in the glassed-in porch.

French. Lunch, dinner. Bar. Reservations recommended. Outdoor seating. Closed Monday; also December-mid-May. $36-85

CHATHAM
★★★★TWENTY-EIGHT ATLANTIC
Pleasant Bay Road, Chatham, 508-432-5400, 800-225-7125; www.wequassett.com

Black truffle risotto, truffled salmon tartare and a petite clambake are among the enticing entrées you'll find here, a waterfront restaurant located in the Wequassett Resort. Also on the menu: a large, open dining room with expansive views of Pleasant Bay.

American. Breakfast, lunch, dinner. Bar. Children's menu. Reservations recommended. Outdoor seating. Closed December-March. $36-85

COTUIT
★★★THE REGATTA OF COTUIT
4631 Falmouth Road, Cotuit, 508-428-5715; www.regattaofcotuit.com

The kitchen at this 1790 stagecoach inn is run by chef Heather Allen, whose cooking is inspired by French, American and Asian themes. Try the lacquered duck, an Americanized version of Peking duck, or the Vietnamese-style fish and chips tempura, made from whatever the local fishermen catch that day. The Regatta is a must-stop for wine lovers—owners Wendy and Brantz Bryan have accumulated a legendary wine list over the years.

American. Dinner. Bar. Reservations recommended. Closed on Sunday, November-April.
$36-85

DENNIS

★★★RED PHEASANT INN
905 Main St., Dennis, 508-385-2133, 800-480-2133; www.redpheasantinn.com

Housed in a 200-year-old barn, this restaurant delivers quaint surroundings and fine American food. The menu emphasizes New England-style fish and meat dishes, though chef Bill Atwood Jr. also adds creative herbs and fresh ingredients. Lamb and game offerings change nightly. The 300-bottle wine list is extensive and features wines from around the world.

American. Dinner. Bar. Reservations recommended. $36-85

HYANNIS

★★★NAKED OYSTER
20 Independence Drive, Hyannis, 508-778-6500; www.nakedoyster.com

When you're craving fresh, dayboat oysters and seafood, why not go directly to the source? The owners of this contemporary bistro struck a deal with local fishermen, who deliver daily catches directly to the kitchen. Here, the oyster-slurping experience is further enhanced by dishes like marinated Wagyu flank steak and parmesan risotto, as well as a lengthy wine list.

Seafood. Lunch, dinner. Bar. Closed Sunday. $16-35

★★★THE PADDOCK
20 Scudder Ave., Hyannis, 508-775-7677; www.paddockcapecod.com

Pressed linens and abundant fresh flowers lend an air of sophistication to this family-friendly restaurant, while equestrian paintings and antiques give it the classic look. The menu is loaded with fresh seafood, though poultry, steak and pasta also make appearances.

American. Lunch, dinner. Bar. Children's menu. Reservations recommended. Closed mid-November-March. $16-35

MARTHA'S VINEYARD

★★★ALCHEMY
71 Main St., Edgartown, 508-627-9999

A smart, casual crowd, including the occasional celebrity, frequents Edgartown's popular Alchemy. The American bistro offers upscale dining in a relaxed, two-story atmosphere. No visit is complete without an order of fried risotto balls and a trip to the buzzing lounge downstairs, always packed with revelers after hours.

American. Lunch, dinner. Bar. Outdoor seating. Closed January. $36-85

★★★BEACH PLUM INN RESTAURANT
50 Beach Plum Lane, Menemsha, 508-645-9454; www.beachpluminn.com

No matter where you sit at this renowned, out-of-the-way restaurant, you're assured an ocean view—this makes the Beach Plum Inn one of the most romantic places on Martha's Vineyard. Here, local ingredients fuel the seafood-heavy menu with standout dishes like pan-seared hazelnut crusted halibut.

American. Dinner. Outdoor seating. Closed January-early May. $36-85

★★★L'ETOILE
22 N. Water St., Edgartown, 508-627-5187; www.letoile.net

Once housed at the Charlotte Inn, L'Etoile is now at home in a more relaxed location on North Water Street. Here, the food is still served in a very formal atmosphere, with a price tag to match. But the overall emphasis has changed—these days the experience emphasizes the food over the environment. The seasonal menu features locally sourced seafood and meat, along with the island's native herbs and produce. A brightly colored bar adjoins the restaurant—either room is a worthy place to dine in style.

French. Dinner. Bar. Jacket required. Reservations recommended. Closed Monday-Thursday off-season. $86 and up

★★★OUTERMOST INN
81 Lighthouse Road, Aquinnah, 508-645-3511; www.outermostinn.com

Here, the dramatic cliff-top location is matched only by the menu—a creative prix-fixe selection of three-course meals made with local seafood, meats and produce so fresh it came from the inn's very own garden. Wine lovers, take note—the restaurant is strictly BYOB.

American. Dinner. Reservations recommended. Closed Wednesday; also mid-October-mid-May. $36-85

NANTUCKET
★★★21 FEDERAL
21 Federal St., Nantucket, 508-228-2121; www.21federal.com

Historic charm and contemporary panache unite at this stylishly clubby spot—a favorite of the island's who's who, both for its delectable New American cuisine and convivial bar scene. The well-rounded menu has a wide selection of meat, poultry and seafood, while the award-winning wine list delights oenophiles.

American. Dinner. Bar. Reservations recommended. Outdoor seating. Closed January-April. $36-85

★★★AMERICAN SEASONS
80 Center St., Nantucket, 508-228-7111; www.americanseasons.com

The varied menu at this upscale bistro is divided to reflect four regional cuisines: New England, Down South, the Wild West and the Pacific Coast. Thanks to meticulous attention to detail and fresh, local produce, the themed meals are a resounding success. Regulars rave about the cooking and the folk art that bedecks the romantic dining room and patio.

American. Dinner. Bar. Reservations recommended. Outdoor seating. Closed January-March. $36-85

★★★BOARDING HOUSE
12 Federal St., Nantucket, 508-228-9622; www.boardinghouse-pearl.com

The restaurant's nouveau cuisine and sexy, youthful scene make for long waits. Smart diners book a table outdoors to people-watch and stargaze while they dine on Asian-inspired seafood and beef dishes. Others prefer the dimly lit downstairs dining room. Wherever you sit, the comprehensive wine list ensures perfect pairings.

American. Lunch, dinner. Bar. Reservations recommended. Outdoor seating. $36-85

★★★CLUB CAR

1 Main St., Nantucket, 508-228-1101; www.theclubcar.com

This unique spot is housed within a renovated train club car that once ran between Steamboat Wharf and Siasconset Village. Lunches and dinners offer sophisticated takes on classic seafood, veal and duck dishes. A live pianist adds to the romantic, yesteryear ambience.

French. Lunch, dinner. Bar. Reservations recommended. Closed November-late May. $86 and up

★★★COMPANY OF THE CAULDRON

7 India St., Nantucket, 508-228-4016; www.companyofthecauldron.com

From its ivy-covered exterior to the soft glow of its candlelit dining room, this restaurant seems like it was crafted straight from a romance novel. The menu emphasizes New American dishes and changes daily. There are two seatings each night, each with a pre-determined menu of locally sourced ingredients.

International. Dinner. Reservations recommended. Closed Monday; also Mid-December-April. $36-85

★★★ORAN MOR

2 S. Beach St., Nantucket, 508-228-8655; www.oranmorbistro.com

Climb the copper flight of stairs to Oran Mor and discover a food lover's haven. Located on the top floor of a historic Nantucket house, the restaurant features an eclectic menu that echoes the restaurant's approachable, though elegant, style. Organic ingredients and fresh seafood dominate the complex dishes. A friendly, knowledgeable staff caps off this fine-dining experience.

International. Dinner. Bar. Reservations recommended. Closed January-March. $36-85

★★★THE PEARL

12 Federal St., Nantucket, 508-228-9701; www.boardinghouse-pearl.com

This spot was among the first to bring an urban-chic vibe to Nantucket. Appealing to a young, fashionable clientele that crowds the bar area on weekends, The Pearl offers Asian-flavored seafood dishes and an excellent cocktail menu of martinis, cosmos and sake in addition to a wine and champagne. There are only two seatings per evening, so reserve early.

International. Dinner, late-night. Bar. Reservations recommended. Closed October-April. $86 and up

★★★SUMMER HOUSE

17 Ocean Ave., Nantucket, 508-257-9976; www.thesummerhouse.com

The Summer House seduces with its oceanfront seating and superb cuisine. White wicker furnishings and ceiling fans set the tone for a refined New American dining experience, with decadent seasonal dishes like duet of beef tenderloin and braised beef short rib. A more casual poolside lunch is also served.

American. Dinner. Bar. Outdoor seating. Closed mid-October-mid-May. $86 and up

★★★★TOPPER'S

120 Wauwinet Road, Nantucket, 508-228-0145, 800-426-8718; www.wauwinet.com

Chef David Daniels lends his extensive New England-honed skills to Toppers. Regulars know to order the seasonal prix-fixe menu, which features locally inspired treats like lobster and chestnut soup, roasted sirloin of venison and homemade ice cream. Daniels' signature dishes include maple-glazed foie gras, potato-crusted Maine scallops and roasted New York duckling. All meals can be paired with a selection from the award-winning 900-bottle wine list.

American. Lunch, dinner, Sunday brunch. Bar. Reservations recommended. Outdoor seating. Closed late October-early May. $86 and up

ORLEANS
★★★CAPTAIN LINNELL HOUSE
137 Skaket Beach Road, Orleans, 508-255-3400; www.linnell.com

Chef-owner Bill Conway delivers a delightful dining experience at this romantic restaurant. A Victorian gazebo, lavender bushes and ocean breezes set the scene for what's inside—oil lamps, fresh flowers and a cozy atmosphere. Highlights of the skillfully prepared menu include veal with crab, bouillabaisse and pork tenderloin. An extensive wine list is offered.

American. Dinner. Bar. Children's menu. Reservations recommended. Closed Monday; also mid-February-March. $36-85

PROVINCETOWN
★★★BISTRO AT CROWNE POINTE INN
82 Bradford St., Provincetown, 508-487-6767; www.crownepointe.com

Paintings, fresh flowers and gleaming hardwood floors set the inspired tone at this bluff-top restaurant. A creative, seasonal menu (heavy on the seafood) is skillfully prepared by chefs who are happy to accommodate health-conscious diners by substituting butter, cream or fatty oils.

American menu. Dinner. Bar. Reservations recommended. Closed Tuesday. $36-85

★★★RED INN RESTAURANT
15 Commercial St., Provincetown, 508-487-7334, 866-473-3466; www.theredinn.com

The best part about this restaurant is its view—a panorama of Providence harbor, Cape Cod Bay, the Long Point lighthouse and the shores of the Outer Cape. Diners get an eyeful as they chomp on the house specialty—a tasty porterhouse steak.

American. Dinner. Bar. Reservations recommended. $36-85

SANDWICH
★★★THE DAN'L WEBSTER INN
149 Main St., Sandwich, 508-888-3623, 800-444-3566; www.danlwebsterinn.com

A former 1800s stagecoach inn once frequented by its namesake, this hotel offers both a tavern and a white-tablecloth dining experience. Chef and co-owner Robert Catania specializes in traditional, New England-style fare— he even buys much of his fish and hydroponic vegetables from a local aquafarm. The wine list complements his culinary aspirations.

American. Breakfast, lunch, dinner, Sunday brunch. Bar. Children's menu. Reservations recommended.

RECOMMENDED

HARWICH

L'ALOUETTE

787 Main St., Harwich Port, 508-430-0405; www.lalouettebistro.com

A charming French bistro located in central Harwich Port, L'Alouette features a casual French menu that emphasizes fresh local produce and seafood. Standout dishes include steak frites with fresh asparagus and soy-lacquered salmon.

French. Dinner. Reservations recommended. $36-85

MARTHA'S VINEYARD

LOLA'S SOUTHERN SEAFOOD

Beach Road, Oak Bluffs, 508-693-5007; www.lolassouthernseafood.com

Seafood gets a spicy, southern accent at this cozy bistro. Steamed lobster is served with maple garlic mashed potatoes, while north Atlantic salmon comes with a honey mango sauce. Stop by in the evening to catch live reggae, jazz and other genres of music.

American, seafood. Dinner, late-night, Sunday brunch. Outdoor bar. $16-35

LOOKOUT TAVERN

8 Seaview Ave., Oak Bluffs, 508-696-9844; www.lookouttavern.com

With its outdoor patio overlooking Oak Bluffs' harbor, this seafood restaurant is a popular spot to eat lobsters, clams and fish tacos. The desserts are excellent, too—for example, the Boston cream pie cheesecake offers a unique take on the classic.

Seafood. Lunch, dinner. Bar. Outdoor seating. Closed November-April. $16-35

LURE GRILL

31 Dunes Road, Edgartown, 508-627-3663; www.winnetu.com

Located at the Winnetu Resort, this casual, family-friendly restaurant serves comfortable seafood, burgers and steaks, all cooked over a wood-fired grill. The restaurant also features an activity area to keep children occupied while their parents dine.

Seafood. Dinner. September-mid-October, closed Monday-Tuesday; Mid-October-November, closed Monday-Thursday; closed December-May. $36-85

SWEET LIFE CAFÉ

63 Circuit Ave., Oak Bluffs, 508-696-0200; www.sweetlifemv.com

Ask for a seat inside this Victorian inn or sit in the beautiful, flower-filled garden—either way, you're assured a comfortable perch for sampling the flavorful, seasonal cuisine produced by chef Scott Ehrlich. Dig into sautéed halibut with sweet pea risotto or grilled duck breast with potato purée. The inn's owner has selected an extensive wine list.

Seafood. Dinner. Reservations recommended. Outdoor seating. Closed January-March. $16-35

NANTUCKET

BLACK EYED SUSAN'S

10 India St., Nantucket, 508-325-0308; www.black-eyedsusans.com

Whether you come for the hearty, creative breakfasts or the romantic, candlelit dinners, you'll need to come early because this small, popular restaurant does not take reservations. A seat at the classic, diner-style counter is prime for watching the staff at work in the open kitchen. The BYOB policy makes this a budget-friendly place to sample locally sourced seafood.

American. Breakfast, dinner. Credit cards not accepted. Closed Sunday; also November-March. $16-35

DOWNYFLAKE

18 Sparks Ave., Nantucket, 508-228-4533

Locals line up at this restaurant for satisfying, classic American breakfasts including fresh blueberry pancakes. The place is most popular, though, for its fresh-made doughnuts, baked each morning and served piping hot.

Breakfast, lunch. $15 and under

FOG ISLAND CAFÉ

7 S. Water St., Nantucket, 508-228-1818; www.fogisland.com

This casual spot is known for its breakfasts—including the popular fog-style chicken hash, cranberry pancakes and build-your-own omelets. But the dinner menu is excellent, too, featuring dishes such as sesame-crusted tuna and grilled salmon with lemon dill butter.

American. Breakfast, Lunch, dinner. Bar. Children's menu. Closed January-February. $15 and under

LE LANGUEDOC

24 Broad St., Nantucket, 508-228-2552; www.lelanguedoc.com

Classic French recipes fill the menu at this uncomplicated restaurant, located in a historic house. Here, the steak frites comes doused with béarnaise and a side of truffled greens, while pan-roasted lobster is served with creamy polenta.

French. Lunch, dinner. Bar. Reservations recommended. Outdoor seating. Closed February-March. $36-85

LOLA 41°

15 S. Beach St., Nantucket, 508-325-4001;www.lola41.com

As the name would suggest, this restaurant sits on the 41st parallel, but it's also close to downtown. While the emphasis is on sushi, this contemporary spot also offers plates like pan-roasted Atlantic halibut and thyme-roasted potatoes. Feel like a nice juicy burger? Visit the sister restaurant, Lola Burger, where you'll find a variety of top-notch burgers with a twist. One suggestion—upgrade to truffle fries to make the burger that much better. Doubling as a hip bar, Lola 41° has an extensive wine and sake list, not to mention a stellar cocktail list. Order up a St. Germain screwdriver for a nice take on the classic.

International. Dinner. $16-35

NANTUCKET LOBSTER TRAP

23 Washington St., Nantucket, 508-228-4200; www.nantucketlobstertrap.com

Lines are long at this traditional lobster restaurant, where the kitchen cranks out simple dishes like steamed lobsters served with fresh corn, boiled potatoes, bread and butter. The menu also includes clams, shrimp, steaks and chowder. Takeout dinners can be ordered ahead of time—they're packed and ready to go for the beach or a picnic.

Seafood. Dinner. Bar. Children's menu. Outdoor seating. Closed October-April. $36-85

PROVISIONS

3 Harbor Square, Nantucket, 508-228-3258

This shop is where all the locals go for freshly made sandwiches. Provisions offers an eclectic menu, with a twist on the favorites. If you've been craving that Thanksgiving turkey sandwich, order the Terrific Turkey filled with stuffing, cranberry sauce, and of course turkey. Another favorite is the Italian, combining sopressata, salami, provolone, hot peppers, red onion, mayo and the traditional oil and vinegar duo.

American. Breakfast, Lunch. May-October. $15 and under

SOMETHING NATURAL

50 Cliff Road, Nantucket, 508-228-0504; www.somethingnatural.com

For a casual, take-and-go breakfast or lunch, check out this terrific local bakery. The off-the-beaten-path shop crafts an array of healthy sandwiches, breads, bagels, salads and of course, not-so-healthy cookies.

American. Breakfast, lunch. $15 and under.

OAK BLUFFS

ORLEANS

MAHONEY'S ATLANTIC BAR AND GRILL

28 Main St., Orleans, 508-255-5505; www.mahoneysatlantic.com

This upscale bistro offers a fresh, gourmet take on classic seafood dishes such as pan-roasted lobster with brandy flambé and blackened tuna sashimi. The bar has an edited menu of smaller, though equally tasty, dishes and an assortment of classic cocktails.

American. Dinner. Bar. $16-35

NAUSET BEACH CLUB RESTAURANT

222 E. Main St., East Orleans, 508-255-8547; www.nausetbeachclub.com

Northern Italian cuisine is the focus at this upscale bistro, where the pastas are made fresh daily and the wine list is heavy on obscure Italian vintages.

Italian. Dinner. Bar. Reservations recommended. $36-85

WOODS HOLE

LANDFALL

2 Luscombe Ave., Woods Hole, 508-548-1758; www.woodshole.com

Perched atop a pier on the waterfront in Woods Hole, this casual restaurant specializes in seafood dishes such as lobster savannah, fresh grilled swordfish and seafood newburg.

Seafood. Lunch, dinner. Bar. Children's menu. Reservations recommended. Outdoor seating. Closed December-March. $16-35

SPAS

NANTUCKET

★★★SPA BY THE SEA

120 Wauwinet Road, Nantucket, 508-228-0145, 800-426-8718; www.wauwinet.com

Indulge all five senses at this luxury spa located at the Wauwinet, a luxury seaside retreat. Signature treatments make use of local and sea-inspired ingredients, as with the garden facial and Atlantic seaweed wrap. After your treatment, lounge in the spa's dedicated herb garden, where you'll find comfortable chaise lounges and the sounds of rolling waves.

CENTRAL MASSACHUSETTS AND THE BERKSHIRES

Just as famous for its landscape as it is for its culture, the Berkshires is a world-class destination filled with galleries, museums, performances and literary legends. In the summer, classical music lovers from throughout the world converge upon the tiny town of Lenox, the summer home of the Boston Symphony Orchestra and its roster of superstar conductors. Lenox is also the site of Edith Wharton's former manse, the Mount. Northampton, on the other hand, is best known for its cluster of bars and rock venues, though the town also hosts an impressive roster of theater companies, restaurants and art galleries.

In nearby North Adams, a cultural revolution is steadily underfoot, thanks mostly to the arrival of Mass MoCA, the biggest modern art museum in the world. Ever since the institution took root in a former factory, North Adams has welcomed a wave of new boutiques and eateries, as well as a crowd of young culture-vultures eager to digest the city's attractions. The once-gritty town of Pittsfield is also enjoying a renewal of its restaurants, shops, theaters and museums. Of course, the longtime destination of Great Barrington continues to lure big-city types with its performing arts events, not to mention its impressive spread of parks.

Other cultural hot spots include Amherst, birthplace and lifelong home to Emily Dickinson, and Stockbridge, home to Norman Rockwell late in his life. Both towns lure fans with museums that celebrate the lives of their most famous daughter and son, respectively.

With so many mountains and fresh, unspoiled waterways, the Berkshires and central Massachusetts offer another form of inspiration, that of the natural sort. Check out the region's plentiful ski areas and nature preserves. In fact, the state's biggest park, October Mountain State Forest, is so beautiful it once inspired Herman Melville. After a busy day of hiking, biking, fishing or skiing, you can rest assured—plenty of innkeepers take advantage of these idyllic settings, so you're sure to find a quaint bed and breakfast wherever you roam.

HIGHLIGHTS

WHAT ARE THE BEST CULTURAL ATTRACTIONS IN THE BERKSHIRES?

EMILY DICKINSON MUSEUM
Explore the birthplace and lifelong residence of the Belle of Amherst. Today, Emily Dickinson's home features biographical exhibits and the poet's restored writing parlor, as well as the adjacent property of Dickinson's brother and beloved sister-in-law Susan, her biggest advocate and fan.

MASS MOCA
This young, 10-year-old museum already has a stellar reputation in the art world, thanks to its cutting-edge exhibits and big-time performing arts presentations. Housed in a former mill, the museum makes great use of its industrial North Adams setting.

STERLING AND FRANCINE CLARK ART INSTITUTE
The Berkshires' arts scene is impressive, especially when you consider the size of the communities that support these institutions. Perhaps no organization is so dazzling as the Clark, a world-class museum with a small collection that includes Renoir, Degas and Monet. Thanks to a recent expansion, the museum now features a dramatic modern building by master architect Tadao Ando.

TANGLEWOOD
This sprawling estate is flecked with indoor and outdoor concert venues. Though the Boston Symphony Orchestra takes residence during the summer, the property also hosts jazz, country and rock concerts the rest of the year.

WHAT TO SEE

AMHERST
AMHERST COLLEGE
100 Boltwood Ave., Amherst, 413-542-2000; www.amherst.edu
One of the best liberal arts colleges in the country, Amherst enrolls some 1,550 students. Check out the tree-shaded campus green in the middle of town. The school's Robert Frost Library owns approximately half of Emily Dickinson's poems, as well as materials by Wordsworth, Eugene O'Neill and others.

EMILY DICKINSON MUSEUM: THE HOMESTEAD AND THE EVERGREENS
280 Main St., Amherst, 413-542-8161; www.emilydickinsonmuseum.org

The Homestead was the birthplace and home of poet Emily Dickinson, whereas the Evergreens housed her brother Austin and Emily's beloved sister-in-law Susan. Select rooms are open for tours on a first-come, first-served basis. *March-May, September-December, Wednesday-Saturday 11 a.m.-4 p.m.; June-August, Wednesday-Sunday 10 a.m.-5 p.m.*

ERIC CARLE MUSEUM OF PICTURE BOOK ART
125 W. Bay Road, Amherst, 413-658-1100; www.picturebookart.org

This 40,000-square-foot facility opened in 2002 as the first museum in the United States exclusively devoted to children's picture-book art. Its founder, Eric Carle, has illustrated more than 70 picture books, including *The Very Hungry Caterpillar*, which has been published in more than 30 languages and has sold more than 18 million copies.

Tuesday-Friday 10 a.m.-4 p.m., Saturday 10 a.m.-5 p.m., Sunday noon-5 p.m.; July-August, Monday-Friday 10 a.m.-4 p.m., Saturday 10 a.m.-5 p.m., Sunday noon-5 p.m.

UNIVERSITY OF MASSACHUSETTS
Massachusetts Avenue and North Pleasant Street, Amherst, 413-545-0111; www.umass.edu

Founded in 1863, UMass-Amherst was the state's first major facility of public higher education. Today, the 1,450-acre campus is packed with 24,000 students and more than 150 buildings—many important modern structures among them, including the W.E.B. DuBois Library. Tours of campus are available.

DEERFIELD
HISTORIC DEERFIELD
Highways 5 and 10, Deerfield, 413-774-5581; www.historic-deerfield.org

The town's lovely main street is lined with 14 historic houses, each furnished with collections of antique furniture, silver, ceramics and textiles. A 28,000-square-foot Collections Study Center features changing exhibits on historic themes. Daily walking tours and antique forums and workshops are available.

Daily 9:30 a.m-4:30 p.m.

MEMORIAL HALL MUSEUM
10 Memorial St., Deerfield, 413-774-3768; www.deerfield-ma.org

Built in 1798, Memorial Hall is one of New England's oldest museums. Today, it boasts impressive collections of colonial furnishings, paintings, textiles and Native American relics.

May-October, daily 11 a.m.-5 p.m.

GREAT BARRINGTON
CATAMOUNT SKI AREA
Highway 23, Great Barrington, 518-325-3200; www.catamountski.com

Night skiing is popular at this mountain, which has four double chairlifts, a ski school, equipment rentals, a cafeteria, a bar and a nursery. The longest run is two miles with a vertical drop of 1,000 feet. Come summertime, the area is a popular destination for treetop ropes courses.

December-March, Monday-Friday 9 a.m.-4 p.m., Saturday-Sunday 8:30 a.m.-4 p.m.

RUBINERS CHEESEMONGERS & GROCERS AND RUBI'S CAFÉ
264 Main St., Great Barrington, 413-528-0488

This cheese shop, grocer and café carries charcuterie boards and beautiful, hard-to-find cheeses from around the world. Fresh, overstuffed sandwiches and tasty coffees are available at the café. Don't miss the entrance—it's located down an alley. Ask the staff to pack a picnic for your drive home.

Monday-Saturday 10 a.m.-6 p.m., Sunday 10 a.m.-4 p.m. Rubi's: Monday-Saturday 7:30 a.m.-6 p.m., Sunday 7:30 a.m.-4 p.m.

SKI BUTTERNUT
380 State Road, Great Barrington, 413-528-2000, 800-438-7669; www.skibutternut.com

The family-friendly Butternut ski area has a quad, triple and four double chairlifts, plus a pomalift, a rope tow and four magic carpets. The cafeteria and wine room are better than average, and the slalom race course frequently attracts professionals. The longest run is approximately 1½ miles; its vertical drop is 1,000 feet. Butternut also features seven miles of cross-country trails as well as ski and snowboard rentals.

December-March, daily.

HANCOCK
JIMINY PEAK
37 Corey Road, Hancock, 413-738-5500; www.jiminypeak.com

This ski area has a six-passenger lift, three double chairlifts, a J-bar, two quads, three triple chairs, a ski school, rentals, a restaurant, two cafeterias, a bar and a lodge. There are various hits and rails for skiers and snowboarders. The longest run is two miles with a vertical drop 1,140 feet. In the summer, the mountain has trout fishing, an 18-hole miniature golf course, an Alpine slide and a tennis center.

Late November-early April, daily.

LEE
OCTOBER MOUNTAIN STATE FOREST
256 Woodland Road, Lee, 413-243-1778; www.mass.gov

The state's largest state forest, October Mountain provides fine mountain scenery overlooking 16,000 acres for hiking, hunting, camping and snowmobiling. The park's name is attributed to the writer Herman Melville, who was impressed by the area's fall foliage.

LENOX
EDITH WHARTON ESTATE (THE MOUNT)
Second Plunkett St., Lenox, 413-551-5104, 888-637-1902; www.edithwharton.org

Built in 1902, Edith Wharton's summer estate was based on the principles outlined in a book she coauthored in 1897, *The Decoration of Houses*. The enormous Classical Revival house is continuously being restored. The house is ringed with formal gardens that incorporate Italian walls, a lime walk and grass terraces.

May-October, daily 9 a.m.-5 p.m.; November-mid-December, Saturday-Sunday 10 a.m.-4 p.m.

SPECIAL EVENT

SHAKESPEARE & COMPANY

70 Kemble St., Lenox, 413-637-1199; www.shakespeare.org
Every summer, this professional theater company performs plays by Shakespeare and Edith Wharton on four stages, one of which is situated outdoors.
Late June-Early September, Tuesday-Sunday.

PLEASANT VALLEY WILDLIFE SANCTUARY

472 W. Mountain Road, Lenox, 413-637-0320; www.massaudubon.org
Operated by the Massachusetts Audubon Society, this sanctuary encompasses 1,500 acres with seven miles of trails that stretch over the slopes of Lenox Mountain. Don't miss the beaver colony at Yokun Brook.
Admission: adults $4, children 3-12 $3. Mid-June-mid-October.

TANGLEWOOD

197 W St., Lenox, 413-637-1600; www.bso.org
This 526-acre estate and music venue is best known as the summer home of the Boston Symphony Orchestra. In truth, Tanglewood features a variety of year-round concerts, everything from rock, country and jazz to classical. Nathaniel Hawthorne famously wrote *Tanglewood Tales* while boarding here, and the owner later renamed the estate in the book's honor.
Daily; free except during concerts.

NORTH ADAMS

MASS MOCA

1040 Mass MoCA Way, North Adams, 413-664-4481; www.massmoca.org
Committed to the visual and performing arts, MASS MOCA is a new museum (just ten years old) specializing in unconventional art exhibits and rare performances by renowned musicians, dancers and theater companies. Children love the hands-on activities in the museums' Kidspace. Meanwhile, architecture aficionados appreciate how the museum's building inhabits a former mill.
July-early September, daily 10 a.m.-6 p.m.; rest of year, Wednesday-Monday 11 a.m.-5 p.m.

MOHAWK TRAIL STATE FOREST

175 Mohawk Trail/Route 2, Charlemont, 413-339-5504; www.mass.gov
A cascading river divides this 6,000-acre woodland, creating high ridges, deep gorges and tall tree growth. The spectacular scenery makes a great backdrop for swimming, fishing, hiking, winter sports, picnicking and camping.

MOUNT GREYLOCK STATE RESERVATION

Rockwell Road, North Adams, 413-499-4262; www.mass.gov
At 3,491 vertical feet, Mount Greylock is the highest point in the state. It's also the site of Massachusetts's first wilderness state park, incorporated in 1898 to preserve the area for fishing, hunting, hiking, cross-country skiing and picnicking.
Mid-May-mid-October.

NATURAL BRIDGE STATE PARK

McCauley Road, off Route 8 North Adams, 413-663-6392; www.mass.gov

This 48-acre park features the world's only naturally formed water-eroded marble bridge, a 550-million-year-old rock formation popularized by Nathaniel Hawthorne. Picnicking is allowed in the park.

Mid-May-mid-October.

WESTERN GATEWAY HERITAGE STATE PARK

115 State St., North Adams, 413 663-6312; www.mass.gov

Once the site of a freight yard, this urban park details the historic construction of the Hoosac Railroad Tunnel, one of the greatest engineering feats of the 19th century.

NORTHAMPTON

ARCADIA NATURE CENTER AND WILDLIFE SANCTUARY, MASSACHUSETTS AUDUBON SOCIETY

127 Combs Road, Easthampton, 413-584-3009; www.massaudubon.org

This park constitutes 550 acres of land along an ancient oxbow of the Connecticut River. Check out the five-mile self-guided nature trail and the observation tower.

Tuesday-Sunday 9 a.m.-3 p.m.

CALVIN COOLIDGE PRESIDENTIAL LIBRARY & MUSEUM

20 West St., Northampton, 413-587-1011; www.forbeslibrary.org

Established in 1920, the library documents the late president's life, from his early years in Vermont to his days as a young lawyer in Northampton to, of course, his years at the White House. Check out displays of Coolidge's papers and correspondence as well as photography and portraits.

Monday-Thursday, Saturday; schedule may vary.

LOOK PARK

300 N. Main St., Florence, 413-584-5457; www.lookpark.org

A recreation site for the whole family, this park features everything from a miniature train and the Christenson Zoo to boating, tennis, picnicking, playgrounds, ball fields and the Pines Theater.

SMITH COLLEGE

33 Elm St., Northampton, 413-584-2700; www.smith.edu

With 2,700 women, this is the largest private women's liberal arts college in the United States. On-campus attractions include Paradise Pond, the Helen Hills Chapel and the William Allan Neilson Library, featuring an impressive collection of more than one million volumes.

SMITH COLLEGE MUSEUM OF ART

Elm Street, Northampton, 413-585-2760; www.smith.edu

Housed in the recently renovated Brown Fine Arts Center, this eight-year-old museum has already accumulated a fine collection with an emphasis on American and European art of the 19th and 20th centuries. The collection includes Winslow Homer, August Rodin and Alberto Giacometti.

September-May, Tuesday-Sunday; rest of year, Tuesday-Saturday.

PITTSFIELD

ARROWHEAD

780 Holmes Road, Pittsfield, 413-442-1793; www.mobydick.org

Herman Melville wrote *Moby Dick* while living here between 1850 to 1863. Today, the writer's former residence is a house museum as well as the headquarters of the Berkshire County Historical Society.

June-October, daily 9:30 a.m.-4 p.m.

BERKSHIRE MUSEUM

39 South St., Pittsfield, 413-443-7171; www.berkshiremuseum.org

This comprehensive museum of art, natural science and history features American 19th- and 20th-century paintings as well as works by British and European masters. The collections also include artifacts from ancient civilizations, exhibits on Berkshire County history, a brand-new hall of innovation and children's programs.

Monday-Saturday 10 a.m.-5 p.m., Sunday noon-5 p.m.

BOUSQUET

101 Dan Fox Drive, Pittsfield, 413-442-8316; www.bousquets.com

A popular destination for night skiing, the Bousquet ski area features two double chairlifts, three rope tows, snowmaking, ski school, rentals, a cafeteria, bar and daycare. The longest run is one mile with a vertical drop of 750 feet. Snowtubing is also offered.

December-March, daily.

HANCOCK SHAKER VILLAGE

Highways 20 and 41, Pittsfield, 413-443-0188; www.hancockshakervillage.org

A Shaker site from 1790 to 1960, Hancock now serves as a museum of Shaker life, crafts and farming. Large collections of furniture and artifacts are found throughout the village's 20 restored buildings, which includes the Round Stone Barn.

SHEFFIELD

COLONEL ASHLEY HOUSE

117 Cooper Hill Road, Sheffield, 413-229-8600; www.thetrustees.org

The elegance of this home reflects Colonel John Ashley's prominent place in society. One political meeting he held here produced the Sheffield Declaration, the forerunner to the Declaration of Independence. Notably, one of the colonel's slaves, Mum Bett, later sued for her freedom—and won. Today, the house museum contains redware, furniture and tools, as well as five miles of adjacent hiking trails.

July-August, Wednesday-Sunday; June, September-mid-October, Saturday-Monday.

SPRINGFIELD

BASKETBALL HALL OF FAME

1150 W. Columbus Ave., Springfield, 413-781-6500; www.hoophall.com

Founded in 1959, this hall of fame celebrates the best games, players and teams in basketball. Check out video highlights, life-size action blow-ups of Hall of Famers and memorabilia.

Daily.

SPECIAL EVENT

EASTERN STATES EXPOSITION (THE BIG E)

1305 Memorial Ave., West Springfield, 413-737-2443; www.thebige.com
The largest fair in the Northeast celebrates New England history, culture and cuisine. Best of all, it includes the impressive Avenue of States, featuring life-size replicas of the original state houses from all six New England states.
September.

INDIAN MOTORCYCLE MUSEUM

33 Hendee St., Springfield, 413-737-2624
This was part of the vast complex where Indian motorcycles were manufactured until 1953. A gear-head's dream, the site now features historic Indian bikes, an early snowmobile, even a 1928 roadster.
Daily.

SPRINGFIELD ARMORY NATIONAL HISTORIC SITE

1 Armory Square, Springfield, 413-734-8551; www.nps.gov
An important site of military innovation, the nation's first armory now contains one of the largest collections of military small arms in the world. Check out the famous exhibit the "Organ of Guns", made famous by Longfellow's poem *The Arsenal at Springfield.*
Daily 9 a.m.-5 p.m.

SPRINGFIELD MUSEUMS AT THE QUADRANGLE

220 State St., Springfield, 413-263-6800; www.springfieldmuseums.org
The site includes four museums and a library. The George Walter Vincent Smith Art Museum houses a collection of Asian armor, arms, jade, bronzes and rugs. The Connecticut River Valley Historical Museum includes genealogy and a local history library. The Museum of Fine Arts has 20 galleries and an outstanding collection of American and European works. The Science Museum has an exploration center, early aviation exhibit, aquarium, planetarium, African hall and dinosaur hall.
All buildings: Tuesday-Sunday.

STORROWTON VILLAGE

Eastern States Exposition, 1305 Memorial Ave., West Springfield, 413-205-5051; www.thebige.com
This group of restored 18th and 19th American buildings includes a meetinghouse, schoolhouse and blacksmith shop, all situated around an old-fashioned town green.
June-August, Tuesday-Saturday; rest of year, by appointment.

STOCKBRIDGE

BERKSHIRE BOTANICAL GARDEN

Highways 102 and 183, Stockbridge, 413-298-3926; www.berkshirebotanical.org
This 15-acre botanical garden features perennials, shrubs, trees, antique roses,

ponds, a wildflower exhibit, vegetable gardens and demonstration greenhouses. Don't miss the on-site garden shop. The garden also schedules occasional special events and lectures. Picnicking is allowed on the grounds.
May-October, daily.

CHESTERWOOD
284 Main St., Stockbridge, 413-298-3579; www.chesterwood.org
This was the early 20th-century summer residence and studio of Daniel Chester French, sculptor of the Minute Man statue in Concord and the Lincoln Memorial in Washington, D.C. The house contains many of French's plaster sketches. The estate also includes formal gardens and woodland paths designed by the artist himself.
May-October, daily.

MISSION HOUSE
1 Sergeant St., Stockbridge, 413-298-3239; www.thetrustees.org
This house was built in 1739 for the missionary Reverend John Sergeant and his wife, Abigail Williams. Today it serves as a museum of colonial life with outstanding antique furniture and decorative arts.
June-mid-October, Thursday-Monday 11 a.m.-3 p.m.

NAUMKEAG
1 Seargeant St., Stockbridge, 413-298-3239; www.thetrustees.org
Stanford White designed this Norman-style "Berkshire cottage" in 1886. The interior features antiques, Oriental rugs and a collection of Chinese export porcelain. The formal gardens include terraces of tree peonies, ornate fountains and a birch walk.
Mid-May-mid-October, daily 10 a.m.-5 p.m.

NORMAN ROCKWELL MUSEUM
9 Glendale Road, Stockbridge, 413-298-4100; www.nrm.org
The museum maintains and exhibits the world's largest collection of original art by Norman Rockwell, with 574 original paintings and drawings. Rockwell lived in Stockbridge for the last 25 years of his life—see the artist's Stockbridge studio, which has been relocated to the museum grounds, when you visit between May and October.
Daily.

TYRINGHAM

SANTARELLA
75 Main Road, Tyringham, 413-243-2819, 760-212-1577; www.santarella.us
This 1920s-era studio is the former workplace of sculptor Sir Henry Kitson, creator of the Minuteman statue in Lexington. The studio's roof was designed to look like the rolling hills of the Berkshires, whereas the fronting rock pillars and grottoes were inspired by similar edifices in Europe. This unique and charming setting is situated on a four-acre estate.

WILLIAMSTOWN
STERLING AND FRANCINE CLARK ART INSTITUTE
225 South St., Williamstown, 413-458-2303; www.clarkart.edu

Rare among small, rural museums is a collection like this—the Clark houses more than 30 paintings by Renoir and other French Impressionists, as well as English and American silver and works by American artists like Homer, Sargent, Cassatt and Remington.

July-early September, daily; rest of year, Tuesday-Sunday.

WILLIAMS COLLEGE
54 Sawyer Library Drive, Williamstown, 413-597-3131; www.williams.edu

A private liberal arts college established in 1793, Williams features an idyllic 450-acre campus in the Berkshires. For visitors, highlights include the Chapin Library of rare books, which houses the four founding documents of the United States. The Hopkins Observatory is another great attraction—the oldest observatory in the United States, it features planetarium shows.

WILLIAMS COLLEGE MUSEUM OF ART
15 Lawrence Hall Drive, Williamstown, 413-597-2429; www.wcma.org

One of the finest college art museums in the country, the WCMA houses approximately 13,000 works that span the history of art—from ancient Greek decorative arts to European classics and 19th-century paintings by Winslow Homer. Because the museum has an educational agenda, admission is always free.

Tuesday-Saturday 10 a.m.-5 p.m., Sunday 1-5 p.m.

WHERE TO STAY

DEERFIELD
★★★DEERFIELD INN
81 Old Main St., Deerfield, 413-774-5587, 800-926-3865; www.deerfieldinn.com

This 1884 inn hasn't changed much over the years. The sitting parlors still exhibit period wallpaper and antiques, and the ten main guest rooms remain decorated with period-style furnishings and antiques. Modern updates include sparkling bathrooms, four-poster beds and a 13-room barn annex. The inn is supposedly haunted, though that hasn't scared away the guests—it's perpetually packed, with some Deerfield Academy parents booking rooms four years in advance of their child's graduation.

23 rooms. Complimentary breakfast. Restaurant, bar. $151-250

LENOX
★★★★★BLANTYRE
16 Blantyre Road, Lenox, 413-637-3556; www.blantyre.com

Gilded Age charm abounds at this Tudor-style inn in the Berkshire Mountains. Blantyre's guest rooms maintain a decidedly British country style, with floral fabric, overstuffed furniture and in some quarters, fireplaces. Activities include croquet, tennis, swimming and convenience to the cultural festivities at nearby Tanglewood and Jacob's Pillow. Dining at Blantyre makes for a special occasion—the chef even packs gourmet picnics for guests to take with them while exploring the region.

25 rooms. Children over 12 years only. Complimentary breakfast. Spa. Restaurant, bar. $351 and up

★★★CRANWELL RESORT SPA AND GOLF CLUB

55 Lee Road, Lenox, 413-637-1364, 800-272-6935; www.cranwell.com

Perfect for active vacationers, this 100-year-old luxury hotel is set atop a hill and surrounded by 380 acres of the beautiful Berkshires. The inn's 18-hole championship golf course is host to Beecher's golf school, a friendly place to learn the game. Meanwhile, inside the stone turreted main home, visitors find an enormous new spa and fitness center, complete with yoga studios and a pool.

108 rooms. Restaurant, bar. Spa. Fitness center. $251-350

★★★GATEWAYS INN

51 Walker St., Lenox, 413-637-2532, 888-492-9466; www.gatewaysinn.com

A white Colonial-style mansion is the setting for this classic country inn. Guest rooms are individually decorated with antiques, some with private fireplaces. The onsite restaurant is more than a breakfast joint—it offers an elegant dining room with nightly helpings of fresh pastas, grilled steaks and seafood.

11 rooms. Complimentary breakfast. Restaurant, bar. $151-250

★★★WHEATLEIGH

Hawthorne Road, Lenox, 413-637-0610; www.wheatleigh.com

Wheatleigh is a country house hotel of the finest order. Housed in a 19th-century Italianate palazzo, the inn is set on 22 acres of hills and Frederick Law Olmsted-designed gardens. Details make the difference here, from the dazzling Tiffany windows to the ornate fireplace in the Great Hall. The guest rooms are comfortably elegant with English soaking tubs, exclusive bath amenities from Ermenegildo Zegna and raw silk coverlets. The restaurant, with its updated French dishes, draws foodies from throughout the Berkshires.

19 rooms. No children under 9. Restaurant, bar. $351 and up

NORTH ADAMS
★★★THE PORCHES INN

231 River St., North Adams, 413-664-0400; www.porches.com

Located directly across the street from Mass MoCA, this unusual inn was converted from row houses where local mill workers used to reside. The inn has been painstakingly restored and decorated with sleek, modern furnishings and original artwork. Sure, there are down duvets and rocking chairs, but most of the guests here are just as interested in hipster flourishes like lunch-pail room service and the bonfire pit.

52 rooms. Complimentary breakfast. Fitness center. $151-250

NORTHAMPTON
★★★THE HOTEL NORTHAMPTON

36 King St., Northampton, 413-584-3100, 800-547-3529; www.hotelnorthampton.com

Built in 1927, this brick Colonial Revival-style inn sits on a busy street opposite the restored Calvin Theater. A narrow glass greenhouse enwraps half the building, and the hotel's public areas are adorned with museum-quality Norman Rockwell prints and Japanese woodcuts. Meanwhile, in the guest rooms, colonial furnishings lend a stately vibe, while the hotel's two restaurants round out the elegant experience.

106 rooms. Complimentary breakfast. Restaurant, bar. $151-250

SPRINGFIELD

★★★MARRIOTT SPRINGFIELD

1500 Main St., Springfield, 413-781-7111, 800-228-9290; www.marriott.com

At this business hotel, it's all about the beds—extra-thick mattresses, duvets, bed skirts, plush pillows. The hotel is conveniently connected via an enclosed walkway to a shopping complex with plentiful restaurants, art galleries, an African-American history museum, even a billiards parlor.

265 rooms. Restaurant, bar. $151-250

★★★SHERATON SPRINGFIELD MONARCH PLACE HOTEL

1 Monarch Place, Springfield, 413-781-1010; www.sheraton-springfield.com

Guest rooms in this contemporary, urban spot have a spacious, airy vibe—after all, they surround an open, 12-story atrium. The public areas feature intimate touches like a folk art mural of Springfield's historical sights. The hotel's Athletic Club is the largest hotel health club west of Boston, and spa services include massages and manicures. Business travelers should ask for a smart room, complete with its own photocopier and fax machine.

325 rooms. Restaurant, bar. $151-250

STOCKBRIDGE

★★★THE RED LION INN

30 Main St., Stockbridge, 413-298-5545; www.redlioninn.com

The Red Lion Inn was once immortalized by Norman Rockwell in his hearty, happy Stockbridge street scenes. Nowadays its guest rooms are just as snug, though the inn added modern amenities like a heated swimming pool and in-suite massage services. For roomier digs, book one of the inn's off-site suites, which are sprinkled among a handful of buildings throughout town. Favorites include the former studio of artist Daniel Chester French and the former home of the Stockbridge Volunteer Fire Department.

100 rooms. Restaurant, bar. $151-250

★★★WILLIAMSVILLE INN

Highway 41, West Stockbridge, 413-274-6118; www.williamsvilleinn.com

Run by a German husband-and-wife team, the Williamsville Inn blends Shaker-style austerity with modern comfort. Its blond-wood floors are spotless, as are its white bed linens and bath towels. But fresh flowers scent each room, and guests are free to enjoy the property's extensive gardens, clay tennis courts and swimming pool. The food is delicious—and authentic—at the onsite Taste of Germany restaurant.

16 rooms. Complimentary breakfast. Restaurant, bar. $61-150

WILLIAMSTOWN

★★★1896 HOUSE

910 Cold Spring Road, Williamstown, 413-458-1896, 888-999-1896; www.1896house.com

The options run from posh to affordable at this historic inn. For example, guests can book the brook-side room, an intimate suite that features Cushman rock maple furniture and a private porch. No matter where you stay, you'll enjoy the landscape of rivers, gardens, footbridges and gazebos.

29 rooms. Complimentary breakfast. Restaurant. $61-150

★★★THE ORCHARDS

222 Adams Road, Williamstown, 413-458-9611, 800-225-1517; www.orchardshotel.com

Grand gates made of Vermont granite welcome visitors to this chateau-style property, located east of the village center. With bay windows and marble-floored baths, the rooms are decorated in English country style. The public spaces feature oriental rugs and Austrian crystal chandeliers. The outstanding onsite restaurant serves a mix of continental and American cuisine—you can even have your meal outdoors in the garden during summer months.

49 rooms. Restaurant, bar. $151-250

RECOMMENDED

GREAT BARRINGTON

THORNEWOOD INN & RESTAURANT

453 Stockbridge Road, Great Barrington, 413-528-3828, 800-854-1008; www.thornewood.com

This turn-of-the-century inn features Dutch colonial-style architecture, period antiques, French doors and private fireplaces. The beautifully landscaped gardens are enhanced by an outdoor pool.

13 rooms. No children under 12. Complimentary breakfast. Restaurant. $151-250

WINDFLOWER INN

684 S. Egremont Road, Great Barrington, 413-528-2720, 800-992-1993; www.windflowerinn.com

Situated on 10 acres of hilly Berkshires terrain, this white clapboard inn features a quaint screen porch, period antiques, four-poster beds and private wood-burning fireplaces. The estate dates back to the 1850s and is convenient to the famous Tanglewood music center.

13 rooms. Complimentary breakfast. $151-250

LENOX

BIRCHWOOD INN

7 Hubbard St., Lenox, 413-637-2600, 800-524-1646; www.birchwood-inn.com

Built in 1767, this columned white Colonial has served as an inn ever since. The bed and breakfast is decorated with antiques and collectibles and features meticulously kept guest rooms and gardens. Breakfast, meanwhile, is a strictly gourmet affair, with freshly baked breads and soufflés. The innkeepers deliver a heaping plate of fresh chocolate-chip cookies to satisfy afternoon cravings.

11 rooms. Complimentary breakfast. No children under 12. Pets accepted. $151-250

BROOK FARM INN

15 Hawthorne St., Lenox, 413-637-3013, 800-285-7638; www.brookfarm.com

An impressive library of poetry, fiction and history lends a literary feel to this property. Located just one mile from Tanglewood, the Victorian inn is convenient for music-lovers, too. Start the day with a complimentary breakfast buffet worthy of a gourmand. Tea and homemade scones are served in the afternoon.

15 rooms. No children under 15. Complimentary breakfast. $151-250

KEMBLE INN

2 Kemble St., Lenox, 413-637-4113, 800-353-4113; www.kembleinn.com

Located on three acres in the center of historic Lenox, this 1881 inn features magnificent views of the Berkshire Mountains. The newly redecorated guest rooms are named for various famous authors—Charles Dickens, Henry James. Enjoy a home-cooked breakfast in the morning and convenience to the cultural attractions of Tanglewood and downtown Lenox.

14 rooms. No children under 12. Complimentary breakfast. $151-250

ROOKWOOD INN

11 Old Stockbridge Road, Lenox, 413-637-9750, 800-223-9750; www.rookwoodinn.com

The guest rooms at this 1885 Victorian inn are furnished with English antiques, some with fireplaces. Located just a block from the center of Lenox, the bed and breakfast is also close to the art, music and theater of Tanglewood

21 rooms. Complimentary breakfast. $151-250

LEE

APPLEGATE

279 W. Park St., Lee, 413-243-4451, 800-691-9012; www.applegateinn.com

This Georgian Colonial mansion was built in the 1920s. Now a charming bed and breakfast, the property features six acres of rose gardens, perennial beds, apple trees, even horse farms. Guests are treated to complimentary breakfasts, afternoon wine and cheese service and bedtime cognacs.

11 rooms. No children under 12. Complimentary breakfast. Pool. $61-150

DEVONFIELD INN

85 Stockbridge Road, Lee, 413-243-3298, 800-664-0880; www.devonfield.com

Located in the heart of the Berkshires, this Federal-era manor house offers a comfortable stay. Guest rooms are individually decorated with antiques, some with fireplaces. Complimentary breakfast is served to the accompaniment of candlelight and classical music.

10 rooms. No children under 10. Complimentary breakfast. $151-250

FEDERAL HOUSE INN

1560 Pleasant St., South Lee, 413-243-1824, 800-243-1824; www.federalhouseinn.com

This 1824 inn borders the Housatonic River and the Beartown State Forest. Guest rooms display a casual, country-style aesthetic with lacy curtains and quilts. Special perks include access to golf and tennis at nearby Stockbridge Country Club, complimentary three-course breakfast and free afternoon wine reception.

10 rooms. No children under 12. Complimentary breakfast. Bar. $151-250

HISTORIC MERRELL INN
1565 Pleasant St., South Lee, 413-243-1794, 800-243-1794; www.merrell-inn.com

This old stagecoach inn sits on two acres of picturesque Housatonic Riverfront property, with excellent views of the Berkshire Mountains. Guest rooms are decorated in the classic New England country style with antiques and floral bed linens. Guests can personalize their complimentary breakfast—because they order off a menu.

10 rooms. Complimentary breakfast. $61-150

RECOMMENDED

INN AT STOCKBRIDGE
Highway 7 N., Stockbridge, 413-298-3337; www.stockbridgeinn.com

An in-room decanter of port. Breakfast in a formal dining room. A large parlor with fireside chairs. A stroll through 12 secluded acres. Sound appealing? This 1906 Georgian-style inn has just eight guest rooms, but it's so private the guests get to savor the topnotch amenities. The Cottage House has four junior suites, and The Barn provides four deluxe suites.

16 rooms. No children under 12. Complimentary breakfast. Fitness center. Spa. $251-350

THE TAGGART HOUSE
18 W. Main St., Stockbridge, 413-298-4303, 800-918-2680; www.taggarthouse.com

This lovingly restored 1800s country house fronts the Housatonic River. Guest rooms are comfortable and intimate, with heated towels and fine antiques. Other perks include complimentary candlelit breakfast and an afternoon reception with wine and fresh local cheese.

4 rooms. Complimentary breakfast. $251-350

WHERE TO EAT

DEERFIELD

★★★CHAMPNEY'S
81 Old Main St., Deerfield, 413-774-5587, 800-926-3865; www.deerfieldinn.com

The inn's dining room is among the finest in the area, with fresh, local ingredients fueling classic New England dishes like lobster cakes and Berkshire pork chops. Reservations are a must, though, since Deerfield students routinely pack the place.

American. Breakfast, dinner. Bar. Children's menu. Reservations recommended. $16-35

★★★SIENNA
6B Elm St., Deerfield, 413-665-0215; www.siennarestaurant.com

American cooking gets a French-inspired flourish at this contemporary, 45-seat restaurant. Chef-owner Karl Braverman is committed to using seasonally available ingredients. Don't miss his duck with white potato, blood orange, bok choy and Spanish vinegar demi-glace.

American. Dinner. Closed Sunday and Tuesday. $16-35

GREAT BARRINGTON

★★★CASTLE STREET CAFÉ
10 Castle St., Great Barrington, 413-528-5244; www.castlestreetcafe.com

Chef-owner Michael Ballon's lively restaurant is divided into two parts: a fine-dining room and the more casual Celestial Bar. White tablecloths and candles decorate the former, while live music and multicolored pendant lamps set the tone in the lively bar. Think burgers and salads. No matter what you order, the eatery's classic American food is consistently fresh.

American. Dinner. Bar. Closed Tuesday. $16-35

LENOX

★★★BISTRO ZINC
56 Church St., Lenox, 413-637-8800; www.bistrozinc.com

Convenient to Tanglewood, this hotspot is a good choice for pre-concert meals. Guests appreciate the contemporary décor, a tasteful array of black-and-white tile, tin ceilings, burgundy banquettes and a large copper bar. The French-American menu is the standout, thanks to favorites like ginger-encrusted salmon and entrecote aux oignons.

French. Lunch, dinner, late-night. Bar. Reservations recommended. $36-85

★★★BLANTYRE
16 Blantyre Road, Lenox, 413-637-3556; www.blantyre.com

This 1902 mansion offers a rare culinary experience. First, the impeccable wait staff treats diners to pre-dinner champagne and canapes on the terrace or in the Music Room. Next, everyone retreats to the dining room: antique glassware and place settings set the romantic tone for a feast on chef Christopher Brooks' rich, sophisticated fare.

French. Breakfast, lunch, dinner. Jacket required. Reservations recommended. Bar. $36-85

★★★GATEWAYS INN
51 Walker St., Lenox, 413-637-2532, 888-492-9466; www.gatewaysinn.com

At the Gateways, the chefs incorporate local produce and dairy products in every dish. The restaurant features a diversity of seating options, though the best tables are in the main dining room—its French doors and terra cotta walls recall a Tuscan country inn.

American. Breakfast, lunch, dinner. Bar. Reservations recommended. Closed Monday September-June. $36-85

★★★WHEATLEIGH
Hawthorne Road, Lenox, 413-637-0610; www.wheatleigh.com

Polished mahogany doors lead to the hotel's regal dining room, which was modeled in 1893 after a 16th-century Florentine palazzo. Dine on contemporary French cuisine in a sun-drenched room filled with oil paintings, hand-carved Chippendale chairs and a large wood-burning fireplace. Favorite dishes include the roasted Maine lobster and the sweet corn soufflé with cassis ice cream.

French. Dinner, Sunday brunch. Bar. Reservations recommended. $86 and up

★★★THE WYNDHURST RESTAURANT

55 Lee Road, Lenox, 413-637-1364, 800-272-6935; www.cranwell.com

Cranwell Resort's main dining room is located on the first floor of the 100-year-old Tudor mansion. Large windows offer vistas of the Berkshire Hills and the fireplace keeps guests warm on cold New England nights. The French and American cuisine highlights local ingredients, with an emphasis on game and cheese.

American, French. Lunch, dinner. Reservations recommended. $251-350

STOCKBRIDGE

★★★THE RED LION

30 Main St., Stockbridge, 413-298-5545; www.redlioninn.com

It doesn't get any more classic than this fine dining restaurant. This inn's candlelit dining room is filled with antiques, colonial pewter and crystal. Meanwhile, the contemporary New England menu emphasizes local, seasonal produce—including several vegetarian options. Try the chicken pot pie or the maple cured pork tenderloin if either is on the menu.

American. Lunch, dinner. Bar. Children's menu. Reservations recommended. Outdoor seating. $36-85

★★★WILLIAMSVILLE INN

Highway 41, West Stockbridge, 413-274-6118; www.williamsvilleinn.com

This cozy dining room features an open fireplace and plenty of candlelight. But what's really special about the German eatery is its open kitchen. Guests are free to observe chef-owner Erhard Wendt in his yellow-walled workspace—in fact, he often invites them to take a closer look. The food is rich and savory. In other words, don't pass on dessert.

French, German. Dinner, brunch. Bar. Reservations recommended. Outdoor seating. $36-85

WILLIAMSTOWN

★★★GALA RESTAURANT & BAR

222 Adams Road, Williamstown, 413-458-9611, 800-225-1517; www.galarestaurant.com

Gold and red brocade chairs and white tablecloths dress the room's interior at Gala, located in the Orchards Hotel. Here, the chef incorporates high-quality local ingredients into classic American dishes like apple and cheddar-stuffed pork chop, merlot-braised New Zealand lamb shank and seared Atlantic salmon. A wine cellar with a tasting room is used for chef's tables and private functions.

American menu. Breakfast, lunch, dinner, Sunday brunch. Bar. Reservations recommended. Outdoor seating. $16-35

RECOMMENDED

LEE

CORK N' HEARTH

Route 20 Laurel Lake, Lee, 413-243-0535; www.corknhearth.com

This classic New England restaurant boasts views of Laurel Lake and a cozy wood-beamed interior. The menu is the true showstopper—it features innovative takes on classics like grilled Atlantic salmon, roast duck and roasted pork prime rib.

Seafood, steak. Dinner. Bar. Children's menu. Closed Monday. $16-35

NORTHAMPTON
EASTSIDE GRILL
19 Strong Ave., Northampton, 413-586-3347; www.eastsidegrill.com

With a lengthy menu offering a range of eclectic dishes, this casual bistro offers something for everyone. Entrées include classics like baked Atlantic cod with lobster bisque as well as more eclectic dishes like blackened rib-eye and chicken etouffée.

American. Dinner. Bar. $16-35

SPRINGFIELD
STUDENT PRINCE & FORT
8 Fort St., Springfield, 413-788-6628; www.studentprince.com

Known for its classic German menu, this dark, cozy restaurant has been in operation for 75 years. Check out the large selection of imported German beers, the perfect pairing for schnitzels, sauerbratens or Hungarian-style goulash.

German. Lunch, dinner. Bar. $16-35

WELCOME TO MAINE

MAYBE IT'S THE FLANNEL-CLAD LOBSTERMEN, OR MAYBE

it's the salty sea air. Whatever it is, there's definitely something special about Maine. With the highest tides in the country and the full spectrum of seasons on display, Maine is sure to promise an intense sensory experience.

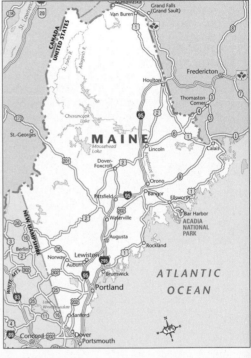

The state offers a vast playground of natural beauty, populated (in some places sparsely) by 1.2 million hearty Mainers who earn their stripes by surviving the long, dark winters. The state boasts 17.6 million acres of protected woodlands. Acadia National Park is one of the nation's wildest and most beautiful areas, filled with a resurgent bald eagle population. Six-thousand lakes and 3,500 miles of coastline make Maine a great place to spy sea life, too. Penobscot Bay, for example, is a popular destination for seals, porpoises and migratory whales. But these waters aren't so hospitable to humans, with summertime water temperatures hovering at 50 F.

Come summertime, the state fills with sojourners who feast on lobster, poke through antique shops, and sail the rugged, rocky coast. Many visitors skip the lighthouses and country inns altogether, opting instead for the cosmopolitan scenes they find in Portland, Augusta and Bangor.

Of course, fall rivals summer as the most popular time to visit New England's largest state, and the locals have a curious name for all the tourists who come to ogle the autumn landscape—leaf peepers. In any case, their presence keeps the state's inns, restaurants and roadways packed to capacity through October.

HIGHLIGHTS

MAINE'S BEST ATTRACTIONS

ACADIA NATIONAL PARK

This national park is a playground for bald eagles and those who love to observe them. Located off the central coast of Maine, the rugged granite terrain is perfect for hiking and rock-climbing. Meanwhile, the surrounding sea, with its many bays and inlets, makes for excellent sailing.

LOBSTER FESTIVALS

Nothing says Maine like a piping hot steamed lobster. Celebrate the state's premier crustacean at the annual Maine Lobster Festival in Rockland with harbor cruises, a parade and more lobster-inspired dishes than you can possibly eat.

KENNEBUNKPORT

The Bush family isn't the only gang of bluebloods that flocks to this fishing village. Perched at the mouth of the Kennebunk River, the coastal town is chock-full of antique shops, Victorian inns and dockside restaurants. Although summer is the area's busiest season, the fall foliage provides a handy excuse to visit off-season.

FREEPORT

When in Maine, you'll want to dress like a Mainer, and you can stock up on chinos and flannel at the famous outlets in Freeport. Along with more than 170 different outlet stores, Freeport is also home to L.L.Bean's flagship, a mega-store that stays open 24 hours a day.

SOUTHWEST COAST

Most Americans know about the Bush family's warm-weather compound in Kennebunkport, a picture-perfect town along Maine's southwest coast. Fewer people know about the town's history—it's been a blueblood magnet for more than a century, thanks to stalwart establishments like the Colony Hotel. Today, the town is packed with upscale establishments, from fine restaurants and Victorian inns to fashionable boutiques and world-class destination spas, such as the one at the White Barn Inn.

Venture south from Kennebunkport and you encounter a string of villages that are equally beautiful, though most are less exclusive. Maine's oldest settlement, Kittery features cobblestone streets, beautiful old houses and other historic structures. Today, the historic shipbuilding town is also a popular shopping destination, thanks to its many antique shops and outlet stores.

The town of York is, in spirit, four separate communities—Cape Neddick, York Harbor, York Village and York Beach were once separate municipalities, though now they share a single city government. While these family-friendly spots feature quintessential Maine sights like lighthouses and craggy coastal scenes, the area is also famous for its sandy beaches.

In fact, the Southwest Coast is blessed with the state's friendliest beaches. But the sandiest, whitest stretch is found near Ogunquit, a resort community with an artistic streak. The town's public beach is considered one of the finest on the Atlantic coast. As for the town itself, it offers plenty more than coastline to occupy its guests: excellent restaurants, funky galleries, quirky shops, even its own theater company.

WHAT TO SEE

KENNEBUNKPORT AND KENNEBUNK
BRICK STORE MUSEUM
117 Main St., Kennebunk, 207-985-4802; www.brickstoremuseum.org

This block of restored 19th-century buildings is the one-time home of William Lord's Brick Store, once owned by the richest man in Kennebunk. Today, the beautiful block functions as a regional history and archives center. It also features regular exhibits of fine and decorative arts, historical and maritime collections.

Tuesday-Friday, 10 a.m.-4.30 p.m., Saturday 10 a.m.-1 p.m. Parking available.

SCHOOL HOUSE
135 N. St., Kennebunkport, 207-967-2751; www.kporthistory.org

The 1899 schoolhouse is now the headquarters of the Kennebunkport Historical Society, a great place to peruse collections of genealogy, photography, maritime history and many artifacts and documents from throughout Kennebunkport's history.

Tuesday-Friday.

HIGHLIGHTS

WHAT ARE THE TOP THINGS TO DO IN THE SOUTHWEST COAST?

UNWIND AT OLD ORCHARD BEACH

A destination for more than 170 years, Old Orchard Beach features an old-fashioned pier flanked by miles upon miles of sandy beach. In warm weather months, the pier features nightly entertainment like dancing, live concerts and fireworks.

GALLERY-HOPPING IN OGUNQUIT

Ogunquit is a resort town with an artistic heart and a cluster of galleries to match. When you're done perusing the town's galleries, check out the Ogunquit Museum of American Art, one of the country's most beautiful small museums.

SHOPPING IN KITTERY

A quaint town with plentiful discounts, Kittery features 120 outlet stores for upscale retailers like Izod, J. Crew and Calvin Klein.

KITTERY

FORT FOSTER PARK

Northeast via Highway 103 to Gerrish Island, 207-439-3800; www.kittery.org

This 92-acre park offers everything you expect from a park: a pavilion, a beach, a baseball field and a fishing pier. Cross-country skiing is available in winter. What's different, though, are the crumbling WWII-era cement forts and the spectacular path that hugs the rocky shoreline. Entrance fee per individual and per vehicle.

June-August, daily; May, September, Saturday-Sunday.

KITTERY HISTORICAL AND NAVAL MUSEUM

Highway 1 and Rogers Road, Kittery, 207-439-3080; www.kitterymuseum.com

This tiny museum captures the history of Kittery, Maine's oldest incorporated town, with an emphasis on maritime artifacts like U.S. Navy uniforms, ship models, lighthouse artifacts and vintage diving gear.

June-October, Tuesday-Saturday 10 a.m.-4 p.m.

OGUNQUIT

OGUNQUIT MUSEUM OF AMERICAN ART

543 Shore Road, Ogunquit, 207-646-4909; www.ogunquitmuseum.org

In every way, this institution reflects the funky town in which it's situated. The museum overlooks the ocean and nearby sculpture gardens, and also features an excellent collection of 20th-century American sculpture and painting, with a special emphasis on arts affiliated with the Ogunquit arts colony.

July-mid-October, daily.

OGUNQUIT PLAYHOUSE

10 Highway 1, Northeast Harbor, 207-646-2402; www.ogunquitplayhouse.org

Established in the early 1930s, this playhouse is more than a small-town stage. It features top plays and musicals, often starring familiar actors from television and film.

Late June-Early September.

OLD ORCHARD BEACH
THE PIER

Old Orchard Beach

One of Maine's few sandy beaches, Old Orchard Beach is a seven-mile beach. The centerpiece, though, is the 113-year-old pier that extends 475 feet into the harbor and features shops, boutiques and a restaurant.

Daily, May-September.

SOUTH BERWICK
SARAH ORNE JEWETT HOUSE

5 Portland St., South Berwick, 207-384-2454; www.spnea.org

Novelist Sarah Orne Jewett spent most of her life in this 1774 Georgian residence. Now a museum, the house's interior has been restored to look as it did during Jewett's lifetime (1849-1909). But some things haven't changed: the house contains some original 18th- and 19th-century wallpaper and fine paneling as well as Jewett's bedroom-study, which was left exactly as it was.

June-mid-October, Friday-Sunday.

YORK
EMERSON-WILCOX HOUSE

York and Lindsey Roads, York; www.oldyork.org

Built in 1742, with later additions, the Emerson-Wilcox House intermittently served as a general store, a tavern and a post office, as well as the home of two of the town's prominent early families. It now contains a series of period rooms dating to 1750 and is furnished with the era's antiques.

June-mid-October, Tuesday-Saturday.

JOHN HANCOCK WAREHOUSE

York and Lindsey Roads, York, 207-363-4974; www.oldyork.org

Owned by John Hancock until 1794, this is the city's only remaining commercial building from the Colonial period. It's also the state's oldest surviving customs house, a place where taxes were collected on imported goods. The building is now used to interpret York's maritime and commercial history.

June-mid-October, Tuesday-Saturday.

OLD GAOL

Lindsay Road, York

Built in 1719 with 18th-century additions, the jail is one of the oldest English public buildings in the United States. It was, in fact, used as a jail until 1860. Now it's open to law-abiding citizens who want to peek at the dungeons and cells that once held felons and debtors. Visitors will also find galleries of local historical artifacts and an exhibit of late 1800s photography.

June-mid-October, Tuesday-Saturday.

YORK HARBOR
SAYWARD-WHEELER HOUSE
9 Barrell Lane, York Harbor, 207-384-2454; www.spnea.org

This conservatively furnished 18th-century house was once owned by Jonathan Sayward, a merchant, civic leader and loyalist to the British patriarch till his dying day. Today, it's open to visitors as a historic house museum.

Tours. June-mid-October, second and fourth Saturdays of the month.

WHERE TO STAY

KENNEBUNKPORT
★★★THE COLONY HOTEL
140 Ocean Ave., Kennebunkport, 207-967-3331, 800-552-2363; www.thecolonyhotel.com

Located on a rock promontory overlooking the Atlantic Ocean and the mouth of the Kennebunk River, this hotel features a heated saltwater pool, beach and gardens. Other nearby activities include golfing, tennis, kayaking, bicycling, boating, shopping and touring art galleries. Best of all, you'll find Maine lobster and local seafood on the menu at the in-house restaurant.

125 rooms. Restaurant, bar. Beach. Pool. Closed November-mid-May. $151-250

★★★KENNEBUNKPORT INN
One Dock Square, Kennebunkport, 207-967-2621, 800-248-2621; www.kennebunkportinn.com

Built by a wealthy tea and coffee merchant in 1899, the Victorian mansion was renovated and reopened as an inn in 1926. Conveniently located in the heart of historic Kennebunkport, the inn is an easy walk to the harbor and all the shops and galleries of Dock Square. Guest rooms are decorated in period detail, with antiques and reproductions alike. Four-poster beds, elegant fabrics and floral carpeting round out the look.

49 rooms. Complimentary breakfast. Restaurant, bar. Spa. Pool. $251-350

★★★NONANTUM RESORT
95 Ocean Ave., Kennebunkport, 207-967-4050, 800-552-5651;www.nonantumresort.com

Founded in 1883, this is one of the longest operating inns in the state. The beach is nearby, as is the Bush family compound. But you won't give a thought to president-peeping once you experience the onsite restaurant and its selection of tasty Maine seafood.

111 rooms. Restaurant, bar. Pool. Closed mid-November-April. $61-150

★★★★THE WHITE BARN INN
37 Beach Ave., Kennebunkport, 207-967-2321; www.whitebarninn.com

This quaint, coastal resort is made up of cottages, restored barns and a circa-1860s main house. No matter where you book your room, you're sure to enjoy the elegant appointments: antiques, wood-burning fireplaces, whirlpool tubs and flat-screen TVs. Simple pleasure here include swimming in the stone pool, biking the coast, experiencing a spa treatment or taking afternoon tea by the fire in the comfortable sitting room. The inn houses one of the region's most acclaimed restaurants, where diners enjoy New England cuisine in a rustic, candlelit setting.

25 rooms. Complimentary breakfast. Restaurant, bar. Spa. Pool. Business center. $351 and up

OGUNQUIT

★★★ANCHORAGE BY THE SEA

125 Shore Road, Ogunquit, 207-646-9384; www.anchoragebythesea.com

This airy, family-friendly property is perched directly beside the ocean, with spacious rooms spread over several different buildings. Accommodations are simple, elegant and private, with many rooms featuring fireplaces. Be sure to meet your fellow resort-goers at the several indoor and outdoor pools—or better yet, at the poolside bar and grill.

212 rooms. Complimentary breakfast. Restaurant. Pool. $61-150

YORK HARBOR

★★★STAGE NECK INN

8 Stage Neck Road, York Harbor, 207-363-3850, 800-340-1130; www.stageneck.com

This boutique resort is located on a craggy peninsula, but it's also next door to a sandy private beach. With a full-service spa, seasonal clay tennis courts and a British Colonial aesthetic, it offers all the luxuries a tasteful vacationer needs. When it's time to venture out, though, you'll find plenty of attractions nearby, including the Kittery outlet malls, antiques shops, art galleries and historic downtown York.

58 rooms. Restaurant, bar. Fitness room. Beach. Pool. Tennis. Spa. $151-250

RECOMMENDED

KENNEBUNK

THE BEACH HOUSE

211 Beach Ave., Kennebunk, 207-967-3850; www.beachhseinn.com

This circa-1890 inn is located on Kennebunk Beach, just two miles from Kennebunkport. Rooms are crisp and contemporary, with plush duvet-topped beds. Afternoon tea is served up in the sitting room, along with a breathtaking view of the ocean.

34 rooms. Complimentary breakfast. Reservations recommended. $351 and up

THE KENNEBUNK INN

45 Main St., Kennebunk, 207-985-3351; www.thekennebunkinn.com

Colonial on the outside, contemporary on the inside—this 1799 inn was recently updated with sleek, modern décor. The property also features a terrific onsite restaurant and is convenient to downtown Kennebunk.

22 rooms. Complimentary breakfast. Restaurant. $61-150

KENNEBUNKPORT

BUFFLEHEAD COVE

Bufflehead Cove Lane, Kennebunkport, 207-967-3879; www.buffleheadcove.com

This Victorian inn is spacious, old-fashioned and private—it's situated off the beaten path on the banks of the Kennebunk River. But it's still convenient to the nearby beaches and downtown Kennebunkport, with its restaurants, galleries, antique shops and bookstores.

6 rooms. No children under 11. Complimentary breakfast. $251-350

CAPE ARUNDEL INN

208 Ocean Ave., Kennebunkport, 207-967-2125; www.capearundelinn.com

At this charming, Victorian-style inn, guests can choose between the 1890 cottage or the ultra-private carriage house. Most rooms overlook the ocean; all are individually decorated in the cozy English country style.

14 rooms. Complimentary breakfast. Restaurant. Closed mid-December-mid-April. $151-250

CAPTAIN FAIRFIELD INN

8 Pleasant St., Kennebunkport, 207-967-4454, 800-322-1928; www.captainfairfield.com

This 1813 bed and breakfast provides a classic example of Federal-style architecture. Guest rooms are fitted with antique and period furniture, each with a private bath and sitting area. Though the inn is centrally located in the heart of Kennebunkport, close to shopping and beaches, it has an aura of privacy thanks to the lush cover of trees and gardens.

9 rooms. No children under 6. Complimentary breakfast. $151-250

THE CAPTAIN JEFFERDS INN

5 Pearl St., Kennebunkport, 207-967-2311, 800-839-6844; www.captainjeffersinn.com

This 1804 inn is filled with antiques and period reproductions, though the guest rooms boast many modern indulgences: private baths, fresh flowers, down-filled comforters and fireplaces. A three-course breakfast and afternoon refreshments are also part of the package.

15 rooms. No children under 8. Complimentary breakfast. Closed last two weeks in December. $251-350

THE CAPTAIN LORD MANSION

6 Pleasant St., Kennebunkport, 207-967-3141, 800-522-3141; www.captainlord.com

Here, the innkeepers used period furnishings and antiques to create guest rooms with varied historic themes: Lincoln, Ophelia, Excelsior and more. Set on an acre of gardens, this luxury inn has a romantic

---

WHAT ARE THE MOST HISTORIC HOTELS?

The Colony Hotel: Ocean porches, gazebos, poolside bar service—it's no wonder this historic, family-owned hotel has such a long history of reeling Brahmin types.

White Barn Inn: Built in the 1820s, this impeccable, New England-style inn is the ultimate romantic getaway. Five-star dining and a new, high-end destination spa are just two of the resort's irresistible services.

Kennebunkport Inn: The former home of a successful tea merchant, this mansion now houses a sophisticated, Victorian-style inn with a great restaurant, onsite spa services and exceptional service.

and sophisticated feel, though there's also a touch of quirk: after their tenth stay, repeat visitors are rewarded with an engraved stone in the Memory Garden.
17 rooms. No children under 12. Complimentary breakfast. $61-150

ENGLISH MEADOWS INN
141 Port Road, Kennebunkport, 207-967-5766, 800-272-0698; www.englishmeadowsinn.com
Housed in a Victorian farmhouse and an attached carriage house dating to the 1860s, this spacious inn is located amid sprawling grounds and gardens, though it's only an eight-minute walk from downtown. Guests enjoy individually decorated, English country-style rooms and high tea in a proper tearoom.
12 rooms. Complimentary breakfast. Closed January. $61-150

OLD FORT INN
8 Old Fort Ave., Kennebunkport, 207-967-5353, 800-828-3678; www.oldfortinn.com
Housed within a turn-of-the-century carriage house built of red brick and local stone, this inn brims with colonial nostalgia. With 15 acres of protected woodlands, an onsite tennis court and heated freshwater pool, it's also an excellent place for sporty vacation-goers. It's located just one block from the Atlantic Ocean, so it's convenient for seafaring types, too.
16 rooms. Complimentary breakfast. Pool. Tennis. Closed mid-December-mid-April. $251-350

OGUNQUIT
HARTWELL HOUSE
312 Shore Road, Ogunquit, 207-646-7210, 800-235-8883; www.hartwellhouseinn.com
At this bed and breakfast, most of the rooms feature French doors that open to terraces or balconies, all of which overlook the property's romantic gardens. Guests are also treated to a full gourmet breakfast and afternoon tea.
16 rooms. No children under 14. Complimentary breakfast. $151-250

YORK
DOCKSIDE GUEST QUARTERS
22 Harris Island Road, York, 207-363-2868, 888-860-7428; www.docksidegq.com
This unique property is more like a compound than an inn, with rooms spread over seven acres of buildings, from the main house to the faraway captain's quarters. Rooms feature contemporary furnishings in bright, cheerful colors and great views of the surrounding harbor.
25 rooms. Restaurant, bar. Closed weekdays late October-December, March-May, December-February. $151-250

YORK HARBOR
EDWARDS HARBORSIDE INN
Stage Neck Road, York Harbor, 207-363-3037; www.edwardsharborside.com
This turn-of-the-century bed and breakfast features period furnishings, fireplaces and an old-fashioned sun porch. When it's time to get closer to the water, there's also a private beach and a deep-water dock, perfect for those who want a better look at the local loberstermen.
9 rooms. Beach. $251-350

YORK HARBOR INN

Coastal Highway 1A, York Harbor, 207-363-5119, 800-343-3869; www.yorkharborinn.com

For the ultimate in cozy, check out the country prints, quilts and antiques that decorate this inn. Some rooms go a step further, with fireplaces or Jacuzzi tubs. The onsite pub is one of the locals' favorite spots for casual dining, while the restaurant offers a more upscale environment.

54 rooms. Complimentary breakfast. Restaurant, bar. Beach. $151-250

WHERE TO EAT

CAPE NEDDICK
★★★CLAY HILL FARM

220 Clay Hill Road, Cape Neddick, 207-361-2272; www.clayhillfarm.com

If you really want to eat in peace, make a dinner reservation at this high-end culinary hideout—it resides in a 1780 farmhouse on 30 acres of protected woodlands. The menu is delightfully epicurean, featuring fresh and seasonal dishes such as basil-roasted haddock with tomato, roasted pork tenderloin and veal marsala.

Seafood. Dinner. Bar. Closed Monday-Wednesday, November-April. $36-85

KENNEBUNK
★★★GRISSINI

27 Western Ave., Kennebunk, 207-967-2211; www.restaurantgrissini.com

Grissini offers Tuscan cooking in an airy, loft-like setting. Features include a large stone fireplace, an open kitchen and an outdoor garden dining area. The pastas and pizzas are made fresh daily in true Tuscan form.

Italian. Dinner. Bar. Reservations recommended. Outdoor seating. $16-35

KENNEBUNKPORT
★★★STRIPERS

131-133 Ocean Ave., Kennebunkport, 207-967-5333; www.thebreakwaterinn.com

The décor of this waterside restaurant is contemporary yet cozy—think light green surfaces, steel-rimmed tabletops and a see-through aquarium wall that divides the entry from the main dining room. Along those very lines, the menu demonstrates a commitment to eating local with Kennebunkport oysters, farm-raised striped bass, halibut and scallops. Located within the Breakwater Inn and Spa, Stripers is close to Dock Square's shops and galleries.

Seafood. Dinner, brunch. Bar. Reservations recommended. Outdoor seating. Closed late October-early April. $36-85

★★★★★THE WHITE BARN INN RESTAURANT

The White Barn Inn, 37 Beach Ave., Kennebunkport, 207-967-2321; www.whitebarninn.com

A New England classic, this charming candlelit space is bedecked with fresh flowers and white linen-topped tables. Executive chef Jonathan Cartwright creates delicious regional dishes accented with European flair. His four-course prix-fixe menu changes weekly, highlighting seasonal seafood from Maine's waters as well as native game and poultry. Best of all, the restaurant has a vast wine selection that complements the cuisine, and a rolling cheese cart that features some of the finest local artisans.

American. Bar. Jacket required. Reservations recommended. Closed three weeks in January. $86 and up

OGUNQUIT

★★★98 PROVENCE

262 Shore Road, Ogunquit, 207-646-9898; www.98provence.com

The clapboard house and cottage-like setting provides a warm, comfortable atmosphere for this country French-style restaurant. The menu changes seasonally, though it often features classics like fisherman soup, escargot, duck confit and cassoulet.

French. Dinner. Bar. Closed Tuesday; mid-December-mid-April. $16-35

★★★ARROWS

Berwick Road, Ogunquit, 207-361-1100; www.arrowsrestaurant.com

Housed in an idyllic 18th-century farmhouse, this restaurant is operated by a pair of serious seasonal dining enthusiasts. Co-owners and co-chefs Clark Frasier and Mark Gaier bake their own breads, grow their own organic vegetables and offer a creative, elegant menu with plenty of local seafood options. The dining rooms are filled with fresh flowers from the onsite gardens, and the service is great, too.

American. Dinner. Bar. Reservations recommended. Closed Monday; also December-early April. $36-85

★★★JONATHAN'S

92 Bourne Lane, Ogunquit, 207-646-4777; www.jonathansrestaurant.com

This restaurant is located in a house surrounded by flower and vegetable gardens that once belonged to the owner's parents. Fittingly, the house specialty is fresh, seasonal ingredients with fruits, vegetables and even the lamb coming from the restaurant's own farm.

American. Dinner. Bar. Closed Monday. $16-35

OLD ORCHARD BEACH

★★★JOSEPH'S BY THE SEA

55 W. Grand Ave., Old Orchard Beach, 207-934-5044; www.josephsbythesea.com

This upscale waterfront restaurant might look old-fashioned, but the food is comfortably modern, offering tasty updates to several American classics—seared scallops with arugula and mustard vinaigrette, baked stuffed lobster and braised pork shank in orange-ginger sauce.

American, seafood. Breakfast, dinner. Bar. Reservations recommended. Outdoor seating. $16-35

YORK

★★★YORK HARBOR INN

Highway 1A, York Harbor, 207-363-5119; www.yorkharborinn.com

Antique furnishings, floral wallpaper and lace curtains set the mood at this quaint, Colonial inn. The menu is similarly nostalgic, emphasizing well-prepared, classic seafood—much of which is caught extremely close to the restaurant.

Seafood. Dinner, Sunday brunch. Children's menu. Reservations recommended. Closed Monday-Thursday (fall-spring). $16-35

RECOMMENDED

KITTERY

WARREN'S LOBSTER HOUSE
11 Water St., Kittery, 207-439-1630; www.lobsterhouse.com

This waterfront restaurant features an extensive menu of seafood dishes, including the house specialty, a lobster thermidor that offers a gourmet take on the classic recipe. The clam chowder, however, is also a standout. It's made with a creamy base and loaded with rich, plump clams.

Seafood. Lunch, dinner, Sunday brunch. Bar. Children's menu. Outdoor seating. $16-35

YORK

DOCKSIDE
22 Harris Island Road, York, 207-363-2722, 888-860-7428; www.docksidegq.com

Here, a contemporary American menu consists of seasonal, organic and local ingredients. Menu highlights include pan-roasted native cod or grilled wild salmon with truffled potato purée.

Seafood, steak. Lunch, dinner. Bar. Reservations recommended. Outdoor seating. Closed Monday; Mid-October-late May. $16-35

SPA

KENNEBUNKPORT

★★★★THE WHITE BARN INN SPA
The White Barn Inn, 37 Beach Ave., Kennebunkport, 207-967-2321; www.whitebarninn.com

The White Barn Inn Spa delivers tasteful minimalism without compromising luxury. Guests can order a soothing aroma sea bath, or if they're feeling more indulgent, they can request a light-of-the-moon plunge, a fizz of marine pebbles infused with mandarin orange and lemon essential oils. What's most impressive, though, is how the spa incorporates its local surroundings: The Kennebunk River provides the ingredients used for the signature stone massage, while natural marine algae and Maine sea salts are incorporated into the moisturizing body wraps.

GREATER PORTLAND AND CASCO BAY

Sure, Portland, Oregon gets all the attention, but Portland, Maine is just as deserving. With cobblestone streets, red brick buildings and plentiful public parks, the city of 60,000 evokes a relaxed, old-world feel. But these days the town is enjoying a modern renaissance, thanks to a new wave of stylish boutiques, stunning art galleries and red-hot restaurants.

As urban retreats go, this one is convenient to several small-town escapes. Just off the coast of Portland, in Casco Bay, Little Chebeague and Great Chebeague islands are small enough to explore on foot or by bike. The islands are rich with Native American history, too. An interesting fact: The Native Americans apparently loved to eat clams, because the European settlers found scads of shells scattered across the island. Those very shells were later used to pave many of the islands' roadways, some of which still exist.

From Portland's charming Old Port district, a visitor can easily venture 17 miles north to the historic town of Freeport. It was here, in a local tavern, that colonists first launched a separation movement from Massachusetts (Maine became a separate state in 1820). Today, the town is best known for its shopping scene. Home to 200 outlet stores and the 24-hour L.L. Bean flagship, Freeport is a great place to buy a bike, a kayak or a pair of thermal underwear.

WHAT TO SEE

CAPE ELIZABETH
PORTLAND HEAD LIGHTHOUSE MUSEUM
1000 Shore Road, Cape Elizabeth, 207-799-2661; www.portlandheadlight.com

George Washington himself ordered the construction of this lighthouse, built in 1791 on a beautiful and rocky coast. It's said to be the first authorized by the United States and state's the oldest lighthouse still in use. The lighthouse tower is not open to the public, though the former keepers' quarters now function as a museum with old lighthouse lenses and interpretive displays.

June-October, daily. November-December and April-May, weekends 10 a.m.-4 p.m.

CHEBEAGUE ISLAND
CHEBEAGUE FERRY
123 Roy Hill Road, Chebeague Island, 207-846-3700; www.chebeaguetrans.com

Step aboard this passenger ferry for a 15-minute trip from Chebeague Island to Cousins Island. Off-site parking is available with free shuttle service to and from the ferry.

Daily.

FALMOUTH
MAST LANDING SANCTUARY
20 Gilsland Farm Road, Falmouth, 207-781-2330; www.maineaudubon.org

Migrant shorebirds and songbirds are drawn to this 140-acre sanctuary consisting of open fields, a freshwater stream, a salt marsh, an apple orchard, a freshwater stream and an evergreen forest. In addition to bird-watching, activities include hiking and cross-country skiing.

Daily.

FREEPORT
ATLANTIC SEAL CRUISES
25 Main St., South Freeport, 207-865-6112; www.freeportusa.org

This 40-foot, 28-passenger vessel cruises across Casco Bay to Eagle Island and the Robert E. Peary house museum. The company also offers seal- and bird-watching cruises, as well as fall foliage tours. Schedules vary and tickets can be purchased at the Main Street office and cruises depart from Town Wharf.

Daily 8 a.m.-7 p.m.

PORTLAND
CASCO BAY LINES
56 Commercial St., Portland, 207-774-7871; www.cascobaylines.com

Casco Bay Lines provides year-round ferry service to the islands of Casco Bay

HIGHLIGHTS

WHAT ARE PORTLAND'S BEST NEIGHBORHOODS TO EXPLORE ON FOOT?

ARTS DISTRICT
Situated along Congress Street, these bohemian blocks are populated by galleries, arts studios and the terrific Portland Museum of Art.

MUNJOY HILL
This emerging neighborhood features two must-see sights—the Portland Observatory and the Eastern Promenade, both offering great views of Casco Bay.

OLD PORT AND WATERFRONT
A classic warehouse district, Old Port has been so successfully revitalized it's now filled with independent restaurants, bars and hip boutiques. Cobblestone streets connect the area with the nearby waterfront and all of its classic fishing piers.

from Portland, at Commercial and Franklin streets. The trip is a one-hour crossing.
Daily.

CHILDREN'S MUSEUM OF MAINE
142 Free St., Portland, 207-828-1234; www.childrensmuseumofme.org
This hands-on museum features interactive exhibits that allow children to test a variety of occupations—Maine lobsterman, storekeeper, fireman, auto mechanic, computer expert or astronaut. Other interactive features include a 40-foot pirate ship, a dress-up stage and a puppet theater.
Admission: adults $9, children under 1 free. June-August, daily; rest of year, Tuesday-Saturday, 10 a.m.-5 p.m., Sunday, noon-5 p.m.

MAINE HISTORY GALLERY
489 Congress St., Portland, 207-774-1822; www.mainehistory.com
In the art gallery, visitors can admire the museum's collection of more than 2,000 paintings, prints and other original works, but this exhaustive museum also holds approximately 8,000 artifacts, including costumes, textiles, decorative arts, archaeological material, political items, military relics and other traces of the state's history. Gallery talks and hands-on workshops are also offered.
Monday-Saturday 10 a.m.-5 p.m., Sunday noon-5 p.m.

PORTLAND MUSEUM OF ART

7 Congress Square, Portland, 207-775-6148; www.portlandmuseum.org

The largest and oldest art museum in the state, this organization has three buildings full of American and European paintings, sculpture, prints and decorative art. Of particular interest is the State of Maine Collection, featuring works by Andrew Wyeth and other artists associated with the state. The museum also boasts a deep Winslow Homer collection.

Admission: adults $10, seniors and students $8, children 6-17 $4, children 5 and under free. Free Friday 5-9 p.m. Memorial Day-Columbus Day, Monday-Thursday, Saturday-Sunday 10 a.m.-5 p.m., Friday 10 a.m.-9 p.m.; November-April, Tuesday-Thursday, Saturday-Sunday 10 a.m.-5 p.m., Friday 10 a.m.-9 p.m.

PORTLAND OBSERVATORY

138 Congress St., Portland, 207-774-5561; www.portlandlandmarks.org

The only remaining maritime signal tower in the nation, this octagonal, shingled tower was built in 1807. The observatory provides spectacular harbor views to anyone willing to climb the 102 steps to the top.

June-mid-October, daily.

TATE HOUSE

1267 Westbrook St., Portland, 207-774-6177; www.tatehouse.org

Built in 1755 for Captain George Tate, a mast agent for the British Navy, this Georgian mansion offers a rare glimpse inside a pre-Revolutionary home. Unique architectural features include original, unpainted clapboards and an indented gambrel roof. The home is furnished and decorated in accordance with the period of Tate's residence, from 1755 to 1800.

Admission: adults $8, seniors $6, children 6-12 $3. Early June-early October, Wednesday-Sunday 10 a.m.-4 p.m., Sunday 1-4 p.m.

VICTORIA MANSION

109 Danforth St., Portland, 207-772-4841; www.victoriamansion.org

One of the finest examples of 19th-century architecture surviving in the United States, this opulent 1858 home is decked out with frescoes, carved woodwork, original furnishings and stained and etched glass.

Admission: adults $15, seniors $13.50, students 6-17 $5, children 5 and under free. May-October, Monday-Saturday 10 a.m.-4 p.m., Sunday 1-5 p.m.

WADSWORTH-LONGFELLOW HOUSE

489 Congress St., Portland, 207-772-1807; www.mainehistory.org

The boyhood home of Henry Wadsworth Longfellow was built in 1785 by the poet's grandfather, General Peleg Wadsworth. It is now maintained by the Maine Historical Society and features original furnishings, portraits, personal possessions and other mementos of the writer and his family.

Monday-Saturday, 10:30 a.m.-4 p.m., Sunday, noon-4 p.m.

WHERE TO STAY

CAPE ELIZABETH

★★★INN BY THE SEA

40 Bowery Beach Road, Cape Elizabeth, 207-799-3134, 800-888-4287; www.innbythesea.com

Contemporary décor permeates this all-suite resort property, though you'll also find old-fashioned comforts like turndown service, terrycloth robes and porches with great views of the ocean. Other amenities include onsite tennis, shuffleboard and volleyball, and a brand-new spa offering a full menu of treatments.

57 rooms. Restaurant. Pool. Spa. Tennis. $151-250

FREEPORT

★★★HARRASEEKET INN

162 Main St., Freeport, 207-865-9377, 800-342-6423; www.harraseeketinn.com

The inn is constituted of three structures: the Federalist House (1798), the Early Victorian House (1850) and a modern, colonial-style inn. Spacious guest rooms are decorated with antiques and outfitted with cozy fireplaces. For further creature comforts, check out the everyday extras: a breakfast buffet and teatime in the paneled drawing room. Located just two blocks from the L.L. Bean flagship and the town's discount outlets, the inn makes an especially great getaway for power-shoppers.

84 rooms. Restaurant, bar. Pets accepted. Complimentary breakfast. Pool. $151-250

PORTLAND

★★★PORTLAND HARBOR HOTEL

468 Fore St., Portland, 207-775-9090, 888-798-9090; www.portlandharborhotel.com

Part of the Old Port district of downtown Portland, a fully restored area of Victorian buildings, this hotel is close to charming restaurants, shops, galleries and the waterfront. It's a great spot for night owls, too, since the hotel is close to many bars. Come wintertime, the hotel itself lures revelers with a novel late-night destination—a bar made entirely of ice. Perfect for business travelers, guest rooms feature toile spreads, custom mattresses, luxury linens, feather pillows and two-level desks with leather chairs. The onsite restaurant goes for extra ambience with its enclosed garden patio and fountain, located just off the lobby dining room.

97 rooms. Restaurant, bar. Fitness center. Business center. Pets accepted. $151-250

★★★PORTLAND REGENCY HOTEL & SPA

20 Milk St., Portland, 207-774-4200, 800-727-3436; www.theregency.com

A small, European-style hotel located in Portland's Old Port district, this getaway lives within an 1895 red brick building. True to the structure's heritage, the lobby and public rooms feature mahogany woodwork, Victorian furnishings and a "map room" tossed with burgundy leather chairs. Period décor in the guest rooms includes four-poster beds, antiques and period reproductions. An onsite spa offers a complete menu of treatments. The hotel is convenient to dozens of galleries, shops and restaurants.

95 rooms. Restaurant, bar. Fitness center. Spa. Business center. $151-250

SCARBOROUGH
★★★BLACK POINT INN

510 Black Point Road, Scarborough, 207-883-2500, 800-258-0003; www.blackpointinn.com

Located on a promontory at the tip of Prout's Neck, this seaside resort is wrapped in the natural beauty of Maine's coast. Each room is clad in period wallpaper and furnishings, with porcelain and crystal lamps at the bedsides. While some of the rooms have histories as sea captains' quarters, all feature gorgeous views of the nearby cliffs and ocean.

65 rooms. Closed December-April. Restaurant, bar. Fitness center. Beach. Pool. $251-350

SOUTH PORTLAND
★★★PORTLAND MARRIOTT AT SABLE OAKS

200 Sable Oaks Drive, South Portland, 207-871-8000, 800-752-8810; www.marriott.com

Despite the quiet, rural setting, this Marriot is just a few miles from the Portland International Jetport and close to downtown. Convenient as that is, however, guests are still assured a proper welcome—a covered portico, pond and fountain greets you upon arrival. Nearby activities include golf, tennis, a spa and the beach.

227 rooms. Restaurant, bar. Fitness center. Pool. Business center. Golf. $151-250

RECOMMENDED

FREEPORT
BREWSTER HOUSE BED & BREAKFAST

180 Main St., Freeport, 207-865-4121, 800-865-0822; www.brewsterhouse.com

Built in 1888, this waterfront inn is bedecked with floral prints and antique furniture. It also features a cozy parlor with a warm, inviting fireplace that's ideal for lounging.

7 rooms. No children under 8. Complimentary breakfast. $251-350

KENDALL TAVERN BED AND BREAKFAST

213 Main St., Freeport, 207-865-1338, 800-341-9572; www.kendalltavern.com

Built in 1832, this laid-back, colonial-style getaway specializes in unpretentious, old-fashioned comfort. The inn features handmade quilts, tapestry wallpapers and antiques. A country-style breakfast is served every morning in the dining room.

7 rooms. No children under 8. Complimentary breakfast. Pets accepted. $151-250

PORTLAND
POMEGRANATE INN

49 Neal St., Portland, 207-772-1006, 800-356-0408; www.pomegranateinn.com

Located in the historic Western Promenade neighborhood, this 1884 inn is small but sophisticated. The property is adorned with antiques and art, with an urban garden for guests to enjoy. It seems appropriate, then, that the inn is close to the midtown arts district, which offers plenty of museums, art galleries, boat rides, fine restaurants and recreational activities.

8 rooms. No children under 16. Complimentary breakfast. $151-250

WHERE TO EAT

FREEPORT

★★★THE MAINE DINING ROOM

162 Main St., Freeport, 207-865-9377, 800-342-6423; www.harraseeketinn.com

Located in the Harraseeket Inn, this restaurant offers a cozy atmosphere with two wood-burning fireplaces and windows that overlook the stately gardens. Organic and homegrown foods are the focus of the menu, which changes seasonally. There's always plenty of fresh seafood on order, and the wine selection is one of the largest in the state.

American. Breakfast, dinner, brunch. Bar. Reservations recommended. $36-85

PORTLAND

★★★BACK BAY GRILL

65 Portland St., Portland, 207-772-8833; www.backbaygrill.com

Located in downtown Portland in a restored 1888 pharmacy, this local hangout dishes up innovative cuisine in a vintage setting. The restaurant is a certified member of the Maine Organic Farmers Growers Association, so the daily menu is sure to feature the area's best seasonal ingredients. Special events include prix-fixe menus, wine tastings, wine dinners and lobster evenings.

American. Dinner. Bar. Reservations recommended. Closed Sunday. $36-85

★★★FORE STREET

288 Fore St., Portland, 207-775-2717; www.forestreet.biz

James Beard award-winning chef Sam Hayward directs a kitchen devoted to fresh, seasonal, inspired cooking at this cozy restaurant in Portland's Old Port District. Local producers provide the ingredients, everything from day-boat scallops to organic arugula. A favorite dish is the wood-oven roasted mussels, though other standouts include the marinated hangar steak and lamb. Be sure to save room for the delicious housemade desserts, especially the ice cream and cakes.

Seafood, steak. Dinner. Bar. Reservations recommended. $16-35

★★★THE ROMA CAFÉ

769 Congress St., Portland, 207-773-9873; www.theromacafe.com

Located in an 1887 Victorian mansion, this restaurant features nook-and-cranny dining rooms, each with its own fireplace. A beautiful carved wood staircase and beveled glass windows add to the classy ambience. The menu is sophisticated, too, with plenty of local seafood, lobster and Italian dishes.

Italian, seafood. Lunch, dinner. Bar. Reservations recommended. Closed Sunday-Monday. $36-85

★★★STREET & CO.

33 Wharf St., Portland, 207-775-0887

Located in the Old Port District on a cobblestone street, this 19th-century building was formerly a fish warehouse. In accordance with that history, the restaurant is done up with rustic style, featuring exposed bricks, original plank hardwood flooring and beamed ceilings. The tables continue to riff on that theme. They're made of heavy black stone slabs with rough-hewn wooden legs.

But the best part? The open kitchen, which reflects the dining room and churns out seafood dishes with sides of seasonal organic produce. Visitors can also choose a table in "the burbs," a quiet dining room that's far away from all the fuss. For a perfect evening, order the daily catch and a craft cocktail.

American, seafood. Dinner. Bar. Reservations recommended. $36-85

WHERE TO SHOP

FREEPORT
FACTORY OUTLET STORES
42-28 Main St., Freeport, 800-865-1994; www.freeportusa.com
Freeport is home to more than 170 outlet stores, where picky shoppers can snag brand-name merchandise at discounted prices. Rugged, outdoorsy types will love the town's most famous shopping destination, the flagship L.L. Bean with its vast selection of clothing and sporting goods, and convenient store hours—it stays open 24 hours a day.

PORTLAND
ASIA WEST
219 Commercial Street, Portland, 888-775-0066; www.asiawest.net
This Old Port shop specializes in Asian imports, especially furnishings, home décor, architectural salvage, garden decorations and jewelry. Come here for unique candles, lamps, statues and antique cabinets. Don't be afraid of those hulking armoires—the staff is willing to ship to your home if necessary.
Daily 10 a.m.-6 p.m.

EDGECOMB POTTERS GALLERY
49 Exchange Street, Portland, (207) 780-6727; www.edgecombpotters.com
Richard and Chris Hilton founded Edgecomb Potters in a one-room schoolhouse in 1976. Needless to say, their hand-glazed bowls, vases and dishware made a resounding impact. Today, the Hiltons have three locations—one in Portland, the others in Freeport and Edgecomb.
Daily 10 a.m.-6 p.m.

LISA-MARIE'S MADE IN MAINE
35 Exchange Street, Portland, 207-828-1515; www.lisamariesmadeinmaine.com
For Maine-made gifts, look no further than this lovely boutique. More than 100 artisans are represented here with handmade jewelry, crafts, chocolates,

photography, pottery and more.
Monday-Wednesday, 10 a.m.-6 p.m., Thursday-Saturday, 10 a.m.-8 p.m., Sunday 11 a.m.-5 p.m.

PLANET DOG
211 Marginal Way, Portland, 207-347-8606; www.planetdog.com
Intent on pleasing your pup, Planet Dog stocks premium dog food, training tools, grooming supplies, gifts and a signature line of eco-friendly toys. Of course, Fido is welcome to shop along with you.
Tuesday-Saturday, 9 a.m.-7 p.m., Sunday 11 a.m.-6 p.m.

MIDDLE COAST

Home to quaint bed and breakfasts, fishing villages and breathtaking outdoor sights, Maine's Middle Coast is a great place for restful and rugged vacations alike. One of the prettiest towns in the region, Camden is perfectly situated between the waters of Penobscot Bay and the peaks of the Camden Hills. Home to great restaurants and historic bed and breakfasts, Camden has long been a popular vacation destination. However, a large year-round population saves the town from being overly resort-oriented.

Set on the peninsula between the Sheepscot and Damariscotta rivers, the town of Boothbay Harbor is the scene of well-attended regattas several times each summer. The bustling harbor scene, with active commercial fisher- and lobstermen, lends the town an authentic maritime feel. Boothbay Harbor is also a popular spot for sport fishing expeditions, whale-watching cruises and puffin tours.

While Middle Coast communities like Camden and Rockport have impressive arts communities, none has a cultural scene quite like Rockland's. During the past few years the town has seen a swell of fashionable new restaurants, shops and galleries. Meanwhile, the acclaimed Farnsworth Art Museum continues to lure visitors with its famous collection of Wyeth family paintings. Of course, Rockland has its share of classic Maine charm. The Winjammer fleet, for example, consists of 12 vintage schooners that take visitors for 12-hour or multi-day tours. Rockland is also home to the beloved Maine Lobster Festival, a five-day celebration of Maine's signature catch.

WHAT TO SEE

BOOTHBAY
BOOTHBAY RAILWAY VILLAGE
586 Wiscasset Road, Highway 27, Boothbay, 207-633-4727; www.railwayvillage.org
Check out the collection of vintage vehicles—60 in all, including a steam train. This historic village also features early fire equipment, a general store, a one-room schoolhouse, restored train stations, artifacts and other relics of 19th century small-town life.
Mid-June-September, daily.

HIGHLIGHTS

WHAT ARE THE TOP THINGS TO DO IN THE MIDDLE COAST?

HIT THE SLOPES
Pack up your skiing gear and head to Camden Snow Bowl. The community-owned ski and recreation area uses a double chairlift and two T-bars to climb 1,300-foot Mount Ragged. Once skiers reach the top, they're treated to great views of the Atlantic Ocean.

SAIL AWAY
Book a Windjammer sailing trip on an old-time schooner departing from Camden or Rockport Harbor. You'll be gone anywhere from 12 hours to six days, whatever you choose. While you're at sea, you're treated to views of lighthouses, seabirds, seals and whales.

VISIT THE MONHEGAN ISLAND LIGHTHOUSE AND MUSEUM
Constructed in 1824, this historic lighthouse sits atop a hill on Monhegan Island. Today, it's surrounded by a museum and an art gallery, both filled with artifacts of the island's history.

BOOTHBAY HARBOR
BOOTHBAY REGION HISTORICAL SOCIETY MUSEUM
72 Oak St., Boothbay Harbor, 207-633-0820; www.boothbayhistorical.org

Housed within the 1874 Reed family house, this museum displays local artifacts and documents from the Boothbay Region, as well as heirlooms from the prominent Reed family.

July-August, Wednesday-Saturday 10 a.m.-2 p.m.; rest of year, Friday-Saturday.

CAMDEN
CAMDEN HILLS STATE PARK
280 Belfast, Camden, 207-236-3109; www.state.me.us

Thirty miles of hiking trails surround 1,380-foot Mount Megunticook at Camden Hills, Maine's third-largest state park. The climb to Mount Megunticook is sure to be rigorous, but the park offers a handy alternative: 800-foot Mount Battie, accessible by car.

June-Mid-October.

CAMDEN OPERA HOUSE

29 Elm St., Camden, 207-236-7963; www.camdenoperahouse.com

You won't find an opera here, though you're treated to just as classic an art form: a lovingly preserved Victorian playhouse with antique moldings, chandeliers, painted friezes and gold stenciling. Check the performance calendar for the lineup of musical theater, dance and concerts.

See website for ticket pricing and event details.

CAMDEN SNOW BOWL

Hosmer Pond Road, Camden, 207-236-3438; www.camdensnowbowl.com

The community-owned ski and recreation area uses a double chairlift and two T-bars to climb 1,300-foot Mount Ragged. Once skiers reach the top, they're treated to great views of the Atlantic Ocean. Other features include a toboggan chute, snowmaking machines, snack bar and lounge. Ski patrol runs regularly. Novices can rent equipment and attend ski school. Snowboarding is allowed.

Late December-mid-March, daily.

CONWAY HOMESTEAD-CRAMER MUSEUM

Highway 1 and Conway Road, Camden, 207-236-2257; www.crmuseum.org

This authentically restored 18th-century farmhouse has collections of antique carriages, sleighs and farm equipment. Visitors will also encounter a black-smith shop, a sugarhouse and an herb garden. Step inside Cramer Museum to see a spread of paintings, ship models, quilts, costumes, documents and other reminders of our historic past.

July-August, Tuesday-Friday.

WINDJAMMER SAILING

Camden Harbor, 800-807-9463; www.sailmainecoast.com

Book a trip on an old-time schooner departing from Camden or Rockport Harbor. You'll be gone anywhere from 12 hours to six day, whatever you choose. While you're at sea, you're treated to views of lighthouses, seabirds, seals and whales. You'll be well fed, too. The operators provide generous meals, including a traditional Maine lobster feast.

May-October.

LINCOLNVILLE BEACH

MAINE STATE FERRY SERVICE

McKay St., and Highway 1, Lincolnville Beach, 207-789-5611; www.state.me.us

Step aboard the *Margaret Chase Smith* for a 20-minute trip to Islesboro, a deeply forested, mostly rural island just three miles from port.

Mid-May-late October, weekdays, nine trips; Sunday, eight trips; rest of year, six trips daily.

NEW HARBOR

COLONIAL PEMAQUID STATE HISTORIC SITE

Colonial Pemaquid Road, New Harbor, 207-677-2423

The site of a very early English outpost and fishing station, this peninsula has a storied past. Excavations have uncovered foundations of a jail, a tavern and private homes. The nearby museum features artifacts unearthed during those digs, everything from rare China to tools. Once you've toured the archeological sites, check out Fort William Henry, a replica of the site's original 1692 stone fort. It contains relics, portraits, maps and copies of Native American deeds. *June-August, daily.*

PEMAQUID POINT LIGHTHOUSE PARK

Pemaquid Lighthouse, New Harbor, 207-677-2494; www.lighthouse.cc

This 1827 lighthouse is so picturesque that Mainers picked it to represent them on their state quarter. The tower rises above unfriendly rock formations and pounding surf (not open to the public). Don't miss the Fishermen's Museum, located in the old lightkeeper's dwelling.

June-mid-October, daily; rest of year, by appointment.

MONHEGAN ISLAND

MONHEGAN LIGHTHOUSE/MUSEUM

1 Lighthouse Hill, Monhegan Island, 207-596-7003; www.monheganmuseum.org

Constructed in 1824, this historic lighthouse sits atop a hill on Monhegan Island, and is surrounded by a museum and an art gallery, both filled with artifacts of the island's history. Notably, the museum also owns the large bell portrayed by Jamie Wyeth in his famous painting Bronze Age, on display at the nearby Farnsworth Museum.

July-August, 11:30 a.m.-3:30 p.m.; select days in June and September 1:30-3:30 p.m.

ROCKLAND

FARNSWORTH ART MUSEUM AND WYETH CENTER

16 Museum St., Rockland, 207-596-6457; www.farnsworthmuseum.org

Dedicated to Maine art, this museum is a cultural center for the region. Its impressive collections include more than 10,000 works of 18th- to 20th-century American art, including a cache of paintings and archival material from Maine's beloved Wyeth family N.C., Andrew and Jamie.

June-mid-October, daily; January-March, Wednesday-Sunday 10 a.m.-5 p.m.; rest of year, Tuesday-Sunday 10 a.m.-5 p.m.

MAINE LIGHTHOUSE MUSEUM

1 Park Drive, Rockland, 207-594-3301; www.mainelighthousemuseum.com

This museum seeks to illuminate the heroic, life-saving role played by lighthouses in our maritime history. Check out the large collection of complexly beautiful lenses. Other artifacts include buoys, foghorns, lighthouse models and historic Coast Guard tools.

Admission: adults $5, seniors $4, children under 12 free. June-November, Monday-Friday 9 a.m.-5 p.m., Saturday-Sunday 10 a.m.-4 p.m.

MAINE STATE FERRY SERVICE

517A Main St., Rockland, 207-596-2202; www.state.me.us

Catch a ferry for the 15-mile trip to Vinalhaven, or the 12 ½-mile trip to North Haven. Either way, travel time is just over an hour. The ferry service runs two to three trips daily year round, but it also offers a once-a-month excursion to Matinicus Island, 23 miles away.

SPECIAL EVENT

MAINE LOBSTER FESTIVAL

Harbor Park, or at the public landing, Rockland, 207-596-0376, 800-562-2529;
www.mainelobsterfestival.com

Mainers give a hero's welcome to their favorite crustacean with five days of food, parades, harbor cruises, entertainment and, yes, more food.

First weekend in August.

WHERE TO STAY

BOOTHBAY HARBOR

★★★SPRUCE POINT INN

88 Grandview Ave., Boothbay Harbor, 207-633-4152, 800-553-0289;
www.sprucepointinn.com

Located on a quiet peninsula on the east side of Boothbay Harbor, this ocean-front resort makes an ideal getaway for families. Activities include berry-picking, swimming in salt and freshwater pools, kayaking, bicycling, fishing and hiking through the resort's 57 secluded acres.

85 rooms. Closed mid-October-mid-May. Pets accepted. Restaurant, bar. Fitness center. Spa. Pool. Tennis. Business center. $151-250

CAMDEN

★★★BLUE HARBOR HOUSE, A VILLAGE INN

67 Elm St., Camden, 207-236-3196, 800-248-3196; www.blueharborhouse.com

Built in 1768 by James Richards, the first settler of Camden, this inn features guest rooms filled with quilts and antiques. Located just a few blocks from the harbor and downtown shops, lodgings come with a gourmet breakfast, the perfect starter to a day of hiking in Camden Hills State Park or boating through Penobscot Bay.

11 rooms. Complimentary breakfast. $151-250

★★★CAMDEN HARBOUR INN

83 Bayview St., Camden, 800-236-4266; www.camdenharbourinn.com

Dutch proprietors inject Camden Harbour Inn with a cosmopolitan feel, from the impeccable service to the luxurious amenities and lovely ocean views. Guests can expect to be spoiled with fine linens and plush towels, a king-size pillow-top mattress, luxe bathrobes, flat-screen TV and complimentary breakfast from Natalie's, the in-house fine dining establishment.

18 rooms. Complimentary breakfast. $151-250

NEW HARBOR

★★★THE BRADLEY INN

3063 Bristol Road, New Harbor, 207-677-2105, 800-942-5560; www.bradleyinn.com

Built by a sea captain for his bride in 1880, this full-service inn has a romantic perch at the tip of Pemaquid Peninsula, not far from John's Bay and the Pemaquid Lighthouse. Rooms are decorated with original art, antiques and feather beds,

WHAT IS THE MOST HISTORIC HOTEL IN THE MIDDLE COAST?

Whitehall Inn:
When it comes to the Whitehall, the superstar credentials go on and on. It was featured in two films, the original 1957 *Peyton Place* and Stephen King's 1996 *Thinner.* The Whitehall also played a role in launching the poetry career of native Mainer Edna St. Vincent Millay.

some with fireplaces. Also of note, guests can order of off two in-house menus: one offers delicious seafood, the other spa services.

16 rooms. Closed January-March. Complimentary breakfast. Restaurant. Spa. $251-350

★★★NEWCASTLE INN

60 River Road, Newcastle, 207-563-5685, 800-832-8669; www.newcastleinn.com

A Federal-style 1850 country inn, Newcastle overlooks magnificent gardens and the Damariscotta River. Rooms and suites come with four-poster or canopy beds, private sitting areas and fireplaces. Start your evening with complimentary hors d'oeuvres, followed by a four-course dinner in one of two dining rooms. End the day at the inn's private pub, available only to guests.

15 rooms. No children under 12. Restaurant, bar. Complimentary breakfast. Pets accepted. $151-250

ROCKLAND

★★★SAMOSET RESORT

220 Warrenton St., Rockport, 207-594-2511, 800-341-1650; www.samoset.com

Named for the Pemaquid chief who greeted the Pilgrims, this inn has welcomed guests since 1889. Best known for its dramatic seaside golf resort, Samoset is set on 230 acres that hug the rugged coast of Maine. Perfect for families and couples alike, the resort also features tennis courts, a new outdoor pool and great dining.

178 rooms. Restaurant, bar. Fitness center. Pool. Tennis. $151-250

RECOMMENDED

CAMDEN

CAMDEN WINDWARD HOUSE

6 High St., Camden, 207-236-9656, 877-492-9656; www.windwardhouse.com

Located in the center of Camden's historic district, this 1854 inn is within walking distance of many restaurants and shops, and Camden Harbor. Mount Battie and Camden Hills State Park are nearby, too. Rooms are individually decorated with antiques, and some even have private decks and Jacuzzis. When it comes to breakfast, guests can order off a menu, complete with vegetarian options.

8 rooms. No children under 12. Complimentary breakfast. Bar. $151-250

HAWTHORN INN

9 High St., Camden, 207-236-8842, 866-381-3647; www.camdenhawthorn.com

This 1894 Victorian inn is big on romance—think candlelight, fresh flowers and luxury bathrobes. Some rooms come with private fireplaces, whirlpools and decks with harbor views. It's convenient, too, located just steps from Camden's downtown area and Penobscot Bay. The Hawthorn Inn strives to be eco-friendly.

10 rooms. Closed January. No children under 12. Complimentary breakfast. $151-250

INN AT OCEAN'S EDGE

24 Stonecoast Road, Lincolnville, 207-236-0945; www.innatoceansedge.com

A contemporary inn overlooking Penobscot Bay, this destination features spacious rooms with down duvet-topped beds, Jacuzzi tubs and ocean views. Families love it here, thanks to 22 miles of gardens, lawns and woods, not to mention the outdoor infinity-edge swimming pool. The onsite restaurant, The Edge, specializing in fresh, seasonal fare.

30 rooms. No children under 14. Complimentary breakfast. Fitness center. $151-250

INN AT SUNRISE POINT

Highway 1, Camden, 207-236-7716, 800-435-6278; www.sunrisepoint.com

Choose a room in the shingled main house or a cottage at the water's edge. Either way, you're assured a quiet, secluded hideout with splendid ocean views and the sounds of crashing waves. A gourmet breakfast is served in the conservatory, while afternoon hors d'oeuvres are available in the library.

13 rooms. No children under 12. Complimentary breakfast. $251-350

MAINE STAY BED AND BREAKFAST

22 High St., Camden, 207-236-9636; www.mainestay.com

Situated inside an 1802 farmhouse, this bed and breakfast features bright, cheerful rooms scattered with oriental rugs and whimsical antiques, like a 17th-century samurai chest. There's even a big country kitchen, where guests are welcome to raid the cookie jar or help themselves to ice cream.

8 rooms. No children under 12. Complimentary breakfast. $151-250

WHAT ARE THE MOST LUXURIOUS HOTELS IN THE MIDDLE COAST?

Camden Harbour Inn: Guests of this cosmopolitan inn can expect to be spoiled with luxe amenities and impeccable service.

Inn at Ocean's Edge: With 22 acres of landscaped gardens, lawns and woods—not to mention a swimming pool and a terrific restaurant specializing in seasonal fare—this contemporary inn is the perfect place for relaxation.

Samoset Resort: Perfect for active vacation-goers, this recently renovated resort features 230 acres of oceanside property with everything from tennis courts and a championship golf course to fine dining.

NORUMBEGA INN

63 High St., Camden, 207-236-4646; www.norumbegainn.com

A stone, Gothic-like castle that towers over Penobscot Bay, this inn doubles as architectural landmark and charming retreat. Guests are treated to remarkable ocean views, as well as rich interior detail like stained-glass windows, coffered ceilings and carved Gothic fireplaces.

13 rooms. No children under 7. Complimentary breakfast. $151-250

WHITEHALL INN

52 High St., Camden, 207-236-3391, 800-789-6565; www.whitehall-inn.com

Built in 1834, this picturesque inn has a glamorous past. It was featured in two films, the original 1957 *Peyton Place* and Stephen King's *Thinner*. It has hosted notables like President Bill Clinton and supermodel Christie Brinkley. But the inn is most proud of the role it played in the career of poet Edna St. Vincent Millay—it was here in 1912 that Camden native Millay read a poem to a well-connected guest, who arranged a scholarship to Vassar College and introduced her to literary luminaries in New York City.

50 rooms. Closed mid-October-mid-May. Restaurant, bar. Tennis. Complimentary breakfast. $151-250

WHERE TO EAT

BOOTHBAY HARBOR
★★★88 GRANDVIEW

88 Grandview, Boothbay Harbor, 207-633-4152, 800-553-0289; www.sprucepointinn.com

Located inside the Spruce Point Inn, this high-end restaurant strikes the perfect tone: It covers its tables in white linens and sets them with fine china. It also invites a pianist to perform nightly. If the formal dining room doesn't strike your fancy, opt for a seat on the enclosed sun-porch overlooking the Atlantic Ocean. House specialties include candied duck breast and beef with Bordelaise sauce.

Continental. Dinner. Bar. Reservations recommended. Outdoor seating. Closed late October-mid-May. $36-85

CAMDEN
★★★VINCENT'S

52 High St., Camden, 207-236-3391, 800-789-6565; www.whitehall-inn.com

Located in the quaint Whitehall Inn, this restaurant is a favorite of frequent visitors and locals alike. Dishes are creative, with a heavy emphasis on seafood, as with the pasta conil pesce and the whitetail lobster. Choose a table in the main dining room, the glass-enclosed dining porch or the seasonal side patio. For casual occasions, stick to the lounge and its tasty bar menu.

American. Breakfast, dinner. Bar. Reservations recommended. Outdoor seating. $16-35

ROCKLAND
★★★PRIMO

2 S. Main St., Rockland, 207-596-0770; www.primorestaurant.com

An ardent supporter of sustainable agriculture, chef Melissa Kelly keeps her own garden on the premises. Diners will encounter fresh, organic vegetables in every meal, even the meaty ones. Kelly changes her menu weekly, but one thing stays the same: She always draws from coastal Italy and France. Past favorites include asparagus soup with goat cheese, olive oil-poached salmon with bitter greens and beets, and wood-roasted oysters. For something sweet, save room for desserts by pastry chef and co-owner Price Kushner.

American. Dinner. Bar. Reservations recommended. Closed Tuesday. $36-85

RECOMMENDED

ATLANTICA
1 Bayview Landing, Camden, 207-236-6011; www.atlanticarestaurant.com

This seafood bistro is decorated in a bright, contemporary style to match the vibrant dishes on its menu. House specialties include the lobster pot-pie with matchstick fries and the grilled scallops with pumpkin risotto.

Seafood. Dinner. Bar. Reservations recommended. Outdoor seating. Closed Tuesday in winter. $36-85

WATERFRONT
40 Bayview St., Camden, 207-236-3747; www.waterfrontcamden.com

Originally built as a boat shed, this restaurant is perched so close to Camden Harbor it even has its own docking for boaters. The true specialty, however, is bringing the sea to the plate. Favorite dishes include traditional takes on clam chowder and creative versions of fish soup. The dining room is casual and open, with beamed ceilings, hanging lanterns and a double fireplace, though the outdoor deck is the place to be for exceptional harbor views.

Seafood, steak. Lunch, dinner. Bar. Children's menu. Outdoor seating. $16-35

DOWNEAST AND ACADIA

An outdoorsman's paradise, the Acadia National Park region bears the tempting tagline "Where the mountains meet the sea." The glacier-cut park stretches over 41,000 acres of rock-bound coastline along Mount Desert Island, with gorgeous bays and inlets all along the way. With a population of more than 20,000 people, Bar Harbor is the biggest community on Mount Desert Island. An ideal destination for hikers, sailing enthusiasts and leaf-peepers, the city is concentrated with hotels, resorts and traditional New England inns. For extra tranquility, opt instead for a room in Southwest Harbor or Northeast Harbor, two of Mount Desert Island's smaller towns.

Just a 30-minute ferry ride from Bar Harbor, the Cranberry Isles are home to rural communities of fishmongers, loberstermen and craftspeople. Named for their rich red cranberry bogs, the islands consist of Great Cranberry Isle (the biggest at 900 acres), as well as Little Cranberry, Bear, Baker and a privately owned island called Sutton. Here, visitors enjoy a slow pace and gorgeous views of Acadia.

Naturally, beauty like this inspires art, so painters, potters, woodworkers and other artisans are drawn to this area. You'll find many creative people living and working in Blue Hill, a 200-year-old, gallery-filled seaport on Blue Hill Bay, which borders Acadia. Similarly, the rural outpost of Deer Isle is a classic New England lobstering town with its own arts and crafts movement.

WHAT TO SEE

BAR HARBOR
ABBE MUSEUM
26 Mount Desert St., Bar Harbor, 207-288-3519; www.abbemuseum.org

Dedicated to preserving Maine's Native American heritage, the Abbe features artifacts, interpretive displays, craft workshops and archeology field tours. Though the museum is now located in downtown Bar Harbor, it was first located in Acadia National Park. June through October, visitors can still check out the vintage displays at this original site.

Daily 10 a.m.-6 p.m.; closed January.

BAR HARBOR HISTORICAL SOCIETY MUSEUM
33 Ledgelawn Ave., Bar Harbor, 207-288-0000; www.barharborhistorical.org

The museum documents the history of Bar Harbor with early photographs of hotels, summer cottages and the Green Mountain cog railroad. Other artifacts include maps, antique clothing, hotel registers from the early to late 1800s and a scrapbook that documents the town's big fire of 1947.

June-October, Monday-Saturday 1-4 p.m.; November-March, by appointment.

BAR HARBOR WHALE WATCH COMPANY
1 West St., Bar Harbor, 207-288-2386, 888-533-9253; www.whalesrus.com

This company offers a variety of themed cruises aboard catamarans *Friendship V* or *Helen H*. Choose between whale-, seal-, puffin- and osprey-watching tours, or go with the straight-ahead nature cruise. The route and duration of each trip varies.

May-October daily. Depart from Bluenose Ferry Terminal.

BLUE HILL
HOLT HOUSE
Water Street, Blue Hill, 207-326-8250; www.bluehillhistory.org

The Blue Hill Historical Society occupies one of the town's oldest houses, built for the Holt family in 1815. Dedicated to preserving the area's history, the museum features exhibits on shipbuilding and seafaring, as well as town memorabilia and genealogical resources.

July-September, Tuesday, Friday-Saturday 11 a.m.-2 p.m.

RACKLIFFE POTTERY
132 Elsworth Road, Blue Hill, 207-374-2297; www.rackliffepottery.com

This fourth-generation family-owned business turns out traditional, hand-thrown pots, bowls, mugs and plates. Each creation is made of native clay, incorporating colors and designs that draw from Blue Hill's natural surroundings—blueberries, cranberries, leaves, animals and, of course, the sea. Watch the potters work in the open workshop, or pick up a set of one-of-a-kind dinnerware from the onsite pottery store.

July-August, daily; rest of year, Monday-Saturday.

HIGHLIGHTS

WHAT ARE THE BEST PLACES FOR OUTDOOR ADVENTURE?

ACADIA MOUNTAIN TRAIL
By all accounts, it's a strenuous hike to the top of Acadia Mountain. But once you reach the summit, you're rewarded with dream-like views of Somes Sound, the mountains and the ocean.

AQUATERRA ADVENTURES
If you get the hankering to glide across the waters of Bar Harbor, check out this outdoor outfitter. They employ the finest guides to lead sea-kayaking tours.

ATLANTIC CLIMBING SCHOOL
You, too, can scale the unfriendly granite cliffs of Acadia National Park with the help of these experienced climbers and guides.

CRANBERRY ISLES
FERRY SERVICE
33 Main St., Cranberry Isles, 207-244-3575
Find this ferry operator in Northeast Harbor, at the town pier, and catch a 30-minute lift to Great Cranberry, Little Cranberry or, on request, Sutton Island.
June-August, daily; rest of year: schedule varies.

ISLESFORD HISTORICAL MUSEUM
Main Street, and Sand Beach Road, Cranberry Isles, 207-244-9224; www.mainemuseums.org
Antique guns, harpoons, cooking utensils, even a store ledger—this collection of historic tools tells the story of everyday life for the hearty inhabitants of Little Cranberry Island.
Mid-June-September, daily.

DEER ISLE
ISLE AU HAUT BOAT SERVICES
Seabreeze Avenue, Stonington, 207-367-6516; www.isleauhaut.com
With forested shores, cobblestone beaches and hills that reach higher than 500 feet, this island is home to portions of Acadia National Park and well worth the 45-minute mailboat ride from Stonington. No cars allowed.

NORTHEAST HARBOR
WOODLAWN MUSEUM (THE BLACK HOUSE)
172 Surrey Road, Northeast Harbor, 207-667-8671; www.woodlawnmuseum.com

This 180-acre estate incorporates majestic gardens, parks and even a carriage barn, still filled with riding gear, carriages and sleighs. The primary attraction is the 1820 Federal-style mansion, owned until 1928 by the Black family and now featuring three generations of their acquisitions, including paintings, European and American furniture, exotic carpets, china, books and more.

May-October, Tuesday Sunday; rest of year, by appointment.

SOUTHWEST HARBOR
CRANBERRY COVE BOATING COMPANY
Southwest Harbor and Manset, 207-244-5882

Departing from the Upper Town Dock in Southwest Harbor, these convenient 40-minute cruises to the Cranberry Islands double as lessons in native wildlife and island history.

Mid-June-mid-September, daily.

MAINE STATE FERRY SERVICE
Grandville Road, Bass Harbor, 207-244-3254; www.maine.gov

From Bass Harbor, this ferry makes a six-mile, 40-minute trip to Swans Island and an 8 ¼-mile, 50-minute trip to Frenchboro.

Daily.

MOUNT DESERT OCEANARIUM
172 Clark Point Road, Southwest Harbor, 207-244-7330; www.theoceanarium.com

This waterfront oceanarium features more than 20 tanks filled with Gulf of Maine marine creatures. Perfect for kids, the museum also has exhibits on tides, seawater and plankton as well as displays of industrial fishing gear, boats to climb in and a tide-pool touch tank.

Mid-May-mid-October, Monday-Saturday.

WENDELL GILLEY MUSEUM
4 Herrick Road, Southwest Harbor, 207-244-7555; www.wendellgilleymuseum.org

Beloved to Mainers, Wendell Gilley was a pioneer in decorative bird carving. His namesake museum is a trailblazer in its own right. Not only does it feature displays of Gilley's work, but it also does ecological exhibits and hands-on workshops that teach visitors the art of bird carving.

June-October, Tuesday-Sunday 10 a.m.-4 p.m.; May, November-December, Friday-Sunday 10 a.m.-4 p.m.

UNION
ROWANTREES POTTERY
84 Union St., Union, 207-374-5535

Founded in 1939, this company specializes in heirloom-quality pottery, from crocks and jars to wheel-thrown, handcrafted dinnerware.

June-September, Monday-Saturday.

WHERE TO STAY

BAR HARBOR

★★★BAR HARBOR HOTEL-BLUENOSE INN

90 Eden St., Bar Harbor, 207-288-3348, 800-445-4077; www.barharborhotel.com

From its hilltop perch on Mount Desert Island, this hotel offers glorious views of Frenchman Bay. It's also convenient to Acadia National Park and a host of ferry services to the surrounding islands, with four-poster beds and private balconies awaiting tired sightseers back in their rooms. After a rigorous day of hiking, head to the onsite Rose Garden Restaurant for a well-deserved gourmet supper.

98 rooms. Closed November-mid-April. Restaurant, bar. Fitness center. Pool. Business center. $151-250

★★★THE BAYVIEW

111 Eden St., Bar Harbor, 207-288-5861, 800-356-3585; www.thebayviewbarharbor.com

Located just 75 feet from the shore, this eight-acre oceanfront property is perfect when you want the waves to lull you to sleep. Each room is outfitted with French doors that lead to wide, private decks overlooking the water. It's perfect for guests on longer stays, because each room features an inlaid wooden table and an armoire. For those extra-extended trips, go for the two- or three-bedroom townhouses.

26 rooms. Closed November-mid-May. Complimentary breakfast. Fitness center. Tennis. Business center. $151-250

BLUE HILL

★★★BLUE HILL INN

40 Union St., Blue Hill, 207-374-2844, 800-826-7415; www.bluehillinn.com

A Federal-style retreat overlooking Blue Hill Bay, this bed and breakfast has been in operation since 1840—it's even on the National Register of Historic Places. Guest rooms are decorated with comfort in mind, with down comforters, designer linens and plush bathrobes. For a more private retreat, book a room in the adjacent Cape House suite. When it comes to breakfast, there's just one word to describe the innkeeper's approach: accommodating.

12 rooms. Restaurant. $151-250

DEER ISLE

★★★PILGRIMS INN

20 Main St., Deer Isle, 207-348-6615, 888-778-7505; www.pilgrimsinn.com

Built in 1793, this post-and-beam building offers a cottage-style getaway, complete with eight-foot-wide fireplaces and cushy leather sofas. Extra indulgences include in-room massages and fresh flower delivery, as well as an onsite restaurant specializing in local seafood, produce and fresh-grown ingredients from the inn's very own garden.

16 rooms. Closed November-mid-May. Restaurant. Complimentary breakfast. Pets accepted.

NORTHEAST HARBOR
★★★ASTICOU INN
15 Peabody Drive, Northeast Harbor, 207-276-3344, 800-258-3373;
www.asticou.com

Situated on Northeast Harbor, at the foot of Eliot Mountain, this sprawling 1883 Victorian inn is decorated with oriental rugs and traditionalist furniture. The grounds are just as magnificent, with beautifully landscaped gardens, clay tennis courts and an outdoor heated pool.

31 rooms. Restaurant, bar. Pool. Tennis. Spa. $251-350

RECOMMENDED

BAR HARBOR
BAR HARBOR INN
Newport Drive, Bar Harbor, 207-288-3351, 800-248-3351; www.barharborinn.com

The Adirondack chairs on the grassy lawn of Bar Harbor Inn—set on eight nicely groomed acres—overlook Frenchman Bay and are the perfect place to take a book or to just sit and watch the boats sail by Bar and Sheep Islands. Service is friendly, and three guest buildings feature rooms with patios overlooking the ocean or manicured grounds. Take a meal in the hotel's Reading Room Restaurant or Terrace Grill—both with water views—or enjoy a spa treatment in the inn's brand-new spa facility.

153 rooms. Complimentary breakfast. Restaurant, bar. Fitness center. Pool. Beach. Spa. $151-250

BAR HARBOR REGENCY
123 Eden St., Bar Harbor, 207-288-9723, 800-234-6835; www.barharborregency.com

Fronting the water, this large gray stone property offers oceanfront or garden view rooms and is approximately one mile from downtown Bar Harbor and near Acadia National Park. Guest accommodations are spacious, and rooms include refrigerators. A putting green, marina and walking trail are offered onsite, and a coin laundry is available to guests who are traveling light.

278 rooms. Closed November-April. Restaurant, bar. Fitness center. Tennis. Pool. $151-250

CASTELMAINE
39 Holland Ave., Bar Harbor, 207-288-4563, 800-338-4563; www.castlemaineinn.com

Tucked away on a quiet side street, this 1886 Victorian-style inn is as restful as they come. Located just one mile from Acadia National Park, and even closer to the ocean, the inn makes for a third sanctuary with period antiques, fireplaces and whirlpool paths.

17 rooms. Closed November-April. Complimentary breakfast. $61-150

INN AT BAY LEDGE
150 Sand Point Road, Bar Harbor, 207-288-4204; www.innatbayledge.com

Built in 1907 atop an 80-foot cliff on Mount Desert Island, this cozy inn features rustic appointments—think antiques tossed in with furniture made by local artisans. Fresh-baked breads, hashes and blueberry breakfast pudding served with English custard sauce are just some of the treats you'll find at the inn's gourmet breakfast, served daily in a charming sunroom overlooking Frenchmans Harbor.

10 rooms. No children under 16. Complimentary breakfast. Closed late October-April. Bar.
$251-350

SOUTHWEST HARBOR
THE CLARK POINT INN
109 Clark Point Road, Southwest Harbor, 207-244-9828, 888-775-5953; www.clarkpointinn.com

Situated within an 1857 Captain's house, this sophisticated inn caters to big-city types with its full-service espresso bar. Other indulgences include fresh-baked cookies, homemade truffles, three-course breakfasts, fireplaces and English country-style guestrooms, the perfect rewards after long days of hiking in nearby Acadia National Park.

5 rooms. Closed mid-October-April. No children under 8. Complimentary breakfast. Bar.
$151-250

KINGSLEIGH INN
373 Main St., Southwest Harbor, 207-244-5302; www.kingsleighinn.com

Built in 1904, this Queen Anne Victorian-style inn features striking architectural flourishes like steeply pitched roofs, cedar shingles and a wraparound porch. Guest rooms are decorated in the English country-style with down duvets, pillow-top mattresses and fresh flowers. In the morning, sit down to a gourmet breakfast of fresh fruit, homemade granola and hot, savory omelets and hashes. Homemade desserts are served every afternoon—the menu varies, but typical treats include almond lace florentines and chocolate caramel fudge brownies.

8 rooms. No children under 10. Complimentary breakfast. Bar. $61-150

WHERE TO EAT

BAR HARBOR
★★★READING ROOM
Newport Drive, Bar Harbor, 207-288-3351, 800-248-3351; www.barharborinn.com

An oceanfront restaurant with panoramic views of the harbor, this restaurant has an obvious specialty—seafood. House specialties include crab cakes, sea scallops wrapped in applewood bacon, broiled haddock and lobster-filled Maine pie. Best of all, this fine dining experience is delivered in a casual, less formal environment. Leave your jackets back at the hotel.

American. Breakfast, lunch, dinner, Sunday brunch. Bar. Children's menu. Reservations recommended. Closed December-March. $36-85

RECOMMENDED

BAR HARBOR
MAGGIE'S
6 Summer St., Bar Harbor, 207-288-9007; www.maggiesbarharbor.com

For the ultimate locavore experience, try this sweet, local bistro. The owner started growing her own produce back in the 1990s. Before that, in the 1970s, she operated a fish market, where she learned to buy the freshest catch directly from local fisherman. Today, the restaurant is a beloved local establishment housed in a tiny blue house and specializing in tasty plates of lobster crepes, stuffed flounder and braised monkfish. The warm, dark chocolate pudding cake offers the perfect end to a meal.

International. Dinner. Reservations recommended. Outdoor seating. Closed Sunday; late October-mid-June. Bar. $16-35

INLAND MAINE, AUGUSTA, BANGOR AND AROOSTOCK COUNTY

There are no lighthouses or lobstering boats, but even so, central Maine is a pleasant vacation destination, especially for outdoor enthusiasts and history lovers. Start your exploration in Augusta, the state's unusually quaint capital city. The 180-foot dome over Maine's capitol is Augusta's signature landmark, though visitors are just as pleased to see the expansive Maine History Museum and the Old Fort Western, the nation's oldest surviving wooden fort.

Bangor, meanwhile, is a historic lumbering town—it even has a 30-feet tall Paul Bunyon statue to prove it. For more evidence of the city's flush past, take a stroll to see the Federalist-style mansions in the Broadway region (where novelist Stephen King now lives). Maine's third-largest city, this city beside the Penobscot River also boasts restaurants, shopping and a thriving arts scene.

Finally, if you drive to the top of Highway 1, you'll land at Fort Kent, directly across the St. John River from New Brunswick. Another of the city's famous lumbering towns, Fort Kent is now a gathering ground for canoeists, skiers and snowmobilers.

WHAT TO SEE

AUGUSTA

BLAINE HOUSE
State and Capitol streets, Augusta, 207-287-2121; www.blainehouse.org

Originally, this 1883 mansion was home to James G. Blaine, Speaker of the U.S. House of Representatives and an 1884 presidential candidate. Since 1919, however, this 28-room house has functioned as the official residence of Maine's governors. Originally built in the Federal style, it was remodeled several times and today appears semi-colonial.

Self-guided tours: by appointment only. May-September, Tuesday-Thursday, 2-4 p.m.

MAINE STATE MUSEUM
83 State House Station, Augusta, 207-287-2301; mainestatemuseum.org

Dating back to 1837, this state museum features exhibits on Maine's natural environment, prehistory, social history and manufacturing heritage. The vast collection ranges from fossils and ancient Native American relics, to colonial furniture, glass, textiles and vintage industrial equipment.

Monday-Friday 9 a.m.-5 p.m., Saturday 10 a.m.-4 p.m.

OLD FORT WESTERN
City Center Plaza, 16 Cony St., Augusta, 207-626-2385; www.oldfortwestern.org

Built in 1754 by wealthy Boston merchants, this is America's oldest surviving wooden fort. Today, the grounds feature the original fort, watch boxes and

HIGHLIGHT

ACADIA NATIONAL PARK

The majestic rocky coastline and thich woodlands filled with wildlife make Acadia National Park a favorite spot to visit in Maine. The 47,633-acre park takes up almost half of Mount Desert Island, a 14-by-12-mile lobster claw–shaped island made predominantly of rugged granite. The park also comprises smaller areas on Isle au Haut, Little Cranberry Island, Baker Island, Little Moose Island and part of the mainland at Schoodic Point. Created by the force of glaciers more than 20,000 years ago, the coastal Acadia area has countless valleys, lakes and mountains that were forever changed by the great fire of 1947, which burned for over four weeks and scorched more than 17,000 acres. As a result, instead of only fir, pine and spruce, the forests in the area now include younger, more varied tree species. Although small compared to other national parks, Acadia still hosts more than 2 million visitors annually, and it's the only national park in the northeastern United States. Situated 160 miles north of the state's capital, Augusta, Acadia can be reached by plane through Bangor, Maine (50 miles), the closest airport that serves national airlines.

Native Americans were the first inhabitants of the Acadia area, and they lived here for more than 6,000 years before Europeans began arriving in search of natural resources. French explorer Samuel de Champlain officially founded a settlement on Mount Desert Island in 1604. Shortly thereafter, French Jesuit missionaries settled here until they were driven off by an armed vessel from Virginia in the first act of overt warfare between France and England for control of North America. Until 1713, the island was a part of French Acadia, and not until after the Revolutionary War was it officially settled. It soon became a popular summer destination for wealthy vacationers who bought land and built mansions or "summer cottages." In 1916, President Woodrow Wilson proclaimed 6,000 acres of land as Sieur de Monts National Monument. It was changed to Lafayette National Park in 1919, and finally, in 1929, it was enlarged and renamed Acadia National Park.

The expansion of the park is largely thanks to land donated by private citizens who loved the area and wanted to preserve its natural beauty. One of the best-known contributors to the park was John D. Rockefeller, Jr., who built the popular carriage road system to avoid motorized vehicles. He later donated 11,000 acres of land, roughly one-quarter of the park's current acreage. Because of private gifts like these, the park grew piecemeal throughout the 20th century, so much so that Congress could only establish its official boundaries in 1986.

Only limited camping is available in Acadia National Park. On Mount Desert Island, the 306-site Blackwoods Campground is open year-round (Route 3, five miles south of Bar Harbor; reservations recommended May 1-October 31, 877-444-6777; www.recreation.gov), while the Seawall campground's 214 sites are available late May to September 30 (Route 102A, four miles south of Southwest Harbor; first-come, first served). Both campgrounds are located in the woods within a short walk from the ocean. On the Isle au Haut, the primitive Duck Harbor campground only has five sites and is open May 15 to October 15. Reservations are required; call 207-288-3338 or use the form at www.nps.gov/acad.

HIGHLIGHTS

WHAT ARE SOME EXAMPLES OF GREAT HISTORIC ARCHITECTURE IN AUGUSTA?

THE BLAINE HOUSE
Check out this mish-mosh of New England architectural styles that functions as the governor's mansion. Originally built in 1883 as a Federal-style mansion, the Blaine House was remodeled over the years so that it now looks semi-Colonial.

OLD FORT WESTERN
Built in 1754 as part of an effort to promote settlement near Augusta, Old Fort Western has two distinctions: First, it has never been attacked. Second, because of this it's still possible to visit America's oldest surviving wooden fort.

STATE HOUSE
This classical granite marvel was built in 1827 by Charles Bulfinch, the architect who designed the U.S. Capitol. The State House was continually remodeled over the years, and later given the city of Augusta's most distinctive architectural feature: the building's dollhouse-like copper dome.

palisade as well as a reproduction blockhouse. Take a tour with a costumed interpreter to get a feel for 18th-century life on the Kennebec River.
June-August, daily 1-4 p.m.; after September-early October, weekends only 1-4 p.m.; November-March, limited Sundays.

STATE HOUSE
83 State House Station, Augusta, 207-287-2301
The original 1827 design for this impressive building was by Charles Bulfinch, celebrated architect of the Massachusetts State House and the United States Capitol in Washington, D.C. However, the building has been continually remodeled and enlarged over the years, including a major renovation in 1910 that established the capitol's current look. Also of note, the building's 150-foot copper dome is crowned by a statue that depicts the female character Wisdom. It was designed by W. Clark Noble and installed, along with the building's new dome, in 1910.
Monday-Friday.

BANGOR

BANGOR MUSEUM AND CENTER FOR HISTORY

159 Union St., Bangor, 207-942-1900; www.bangormuseum.com

Founded in 1864, this museum has been documenting life in the Penobscot Valley for more than 140 years. Highlights include an exhaustive collection of daguerreotypes, tintypes and other early photography processes, as well as the Quipus collection of historic clothing.

Tuesday-Saturday.

COLE LAND TRANSPORTATION MUSEUM

405 Perry Road, Bangor, 207-990-3600; www.colemuseum.org

Showcasing the history of transportation in the American Northeast, the Cole Museum does a good job of reflecting its environment—it has one of the largest collections of snow removal equipment in the country. It also features antique cars, military vehicles, firetrucks, farm equipment, motorcycles and horse-drawn carriages.

May-mid-November, daily 9 a.m.-5 p.m.

MONUMENT TO PAUL BUNYAN

Bass Park, Main Street, Bangor

You can't miss the supposed birthplace of Paul Bunyan. It's marked by a 31-foot-tall statue of the ax-wielding lumberjack. It's worth noting, however, that Akeley, Minnesota makes a competing claim to Bunyan's heritage.

FORT KENT

FORT KENT BLOCKHOUSE

North edge of town, 207-941-4014

This 839 blockhouse was built as a guard post during the Aroostook "Bloodless" War with Great Britain, a dispute regarding the boundary between Maine and New Brunswick. A fascinating example of 19th century military construction, the heavy-duty structure is built from extra-thick, square-hewn cedar longs. Today, the blockhouse contains a museum featuring antique hand tools and interpretive displays. Picnicking is allowed onsite.

June-August, daily.

FORT KENT HISTORICAL SOCIETY MUSEUM AND GARDENS

54 W. Main St., Fort Kent, 207-834-5121

Built in 1902, this railroad station was the northernmost point along the Fish River Railroad. The simple station houses a museum that traces the history of the railroad as it relates to Fort Kent.

June-August, Tuesday-Friday 1-4 p.m.

LONESOME PINE TRAILS

Forest Avenue, Fort Kent, 207-834-5202; www.lonesomepines.org

Maine's northernmost ski area features 13 trails for Nordic and alpine skiers alike. Experienced shredders will love the dramatic 2,300-foot slope with a 500-foot drop, whereas novices will feel more comfortable with the beginners slope. Cross-country skiers, meanwhile, can pick from 25 kilometers of trail. The ski patrol is on duty daily.

December-April.

SPECIAL EVENT

CAN-AM CROWN INTERNATIONAL SLED DOG RACES

West Main Street, Fort Kent, 207-834-3312, 800-733-3563; can-am.sjv.net

Cheer for the mushers as they compete in three races of varying length: 30, 60 and 250-miles, the last of which is a qualifier for Alaska's prominent Iditarod and Yukon Quest races. Each event begins on Main Street in downtown Fort Kent and each finishes at the Lonesome Pine Ski Lodge.

March.

WHERE TO STAY

AUGUSTA

★★★SENATOR INN & SPA

284 Western Ave., Augusta, 207-622-5804, 877-772-2224; www.senatorinn.com

This hotel makes the perfect base camp for those wanting to explore Acadia or Maine's western mountains. Then again, the lodgings are so nice you might stay put to luxuriate in its colonial-style rooms, its relaxing spa or its excellent onsite restaurant, aptly named Cloud 9.

125 rooms. Complimentary breakfast. Restaurant, bar. Fitness center. Spa. Pool. $151-250

WELCOME TO NEW HAMPSHIRE

THE NEW HAMPSHIRE STATE MOTTO, AS PROUDLY proclaimed on its motorists' license plates, is "Live Free or Die." Though the maxim is a reference to the state's revolutionary history, it inspires a little ribbing at the granite state's expense. "Do you mean to say 'Live Free and Die?,'" ask New Hampshire's neighbors. After all, the state has markedly fewer laws restricting personal freedoms than any other state, including no helmet laws for motorcyclists and no seatbelts laws for automobile drivers.

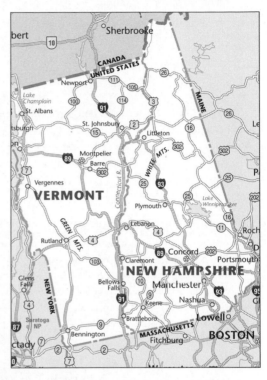

But this very atmosphere is what attracts newcomers: Entrepreneurs come for the low taxes; vacationers come for the wild mountain scenes. Journalists descend, too, usually to puzzle over New Hampshire's famously independent voters, who participate in the nation's first presidential primary every four years.

When it comes to tourist attractions, New Hampshire's White Mountains region is the most popular. Here, explorers encounter all manner of hotel resorts, skiing areas and "notches," a.k.a. passes in the rest of the country. Perched along the state's tiny 18-mile shoreline, the city of Portsmouth also offers plenty to occupy the traveler—historic forts, classic architecture and quintessential New England coastal scenes. Meanwhile, the state's central and southern corridors contain the economic and political powerhouses of Manchester and Concord. Though tourists often overlook these areas, they're packed with gentle hills, river valleys and time-locked colonial villages.

HIGHLIGHTS

NEW HAMPSHIRE'S BEST ATTRACTIONS

GRANITE STATE CANDY SHOPPE
There's nothing like a hand-dipped chocolate, especially when it's made from a family recipe dating back 80 years.

LEAF-PEEPING IN THE WHITE MOUNTAINS
In October, the White Mountains countryside comes alive with reds, golds and oranges. For the ultimate enjoyment, set up camp at a cozy bed and breakfast. Many of these establishments feature great leaf-peeping from the comfort of their guest rooms.

PALATIAL RESORT-HOTELS
The White Mountains boast some the nation's grandest castle-like resort-hotels. Choose between the elegant Omni Mount Washington Resort, or the delightfully old-fashioned Balsams Resort. Either way, you're sure to enjoy wholesome outdoor activities, topnotch service and terrific gourmet meals.

SOUTH, CENTRAL AND SEACOAST

Once upon a time, Portsmouth was the New Hampshire state capital. Luckily for this pleasant city it has plenty of other virtues, enough to console the inhabitants when their city lost the title more than 200 years ago. For starters, Portsmouth and its visitors are the beneficiaries of a decades-old initiative to restore, rather than bulldoze, the town's colonial landmarks. As a consequence, the city makes a great destination for history-lovers and architecture aficionados alike—check out the city's bounty of house museums. From Portsmouth, it's easy to decamp to nearby New Castle, another history trove with both British and American military sites.

As you travel inland from Portsmouth, New Hampshire's only primary port, you encounter the state's string of bucolic villages. Exeter is famous as the home of Philips Exeter Academy, a prestigious preparatory school. Likewise, Hanover is associated with Dartmouth University, the city's largest landowner. Yet each town is charming in its own right, with colonial buildings, gorgeous outdoor scenery and old-fashioned country inns. Notably, southern and central New Hampshire boast another, more unusual variety of idyll: old Shaker villages, which still bear evidence of their founders' idealism.

Meanwhile, in the big city, Manchester is seeing hints of a cultural renaissance, thanks in part to its excellent museums. As for Concord, it's hardly a metropolis, but the fair city has bountiful parks and gorgeous granite buildings.

WHAT TO SEE

CANTERBURY
CANTERBURY SHAKER VILLAGE
288 Shaker Road, Canterbury, 603-783-9511; www.shakers.org

Pay homage to New Hampshire's Shaker heritage by visiting this National Historic Landmark museum offering guided and self-guided tours of the village's dwellings, workshops, gardens and barns. Notably, the site also includes a Shaker-inspired restaurant and gift shop.

Admission: adults $17, children 6-17 $8, children 5 and under free. Mid-May-late-October, daily 10 a.m.-5 p.m.; November, Saturday-Sunday; December, select days.

CONCORD
CHRISTA MCAULIFFE PLANETARIUM
2 Institute Drive, Concord, 603-271-7831; www.starhop.com

Named for New Hampshire teacher Christa McAuliffe, who died aboard the U.S. space shuttle Challenger on January 28, 1986, this 92-seat planetarium offers a variety of shows on black holes, solar systems and starry skies. While some presentations are designed specifically for the young, others boast 3-D graphics so cool they'll impress all ages.

Saturday-Thursday 10 a.m.-5 p.m.; Friday until 9 p.m.

GRANITE STATE CANDY SHOPPE
9-17 Warren St., Concord, 603-225-2591, 888-225-2531; www.nhchocolates.com

Founded in 1927 by a Greek immigrant, Granite State Candy Shoppe is an old-fashioned candy store with a cult following. The shop is now owned by the founder's grandchildren, who still use their grandfather's original copper kettles and painstakingly dip each chocolate by hand.

Monday-Saturday 10 a.m.-6 p.m., Thursday-Friday until 8 p.m., Sunday noon-5 p.m.

MUSEUM OF NEW HAMPSHIRE HISTORY
6 Eagle Square, Concord, 603-228-6688; www.nhhistory.org

Founded in 1823, this history museum features exhibits on the state's history and heritage. Collections include handicrafts, Native American artifacts, photographs of noteworthy people and events, and even old stagecoaches.

Admission: adults $5.50, seniors $4.50, children 6-18 $3, children 5 and under free. Tuesday-Saturday 9:30 a.m.-5 p.m., Sunday noon-5 p.m.; July-mid-October, December, Monday-Saturday 9:30 a.m.-5 p.m., Sunday noon-5 p.m.

PIERCE MANSE
14 Penacook St., Concord, 603-225-4555; www.piercemanse.org

Our nation's 14th president, Franklin Pierce, lived here from 1842 to 1848. The

HIGHLIGHTS

WHAT ARE THE REGION'S TOP MUSEUMS?

CURRIER MUSEUM OF ART
Despite a recent expansion, the Manchester museum remains manageable and small, especially when you consider the big-time art collection with works by Monet, Picasso and O'Keeffe.

HOOD MUSEUM OF ART
Located on the Dartmouth campus, this museum boasts pieces by superstars like Rembrandt, Picasso and other European masters. The massive collection also features art from Africa, Asia and the Americas, not to mention a significant cache of contemporary art.

STRAWBERRY BANKE MUSEUM
This preserved urban neighborhood features some 40 historic homes, some dating as far back as the 17th century. Be sure to enlist a tour guide to fully appreciate this storied immigrant neighborhood.

modest house now serves as a history museum. Filled with period furnishings, documents and personal artifacts, the property captures what life was like for the Pierce family.
Mid-June-mid-October, Tuesday-Saturday 11 a.m.-3 p.m.; also by appointment.

STATE HOUSE
107 N. Main St., Concord, 603-271-2154
Built in 1812, this Greek Revivalist state capitol features Corinthian columns and Beaux-Arts embellishments. Inside, guests are treated to statues, portraits of notable New Hampshirites and the impressive Hall of Flags.
Monday-Friday.

CORNISH
SAINT-GAUDENS NATIONAL HISTORIC SITE
139 Saint-Gaudens Road, Route 12A, Cornish, 603-675-2175; www.nps.gov
This former residence and studio of Augustus Saint-Gaudens is now a public building displaying more than 100 of the 19th-century sculptor's works. The most famous Saint-Gaudens pieces include The Puritan, Adams Memorial and Shaw Memorial, though the site also features works by other artists, formal gardens and a sculptor-in-residence program.
June-October, daily 9 a.m.-4:30 p.m.

ENFIELD

ENFIELD SHAKER MUSEUM

24 Caleb Dyer Lane, Enfield, 603-632-4346; www.shakermuseum.org

The site of a former Shaker community, this museum includes history exhibits, craft demonstrations, workshop services, special programs and extensive gardens.

Monday-Saturday 10 a.m.-5 p.m., Sunday noon-5 p.m.

EXETER

AMERICAN INDEPENDENCE MUSEUM

1 Governors Lane, Exeter, 603-772-2622; www.independencemuseum.org

During the American Revolution, the Ladd-Gilman House and the Folsom Tavern functioned as epicenters of local political life. Today, the combined sites are dedicated to the stories of Exeter's brave revolutionary community.

May-October, Wednesday-Saturday 10 a.m.-4 p.m.

PHILLIPS EXETER ACADEMY

20 Main St., Exeter, 603-772-4311; www.exeter.edu

Founded in 1781 by John Phillips, a visionary who sought an education for "students from every quarter," Exeter is known for its students' socioeconomic diversity. With a sprawling 400-acre campus and more than 100 buildings, the prestigious prep school is also a charming place to visit. Noteworthy buildings include the 1971 library by Louis I. Kahn, the Frederick R. Mayer Art Center and the Lamont Art Gallery.

HANOVER

DARTMOUTH COLLEGE

Main and Wheelock Streets, Hanover, 603-646-1110; www.dartmouth.edu

This Ivy League school is known for its rural campus, with Georgian-style buildings spread over a five-acre green. That physical isolation ensures high student participation in athletics, sororities and fraternities. It also makes Dartmouth an idyllic place to visit.

WEBSTER COTTAGE

32 N. Main St., Hanover, 603-643-6529

Nineteenth-century statesman Daniel Webster supposedly lived here, a tiny 1780 cottage, during his final year at Dartmouth. Though his residence in the house has never been proven, the cottage has become an important part of Dartmouth identity and campus lore.

June-mid-October, Wednesday, Saturday-Sunday.

MANCHESTER

CURRIER MUSEUM OF ART

150 Ash St., Manchester, 603-669-6144; www.currier.org

This is one of New England's leading small museums, featuring 13th- to 20th-century European and American paintings and sculpture by superstars like Monet, Picasso and O'Keeffe. It also houses New England decorative art, furniture, glass and silver. The museum also offers concerts, films and tours of the nearby Zimmerman House, the only public Frank Lloyd Wright-designed house in the state.

Admission: adults $10, seniors $9, students $8, children 17 and under free. Sunday-Monday, Wednesday-Friday 11 a.m.-5 p.m., Saturday 10 a.m.-5 p.m. (free admission 10 a.m.-noon); extended hours the first Thursday of the month; closed Tuesday.

MANCHESTER HISTORIC ASSOCIATION MILLYARD MUSEUM

129 Amherst St., Manchester, 603-622-7531; www.manchesterhistoric.org

This museum and library documents life in Manchester from pre-colonial times to the present. The permanent collection includes vintage firefighting equipment, decorative arts, costumes and paintings.

Wednesday-Saturday 10 a.m.-4 p.m.

SCIENCE ENRICHMENT ENCOUNTERS MUSEUM

200 Bedford St., Manchester, 603-669-0400; www.see-sciencecenter.org

Dedicated to teaching basic science principles, this museum features more than 60 interactive exhibits on subjects like forces, light and electricity. Kids also love the LEGO Millyard, the largest permanent LEGO installation in the world.

Monday-Friday 10 a.m.-4 p.m., Saturday-Sunday 10 a.m.-5 p.m.

NEW CASTLE
FORT CONSTITUTION

New Castle, 603-436-1552; www.nhstateparks.com

The site of one of the first covert acts of the American Revolution, Fort Constitution was once a British defensive post called Fort William and Mary. On December 14, 1774, a ragtag group of revolutionaries overwhelmed the British captain and his garrison, then stole five tons of gunpowder. Little remains of the original British fort, only the base of its walls. Fort Constitution was built on the site in 1808. Granite walls were added during the Civil War.

Mid-June-August, daily; late May-mid-June, September-mid-October, Saturday-Sunday.

FORT STARK STATE HISTORIC SITE

Wild Rose Lane, New Castle, 603-436-1552; www.nhstateparks.com

Situated on Jerry's Point, overlooking the Piscataqua River and the ocean, the fort was built to protect Portsmouth Harbor. The fort stands as a testament to American military innovation, with its stonework and earthwork fortifications dating to the Spanish American War.

Late May-mid-October, daily.

PORTSMOUTH
GOVERNOR JOHN LANGDON HOUSE

143 Pleasant St., Portsmouth, 603-436-3205; www.spnea.org

This magnificent estate was once home to John Langdon, an early American statesman who served three terms as governor of New Hampshire and who was the first president pro tempore of the U.S. Senate. George Washington was entertained here in 1789. To this day, the 1784 house is surrounded by beautifully landscaped gardens. The exterior features Rococo-style woodcarving, whereas the interior is filled with fine Portsmouth-area furniture.

Tours: June-mid-October, Friday-Sunday.

ISLES OF SHOALS

315 Market St., Portsmouth, 603-431-5500; www.islesofshoals.com

The *M/V Thomas Laighton* makes cruises to historic stops throughout Portsmouth Harbor and the Piscataqua River Basin, with special events like lobster clambake river cruises, fall foliage excursions and more.
Mid-June-August, daily.

JOHN PAUL JONES HOUSE

43 Middle St., Portsmouth, 603-436-8420; www.seacoastnh.com

The famous naval commander boarded here with his steward during two visits to Portsmouth. The 1758 house is now a museum containing period furniture, and collections of costumes, china, glass, documents and weapons.
June-mid-October, daily.

MOFFATT-LADD HOUSE

154 Market St., Portsmouth, 603-436-8221; www.moffattladd.org

Built in 1763 by Captain John Moffatt, this Georgian mansion was later home to General William Whipple, Moffatt's son-in-law and a signer of the Declaration of Independence. Many original 18th- and 19th-century furnishings are on display, reflecting the estate's use as a private home from 1763 to 1900.
Mid-June-mid-October, daily.

RUNDLET-MAY HOUSE

364 Middle St., Portsmouth, 603-436-3205; www.seacoastnh.com

This Federalist, three-story 1807 mansion sits on a terraced rise, surrounded by its original 1812 courtyard and gardens. Inside the house, visitors find Rundlet family heirlooms from the 19th century, including many fine examples of Federalist craftsmanship and what were the latest technologies of the time. Guided tours are available.
June-October, first Saturday of the month.

STRAWBERY BANKE MUSEUM

454 Court St., Portsmouth, 603-433-1100; www.strawberybanke.org

More than a museum, this site connects visitors with history via the restoration of a historic waterfront neighborhood. Check out the architectural exhibits, family programs and tours to learn more about the immigrant families who once lived here.
May-October, daily 10 a.m.-5 p.m.; December, hours vary.

WARNER HOUSE

150 Daniel St., Portsmouth, 603-436-5909; www.warnerhouse.org

This 1716 house is one of New England's finest Georgian houses, with ornamental plasterwork in the dining room, restored mural paintings decorating the staircases, a lightning rod said to have been installed by Benjamin Franklin in 1762 and five portraits by Joseph Blackburn.
Guided tours: June-mid-October, Monday-Sunday, hours vary.

WENTWORTH-GARDNER HOUSE

50 Mechanic St., Portsmouth, 603-436-4406; www.wentworthgardnerandlear.org

Built by the wealthy Wentworth family in 1760, this Georgian mansion is filled

with heavy carvings and period furniture.
Mid-June-mid-October, Thursday-Sunday noon-4 p.m.

WHERE TO STAY

BEDFORD
★★★BEDFORD VILLAGE INN
2 Olde Bedford Way, Bedford, 603-472-2001, 800-852-1166; www.bedfordvillageinn.com
Housed in a converted 1800s barn, this stately New England inn offers all-suite rooms with four-poster beds, Italian marble and whirlpool bathtubs. Guests and locals alike line up for breakfast and dinner at the cozy on-site restaurant, specializing in hearty takes on classic American recipes.
14 rooms. Restaurant, bar. $251-350

HANOVER
★★★HANOVER INN
Main and Wheelock streets, Hanover, 603-643-4300, 800-443-7024; www.hanoverinn.com
Located just minutes from Dartmouth College, this inn serves up comfy accommodations with a colonial motif. When it comes time to work out, you won't have to sweat it out in a cramped fitness center; as a guest of the hotel, you're welcome to use the university's athletic facilities. The inn features a lovely fine-dining restaurant that serves breakfast, lunch and dinner.
92 rooms. Restaurant, bar. Fitness center. Airport transportation available. $251-350

PORTSMOUTH
★★★SHERATON HARBORSIDE HOTEL PORTSMOUTH
250 Market St., Portsmouth, 603-431-2300, 800-325-3535; www.sheratonportsmouth.com
An expansive New England-style hotel, this Sheraton features a stately brick-and-granite exterior with large-paneled windows. The interior, however, is far more contemporary—sleek, comfortable and stylish. Best of all, the hotel is conveniently located in the downtown historic district on the Piscataqua River.
220 rooms. Restaurant, bar. Fitness center. Pool. Business center. $151-250

RECOMMENDED

THE PORT INN
505 Highway 1 Bypass South, Portsmouth, 603-436-4378, 800-282-7678; www.theportinn.com
This independent inn decorates its rooms with cheerful chintzes and wall coverings. Business travelers will appreciate the special touches like upscale bath products and kitchenettes. Barbecue enthusiasts will be especially pleased: The outdoor pool area features a grill.
57 rooms. Complimentary breakfast. Pool. $61-150

WHERE TO EAT

BEDFORD
★★★BEDFORD VILLAGE INN
2 Village Inn Way, Bedford, 603-472-2001, 800-852-1166; www.bedfordvillageinn.com
Originally part of a working farm, this country inn is surrounded by gardens and verdant hillsides. Come mealtime, guests can choose between the high-end

BVI Restaurant, Corks wine bar or the casual tavern. Either way, they'll enjoy finely crafted dishes made from fresh, local ingredients.

American. Breakfast, lunch, dinner. Reservations recommended. Bar. $36-85

RECOMMENDED

CONCORD

ANGELINA'S RISTORANTE ITALIANO

11 Depot St., Concord, 603-228-3313; www.angelinasrestaurant.com

A casual Italian bistro with simple, whitewashed walls and linen-covered tables, this restaurant is a reliable spot for freshly made pastas and classics like veal parmesan. The wine list is noteworthy for its reasonably priced bottles, not to mention its focus on Italy's great wines.

Italian. Lunch, dinner. Reservations recommended. Lunch (Monday-Friday), dinner (Monday-Saturday). Closed Sunday. $16-35

HANOVER

JESSE'S

Lebanon Road, Hanover, 603-643-4111; www.blueskyrestaurants.com

This steakhouse delivers on more than tasty grilled meats. It delivers on ambiance, too, with a log cabin feel and a charming wood-burning fireplace. To top things off, the brand-new martini bar specializes in craft offerings such as the so-called espressotini and the sour apple martini.

Steak. Lunch, dinner. Bar. Children's menu. Outdoor seating. $16-35

WHITE MOUNTAINS AND THE GREAT NORTH WOODS

New England's highest peak, Mount Washington, attracts some of the world's most monstrous weather. Even so, the mountain is ringed with heavenly valleys, mountain lakes and luxury hotel-resorts, enough to sustain a hearty year-round tourist industry. Visitors flock to the Bretton Woods, for example, a popular resort area located on a long glacial plain beside the mountain. North Conway, meanwhile, is a posh town that serves up dramatic views of the area's mountaintops and ledges, not to mention a growing anchor of outlet stores to attract bargain-hunters. Popular with leaf-peepers, popular with winter sports enthusiasts, the White Mountains region features something to please practically everyone.

Constituting the northernmost third of the state, the Great North Woods almost kisses Canada. This gorgeous backcountry is popular with vacationing outdoorsmen, thanks to abundant moose populations, and excellent skiing, hunting and fishing. Notably, the wholesome Balsams Resort is located in a blink of a town called Dixville Notch. The town may be familiar to news junkies—every fours years, the town's registered voters (all 20 or so) are the first Americans to vote for U.S. president. They cast their ballots just past midnight.

HIGHLIGHTS

WHAT ARE THE BEST PLACES FOR OUTDOOR ADVENTURE?

FRANCONIA NOTCH STATE PARK
For low effort and high reward, take an easy-breezy hike along the wooden boardwalk that hugs the mossy cliffs of Flume Gorge.

OMNI MOUNT WASHINGTON RESORT
Where opulence meets the outdoors, this resort offers zipline canopy tours, mountain biking, alpine skiing, even dogsledding. At the end of the day, adventurers can rest their weary feet at the resort's upscale spa or its nice restaurant.

TUCKERMAN RAVINE TRAIL
The most common way to ascend Mount Washington is by way of this popular trail. From Pinkham Notch, it's a strenuous four-mile hike to the summit.

WHAT TO SEE

BRETTON WOODS
BRETTON WOODS SKI AREA
Highway 302, Bretton Woods, 603-278-1000; www.brettonwoods.com
New Hampshire's largest ski area features more than slopes, lifts and trails for Nordic skiing. The property is a popular destination for summertime activity, too, including zipline tours, horseback riding and golf. When visitors get hungry, they can choose from the onsite pub, food court or summit house.
Late November-April, daily. Night skiing: early December-March, Friday-Saturday.

COG RAILWAY
Highway 302, Bretton Woods, 603-278-5404, 800-922-8825; www.thecog.com
Mount Washington is home to the world's first cog railway, a rack-and-pinion trail that enables train travel on steep surfaces. Visitors can ride the vintage track by way of steam engine and biodiesel trains. It's a leisurely mode of travel, to be sure. It takes three hours to reach the scenic summit and come back.
May, Saturday-Sunday; June-November, daily.

CRAWFORD NOTCH STATE PARK
Highway 302, Bretton Woods, 603-374-2272; www.nhstateparks.com
This notch is one of the state's most spectacular passes. Once you reach the pass, you'll see mounts Nancy and Willey rising to the west, with mounts Crawford, Webster and Jackson visible to the east. Park headquarters are located in the former site of the famous Samuel Willey house, a structure that miraculously

survived the catastrophic landslide of 1826. The parks also features hiking and walking trails on the Appalachian system. Camping is allowed.
Late-May-mid-October.

DIXVILLE NOTCH

BALSAMS/WILDERNESS SKI AREA

1000 Cold Spring Road, Dixville Notch, 603-255-3400, 877-225-7267; www.thebalsams.com

This uncrowded winter recreation area features 16 alpine trails of varying difficulty, 95 kilometers of Nordic ski trails, even a ski-play area for children. Best of all, the base lodge features high-quality, gourmet meals and snacks, thanks to the oversight of chef Josh Berry from the affiliated Balsams Grand Resort.
December-March, daily.

FRANCONIA

CANNON MOUNTAIN SKI AREA

Franconia Notch State Parkway, Franconia, 603-823-8800; www.cannonmt.com

One of the state's most scenic ski areas, Cannon Mountain features 72 trails, nine lifts, snowboarding facilities and terrific views of Northern New Hampshire and Vermont. Diehards are especially pleased by the New England Ski Museum, an onsite retrospective of East Coast skiing.
Late November-mid-April, June-mid-October, daily; rest of year, Saturday-Sunday (weather permitting).

FLUME GORGE & PARK INFORMATION CENTER

Franconia Notch State Parkway, Franconia, 603-745-8391; www.flumegorge.com

Flume Gorge is a narrow, natural gorge and waterfall located at the base of Mount Liberty. It's a grueling hike, but the gorge is accessible by walkways and stairs. When visitors arrive at the park, they are advised to drop by the information center. There, staffers screen a 15-minute movie that introduces newcomers to the park.
Mid-May-October, daily 9 a.m.-5.30 p.m.

FRANCONIA NOTCH STATE PARK

A top tourist destination since the 19th century, this seven-mile pass and state park runs along a deep valley of 6,440 acres between the Franconia and Kinsman ranges of the White Mountains. Mounts Liberty (4,460 feet), Lincoln (5,108 feet) and Lafayette (5,249 feet) loom in the east, whereas nearby Cannon Mountain (4,200 feet) presents a sheer granite face. The Pemigewasset River follows the length of the Notch. The park offers various recreational activities, including swimming at Sandy Beach.

FROST PLACE

Ridge Road, Franconia, 603-823-5510; www.frostplace.org

The poet's former homestead now functions as a house museum. Visitors won't find much in the way of interpretive displays. They will, however, glimpse the small, uncorrupted house where great American poet Robert Frost worked and lived.
July-mid-October, Wednesday-Monday; June, Saturday-Sunday.

NEW ENGLAND SKI MUSEUM
Franconia Notch Parkway, Franconia, 603-823-7177, 800-639-4181; www.nesm.org
Dedicated to the East Coast's history of skiing, the museum features displays of
vintage skis and bindings, antique clothing and gear, and skiing-relating photo-
graphs and art. The are also occasional screenings of classic ski films.
Admission: free. June-mid-October, December-March, daily 10 a.m.-5 p.m.

OLD MAN OF THE MOUNTAIN HISTORIC SITE
Notch State Parkway
Discovered in 1805, these craggy, glacier-carved cliff edges seemed to form the
profile of a man's face. Sadly, the granite boulders came tumbling down on May
3, 2003. A nonprofit group is in the midst of building a ground-level memorial
on the site.

MOUNT WASHINGTON
GREAT GLEN TRAILS
Highway 16, Gorham, 603-466-2333; www.greatglentrails.com
Located at the base of Mount Washington, these all-season recreational trails
are great for biking and hiking. Drop by the Outdoor Center to inquire about
bicycle rentals and guided hikes. Cross-country skiing, snowshoeing and snow
tubing are offered in the winter. Kayak and canoe tours are also offered on the
nearby Androscoggin River.
Daily; closed April.

MOUNT WASHINGTON AUTO ROAD
Highway 16, Gorham, 603-466-3988; www.mt-washington.com
It takes just 30 minutes to reach the summit of Mount Washington by car.
Before you go, make sure your car is in good condition, especially the brakes.
Guided tours are also available.
Mid-May-mid-October, daily (weather permitting).

MOUNT WASHINGTON SUMMIT MUSEUM
Highway 302, Top of Mount Washington; 603-466-3388; www.mountwashington.org
The Mount Washington Observatory features a small museum with displays
and exhibits about the summit's severe weather, the mountain's rare flora and
fauna, and the range's geological history.
June-mid-October, daily.

JACKSON
BLACK MOUNTAIN
Highway 16B, Jackson, 603-383-4490; www.blackmt.com
For more than 75 years, this family-friendly, family-owned ski resort has
provided something to suit all ages and abilities. These days, the mountain
features 145 acres of ski-able terrain, everything from gentle learning hills to
steep chutes. After a day on the slopes, grab a meal and a beer at the onsite
Lostbo Pub.

JACKSON SKI TOURING FOUNDATION
153 Main St., and Highway 16A, Jackson, 603-383-9355; www.jacksonxc.org
Dedicated to Nordic skiing, the foundation maintains 95 miles of cross-country

trails that connect the area's inns and ski areas. Instruction, rentals and rescue service are also provided.
December-mid-April, daily.

NORTH CONWAY
CONWAY SCENIC RAILROAD
38 Norcross Circle, North Conway, 603-356-5251; www.conwayscenic.com
Take a nostalgic tour aboard steam and diesel trains, which depart from a restored Victorian station for 11-mile trips. The railway runs a Valley Train that explores the Saco River valley, and a Notch Train that travels through Crawford Notch. Special events include dinner trains, foliage tours and kid-friendly tours. A small onsite railroad museum reflects upon the area's locomotive history.
Valley Train: Mid-May-October, daily; mid-April-mid-May, November-December, Saturday-Sunday. Notch Train: Mid-September-mid-October: daily; late June-mid-September, Tuesday-Thursday, Saturday.

ECHO LAKE STATE PARK
Highway 302, North Conway, 603-356-2672
Travel the mile-long auto road to the 700-foot Cathedral Ledge, a dramatic rock formation that towers over beautiful Echo Lake. While you're there, take in the panoramic views of the White Mountains and the Saco River Valley. Swimming and picnicking are permitted in the park.
Late June-August.

MOUNT CRANMORE
Route 16 North Conway, 800-786-6754; www.cranmore.com
Opened in 1937, this White Mountains getaway is one of the country's oldest continually operated ski resorts. With alpine skiing, snowboarding and a snow tubing park, Mount Cranmore has something to offer winter sports enthusiasts of every stripe. Perks include an onsite restaurant with full bar service and even daycare services.
November-April, daily.

WHERE TO STAY

BRETTON WOODS
★★★OMNI MOUNT WASHINGTON HOTEL
Highway 302, Bretton Woods, 603-278-1000, 800-258-0330; www.mountwashingtonresort.com
Opened in 1902 as a summer resort for wealthy city-dwellers, this landmark hotel features a sprawling, well-preserved example of Spanish Renaissance architecture. Tucked at the foot of the White Mountains, the resort features rooms with Colonial-style furnishings, a full-service spa offering mountain-inspired treatments, and solid dining options.
200 rooms. Restaurant, bar. Fitness center. Pool. Golf. Tennis. Business center. $251-350

DIXVILLE NOTCH

★★★THE BALSAMS

1000 Cold Spring Road, Dixville Notch, 603-255-3400, 877-225-7267; www.thebalsams.com

Staying here is like traveling through time. Built just after the Civil War, this 15,000-acre resort maintains a delightfully old-fashioned attitude: service is friendly, guests treat each other like family, and men are required to wear jackets to dinner. During the winter, visitors (usually families) partake in downhill skiing, cross-country skiing, snowboarding and ice skating. During the warmer months, everyone whiles away the time with golf, tennis, swimming and nature walks. Best of all, the food is delicious and it's included in the cost of your room.

212 rooms. Restaurant, bar. Fitness center. Pool. Golf. Tennis. Ski in/ski out. $151-250

FRANCONIA

★★★FRANCONIA INN

1300 Easton Road, Franconia, 603-823-5542, 800-473-5299; www.franconiainn.com

Located in a picturesque valley in the White Mountains, this white clapboard, colonial-style inn has a countrified look to welcome its guests, which includes verandas, oak paneling and fireplaces. Onsite activities include horseback riding, mountain biking, croquet, and swimming in the pool. At the end of the day, visitors retreat to the inn's dining room for upscale comfort food.

34 rooms. Complimentary breakfast. Restaurant, bar. Pool. Tennis. Closed April-mid-May. $61-150

RECOMMENDED

SUGAR HILL INN

Highway 117, Franconia, 603-823-5621, 800-548-4748; www.sugarhillinn.com

Built from a 1789 farmhouse, this country inn delivers charm and style in a traditional New England setting. Inside, though, there are some pleasant surprises—bright, cheerful rooms decorated in fresh florals and checks. The innkeeper has a culinary background, so the focus here is on food, warmth and hospitality. Breakfast and afternoon tea are offered in the lovely dining room, where you can also consume views of Cannon Mountain and Mount Lafayette. For added relaxation, book a hot stone massage in the onsite spa room.

15 rooms. Complimentary breakfast. Restaurant, bar. Spa. Closed one week in April. $151-250

JACKSON

★★★INN AT ELLIS RIVER

17 Harriman Road, Jackson, 603-383-9339, 800-233-8309; www.innatellisriver.com

Sure, the hotel has views of the White Mountains, but this luxury retreat is so relaxing it even has its own bubbling trout stream. Specializing in romantic getaways, the inn features colonial-style guest rooms with whirlpool baths, private balconies and fireplaces. A gourmet breakfast is served in the morning.

21 rooms. No children under 12. Complimentary breakfast. Restaurant, bar. Pool. Reservations recommended. $61-150

★★★INN AT THORN HILL
Thorn Hill Road, Jackson, 603-383-4242, 800-289-8990; www.innatthornhill.com

This modern country-style inn puts a premium on luxury. Choose a room in the main house, the carriage house or one of three private cottages. No matter where you stay, you're treated to down duvet-topped beds, colonial-style furnishings, turndown service and a choice of gourmet breakfasts. Make an appointment at the onsite spa for the ultimate relaxation.

25 rooms. No children under 8. Complimentary breakfast. Restaurant, bar. Fitness center. Spa. Pool. Ski in/ski out. $251-350

★★★WENTWORTH RESORT HOTEL
1 Carter Notch Road, Jackson, 603-383-9700, 800-637-0013; www.thewentworth.com

Built in 1869, this elegant country resort features French provincial-style furnishings, sleigh beds and fireplaces. Guests can choose from suites or budget-friendly standard rooms, though families and business travelers might consider the condo-style accommodations. Gourmet breakfast and dinner are served (at an additional cost) in the onsite dining room.

51 rooms. Restaurant, bar. Pool. Golf. Tennis. Ski in/ski out. $151-250

NORTH CONWAY

★★★WHITE MOUNTAIN HOTEL & RESORT
West Side Road, North Conway, 603-356-7100, 800-533-6301; www.whitemountainhotel.com

This hotel features a breathtaking setting. It's situated at the base of the White Horse Ledge, not far from Cathedral Ledge and Echo State Park. Of course, the English country-style inn makes good on its beautiful surroundings by offering plentiful outdoor activities like cross-country skiing, hiking and rock climbing. Back in their rooms, guests find period-style furnishings and plush linens. At the end of the day, the Ledges Dining Room offers romantic candlelit dinners, live piano music and gourmet meals made from fresh, local ingredients.

80 rooms. Restaurant, bar. Fitness center. Pool. Golf. Tennis. Ski in/ski out. $151-250

SUGAR HILL
RECOMMENDED
SUNSET HILL HOUSE–A GRAND INN
231 Sunset Hill Road, Sugar Hill, 603-823-5522, 800-786-4455; www.sunsethillhouse.com

Built in 1882, this colonial-style property is situated atop a White Mountains ridge, which makes for gorgeous views of the surrounding peaks. The innkeepers are dedicated to preserving that natural beauty, too, offering eco-friendly dining, cleaning services and bath products.

28 rooms. Complimentary breakfast. Restaurant. Pool. Golf. $251-350

WHERE TO EAT

FRANCONIA
★★★THE FRANCONIA INN
1300 Easton Road, Franconia, 603-823-5542, 800-473-5299; www.franconiainn.com

This stately dining room offers inspiring views of the White Mountains. The menu, in turn, exalts that landscape. Comfort foods like filet mignon with crab cakes and pepper-seared Atlantic salmon are made with fresh, local herbs and

HIGHLIGHT

WHICH PLACE MAKES THE BEST WHOOPIE PIES?

This New England treat is supposedly native to Maine, though a tiny New Hampshire pastry shop is known for making some of the best whoopies in the country. To taste this confection in perfection, head to the tiny town of Weare, just 18 miles northwest of Manchester. That's where you'll find **Just Like Mom's Pastries** (*353 Riverdale Road, 603-529-6667; justlikemomspastries.com*). Once you're there, choose between the 18- or the 36-piece platter and from a variety of flavors, though the classic whipped marshmallow and chocolate cake iteration is the reigning favorite.

produce. When the meal is over, there's still plenty to keep guests occupied. Go for a nightcap at the rustic lodge, then end the evening with pinball at the adjacent game room.

American. Breakfast, dinner. Closed April-mid-May. Bar. Children's menu. Reservations recommended. $16-35

JACKSON

★★★INN AT THORN HILL

Thorn Hill Road, Jackson, 603-383-4242, 800-289-8990; www.innatthornhill.com

For the ultimate in cozy dining, this restaurant features mountain views and a wood-burning fireplace. Though the menu changes seasonally, it's known for fine-dining specialties like pan-seared tuna, grilled beef tenderloin and petite rack of veal. The establishment's other virtues include terrific housemade pastries and an extensive wine list.

American. Breakfast, dinner. Bar. Reservations recommended. Outdoor seating. $36-85

NORTH CONWAY

★★★1785 INN

3582 White Mountain Highway, North Conway, 603-356-9025, 800-421-1785; www.the1785inn.com

The atmosphere in the dining room is casual, but the menu is far more painstaking. Choose from creative selections like veal chops with mushrooms and cabernet sauvignon reduction, or seared sea scallops with leeks and artichokes. What's more, the inn is famous for its wide selection of housemade desserts, especially the popular coffee buttercrunch pie.

American, continental. Dinner. Bar. $16-35

WELCOME TO RHODE ISLAND

LITTLE RHODEY, AS IT IS AFFECTIONATELY KNOWN, IS THE

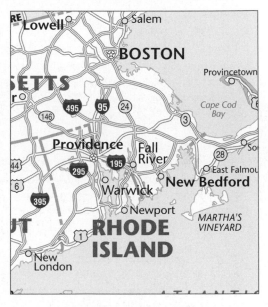

biggest little state in the nation. In fact, Rhode Island's pint size belies its sphere of historical and cultural influence. For starters, there's the Ocean State's 400 miles of coastline, which is lined with lovely sunning, swimming, sailing and fishing enclaves. The glittering coastal city of Newport is one of the nation's most significant and historically rich summer communities. Meanwhile, the state's inland is flecked with postcard-perfect farms, quaint Colonial inns and at least one metropolis. Providence was historically known as the state capital and an industrial town, though lately the city is gaining speed as a center for art, design and cuisine.

Founded in 1636, Rhode Island originally served as a refuge to those fleeing the puritanical tyranny of Massachusetts. As a consequence, Rhode Islanders were early adopters of open-mindedness and religious tolerance. Newport, for example, boasts the nation's first synagogue and its first Anglican church. Notably, Newport is also the site of an important Quaker worship center. In accordance, the state claims a number of other firsts: Rhode Islanders were among the first colonists to attack the British. On May 4, 1776, two months before the signing of the Declaration of Independence, the state was the first to proclaim independence from the British. Rhode Island saw a number of industrial firsts, too, like the first water-powered cotton mill. And while it probably wasn't the first watering hole ever built, Newport's 1673 White Horse Tavern is the oldest operating pub in the United States. Today, the pub is small but sturdy and still going strong—just like its home state.

HIGHLIGHTS

RHODE ISLAND'S BEST ATTRACTIONS

WHITE HORSE TAVERN

Don't leave Newport without a visit to the White Horse Tavern, the oldest operating pub in the nation. Order a Narragansett beer, then stay for dinner—the menu boasts New England favorites like poached Maine lobster and clam chowder.

WATERFIRE

Come summertime, Providence really heats up thanks to the fiery art installation that illuminates its rivers and historic buildings. Grab an outdoor table at a downtown restaurant, or simply camp on a riverbank. Either way, these traveling torch lights are sure to leave you transfixed.

NEWPORT MEGAMANSIONS

Newport's grand estates must be seen to be believed. You'll be amazed as you stroll along Cliffwalk, a scenic pathway sandwiched between the Atlantic Ocean and Newport's gilded-era showpieces.

BLOCK ISLAND

For a taste of nature, catch a ferry from Narragansett to Block Island and spend the day bicycling, hiking or otherwise absorbing the unspoiled splendors. Thanks to historic conservation efforts, almost half the island is protected nature land where rare plant and animal species flourish.

GREATER PROVIDENCE

Longtime locals tell no lies: 15 years ago, they say, you could've rolled a bowling ball through the middle of the city and hit no one. After World War II, the capital of the nation's smallest state was hit hard by suburban sprawl. With rising crime rates and diminishing street life, Providence was little more than a thoroughfare to Boston.

Not so today. Dubbed "The Creative Capital" by lawmakers promoting their city, Providence hit its stride with beautiful condo developments, rebuilt infrastructure and a deep commitment to the arts. Today's Providence is an intimate urban enclave with historic splendor, stunning waterways and a nightlife befitting the big city. Family-friendly events like WaterFire draw millions of visitors to the capital each year. Historic buildings and textile mills have been converted into artist studios and commercial centers with plentiful boutiques, cafés and condos. Some of those restaurants, meanwhile, garner national attention for their world-class cuisine. Notable schools like Brown University and the Rhode Island School of Design ensure the city's vitality for years to come.

WHAT TO SEE

PROVIDENCE
ARCADE
65 Weybosset St., Providence, 401-273-9700
This 1828 three-story beauty is considered America's first indoor shopping mall. Sadly, the complex no longer features the charming independent shops of yesteryear. Today, it houses only a few stores and food vendors, but the beautiful Greek Revival building is worthy of a visit as you stroll to the shopping district along Weybosset Street.

BROWN UNIVERSITY
45 Prospect St., Providence, 401-863-1000; www.brown.edu
The third-oldest college in New England and seventh-oldest in the country, Brown's intimate campus (enrollment is just under 8,300) features gorgeous grounds and quads for walking and lounging, not to mention libraries and art galleries that are free and open to the public. The campus is located in the College Hill neighborhood on a seven-degree incline, so be sure to wear comfortable shoes when you visit.

CULINARY ARTS MUSEUM AT JOHNSON & WALES UNIVERSITY
315 Harborside Blvd., Providence, 491-598-2805; www.culinary.org
Attention food lovers: Housed at Johnson & Wales University, this premier museum is dedicated to the artifacts and histories of the culinary and hospitality industries. More than 30 years old, the collection features cookbooks from the 1500s, menus, a gallery of vintage and antique stoves, Julia Child mementos, a New England tavern and more.
Tuesday-Sunday 10 a.m.-5 p.m.

HIGHLIGHTS

WHAT ARE THE TOP THINGS TO DO IN PROVIDENCE?

CHECK OUT THE CULINARY ARTS MUSEUM
Foodies will enjoy this unique museum which houses vintage cookbooks, appliances and even some of Julia Child's mementos.

STROLL AROUND BROWN UNIVERSITY
This old college has beautiful grounds and art galleries that are open to the public.

FEDERAL HILL
Atwells Avenue, Providence, www.providencefederalhill.com

Despite the diversification of its residents, Providence's Little Italy retains the old-world feel of Italia. Of course, there's plenty to see in the Federal Hill, but there's more to eat. Don't miss the Venda Ravioli from Costantino's, a massive deli counter. Scialo Bros. Bakery has the neighborhood's best Italian cookies and pastries. For something different, try the upscale Mexican offerings at Don Jose Tequilas. It's not Italian, but to survive on the Hill it has to be very, very good.

FIRST UNITARIAN CHURCH
1 Benevolent St., Providence, 401-421-7970; www.firstunitarianprov.org

Located in the College Hill neighborhood, this majestic 1816 building features the largest bell ever cast by Paul Revere. What's more, the church is blessed with a very friendly 600-member congregation that welcomes tourists and visitors alike.
Sunday 10:30 a.m. Summer Hours: 10 a.m.

GOVERNOR STEPHEN HOPKINS HOUSE
15 Hopkins St., Providence, 401-421-0694; www.stephenhopkins.org

Dedicated to the memory of Stephen Hopkins, Rhode Island's ten-time governor and a signer of the Declaration of Independence, this house museum's features include historic documents, personal artifacts and Hopkins' tomb.
April-December, Wednesday, Saturday 1-4 p.m.; also by appointment.

JOHN BROWN HOUSE
52 Power St., Providence, 401-273-7507; www.rihs.org

John Brown was a member of the group that chartered "The College in the English Colony of Rhode Island and Providence Plantations," a.k.a. Brown University. A well-known merchant and slave trader, and later a Rhode Island congressional representative, Brown left his family's home as a lasting gift to

Providence. Built in 1786 in the Georgian style, it was the city's first mansion. Today, it serves as a museum house featuring 18th-century china, glass, paintings—even Brown's personal chariot, the oldest surviving American-made vehicle.

Tours are intermittent. Check website for updated listings.

MUSEUM OF NATURAL HISTORY AND CORMACK PLANETARIUM

1000 Elmwood Ave., Providence, 401-785-9450; cityof.providenceri.com

Situated within Roger Williams Park, Rhode Island's only natural history museum features more than 200,000 objects encompassing anthropology, geology, astronomy and biology. The state's only public planetarium, meanwhile, concentrates on cosmic spectacles and space travel.

Admission: adults $2, children 2-7 $1. Museum: Daily 10 a.m.-5 p.m. Planetarium: Saturday-Sunday 2 p.m.; July 5-September 5, daily 2 p.m.

OLD STATE HOUSE

150 Benefit St., Providence, 401-222-2678; www.preservation.ri.gov

It was here on May 4, 1776, two full months before the Declaration of Independence was signed, that the General Assembly of Rhode Island proclaimed its independence from Great Britain, becoming the first of the 13 colonies to secede. The 1762 brick Georgian-style building was home to the state General Assembly until 1902. Featuring red brick with rusticated brown-stone and a two-story square cupola, the Old State House is one of five former Rhode Island state houses still standing.

Monday-Friday.

PROVIDENCE ATHENAEUM LIBRARY

251 Benefit St., Providence, 401-421-6970; www.providenceathenaeum.org

This 1838 Greek Revival building constitutes one of the oldest subscription libraries in the United States. Outside, the building features a graceful granite exterior. Inside, the stacks sway with rare books like original Audubon elephant folios and first editions of Louisa May Alcott, Herman Melville and Walt Whitman.

September-May, Monday-Thursday 9 a.m.-7 p.m., Friday-Saturday 9 a.m.- 5 p.m., Sunday 1-5 p.m.; June-Labor Day, Monday-Friday 9 a.m.-7 p.m., Saturday 9 a.m.- 1 p.m. Closed first two weeks in August.

PROVIDENCE CHILDREN'S MUSEUM

100 South St., Providence, 401-273-5437; www.childrenmuseum.org

With 8,000 feet of interactive exhibits, the Providence Children's Museums provides a variety of hands-on adventures. The fun includes Coming To Rhode Island, a time-travel adventure through Rhode Island's multicultural history, and Water Ways, an exploration of how water moves. In nicer weather, try the Climber and Underland outdoor learning environments.

April-Labor Day, daily 9 a.m.-6 p.m. and select Friday evenings until 8 p.m.; September-March, Tuesday-Sunday and Monday holidays 9 a.m.-6 p.m., Friday until 8 p.m.

RHODE ISLAND SCHOOL OF DESIGN

2 College St., Providence, 401-454-6100; www.risd.edu

One of the most prestigious art schools in the world, the Rhode Island School of Design enrolls nearly 2,200 students who study everything from painting and sculpture to illustration and fashion design. Don't miss RISD's Fleet Library, one of the country's oldest independent art college libraries. Check out RISD: Gallery for a glimpse of works by staff and students alike.

RHODE ISLAND STATE HOUSE

82 Smith St., Providence, 401-222-2357; www.rilin.state.ri.us

The 1901 neoclassical-style capitol features one of the largest self-supporting domes in the world. Other noteworthy features include the white Georgian marble exterior, sculpted ceilings and the opulent stateroom that features an original Gilbert Stuart portrait of George Washington.

Tours: Monday-Friday; call for appointment. Closed second Monday in August.

ROGER WILLIAMS PARK

1000 Elmwood Ave., Providence, 401-785-9450; www.rogerwilliamsparkzoo.org

With 430 acres of woodlands, waterways and winding drives, this meticulously landscaped park contains the Roger Williams Park Zoo, the Roger Williams Park Museum of Natural History and Planetarium, Japanese gardens, rose gardens, a botanical center, seven lakes, greenhouses and more.

Daily.

ROGER WILLIAMS PARK ZOO

1000 Elmwood Ave., Providence, 401-785-3510; www.rogerwilliamsparkzoo.org

One of the oldest zoos in the country, this 40-acre zoo features a nature center, a tropical building, a wetlands trail and exhibits on Africa, Australia, Asia and North America. One of the zoo's more unique features, the Marco Polo Trail, retraces the explorer's steps by way of the animals he might have encountered. With more than 600 animals spanning 160 species, the average visit is about three hours.

Daily 9 a.m.-4 p.m. (last admission is at 3:30 p.m.)

SLATER MILL

67 Roosevelt Ave., Pawtucket, 401-725-8638; www.slatermill.org

Just a short drive from Providence's downtown, visitors can discover one of the country's most important textiles museums. During America's Industrial

Revolution, Samuel Slater used Rhode Island's waterways to build the nation's first successful water-powered cotton mill. Needless to say, it changed the face of textile production. Hands-on exhibits and costumed guides—including some children—recreate what it was like to work at the mill.
May-October, Tuesday-Sunday 10 a.m.-4 p.m.

WARWICK

HISTORIC PONTIAC MILLS
334 Knight St., Warwick, 401-737-2700
Once the production site for Fruit of the Loom underpants, this restored 1863 mill complex now houses nearly 80 small businesses—everything from artisan-owned studios and boutiques to open-air markets on the weekends.
Daily.

WALKING TOUR OF HISTORIC APPONAUG VILLAGE
3275 Post Road, Warwick, 401-738-2000, 800-492-7942
Take a tour of Warwick's historic downtown, a heritage district featuring more than 30 historic and architecturally significant buildings. Maps and brochures are available at city hall.

WHERE TO STAY

PROVIDENCE

★★★MARRIOTT PROVIDENCE DOWNTOWN
1 Orms St., Providence, 401-272-2400, 800-937-7768; www.marriott.com
Conveniently located next to I-95, just steps from the state house, this Marriott can't be beat for convenience. The well-appointed rooms make it hard to beat for hospitality as well—think cushy armchairs, stately desks and a pillow menu. In 2009, G Salon opened an onsite outpost for guests who need extra pampering. What's more, the new onsite AQUA Restaurant is a top spot for outdoor dining. Even kids get the royal treatment here, with special events like sandcastle-building competitions and scavenger hunts.
356 rooms. Restaurant, bar. Business center. Fitness center. Pool. Pets accepted. $151-250

★★★THE WESTIN PROVIDENCE
1 W. Exchange St., Providence, 401-598-8000, 800-301-1111; www.westin.com
The downtown Westin is attached via skybridge to Providence Place, the city's primary shopping mall. Even if browsing boutiques isn't your thing, this glistening hotel offers plenty of other distractions: a pleasant enough restaurant-lounge, comfy beds, a better-than-average minibar and a concierge-led running group. What's more, the location is close to dozens of independent eateries, galleries and historic buildings. Not only are canine guests welcome, but they get their own dog beds, too.
364 rooms. Restaurant, bar. Business center. Fitness center. Pool. Pets accepted. $251-350

WARWICK

★★★CROWNE PLAZA
801 Greenwich Ave., Warwick, 401-732-6000, 800-227-6963; www.crowneplaza.com
Stranded travelers will sigh with relief when they check into this Crowne Plaza

SPECIAL EVENTS

JACK-O-LANTERN SPECTACULAR AT ROGER WILLIAMS'S PARK

Elmwood Ave., Providence; www.rogerwilliamsparkzoo.org
The light radiates from thousands of artfully carved pumpkins, which line the park's walkways and greenways. Seeing is believing, but hearing about it helps: The Jack-O-Lantern Spectacular has been recognized for its beauty by CNN, CBS, the Associated Press and *USA Today*.
Yearly, from the second week in October through October 31.

ICE SKATING ON KENNEDY PLAZA

City Hall Park, Providence; www.kennedyplaza.org
Located in the middle of downtown Providence, where all the beautiful buildings are on display, this ice rink is twice the size of Rockefeller Plaza's. Ten dollars buys admittance and skate rental.
November 21-March 21, Monday-Friday 10 a.m.-10 p.m., Saturday-Sunday 11 a.m.-10 p.m.

SPRING FESTIVAL OF HISTORIC HOUSES

21 Meeting St., Providence, 401-831-7440; www.ppsri.org
The Providence Preservation Society organizes this annual event, which is basically an elaborate excuse for gawkers to gain access to the city's grandest private houses and gardens. Ticket holders may also attend lectures on featured homes and other architecture topics.
Third weekend in June.

WATERFIRE

Waterplace Park, 101 Regent Ave., Providence, 401-272-3111; www.waterfire.org
Every now and again, a remarkable art installation goes floating along the three rivers of downtown Providence. It's so spectacular that the locals turn out in droves to see it, a flotilla of torch-lit vessels that illuminate the city's buildings and bridges as they pass. Now in its 13th year, WaterFire happens on pre-scheduled evenings throughout the summer and fall. Check the website for dates and times.
Saturday-Sunday, late May-late October.

outpost, located just three miles from the Providence airport. Here, the guest rooms come with marble baths, mahogany desks and free wireless. For light sleepers, or those who fear the dark, the hotel offers a sleep amenity package with an eye mask, a drape clip, earplugs, lavender spray and a night light.
266 rooms. Restaurant, bar. $151-250

RECOMMENDED

PROVIDENCE

THE BILTMORE

11 Dorrance St., Providence, 401-421-0700; www.providencebiltmore.com

An independent hotel in a sea of name brands, the historic Biltmore marries yesteryear's grandeur with modern amenities, including an onsite Starbucks and Elizabeth Arden Red Door Salon. Check out the 17th-floor ballroom for grew views of the skating rink below. The Biltmore is also convenient to all the major sights, namely Providence Place Mall and College Hill.

292 rooms. $151-250

RENAISSANCE PROVIDENCE HOTEL

5 Avenue of the Arts, Providence, 401-919-5000

Housed in a 1929 Masonic temple, this hotel is the product of the city's largest restoration project. Situated between the State House and Providence Place, the Renaissance is more than a gorgeous stone building—it's big on convenience, too, because all the major attractions are within walking distance. Amenities include comfortable beds, spacious desks and the excellent "Design-A-Bar" package, which allows guests to customize their minibars. Onsite Temple Downtown Restaurant and Lounge is good enough to draw crowds of locals for breakfast.

272 rooms. Restaurant, bar. $151-250

WHERE TO EAT

PROVIDENCE

★★★AL FORNO

577 S. Main St., Providence, 401-273-9760; www.alforno.com

A local favorite with a national reputation, Al Forno has been turning out primo pasta dishes and wood-grilled pizzas for nearly three decades now. Though the rustic, waterfront dining room is plenty charming, the restaurant is more beloved for an Italian menu ruled by Tuscan simplicity. Specialties include the housemade gnocchi with spicy sausage and the baked pasta with tomato, cream and five cheeses. Don't forget dessert—the ice cream is frozen-to-order from bases made fresh every morning.

Italian. Dinner. Bar. Outdoor seating. Closed Sunday-Monday. Reservations recommended. $36-85

★★★★MILL'S TAVERN

101 N. Main St., Providence, 401-272-3331; www.merchantcircle.com

Situated in an old millhouse, this lauded restaurant features a menu that balances the building's classic charms with creatively prepared American seasonal dishes. No matter what you order, it's sure to be cooked using the kitchen's wood-burning oven, wood grill or rotisserie. The paneled walls and wood-burning fireplaces are as warm as the staff, who provide professional and thorough service without being stuffy or intrusive.

Contemporary American. Dinner. Bar. Reservations recommended. $36-85

★★★NEW RIVERS

7 Steeple St., Providence, 401-751-0350;
www.newriversrestaurant.com

Artisan and eclectic describe the decor as well as the menu at this downtown American bistro. Here, the emphasis is all things fresh, local, sustainable and organic. Don't expect a long, fancy menu: Every day, New Rivers concentrates on just six to eight starters, soups, entrees and desserts. One favorite dish is called Two Little Tarts—the first made with fava beans, ricotta, mint and fennel greens, the second with balsamic onions, guanciale and Hannahbelle cheese. Another delicious selection is the tagliatelle pasta, a housemade porcini tagliatelle with roasted morels, grated Asiago, thyme and Re Manfredi olive oil.
American. Dinner. Bar. Reservations recommended. Closed Sunday. $36-85

★★★POT AU FEU

44 Custom House St., Providence, 401-273-8953;
www.potaufeuri.com

Pick between the formal upstairs salon or the rustic, candlelit downstairs dining room. Either way, this traditional French bistro treats you to classic and regional French dishes like onion soup, salad niçoise, and sweet and savory crepes. An extensive list of French wines offers pours by the bottle and some by the glass.
French. Lunch, dinner. Bar. Reservations recommended. Closed Sunday. $16-35

RECOMMENDED

GRACIE'S

194 Washington St., Providence, 401-272-7811;
www.graciesprovidence.com

Here, the chef's guiding philosophy is "to make people happy through food." Thankfully, the food makes good on that lofty sentiment. For starters, the dishes are made with ingredients so local they often come from the restaurant's rooftop garden. Choose between delicious dishes like the hand-made ricotta gnocchi with lobster, chanterelles, fava beans and a buere noisette, or the domestic leg of lamb with boucheron-potato torte, yard beans, pequillo pepper and rosemary lamb reduction. The dining room makes guests happy, too—it features whimsical light fixtures, dark paneling and copper accents.
Contemporary American. Dinner. Bar. Reservations recommended. Closed Sunday-Monday. $16-$35

HARUKI EAST

176 Wayland Ave., Providence, 401-223-0332

A standout among Providence's many Japanese and sushi restaurants, Haruki East features fresh fish (delivered daily) and an eminently friendly wait staff. Don't miss the Hamachi Kama, a perfectly broiled meaty yellowtail jaw, or the Tuna Shitake, featuring shitake mushroom caps stuffed with chopped spicy tuna. The green tea is excellent—it's toasty and delicious. Though the sprawling dining room is big enough to accommodate many, it's often filled by 6:30 p.m.

Japanese. Lunch. Dinner. Bar. Outdoor seating. Reservations recommended. $15 and under

HEMENWAY'S SEAFOOD GRILL

121 South main St., Providence, 401-351-8570; www.hemenwaysrestaurant.com

Here's the first reason to try Hemenway's: the floor-to-ceiling windows deliver outstanding views of Providence's historic courthouse and other architectural sights. The second reason: the excellent seafood dishes, especially the steamers, the lobster rolls, the clam chowder and the lobster ravioli. Don't forget to save room for the mile-high key lime pie.

Seafood. Lunch, dinner. Bar. Outdoor seating. $16-35

LA LAITERIE

184-188 Wayland Ave. Providence, 401-274-7177; www.farmsteadinc.com

Billed as a "New England Bistro," this small space is a cheese-lover's haven. The seasonal, ever-changing menu means every visit holds the promise of a new discovery. Try the cheese and charcuterie plates, featuring a rotating assortment of house-cured meats and condiments. For a more adventurous treat, go for the Southern-style pimiento grilled cheese with Virginia smoky ham, roasted garlic and pink lady apples. Save room for dessert and craft cocktails.

Bistro. Dinner. Bar. Outdoor seating. $16-35

PANE E VINO

365 Atwells Ave., Providence, 401-223-2230; www.panevino.net

An Italian bistro located on Federal Hill, Pane E Vino delivers rustic Mediterranean charm via classic recipes like veal scaloppini and linguine with clams. Don't forget to order off the terrific wine list, which offers a selection of unique bottles from Italy's best wine regions.

Italian. Dinner. Bar. Reservations recommended. $36-85

WHERE TO SHOP

PROVIDENCE

BENEFIT STREET ANTIQUES

140 Wickenden St., Providence, 401-751-9109

Don't be fooled by the name—the store is located on Wickenden Street, in the historic Fox District. Once you find it, though, the destination dazzles with beautiful antiques. Chairs, benches, cutlery sets and drinking glasses are just of few of the treasures you'll find. The prices are reasonable, too. When you're finished shopping for antiques, there's plenty more to see in the Fox District— the area is filled with independent boutiques and restaurants.

Monday-Sunday 10 a.m.-5 p.m., Sunday 1-5 p.m.

FROG AND TOAD

795 Hope St., Providence, 401-831-3434

Despite its storybook name, this boutique features unisex gifts for adults and children alike. Located in the funky Hope neighborhood, the emphasis here is on homespun, eclectic and vaguely Asian-inspired products. From unique jewelry to rice-sack bags, handmade sweaters and dining-table votives, these treasures aren't to be missed.

Monday-Saturday 10 a.m.-6 p.m., Sunday 11 a.m.-4 p.m.

OOP!

220 Westminster St., Providence, 401-270-4366; www.oopstuff.com

You can't miss Oop! as you're walking down Westminster Street, in the Downcity district of downtown Providence. Though the area is filled with independent bookstores and boutiques, this shop pops with whimsy and color, from the artistic toys to the playful selection of books, clocks, ceramics and clothing.

Monday-Saturday 10 a.m.-7 p.m., Sunday 12-5 p.m.

PROVIDENCE PLACE MALL

1 Providence Place, at Francis and Hayes streets, Providence, 401-270-1000; www.providenceplace.com

Conveniently located in downtown, Providence Place is a modern architectural beauty with all the stores you know and love. Here, you'll find The Gap, The Loft, Bed Bath & Beyond, Macy's, Nordstrom, Tiffany's and more.

Monday-Saturday 10 a.m.-9 p.m., Sunday noon-6 p.m.

STUDIO HOP

810 Hope St., Providence, 401-621-2262

Located in Providence's funky Hope neighborhood on the east side of town, this shop-slash-gallery features covetable works by local artists. The husband-and-wife owners are friendly, knowledgeable and happy to steer you toward baubles by Providence's best up-and-coming jewelry-makers. The shop's selection also includes one-of-a-kind pottery, paintings, sculpture and furniture. If you don't find something here, it's easy to keep looking. The neighborhood is filled with similar businesses.

Summer Hours: Monday-Saturday 10 a.m.-6 p.m. Open Sundays after Labor Day

VENDA RAVIOLI, INC.

265 Atwells Ave., Providence, 401-421-9105; www.vendaravioli.com

A Federal Hill fixture, the enormous deli counter and store sells meats, cheeses, pastries, all kinds of frozen pasta, sauces and Italian cooking supplies. Grab a pack of Venda-brand frozen raviolis for later that evening. Rest your feet while grabbing an afternoon espresso and a biscotti. Or simply order a hand-held arancini (rice ball) to munch as you continue your walk through Providence's Little Italy.

Monday-Saturday 8:30 a.m.-6 p.m., Sunday 8:30 a.m.-4 p.m.

NEWPORT COUNTRY

If Jay Gatsby had a second summer home, it might have been in Newport. An epicenter of high society during the gilded age, Newport was a seaside idyll where rich families built opulent summer "cottages," sometimes with as many as 70 rooms. The building spree came crashing down, along with the stock market, in 1929. Though modern bluebloods persist to flock here for seasonal revelries, most prefer the lodgings of a tasteful resort. Meanwhile, the old mansions are open to the public as house museums, a tourist destination in their own right.

Similarly, the nearby seaport of Narragansett was once the site of a lavish Beaux-Arts casino complex. The building was devastated by fire in 1900, though the original tower still stands as a reminder of its excesses. Today, Narragansett is as pleasant a resort town as any.

These towns are more than the sum of their palaces. Newport, for example, has a serious progressive streak, evident in everything from its early synagogue to its Quaker worship center. No Newport vacation is complete without a trip to the mysterious Old Stone Mill and a beer at the White House Tavern, the nation's oldest pub. Of course, Newport and Narragansett make great destinations for fishing and yachting.

As long as you're contemplating the boats, why not hop a ferry to Block Island. Located just 12 miles off the mainland, Block Island is worlds away from the bustle of Newport and Narragansett. The island once served as a low-key fishing and farming community. Thanks to a history of conversation efforts, much of its land is as pristine as ever.

WHAT TO SEE

BLOCK ISLAND
NEW HARBOR
The sprawling New Harbor was formed when town planners cut through a sand bar to merge the sea with the Great Salt Pond. Today, the unusually shaped harbor is scattered with marinas and other moorings.

NORTH LIGHTHOUSE
Corn Neck Road, Block Island, 401-466-3200; www.lighthouse.cc
Built in 1867 on a rocky beach, this former lighthouse now houses a shipwreck museum. Surrounding dunes are home to a seagull rookery and wildlife sanctuary.

SOUTHEAST LIGHTHOUSE
122 Mohegan Trail, Block Island, 401-466-5009; www.lighthouse.cc
From its perch atop the Mohegan Bluffs, this towering 67-foot lighthouse is attached to a hefty keeper's quarters, lending the structure the air of a brick mansion. Inside, a museum details the lighthouse's history. The surrounding bluffs provide visitors with unparalleled ocean views.

HIGHLIGHTS

WHAT ARE THE TOP THINGS TO DO IN NEWPORT COUNTRY?

TOUR THE HOMES
No trip to Newport is complete without touring the majestic and historic homes that once belonged to people like the Vanderbilts. Each is more opulent than the next.

WALK THE CHARMING STREETS OF NEWPORT
This idyllic town is full of pretty shops, cozy pubs and water views, all of which make it perfect for a day of strolling before retreating to one of the pubs for a pint.

NARRAGANSETT

BLOCK ISLAND FERRY
Galilee State Pier, 304 Great Island Road, Point Judith, 401-783-4613; www.blockislandferry.com
Catch this automobile ferry at Point Judith. It provides service to the central part of Old Harbor, Block Island.
Daily.

POINT JUDITH
1460 Ocean Road, Narragansett, 401-789-0444
Though the lighthouse and station are closed to the public, strolling the small cape of Point Judith is free. From here, visitors get an excellent look at Narragansett Bay and Rhode Island Sound.

SOUTH COUNTY MUSEUM
Strathmore St., Narragansett, 401-783-5400; www.southcountymuseum.org
The museum captures the life of Rhode Island's 19th-century farmers, fisherman and homemakers with displays of antique costumes, vehicles, farm equipment, blacksmith artifacts, toys and nautical equipment. Don't miss the historic country kitchen, the general store, the cobbler's shop and the operational 19th-century letterpress, which produces all the museum's posters and brochures.
May-June, September, Friday-Saturday 10 a.m.-4 p.m., Sunday noon-4 p.m.; July-August, Wednesday-Saturday 10 a.m.-4 p.m., Sunday noon-4 p.m.; special arrangements may be made for October visits by calling the museum.

THE TOWERS
35 Ocean Road, Narragansett, 401-782-2597; www.thetowersri.com
The grandiose casino that once stood here was designed by McKim, Mead and White, a prominent architecture firm from the early 20th century. Though the Beaux-Arts landmark was destroyed by fire in 1900, its Romanesque arch

entryway, flanked by conical towers, still stands as testament to the wealthy guests the casino once attracted.

NEWPORT

BELCOURT CASTLE
657 Bellevue Ave., Newport, 401-846-0669; www.belcourtcastle.com

Designed by Richard Morris Hunt in the French château style, this 1891 62-room house was the residence of Oliver Hazard Perry Belmont and his wife, Alva Vanderbilt Belmont. It contains the largest collection of antiques and objets d'art in Newport. Belmont loved horses, so he arranged for his stables to sit inside the main structure. A special note: Before Alva married Oliver, she was married to William V. Vanderbilt, so she lived down the street at the Marble House.
Daily; closed January.

BREAKERS
44 Ochre Point Ave., Newport, 401-847-1000; www.newportmansions.org

Built for steamship and railroad magnate Cornelius Vanderbilt in 1895, the Breakers is Newport's largest, most lavish mansion. Vanderbilt assembled an international team of craftsman and artisans to build his 70-room villa in the style of a 16th-century Italian palace. The end product was a house adorned with relief sculptures, ornate fixtures and artisan furnishings, to name but a few of its luxury appointments. The estate even has a children's playhouse cottage with a scale-size kitchen, a fireplace and a playroom.

BRICK MARKET
121 Thames St., Newport, 401-846-0813; www.brickmarketnewport.com

Home of the Newport Historical Society, the 1762 Brick Market was once a market and warehouse. Today, the charming building houses independent boutiques, eateries and residential tenants.

CHATEAU-SUR-MER
474 Bellevue Ave., Newport, 401-847-1000; www.newportmansions.org

Built in 1852, this Victorian mansion was once the most lavish in Newport until the Vanderbilts starting building their showpieces. Built by William S. Wetmore, a China trade merchant, the mansion was remodeled by Wetmore's daughter during the 1870s. As a consequence, Chateau-Sur-Mer displays all the major design trends of the late 19th century.
Late June-early October, daily.

CLIFF WALK
Memorial Blvd., Newport, 401-847-1355; www.cliffwalk.com

This 3 ½-mile walkway serves up dozens of sights: the Atlantic Ocean, wild-flowers, birds and the famous mansions of Newport's gilded age.

THE ELMS
367 Bellevue Ave., Newport, 401-847-1000; www.newportmansions.org

Modeled after the 18th-century Chateau d'Asnieres near Paris, this restored 1901 cottage boasts elaborate interiors, sunken gardens and marble fountains. Built for Edward J. Berwind, a Philadelphia coal magnate and apparent art-lover,

HIGHLIGHT

WHAT IS THE BEST WAY TO TOUR THE MANSIONS?

Take a stroll along Cliffwalk for a great view of the exteriors. But if you want a peek at the lavish interiors, purchase a combination ticket. Redeemable at Chateau-sur-Mer, the Elms, the Breakers, Kingscote, Marble House and Rosecliff, the ticket is available for purchase at any of these houses for $31.

it also features Venetian paintings, Renaissance ceramics and Oriental jade.
May-October, daily; November-March, Saturday-Sunday.

FRIENDS MEETING HOUSE
82 Touro St., Newport, 401-846-0813; www.newporthistorical.org
Between 1699 and 1905, this Quaker worship center was the site of the New England Yearly Meeting of the Society of Friends. The building was continually expanded over the years, though the utilitarian meetinghouse persists to embody the Society's "plain style" of living.
Mid-June-August, Thursday-Saturday. Tours: hourly 10 a.m.-3 p.m.; also by appointment.

HUNTER HOUSE
54 Washington St., Newport, 401-847-1000; www.newportmansions.org
An outstanding example of Georgian Colonial architecture, the 1748 Hunter House features a gambrel roof, 12-on-12 panel windows and a pediment doorway. Prominent interiors include paintings, a collection of Newport pewter and furniture by the Townsend-Goddard family, famous 18th-century cabinetmakers.
Late June-September, daily.

INTERNATIONAL TENNIS HALL OF FAME & MUSEUM
194 Bellevue Ave., Newport, 401-849-3990, 800-457-1144; www.tennisfame.com
Built in 1880, the world's largest tennis museum chronicles the sport's history with interactive and dynamic exhibits, videos of famous games, and historic displays of tennis equipment, fashions, trophies and memorabilia. When you've finished exploring the museum, grab a racquet and head for the museum's grass courts, the only public competitive grass courts in the country.
Daily. Grass courts available May-October.

KINGSCOTE
253 Bellevue Ave., Newport, 401-847-1000; www.newportmansions.org
A landmark of Gothic Revival architecture, this 1881 mansion features medieval-inspired towers, arches and porch roofs. Highlights of the interiors include a wall of Tiffany glass bricks, Chinese paintings and porcelains, and the "aesthetic" dining room, where eastern and western motifs are used in combination for an elegant effect.
June-October, daily.

MARBLE HOUSE

596 Bellevue Ave., Newport, 401-847-1000; www.newportmansions.org

Borrowing from the look of Versailles, this Vanderbilt family home incorporates d 500,000 cubic feet of marble, gold accents and gilded bronze throughout its interiors. Today, the 1892 estate also features yachting memorabilia and a restored Chinese teahouse where Mrs. Vanderbilt once held suffragette meetings. *April-October, daily; rest of year, Saturday-Sunday.*

NEWPORT ART MUSEUM AND ART ASSOCIATION

76 Bellevue Ave., Newport, 401-848-8200; www.newportartmuseum.com

Housed in the 1864 Griswold House, a remarkable example of American Stick-style architecture, this museum focuses on the art of Newport and Southeastern New England. It features rotating exhibitions on contemporary and historical visual art. Lectures, concerts and guided tours are also available. *June-August, Tuesday-Saturday 10 a.m.-4 p.m., Sunday noon-4 p.m.; September-May, Tuesday-Friday 11 a.m.-3 p.m., Saturday 10 a.m.-4 p.m., Sunday noon-4 p.m.*

OLD STONE MILL

Touro Park, Mill Street and Bellevue Avenue, Newport, 401-846-1398;

The origin of this mysterious circular stone tower is unknown. Some people think it was built by early Norse explorers, though excavations have disproved that. Other theories involve Chinese sailors, and Portuguese navigators.

REDWOOD LIBRARY AND ATHENAEUM

50 Bellevue Ave., Newport, 401-847-0292; www.redwoodlibrary.org

Designed by master Colonial architect Peter Harrison in 1750, this is the oldest lending library in the United States. Many of its books vanished during the Revolutionary War, when the British used the building as an officers' club. However, the vast majority of those books were retrieved. Today, a collection of 160,000 volumes includes many rare books and first editions. The library also houses collections of paintings, furniture and sculpture. *Monday, Friday-Saturday 9:30 a.m.-5:30 p.m., Tuesday-Thursday 9:30 a.m.-8 p.m., Sunday 1-5 p.m.*

ROSECLIFF

548 Bellevue Ave., Newport, 401-847-6543; www.newportmansions.org

Built for silver heiress Theresa Fair Oelrichs in 1902, this mansion was modeled after the Grand Trianon at Versailles. It features the largest private ballroom in all of Newport, as well as a famous heart-shaped staircase. *April-early November, daily.*

SAMUEL WHITEHORNE HOUSE

416 Thames St., Newport, 401-849-7300; www.newportrestoration.org

This 1811 Federal-style mansion boasts collections of exquisite colonial furniture, silver and pewter made by 18th-century artisans like the Townsend-Goddard family, plus Chinese porcelain, Irish crystal and Pilgrim-era furniture. The formal gardens, meanwhile, are filled with antique roses, blueberry bushes and perennials. *May-October, Monday, Thursday-Friday 11 a.m.-4 p.m., Saturday-Sunday 10 a.m.-4 p.m.; November-April, by appointment.*

TOURO SYNAGOGUE NATIONAL HISTORIC SITE

85 Touro St., Newport, 401-847-4794; www.tourosynagogue.org

America's first synagogue is a 1763 Georgian-style masterpiece by the country's first architect, Peter Harrison. Not only is the Touro the country's oldest synagogue, it also contains the oldest Torah in North America as well as examples of 18th-century crafts and a letter from George Washington.

Admission: free.

TRINITY CHURCH

Queen Anne Square, Newport, 401-846-0660; www.trinitynewport.org

Built in 1726, Trinity was the first Anglican parish in the state. President George Washington and philosopher George Berkeley are among the congregants to have worshiped here over the years. The interior features original Tiffany windows and an organ that was tested by Handel before it was shipped from London. The many-sized pews reflect the varying characters from the original congregation. Tours are available.

WANTON-LYMAN-HAZARD HOUSE

17 Broadway, Newport, 401-846-0813; www.newporthistorical.org

This 1675 house is the oldest in Newport and one of the finest Jacobean homes in New England. Once the home to Martin Howard, Jr., a British loyalist, it was the site of the 1765 Stamp Act riot. The Newport Historical Society bought the rundown property in 1926. Since then, the building has been stabilized and its 18th-century gardens restored. Guided tours are available.

Mid-June-August, Thursday-Saturday; five tours daily; closed holidays.

WHITEHALL MUSEUM HOUSE

311 Berkeley Ave., Middletown, 401-846-3116; www.whitehallmuseumhouse.org

This 1729 farmhouse was once the home of Bishop George Berkeley, the Irish philosopher and educator. Later, it served as a tearoom, an inn and a coffeehouse. Today, Whitehall serves as a house museum that recreates daily life for the Berkeley family in 1729.

July-early September, Tuesday-Sunday 10 a.m.-4 p.m.; also by appointment.

RHODE ISLAND'S EASTERN COASTLINE

Summer in Rhode Island's South County means beaches, boating and basking in the sun. It also means tourists galore, but you can avoid road rage by visiting the state's quiet eastern coastline. Here you'll find unpretentious towns like Bristol, Tiverton and Little Compton. From downtown Providence, it's a 40-mile trip. Take Highway 195 east to exit 7, where you'll take Highway 114 South. Pass through the town of Barrington. If you need a pit stop, save it for the next burg— downtown Bristol is lined with dozens of colonial antique and secondhand shops. In any case, Highway 114 becomes Hope Street as you drive through Bristol. Continue on Hope Street until you drive over the Mount Hope Bridge and enter the town of Portsmouth, then turn left on Highway 24. Keep driving until you pass the Sakonnet River Bridge as you enter the town of Tiverton, then turn right on Highway 77 South. Soon you'll see a lone traffic light, at the intersection of Highway 77 and Highway 179. You've reached Tiverton Four Corners. Pause here for shopping and lunch at the town's boutiques and eateries, and definitely don't miss a cone from 1920s-style Gray's Ice Cream (*16 East Road, Tiverton, 401-624-4500; www.graysicecream.com*). Continue south on Highway 77 past the open fields with panoramic views of Narragansett Bay. Soon you'll reach Little Compton, a charming summer community. Here, the restored-farmhouses-cum-estates are a sight to behold. Once you've had your fill of the quiet scene, you can double back to Provincetown on the same route. Or you can turn right onto Highway 24 North in Tiverton and drive into Fall River, Mass., then head west to Providence on Highway 195.

WHERE TO STAY

NEWPORT

★★★CASTLE HILL INN & RESORT
590 Ocean Drive, Newport, 401-849-3800, 888-466-1355; www.castlehillinn.com

A colossal resort on Newport's famous Ocean Drive, the resort spans the main house, the adjacent Harbor House, a guest chalet and several renovated private cottages. Guest rooms feature original antiques, gas fireplaces, marble baths and canopy beds. The setting is quiet and romantic, with ocean views and the prohibition of children in common areas. Don't miss the fireside s'mores event every evening in the lobby.

35 rooms. Complimentary breakfast. Restaurant, bar. Beach. $351 and up

★★★THE CHANLER AT CLIFF WALK
117 Memorial Blvd., Newport, 401-847-1300; www.thechanler.com

Live out your gilded-age fantasies at this extra-opulent mansion, featuring lavish guest rooms decorated in various historic themes. The Ocean Villas are the most indulgent of all—they're outfitted with saunas, whirlpools and private decks with water views. If you're feeling extra decadent, request a butler-drawn bath or in-room massage treatment. Best of all, the hotel is located in a prime oceanfront spot along Cliff Walk, a 3 ½-mile walkway featuring the city's best views.

20 Rooms. Restaurant, bar. $351 and up

★★★THE FRANCIS MALBONE HOUSE
392 Thames St., Newport, 401-846-0392, 800-846-0392; www.malbone.com

This 1760 colonial bed and breakfast features all the proper accoutrements, such as complimentary daily tea service and a full gourmet breakfast. Guest rooms are spacious and tastefully decorated with Jacuzzis, fireplaces and fluffy comforters. The Malbone is convenient to the shops, eateries and other attractions of Newport's downtown waterfront.

20 rooms. Complimentary breakfast. $251-350

★★★HOTEL VIKING
1 Bellevue Ave., Newport, 401-847-3300, 800-556-7126; www.hotelviking.com

Built in 1926 atop Newport's Historic Hill neighborhood, the Viking features

WHAT IS THE MOST LUXURIOUS HOTEL IN NEWPORT?

Though most Newport hotels deal in luxury, the **Chanler** has the feel of a private mansion. Sure, the rooms are spacious and the décor sumptuous, but the Chanler impresses with services, such as that glass of sparkling wine at check-in or the tuxedoed butler who mans the hotel's car service.

sweeping vistas of the city, especially Bellevue Avenue. Guest rooms feature four-poster beds with an elegant mix of period-style and modern furnishings. The full-service, in-house spa is a popular retreat for pampering. *222 rooms. Restaurant, bar. $251-350*

★★★HYATT REGENCY NEWPORT
1 Goat Island, Newport, 401-851-1234, 888-591-1234; www.newport.hyatt.com

Located at the tip of Goat Island, the Hyatt Regency serves up the lovely scenery of Newport's harbor, Narragansett Bay and the Jamestown Bridge. Guest rooms feature more than beautiful views—they're stocked with pillow-top mattresses, plush duvets and Portico bath products. No seaside trip is complete without a clambake and the Hyatt delivers this, too, with two do-it-yourself waterfront fire pits. The hotel also features a kid-friendly outdoor pool.
264 rooms. Restaurant, bar. Pool. Fitness center. Spa. $251-350

★★★MARRIOTT NEWPORT
25 America's Cup Ave., Newport, 401-849-1000, 800-458-3066; www.newportmarriott.com

The maritime-themed Marriott Newport seamlessly blends big-city service with small-town charm. A half-dozen colorful sails are suspended above the lounge, which overlooks the water and greets guests as they check-in. Rooms are decorated in a traditional nautical color scheme, with pretty sailboat-patterned quilts laid over white duvets. Enjoy casual American food in onsite restaurant Fathoms, which also overlooks the harbor.
319 rooms. Restaurant, bar. Fitness center. pool. $251-350

★★★NEWPORT HARBOR HOTEL AND MARINA
49 America's Cup Ave., Newport, 401-847-9000, 800-955-2558; www.newporthotel.com

Located in Queen Ann Square, this comfortable hotel overlooks its own 60-slip marina off Narragansett Bay. So if the up-close sights of the harbor don't lull you, then surely the hotel's soothing palette of blues and grays will do the trick. Pier 49 Seafood & Spirits is the onsite restaurant, specializing in—you guessed it—lobster, salmon, clams and quahogs.
133 rooms. Restaurant, bar. $351 and up

RECOMMENDED

BLOCK ISLAND

SPRING HOUSE

52 Spring St., Block Island, 401-466-5844, 800-234-9263;
www.springhousehotel.com

Housed in its mansard roof and wraparound veranda, this seaside inn is the quintessential New England getaway. The hotel offers guest rooms with basic, comfortable furnishings, pastel décor and floral fabrics. Located on a 15-acre promontory, it also offers terrific ocean views. The on-site restaurant, Victoria's Parlor, serves classic New England fare and craft martinis.

50 rooms. Closed in winter. Complimentary breakfast. Restaurant, bar. $151-250

NEWPORT

MILL STREET INN

75 Mill St., Newport, 401-849-9500, 800-392-1316; www.millstreetinn.com

If you've had all you can handle of historic sights, try this recently renovated, contemporary-style inn. Of course, it's housed in a historic 1850s mill, but the inn is decorated with sleek furnishings and minimalist tones. Guest rooms feature Aveda bath products and rainfall showers.

23 rooms. Complimentary breakfast. $251-350

WHERE TO EAT

BLOCK ISLAND

★★★HOTEL MANISSES DINING ROOM

1 Spring St., Block Island, 401-466-2836; www.blockislandresorts.com

Poets and romantics favor the country-chic dining room, which resembles a glass-enclosed garden room. Gourmands and other hungry people appreciate the contemporary American menu, which is heavy on seafood. Sweet tooths, meanwhile, adore the rich homemade desserts such as layered banana cream cake and Italian-style hot chocolate.

American. Dinner. Closed November-April. Bar. Reservations recommended. Outdoor seating. $36-85

NEWPORT

★★★CANFIELD HOUSE

5 Memorial Blvd., Newport, 401-847-0416; www.canfieldhousenewport.com

This elegant restaurant once housed Newport's only gambling casino. Today, it's a topnotch restaurant serving American classics like steaks, lamb and local seafood. High ceilings, dark wood paneling, crystal chandeliers, and a prominent stained-glass window make the occasion feel special. Alfresco dining is available on the covered porch during the warmer months. Casual meals are available year-round in the cellar pub.

American. Dinner. Bar. Children's menu. Reservations recommended. Outdoor seating. Closed Monday. $16-35

★★★WHITE HORSE TAVERN
26 Marlborough St., Newport, 401-849-3600

If walls could talk, the White Horse Tavern's dark wooden planks would have much to say. Built in 1673, the downtown tavern is America's oldest remaining watering hole. Thankfully, none of the pub's owners ever altered the original brown clapboard exterior, stone fireplaces and exposed ceiling beams. The only thing updated is the menu, which highlights well-executed New England favorites like butter-poached lobster.

American. Lunch, dinner, Sunday brunch. Bar. Reservations recommended. Outdoor seating. $36-85

RECOMMENDED

NARRAGANSETT
COAST GUARD HOUSE
40 Ocean Road, Narragansett, 401-789-0700; www.thecoastguardhouse.com

Check out this beachy, seaside restaurant for a laid-back meal of steamed lobsters or grilled fish. Ask for a seat in the elegant dining room, or better yet, if the weather's nice, go for the bar scene on the rooftop patio.

American, seafood. Lunch, dinner, Sunday brunch. Bar. Children's menu. Outdoor seating. Closed January-mid-February. $16-35

NEWPORT
RHODE ISLAND QUAHOG COMPANY
250 Thames St., Newport, 401-848-2330; www.riquahogco.com

This casual seafood restaurant has a prime location in the heart of Newport's historic district, but that's not the only reason the place is perpetually packed. The eatery serves up a tasty assortment of stuffed quahogs, classic clam chowder, white pizzas, sandwiches and salads.

Seafood. Lunch, dinner. Bar. Children's menu. Reservations recommended. Outdoor seating. Closed January-February. $16-35

WELCOME TO VERMONT

GREEN ROLLING HILLS, PICTURE-PERFECT VILLAGES,

fields dotted with black and white cows—Vermont is every bit as bucolic as its reputation, but under that peaceful surface lies an idealistic spirit that makes Vermont one of the most progressive liberal states in the country. Vermonters are fiercely individualistic. As an extreme example, one town threatened to secede from the U.S. over the Iraq war. Others fought to keep Wal-Mart from opening in the state, though that movement was unsuccessful.

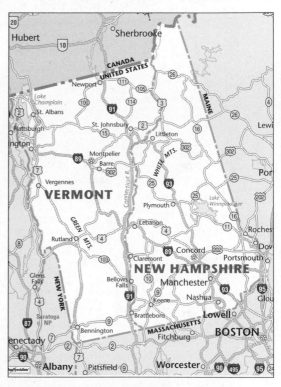

Vermont's progressivism is nothing new. Back in 1777, it was the first state to prohibit slavery. That very year, it became the first to provide universal male suffrage, regardless of property or income. In 2009, it was the first state to legalize same-sex marriage.

Today, that progressive tradition is reflected by the state's economy. With an outstanding agricultural industry, the tiny state of 600,000 people is at the forefront of the national farm-to-table movement, with dozens of terrific new restaurants committed to cooking with fresh, local, eco-friendly ingredients. Of course, excellent restaurants aren't the only reason to visit Vermont. The state's many ski resorts get top marks. From the funky, artsy college town of Burlington to Montpelier, one of the nation's prettiest state capitals— no matter where you wander in this fair state, you're sure to find a quaint bed and breakfast with a view of the gorgeous greenness that is Vermont's great outdoors.

HIGHLIGHTS

VERMONT'S BEST ATTRACTIONS

BEN AND JERRY'S FACTORY TOUR

Your mouth waters as you eavesdrop on the old-fashioned ice cream-making process at this world-famous factory. Luckily, the tour ends with a taste test, which makes this excursion quite satisfying.

NORMAN ROCKWELL MUSEUM

With more than 2,000 illustrations by the superstar artist, this museum offers an exhaustive retrospective plus an escape to a simpler, seemingly happier America. Even the museum's setting—a charming, old red farmhouse—is befitting of Norman Rockwell.

KILLINGTON

Ski "the beast of the east," a.k.a. Killington Peak, the second highest peak in Vermont. Encompassing Killington as well as five other mountains, Killington Resort is known as a magnet for experienced, adventurous skiers, though there's no reason to be fearful—the resort offers plenty of gentler runs for kids, beginners and careful types.

TWIN FARMS

This ultra-upscale resort features every luxury imaginable: posh guest rooms, in-suite spa services, whirlpool bathtubs, museum-gallery artwork, exquisite dining and more. The beauty of those accommodations get upstaged by only one thing—the 300 acres of green gorgeousness that encircles the property.

NORTHERN VERMONT

For lovers of the outdoors, Burlington has it all—Lake Champlain out the front door, the Adirondacks across the border and the Green Mountains in the city's backyard. But Burlington has plenty to please city-dwellers, too—a vibrant cobblestone pedestrian mall, galleries and boutiques galore, and several universities that continually replenish the arts and culture scene. Fall is the favored season, thanks to the fiery colors. Burlington's springs and summers, meanwhile, are studies in green and blue. Yes, winter is a little brisk, but local snowboarding company Burton can offer an extra layer. If that fails to keep you toasty, check out Burlington's indoor hotspots, from brewpubs and bistros to the Flynn Center for the Performing Arts and the indie-rock stop Higher Ground.

Located just 50 miles from Burlington, Stowe boasts one of New England's finest ski resorts. While the snow conditions on Mount Mansfield, Vermont's highest peak at 4,393 feet, generate the most buzz, about half of Stowe's annual visitors land during the summer. Warm-weather guests enjoy the town's charming downtown with abundant inns and organic eateries, not to mention all of the hiking, biking, tennis and golf. Even so, the biggest crowd-pleaser is a tour of the nearby Ben & Jerry's factory.

WHAT TO SEE

BARRE
ROCK OF AGES
560 Graniteville Road, Barre, 800-421-0166; www.rockofages.com

Learn all about the granite industry at this unique visitors' center. Here, families can tour a 600-foot-deep granite quarry, bowl on an outdoor granite lane, observe artisans as they work with the stone and even cut their own souvenirs to take home.

BOLTON VALLEY
BOLTON VALLEY SKI/SUMMER RESORT
4302 Bolton Access Road, Bolton Valley, 877-926-5866; www.boltonvalleyvt.com

Located in the Green Mountains, just 20 miles from Burlington, this four-season resort specializes in alpine and Nordic skiing, snowboarding and snowshoeing. The warm-weather activities are just as enticing, including hiking, biking and autumnal leaf-peeping. The resort is also home to Bailey's Restaurant, which adheres to strict standards for its ingredients: everything is local, organic and delicious.
Daily.

BURLINGTON
CHURCH STREET MARKETPLACE
2 Church St., Burlington, 802-863-1648; www.churchstmarketplace.com

Check out the four traffic-free blocks that run from the historic 1815 Unitarian Church to Burlington City Hall. Church Street features a mix of Art Deco and 19th-century architectural styles along with private houses, restaurants,

HIGHLIGHTS

WHAT ARE THE BEST PLACES FOR OUTDOOR FUN IN NORTHERN VERMONT?

MOUNT PHILO

The foothills of Burlington boast myriad trails for hiking, biking and skiing. One of the finest, and still one of the closest, is the four-mile trek to the top of Mount Philo.

BOLTON VALLEY

The closest full-service ski resort to Burlington is Bolton Valley, which boasts 64 runs and even night skiing. In the summer, Bolton offers hiking and an adventure center with guided excursions.

CATAMOUNT FAMILY CENTER

Based in Williston, this 500-acre outdoor center offers year-round activities of varying intensity levels. Try the mountain biking and running trails in the summer. Winter activities include snowshoeing and cross-country skiing.

galleries and more than 100 shops. Warmer months find the open-air brick promenade packed with vendors and street performers, too.

ECHO LAKE AQUARIUM AND SCIENCE CENTER

1 College St., Burlington, 802-864-1848; www.echovermont.org

From water babies to landlubbers, everyone loves this 28,500 square-foot mega-museum. Most exhibits explore the ecosystem of Lake Champlain, the country's sixth-largest body of fresh water. Here visitors can get a closer look at indigenous turtles, fish and frogs. They can also grab a bite to eat from the green-themed Think Café.

Daily 10 a.m.-5 p.m.

ETHAN ALLEN HOMESTEAD AND MUSEUM

1 Ethan Allen Homestead, Burlington, 802-865-4556; www.ethanallenhomestead.org

Ethan Allen is a folk hero in the state of Vermont, a co-founder of the state with a colorful history as a frontiersman, military leader, land speculator, suspected traitor and prisoner of war. Located on the Winooski River, this preserved pioneer homestead was Allen's final home. Here you'll find Allen's recreated hayfield and kitchen gardens, plus the 1787 farmhouse where he died after just two years of residence. One-hour guided tours are available.

Mid-May-mid-October, Thursday-Monday 10 a.m.-4 p.m.

ETHAN ALLEN PARK

1006 N. Ave Burlington and Ethan Allen Parkway, Burlington, 802-863-3489;

Formerly part of Ethan Allen's large farmstead, this park functions primarily as a nature area with hiking trails, picnic areas and scenic overlooks. Don't miss the sights from Ethan Allen Tower, a 100-year-old monument with views of Lake Champlain, the Adirondacks and the Green Mountains.

Memorial Day-Labor Day, Wednesday-Sunday afternoons and evenings.

LAKE CHAMPLAIN

One hundred and twenty miles long and 400 feet deep, Lake Champlain is both a picturesque backdrop and a vast playground for Burlingtonians. Check out the Community Sailing Center (*802-864-2499*) for sailing courses, kayak clinics and lessons on standup paddleboarding. The center also offers yoga classes on the lake dock. If organized activity isn't your thing, the lake is easy enough to explore on foot or bike. Consult with Local Motion (*802-652-2453*) to rent some wheels. In warmer months, you can pedal the eight-mile Burlington Bike Path all the way to the island town of South Hero.

LAKE CHAMPLAIN CHOCOLATES

750 Pine St., Burlington, 802-864-1808, 800-465-5909; www.lakechamplainchocolates.com

Large glass windows let visitors peek in at the chocolate-making process at this small-scale factory. Tours include a free chocolate tasting. The gift shop often features chocolate-making demonstrations on Saturdays. Don't forget to stock up on truffles, buttercups and chocolate bars.

Factory tours: Monday-Thursday 9 a.m.-2 p.m. on the hour. Factory store: Monday-Saturday 9 a.m.-6 p.m., Sunday noon-5 p.m.

UNIVERSITY OF VERMONT

Waterman Building, 85 S. Prospect St., Burlington, 802-656-3480; www.uvm.edu

Founded in 1791, this university is the fifth oldest in New England. Two of the campus's oldest buildings constitute its finest sights. The 1865 Georgian-style Ira Allen Chapel is named for the founder of the university. The 1865 Old Mill, meanwhile, is a classroom building with its cornerstone laid by General Lafayette in 1825.

SHELBURNE

SHELBURNE FARMS

1611 Harbor Road, Shelburne, 802-985-8686; www.shelburnefarms.org

Built at the turn of the 20th century, this is the former estate of Dr. Seward Webb and his wife, Lila Vanderbilt. Located on the shores of Lake Champlain, the farm boasts magnificent grounds that were originally landscaped by Frederick Law Olmsted, the mastermind behind New York City's Central Park. Check out Shelburne House, the Webbs' 110-room summer "cottage" built in the late 1800s. Don't leave without a hayride and a trip to the cheese shop. Overnight stays at the property are available.

Tours: June-mid-October, daily 9 a.m.-5:30 p.m.; off-season, daily 10 a.m.-5 p.m.

SPECIAL EVENTS

DISCOVER JAZZ FESTIVAL

187 St. Paul St. Burlington, 802-863-7992; www.discoverjazz.com

This ten-day jazz extravaganza features more than 150 live performances every year. It takes place in venues throughout the city including parks, restaurants and nightclubs.

Early June.

VERMONT MOZART FESTIVAL

3 Main St., Burlington, 802-862-7352; www.vtmozart.com

In 1974, a Julliard School music professor noticed the similarities between northern Vermont and Mozart's native Austria. Thus, a perennial music festival was born, featuring upwards of 19 chamber concerts in picturesque Vermont settings like the Trapp Family Meadow, Basin Harbor Club and Shelburne Farms.

Mid-July-early August.

ART HOP

www.seaba.org

During this two-day event, art is on view everywhere you look in Burlington's bohemian South End neighborhood—it's in the factories, in the warehouses, and even in the local restaurants. Now in its 19th year, this gallery crawl is so popular that it draws upwards of 30,000 visitors.

Mid-September.

SHELBURNE MUSEUM

5555 Shelburne Road, Shelburne, 802-985-3346; www.shelburnemuseum.org

Here, more than 150,000 works of art and Americana are displayed in a most unusual way—they're scattered across 37 buildings, including a lighthouse and a boat. Highlights include historic collections of circus posters, toys, weather vanes, trade signs, wildfowl decoys and dolls. But there's enough to please the art aficionado, too. The collection includes American and European paintings and prints by the likes of Monet and Grandma Moses. Travel enthusiasts will adore the 220-foot side-wheel steamboat *Ticonderoga*, which once carried passengers across Lake Champlain. Kids of all ages, meanwhile, will love the 5,000-piece hand-carved miniature depicting a traveling circus. The list of attractions goes on and on—a fully intact lighthouse, a one-room schoolhouse, an authentic country store, a covered bridge and blacksmith shop.

May-October, daily 10 a.m.-5 p.m.

VERMONT TEDDY BEAR COMPANY

6655 Shelburne Road, Shelburne, 802-985-1319; www.vermontteddybear.com

Factory tours answer that pesky question, "Where do teddy bears come from?" Meanwhile, the onsite gift shop ensures no one leaves empty handed.
Daily.

VERMONT WILDFLOWER FARM

4750 Shelburne Ave., Shelburne, 802-425-3641; www.vermontwildflowerfarm.com

More than a farm and flower business, this destination boasts acres of wild-flower gardens, flower fields and woodlands. As an added perk, flowers are discretely marked to help visitors identify them. With a pond, a brook and a fenced patio, the wildflower farm is a great destination for family picnics.
May-October, daily 10 a.m.-5 p.m.

STOWE

BEN & JERRY'S ICE CREAM FACTORY TOUR

Route 100, Waterbury, 866-258-6877; www.benjerry.com

Take a guided half-hour tour through the famous ice cream factory that cranks out favorites such as Cherry Garcia and Chunky Monkey. The tour includes a seven-minute "moovie," views of the production line (except on weekends) and, of course, free samples. Check out the gift shop for those infamous tie-dyed cow T-shirts and a pint or two to take home.
Daily.

MOUNT MANSFIELD GONDOLA

Stowe Mountain Resort, 5781 Mountain Road, Stowe, 802-253-3000, 800-253-4754

An eight-passenger enclosed gondola delivers riders to the summit of Vermont's highest peak. Once you reach the top, you'll find more than gorgeous views— the summit house also features a snack bar and gift shop.
Mid-June-mid-October, daily 10 a.m.-5 p.m.

MOUNT MANSFIELD STATE FOREST

www.vtparks.com

This 38,000-acre forest features a variety of activities—camping, picnicking, but most of all hiking, including four trails that lead to the summit of Mount Mansfield.

STOWE MOUNTAIN RESORT

5781 Mountain Road, Stowe, 802-253-3000, 800-253-4754; www.stowe.com

One of the best ski resorts in New England, Stowe Mountain Resort features longer than average runs and ample powder (thanks to its hard-working snow-making machines). With 45 kilometers of groomed trails, Stowe is also an excellent destination for cross-country skiing. Come summertime, the resort features a variety of outdoor activities, most notably the 2,300-foot alpine slide. The resort also offers mountain biking, gondola rides, hiking trails, tennis, golf, and even an in-line skate park.
Mid-November-mid-April, daily.

VERMONT SKI MUSEUM
1 Main St., Stowe, 802-253-9911; www.vermontskimuseum.org
Dedicated to collecting and preserving Vermont's skiing history, this two-story museum features more than 5,200 pieces of memorabilia. The collections include everything from vintage brochures, photography and film archives.

WHERE TO STAY

BURLINGTON
★★★SHERATON BURLINGTON HOTEL AND CONFERENCE CENTER
870 Williston Road, Burlington, 802-865-6600, 800-677-6576; www.sheratonburlington.com
Convenient to downtown Burlington and five ski areas, this full-service hotel features contemporary furnishings, plush beds and the largest guest rooms in the city. Many rooms feature views of the Green Mountains. Complimentary breakfast and snacks are provided for Sheraton Club members.
309 rooms. Restaurant, bar. Fitness center. Pool. Business center. Pets allowed. $61-150

ESSEX
★★★THE ESSEX
70 Essex Way, Essex, 802-878-1100, 800-727-4295; www.innatessex.com
This recently renovated inn features posh accommodations like fireplace suites and a new 22,000-square-foot spa and salon. Those comforts get surpassed, though, by the quality of the meals served at the inn's restaurant, where everything is prepared by students from the New England Culinary Institute. Occupy yourself between feedings with onsite fly-fishing lessons, rock-climbing excursions or cooking classes.
120 rooms. Restaurant. Fitness center. Pool. Spa. Pets accepted. $151-250

STOWE
★★★GREEN MOUNTAIN INN
18 S. Main St., Stowe, 802-253-7301, 800-253-7302; www.greenmountaininn.com
Located in downtown Stowe, this 1833 Colonial-style inn is surrounded by charming shops, galleries and restaurants. Guest rooms reflect that bucolic setting with country-style furnishings like quilts, deep soaking tubs and fireplaces. A member of the Vermont Fresh Network, the inn features two onsite dining options that specialize in food made from locally sourced ingredients.
104 rooms. Restaurant, bar. Fitness center. Pool. $151-250

★★★STOWE MOUNTAIN LODGE
7412 Mountain Rd., Stowe, 888-478-6938; www.stowemountainlodge.com
Opened in 2008, Stowe Mountain Lodge brings the über-luxury aesthetic of Western ski resorts to New England. The spacious lobby area features vaulted ceilings, leather couches and a large wood-burning fireplace, whereas the contemporary guest rooms are bedecked with Vermont-made art. What's more, the ski-in, ski-out property features a 21,000-square-foot spa, a farm-to-table restaurant and 2,000 acres of conservation land, perhaps for hiking and other outdoor activities.
139 rooms. Restaurant, bar. Fitness center. Spa. Pool. $351 and up

★★★STOWEFLAKE MOUNTAIN RESORT & SPA
1746 Mountain Road, Stowe, 802-253-7355, 800-253-2232; www.stoweflake.com

At this family-owned resort, there are many paths to pampering—the hydrotherapy room, the women's-only fitness section, the plates of fresh-baked cookies, and the 50,000 square-foot spa. Additionally, most guest rooms are outfitted with fireplaces, but all feature pillow-top beds, upscale décor and views of the Green Mountains. The downtown location is convenient to all the best shops, galleries and restaurants, but you won't have to walk for a terrific meal—choose from two onsite eateries, the casual Charlie B's or the more formal Winfield's Bistro.

117 rooms. Restaurant, bar. Fitness center. Spa. Pool. Golf. $250-595

★★★TOPNOTCH RESORT AND SPA
4000 Mountain Road, Stowe, 888-460-5567, 800-451-8686; www.topnotchresort.com

This resort is best known to tennis enthusiasts, thanks to the vast network of indoor and outdoor courts as well as a tennis center open 365 days a year. On Christmas, guests can go skiing at nearby Stowe in the morning, play tennis in the afternoon and then visit the 35,000-square-foot spa before an organic dinner at Norma's onsite restaurant. After all that, no doubt, you'll be ready to collapse on a pillow-topped bed in your cheery, European country-style room. Equipment rentals are available for every Stowe sport imaginable, from flyfishing and horseback riding to snowshoeing and cross-country sledding. Even so, visitors often choose to relax by the pool as they contemplate the stunning views of Mount Mansfield.

68 rooms. Restaurant, bar. Fitness center. Spa. Pool. Business center. Pets accepted. $195-595

RECOMMENDED

BURLINGTON
LANG HOUSE
360 Main St., Burlington, 877-919-9799; www.langhouse.com

Housed in the 1881 house once owned by Ira Allen (Ethan's brother), this bed and breakfast features romantic rooms with period furnishings. Gourmet breakfasts are served every morning in a sunroom, with offerings that incorporate Vermont's famous maple syrups and dairy products. The inn is conveniently situated near the University of Vermont and downtown Burlington.

11 rooms. $151-250

MARRIOTT COURTYARD BURLINGTON HARBOR
25 Cherry St., Burlington, 802-864-4600; www.marriott.com

Boasting spectacular panoramic views of Lake Champlain and the Adirondacks, this eight-floor hotel makes a convenient base camp for those wanting to explore Church Street, Burlington's waterfront and beyond. Here, the guestrooms are decorated with sophisticated, modern décor. Meanwhile, the onsite restaurant specializes in Vermont-inspired dishes made from local ingredients.

150 rooms. Restaurant. Fitness center. Pool. $251-350

WILLARD STREET INN
349 South Willard St., Burlington, 800-577-8712; 802-651-8710; www.willardstreetinn.com

This 1881 Victorian-style mansion is located just a stone's throw from Lake Champlain. Some guest rooms boast views of the water and the Adirondacks, but all feature romantic, turn-of-the-century-style tapestries and furnishings. Complimentary breakfast is served daily in the solarium, where diners have their choice of house-cooked dishes. Best of all, everyone gets a daily delivery of fresh chocolate-chip cookies, dried fruit and Lake Champlain chocolates.

14 rooms. $151-250

STOWE

STONE HILL INN
89 Houston Farm Road, Stowe, 802-253-6282; www.stonehillinn.com

Built especially for couples, this downtown inn is filled with romantic flair, from the candlelit breakfasts to the fireside Jacuzzi bathtubs. Along those lines, the innkeepers offer a host of concierge services of flower delivery, in-room massages and sleigh rides.

Closed April; also mid-November-early-December. No children allowed. Complimentary breakfast. $251-350

TRAPP FAMILY LODGE
700 Trapp Hill Road, Stowe, 802-253-8511, 800-826-7000;
www.trappfamily.com

The hills are alive at this resort run by members of the famous Von Trapp family. The rustic lodge overlooks the beautiful Green Mountains—not exactly the Austrian Alps, though the Von Trapps make the bold connection with their in-house brewery and European cuisine. Throughout the hotel, guests encounter other alpine flourishes, like the building's vaulted ceilings, pitched gables and a cedar shake roof. In addition to cross-country skiing, activities include croquet, mountain biking, hiking, horse-drawn sleigh rides and pastry-making classes.

96 rooms. Restaurant, bar. Fitness center. Pool. Tennis. $151-250

WHERE TO EAT

BURLINGTON
RECOMMENDED
BLUEBIRD TAVERN
317 Riverside Ave., Burlington, 802-540-1786; www.bluebirdvermont.com

The food reflects the restaurant's location near Burlington's Intervale Center, an area concentrated with organic farms. The ingredients are fresh, local and sustainable. The dishes, meanwhile, are eclectic, seasonal and delicious. Signature plates include double burgers, rabbit fritto misto and braised pig shanks.

American. Dinner. Bar. Outdoor seating. $36-85

THE FARMHOUSE TAP & GRILL
160 Bank St., Burlington

Located in a former McDonald's, this downtown pub serves anything but fast food. Rather, the emphasis is on local brews, cheeses and housemade charcuterie, as well as gourmet burgers and comfort foods.

American. Lunch, dinner. Bar. Outdoor seating. $16-35

LEUNIG'S
115 Church St., Burlington, 802-863-3759; www.leunigsbistro.com

With sidewalk tables and picture windows, Leunig's is a great place to people-watch the passers-by on busy Church Street. The menu is equally entertaining—steak frites, mussels and soup au pistou. A comfortable dining room doesn't hurt matters, either. Cozy in the winter and breezy in the summer, Leunig's is usually packed with tourists and locals alike.

French. Lunch, dinner, Sunday brunch. Bar. Outdoor seating. $16-35

A SINGLE PEBBLE
133-35 Bank St., Burlington, 802-865-5200; www.asinglepebble.com

New England isn't known for Chinese food, but this upscale eatery breaks the mold with inventive spreads of Szechuan banquet food. The service is great, too—first the hostess seats you on a red lacquered lazy Susan; then she demonstrates her knowledge of the menu, down to the wines and the individual ingredients. Signature plates include mock eel and fried green beans.

Chinese. Lunch, dinner, Sunday Dim Sum. Bar. Outdoor seating. $16-35

STOWE

SANTOS COCINA LATINA
311 Mountain Road, Stowe, 802-523-3110

This brand-new Latin-American restaurant does upscale iterations of traditional Puerto Rican, Cuban and Peruvian dishes. So far, some of the standouts include pumpkin buñuelos, grilled skirt steak with chimichurri sauce and mojo-marinated fried pork cubes.

Latin. Dinner. Bar. Outdoor seating. $16-35

PIECASSO PIZZERIA & LOUNGE
1899 Mountain Road, Stowe 802-253-4311

This decade-old eatery slings the finest hand-tossed pizzas in Stowe, and the names of these pies are just as interesting as the ingredients: the Tree Hugger features spinach and tomatoes, while the Carcass includes four types of meat. For extra fun, there's free live music every Tuesday and Saturday night.

Italian. Lunch, dinner. Bar. Children's menu. Outdoor seating. $16-35

MATTERHORN
4969 Mountain Road, Stowe, 802-253-8198; www.matterhornbar.com

The original après-ski hotspot, the Matterhorn is equal parts nightclub and casual dining room. It's a great place to sip a PBR after a hard day on the slopes. The food is delicious: burgers, salads, chicken wings and gourmet pizzas are all on the menu.

American. Dinner. Bar. Outdoor seating. $16-35

WHERE TO SHOP

BURLINGTON

ANJOU & THE LITTLE PEAR
53 Main St., Burlington, 802-540-0008; www.anjouvt.com

This consignment shop sells upscale home furnishings and art, with special selections of antique children's furniture and vintage games, too. Shopping here is akin to a treasure hunt, though you might uncover a funky '50s kitchen set, vintage china or a painting from the 1970s.

Tuesday-Saturday 10 a.m.-5 p.m., Sunday 11 a.m.-3 p.m.

BURLINGTON FARMER'S MARKET
City Hall Park, Burlington, 802-399-0149; www.burlingtonfarmersmarket.com

Saturday mornings bring Burlingtonians young and old to City Hill Park, where foodies can buy direct from local producers of maple syrup, fruits, vegetables, wines, meats and more. A winter market is held once a month inside nearby Memorial Auditorium.

May-October, Saturday 8:30 a.m.-2 p.m, rain or shine.

FROG HOLLOW
85 Church St., Burlington, 802-863-6458; www.froghollow.com

Located on Burlington's Church Street Marketplace, this carefully curated gallery represents more than 250 Vermont artists, everyone from printers, painters and photographers to ornament- and jewelry-makers.

Monday-Thursday 10 a.m.-7 p.m., Friday 10 a.m.-8 p.m., Saturday 9 a.m.-8 p.m, Sunday noon-6 p.m.

STOWE

WELL HEELED
2850 Mountain Road, Stowe, 802-253-6077; www.wellheeledstowe.com

Forget Birkenstocks and overalls. Despite the location in an 1800s farmhouse, this Vermont boutique stocks stylish picks of Silver jeans, Frye boots and Junior Drake handbags. While you're there, pick up a cozy cashmere sweater and a chic belt.

Daily 10 a.m.-6 p.m.

STOWE MERCANTILE
Depot St. Building, Main St., Stowe, 802-253-4554; www.stowemercantile.com

An old-fashioned shop located in the center of the Stowe Village, the Mercantile sells penny candy, maple syrup, fudge, beauty products and a host of other Vermont-made goods.

Daily 9 a.m.-6 p.m.

AJ'S SKI & SPORTS
Mountain Road, Stowe, 802-253-4593; www.ajssportinggoods.com

The place to buy anything and everything for a mountain excursion, AJ's stocks skis, snowboards, jackets, footwear, car racks and more. The shop even offers equipment rentals.

Daily 9 a.m.-6 p.m.

CENTRAL VERMONT

From ski towns to small towns, the state's central corridor is flecked with excellent vacation spots. Winter sports enthusiasts converge upon the downhill scenes of Killington and Waitsfield, where they enjoy the finest skiing and freshest powder New England has to offer. Meanwhile, picturesque towns like Montpelier attract visitors with historic architecture, blazing fall foliage, and cozy bed and breakfasts.

Likewise, historic Woodstock features a town green lined with lovingly preserved architecture, though the presence of galleries and boutiques lends the area a cosmopolitan feel. Cute towns like Middlebury and Quechee, meanwhile, boast Victorian inns as well as world-class cultural attractions—the Bread Loaf Writer's Conference and Simon Pearce pottery studio, respectively. If you're a weary skier in want of a bed and breakfast, seek refuge in the tiny hamlet of Warren. If you're a history buff on the hunt for nostalgia, try the town of Plymouth, a place that remains remarkably time-trapped, as if to pay homage to its hometown pride, former U.S. President Calvin Coolidge. No matter what you're looking for—hiking, biking, dining, gallery-hopping—central Vermont offers a vacationer's grab bag with no centralized point, just scattered attractions of the relaxing sort.

WHAT TO SEE

CENTER RUTLAND
WILSON CASTLE
West Proctor Road, Center Rutland, 802-773-3284; www.wilsoncastle.com

Built by a wealthy doctor and his aristocratic wife, this 1867 brick-and-marble mansion features 32 rooms, 19 open proscenium arches, 84 stained-glass windows, 13 imported tile fireplaces, a towering turret and a parapet. The furnishings are equally impressive, including European and Asian antiques, and a sculpture gallery. The 115-acre estate also includes stables and a carriage house. Take a guided tour of the property, then relax at the onsite picnic area.
Guided tours: late May-late October, daily 9 a.m.-6 p.m.; Christmas tours.

EAST HUBBARDTON
HUBBARDTON BATTLEFIELD AND MUSEUM
5696 Monument Hill Road, East Hubbardton, 802-759-2412; www.historicvermont.org

Check out this 1777 battlefield, where the Green Mountain Boys and colonial troops once clashed with the British. Technically, the British won the Battle of Hubbardton, though the struggle left their troops badly bloodied. General Burgoyne surrendered with his entire army just three months later. Today, the battlefield features a visitor center with educational exhibits and historic artifacts.
Late May-mid-October, Thursday-Sunday 9:30 a.m.-5 p.m.

HIGHLIGHTS

WHAT ARE THE TOP THINGS TO DO IN CENTRAL VERMONT?

VISIT THE CROWLEY CHEESE FACTORY
Don't visit Vermont without submerging yourself in cheese—the state's famous cheese-making culture, that is. Drop by Crowley Cheese, the nation's oldest cheese-making factory, for a taste of the old-fashioned techniques.

SKI MOUNT KILLINGTON
Are you tough enough to tackle "the Beast," otherwise known as Killington Peak? Even if you're not, Killington Resort is still a great place to shred—it offers plenty of shorter, simpler trails.

ENJOY THE NORMAN ROCKWELL MUSEUM
What better place to behold Rockwell's iconic American images than the classic American countryside that once inspired the artist? Situated in a charming red farmhouse, this museum boasts a location to match the charm of its collection—an assortment of 2,000 original illustrations by Norman Rockwell.

HEALDVILLE
CROWLEY CHEESE FACTORY
14 Crowley Lane, Healdville, 802-259-2340, 800-683-2606; www.crowleycheese-vermont.com
The oldest cheese factory in the United States was opened in 1882. And lucky for us, Crowley Cheese still makes cheese the way it always did—by hand. Check out the displays of old-fashioned cheese-making tools, then watch the process as it's done today. Save the best for last, though, when you end the tour by sampling the product.
Monday-Saturday 8 a.m.-4 p.m.; call ahead as hours may change.

KILLINGTON
GIFFORD WOODS STATE PARK
34 Gifford Woods, Killington, 802-775-5354; www.vtstateparks.com
Located at the base of Killington and Pico peaks, this 114-acre park boasts lush forests and terrific hiking on the Appalachian Trail network. The park features fishing and boating access to Kent Pond.
June-mid-October.

KILLINGTON RESORT
4763 Killington Road, Killington, 802-422-3261, 800-621-6867; www.killington.com
Spread out over seven mountains, Killington Resort features 141 trails and 70 miles of skiing. With more than 200 runs, the park is best known for its

diversity of terrain, from classic New England tree runs to pipes and bumps. Snowboarding and tubing are also allowed. Special amenities include observation decks, six cafeterias, bars, a children's center and onsite lodging.
October-June, daily.

PICO ALPINE SLIDE AND SCENIC CHAIRLIFT
4763 Killington Road, Killington, 866-667-7426; www.killington.com
First, take the chairlift to the top of Pico Mountain. Then race back down the alpine slide on a sled that lets you control your speed. A sports center and restaurant are waiting below.
Late May-mid-October.

MIDDLEBURY
BREAD LOAF MOUNTAIN CAMPUS
121A S. Main St., Middlebury College, Freeman International Center, Middlebury, 802-443-5418; www.middlebury.edu
Owned by Middlebury College, the Bread Loaf Inn is a the setting for two ultra-exclusive literary events: the world-famous Bread Loaf School of English and the Bread Loaf Writer's Conference. In winter, though, the campus serves as the home for the Carroll and Jane Rikert Ski Touring Center, a destination for Nordic skiers.

CONGREGATIONAL CHURCH
27 N. Pleasant St., Middlebury, 802-388-7634; www.midducc.org
This pretty 1809 church features a five-tiered spire that towers above the treetops, thereby confirming the community's status as a classic New England town. No trip to Middlebury is complete without a look at the church.

MIDDLEBURY COLLEGE
Middlebury College, Route 30, Middlebury, 802-443-5000; www.middlebury.edu
One of the oldest liberal arts colleges in the nation, Middlebury is famous for its firsts: It was the first to grant a degree to an African-American student and the first to go coed. The school also hosts the prestigious Bread Loaf School of English and the Bread Loaf Writers' Conference (see above). As for the campus, it's characterized by mountain views and historic granite, limestone and marble buildings, including an Italianate farmhouse and a Beaux-Arts library.

MIDDLEBURY COLLEGE SNOW BOWL
Route 125, Middlebury, 802-388-4356; www.middlebury.edu
One of Vermont's earliest ski areas, this Middlebury College-owned mountain features 17 trails ranging from challenging to family-friendly. Snowboarders are welcome, too—in fact, they're well served by the onsite Ski and Snowboard Shop. Snowmaking machines ensure fresh powder. When it's time for a break, check out the old-fashioned lodge and full-service cafeteria.
December-early April, daily.

MONTPELIER
MORSE FARM
1168 County Road, Montpelier, 802-223-2740, 800-242-2740; www.morsefarm.com
Visit a maple syrup and vegetable farm set in a rustic, wooded setting. Take

a tour of the sugar house to learn more about the syrup-making process, or simply stroll the nature trails. Wherever you wander, you'll encounter all sorts of whimsical wood carvings by local folk artist Burr Morse. Before you leave, drop by the country store to stock up on maple candies and syrup.

March-April, daily.

STATE HOUSE

115 State St., Montpelier, 802-828-2228, 802-828-1411; www.leg.state.vt.us

The state's 1859 capitol was built in the Renaissance Revival style with 23-carat gold leaf covering its prominent dome. The prior capitol was destroyed by fire in 1857, though its Grecian portico was left standing and was incorporated into the capitol we see today.

Monday-Friday 8 a.m.-4 p.m. Guided tours: July-mid-October, Monday-Friday 10 a.m.-3:30 p.m., Saturday 11 a.m.-2:30 p.m.

THOMAS WATERMAN WOOD ART GALLERY

36 College St., Montpelier, 802-828-8743; www.twwoodgallery.org

This 110-year old gallery features a permanent collection of oils, watercolors and etchings by T. W. Wood and other 19th-century American artists. The gallery served as the official repository for Vermont's W.P.A. art, so it also holds a substantial collection of Depression-era works. The monthly exhibitions, meanwhile, spotlight contemporary works by regional artists.

Tuesday-Sunday noon-4 p.m.

VERMONT HISTORICAL SOCIETY MUSEUM

109 State St., Montpelier, 802-828-2291; www.vermonthistory.org

The museum's centerpiece is a 5,000-square-foot permanent exhibit called "Freedom and Unity: One Ideal, Many Stories," which tells the story of Vermont's residents from 1600 to present day. It includes everything from wigwams to Ethan Allen artifacts and historic firearms.

May-October, Tuesday-Saturday 10 a.m.-4 p.m., Sunday noon-4 p.m.

PITTSFORD

NEW ENGLAND MAPLE MUSEUM

Highway 7, Pittsford, 802-483-9414, 800-639-4280; www.maplemuseum.com

Located in the heart of Vermont's maple syrup country, the museum offers a trip through sugaring history, starting with the Native Americans' discovery about cooked maple sap. One of the world's largest collections of maple sugaring artifacts is complemented by interpretive displays, a narrated slideshow, cooking demonstrations and taste-tests. There is also a craft and maple-product gift shop.

June-October, daily 8:30 a.m.-5:30 p.m.; November-December, mid-March-May, daily 10 a.m.-4 p.m.; closed January-February.

PLYMOUTH NOTCH

PRESIDENT CALVIN COOLIDGE HOMESTEAD

Coolidge Memorial Drive, Plymouth Notch, 802-672-3773; www.historicvermont.org

On the evening of August 3, 1923, Calvin Coolidge was sworn in as president by his father, the local notary public, in this very house. Today, the site remains exactly as it was on that fateful night. The surrounding Plymouth Historic

District hasn't changed much, either. Visitors can explore the General Store that was operated by the president's father, the house where the president was born, even the village dance hall from which he governed during the summer of 1924.

June-mid-October, daily 9:30 a.m.-5 p.m.

QUECHEE
VERMONT INSTITUTE OF NATURAL SCIENCE
Route 4, Quechee, 802-359-5000; www.vinsweb.org

Designed to inspire care for the environment, the center features a raptor museum, a learning space for children, and a one-way viewing window that lets guests peek at birds in rehabilitation. Meanwhile, the surrounding network of trails winds through mixed habitat sites with hawks, owls, eagles and more.

May-October, daily 9 a.m.-5:30 p.m.; November-April, daily 10 a.m.-4 p.m.

RUTLAND
NORMAN ROCKWELL MUSEUM
654 Highway 4 E., Rutland, 802-773-6095; www.normanrockwellvt.com

A collection of 2,000 Norman Rockwell illustrations commemorates his 60-year career with a special emphasis on the 14 years he lived in Vermont. Highlights include the Four Freedoms, Boy Scout series and many magazine covers, including all 323 from the *Saturday Evening Post*.

Daily.

WAITSFIELD
MAD RIVER GLEN SKI AREA
Highway 17, Waitsfield, 802-496-3551; www.madriverglen.com

This ski resort has the country's oldest single chairlift, which was fully restored in 2006. What's more, Mad River Glen is the only cooperatively owned ski area in the nation, so it doesn't have the upscale features you find elsewhere. Operators do minimal grooming and they don't make snow, so the slopes maintain a vintage feel. In other words, no snowboarders allowed.

December-April, daily.

WARREN
SUGARBUSH RESORT
1840 Sugarbush Access Road, Warren, 802-583-6300, 800-583-7669; www.sugarbush.com

One of the largest ski areas in New England, Sugarbush encompasses two mountains, a diversity of terrain and a whopping 111 trails with plenty of great spots for snowboarding. Come summertime, Sugarbush attracts golfers and mountain bikers alike with its mountainous links and singletracks.

November-April, daily.

WOODSTOCK
MARSH-BILLINGS-ROCKEFELLER NATIONAL HISTORICAL PARK
54 Elm St., Woodstock, 802-457-3368; www.nps.gov

Built in 1805, the Marsh-Billings-Rockefeller mansion was later transformed into an American Stick-style residence. Now a house museum, the mansion is known for its extensive collection of American landscape paintings and formal gardens. What's more, it's surrounded by the 550-acre Mount Tom forest with its lush cover of sugar maples and hemlocks.

June-October, daily 10 a.m.-5 p.m.

SUICIDE SIX SKI AREA

South Pomfret Road, Woodstock, 802-457-1100; www.skivermont.com

Despite the intimidating name, this resort boasts plenty of family-friendly slopes. Of course, there's plenty to satisfy the advanced skier, too. Snowboarders are welcome. After a long day of shredding, check out the Out of Bounds restaurant for sandwiches, wine and beer.

December-March, daily.

WOODSTOCK HISTORICAL SOCIETY

26 Elm St., Woodstock; www.woodstockhistorical.org

The 1807 Dana House Museum has 11 rooms representing 150 years of Woodstock history, from 1750 and 1900. The house is full of antique silver, ceramics, furniture, paintings, clothing, photographs and early American toys. The grounds also include a research library, a document and photo archive, and an heirloom perennial garden.

June-October, Monday-Saturday 10 a.m.-4 p.m., Sunday noon-4 p.m.

WHERE TO STAY

BARNARD
★★★★★TWIN FARMS

452 Royalton Turnpike, Barnard, 802-234-9999, 800-894-6327; www.twinfarms.com

As indulgent a resort as you'll find anywhere, this all-inclusive hideaway features ten private cottages and ten sumptuous guest rooms, each decked out on a different theme by renowned interior designer Jed Johnson. The Moroccan-influenced Meadow room is adorned with Persian rugs and a mosaic-tiled fireplace, whereas the Scandinavian Barn has bleached pine floors, walls and rafters. Meals are made to order—enjoy them in the main dining room, the wine cellar or the privacy of your cottage. The resort is tucked away on 300 acres of wildflower meadows, hardwood forests and ponds.

16 rooms. Children not allowed. Complimentary breakfast. Restaurant, bar. Fitness center. Spa. Tennis. Ski-in/ski-out. $351 and up

CRAFTSBURY COMMON
★★★THE INN ON THE COMMON

1162 N. Craftsbury Road, Craftsbury Common, 802-586-9619, 800-521-2233

This classic country inn consists of three restored Federal-style houses, each with its own colorful garden. Guest rooms are individually decorated in the French country style. The dining room, meanwhile, specializes in seasonal dishes made from fresh, local ingredients.

16 rooms. Restaurant, bar. Pool. Tennis. $151-250

CHITTENDEN

★★★MOUNTAIN TOP INN

195 Mountain Top Road, Chittenden, 800-445-2100, 802-483-2311; www.mountaintopinn.com

With terrific views of a mountain lake and the Green Mountains National Forest, this cozy inn is ideal for outdoor enthusiasts. The inn also boasts its own equestrian center as well as the onsite Nordic ski and Snowshoe Center.

60 rooms. Closed April and first three weeks in November. Pets accepted. Restaurant, bar. Pool. Golf. Tennis. $151-250

KILLINGTON

★★★INN OF THE SIX MOUNTAINS

2617 Killington Road, Killington, 802-422-4302, 800-228-4676; www.sixmountains.com

Perfect for skiers, the Inn of the Six Mountains is located just one mile from the Killington ski area. Kick back in your rustic-style guest room before catching the complimentary shuttle to the slopes. Cedars restaurant serves a hearty breakfast buffet, perfect fuel for a long day of skiing. The onsite lounge, meanwhile, is a great place for an après-ski cocktail.

100 rooms. Complimentary breakfast. Restaurant, bar. Fitness center. Pool. Tennis. Spa. $61-150

MENDON

★★★RED CLOVER INN

7 Woodward Road, Mendon, 802-775-2290, 800-752-0571; www.redcloverinn.com

Built in the1840s, this country inn features terrific views of the Green Mountains. A few of the rooms have extra-special touches, like fireplaces and four-poster beds. No matter where you stay, though, you'll appreciate the farm-to-table foods, including fresh-made scones served with local jam and honey.

14 rooms. No children under 12. Complimentary breakfast. Restaurant, bar. $151-250

MIDDLEBURY

★★★SWIFT HOUSE INN

25 Stewart Lane, Middlebury, 802-388-9925, 866-388-9925; www.swifthouseinn.com

Built from a former governor's mansion, this bed and breakfast has character and charm in spades. Guest rooms feature 19th century-style décor with four-poster beds and handmade quilts. Some have fireplaces, too. At the end of the day, retreat to the candlelit dining room for a classic American meal made from fresh, seasonal ingredients.

20 rooms. Complimentary breakfast. Restaurant. $151-250

MONTPELIER

★★★INN AT MONTPELIER

147 Main St., Montpelier, 802-223-2727; www.innatmontpelier.com

Revisit the early 1800s at this historic inn, comprised of two stately Federal-style buildings. Each showcases Greek and Colonial Revival woodwork, numerous fireplaces and spectacular front staircases. One building features a wraparound porch. Guest rooms are decorated with antique furniture and rugs. In the morning, continental breakfast consists of fresh fruits, lemon curd, jams, and an assortment of pastries from a prominent local bakery.

19 rooms. Complimentary breakfast. $61-150

PLYMOUTH

★★★HAWK INN AND MOUNTAIN RESORT

Route 100 South, Plymouth, 802-672-3811, 800-685-4295; www.hawkresort.com

Whether you choose a room in the main house or one of the mountainside villas, this quiet resort treats you to crackling fireplaces, country décor and glorious views. As the resort is situated on 1,200 wooded acres, guests can partake in a variety of outdoor activities like hiking, biking and fly-fishing. The Hawk Spa offers convenient massage and hair styling services.

200 rooms. Restaurant, bar. Fitness center. Tennis. $251-350

QUECHEE

★★★QUECHEE INN AT MARSHLAND FARM

1119 Quechee Main St., Quechee, 802-295-3133, 800-235-3133; www.quecheeinn.com

Built in 1793 this inn features Queen Anne-style furnishings and period antiques. Enjoy views of the Ottauquechee River and Dewey's Mill Pond, or just kick back in the candlelit dining room with a meal of country-style comfort food.

24 rooms. Complimentary breakfast. Restaurant, bar. $151-250

WARREN

★★★THE PITCHER INN

275 Main St., Warren, 802-496-6350, 800-735-2478; www.pitcherinn.com

A classic country inn with an upscale flourish, the Pitcher Inn features rustic appointments with luxury details like in-room spa services and fireplaces. Guest rooms are decorated in a variety of Vermont themes, from fishing to skiing (speaking of which, the Sugarbush Ski Area is nearby). The Pitcher Inn is also ideal for oenophiles—after all, the restaurant boasts a 6,500-bottle wine cellar.

11 rooms. Complimentary breakfast.. Restaurant, bar. $351 and up

★★★SUGARBUSH INN

1840 Sugarbush Access Road, Warren, 802-583-6114, 800-537-8427; www.sugarbush.com

Surrounded by slopes, hills and trails, this activity-oriented inn is nestled between the towns of Waitsfield and Warren. Snowshoeing, snow tubing, ice skating and horse-drawn sleigh rides are available on the property. Back at the inn, enjoy end-of-day crackling fireplaces and other country-style comforts.

143 rooms. Complimentary breakfast. Restaurant, bar. Fitness center. Pool. Golf. Tennis. Ski in/ski out. $151-250

WOODSTOCK

★★★KEDRON VALLEY INN

10671 S. Road, South Woodstock, 802-457-1473, 800-836-1193; www.kedronvalleyinn.com

Located five miles outside of Woodstock, this 185-year-old inn makes a great home base for those focused on antique shopping. After a long day of browsing, relax by the inn's spring-fed pond or explore the nearby hills on horseback. Guest rooms feature wood-burning stoves or fireplaces and country-style décor. The in-house restaurant, meanwhile, serves American classics and vegetarian meals made from fresh, local ingredients.

26 rooms. Restaurant, bar. Closed April. $151-250

★★★WOODSTOCK INN & RESORT

14 The Green, Woodstock, 802-457-1100, 800-448-7900; www.woodstockinn.com

An enormous inn situated on the town green, the 18th-century Woodstock Inn stands as the centerpiece of Woodstock. Guest rooms and suites capture traditional Vermont coziness with handmade quilts, built-in alcoves and original art prints. Despite that intimate feel, however, the inn is big enough to house three restaurants serving everything from gourmet to casual tavern-style fare. Downhill and cross-country skiing are two of the resort's most popular winter activities, while the Woodstock Country Club's prestigious course attracts golfers during the summer. Other popular activities include biking, canoeing, fishing, horseback riding and nature walks.

142 rooms. Restaurant, bar. Fitness center. Spa. Pool. Golf. Tennis. Ski in/ski out. Business center. $251-350

RECOMMENDED

BARNARD
MAPLE LEAF INN

Highway 12, Barnard, 802-234-5342, 800-516-2753; www.mapleleafinn.com

A Victorian-style farmhouse hidden among a forest of maples and birch trees, this bed and breakfast specializes in relaxation. Along those lines, guests enjoy country-style décor, close proximity to nature walks and candlelit morning meals.

7 rooms. Complimentary breakfast. $151-250

EAST MIDDLEBURY
WAYBURY INN

457 E. Main, East Middlebury, 802-388-4015, 800-348-1810; www.wayburyinn.com

One of the nation's most famous inns, the Waybury was featured in the opening credits of Bob Newhart's television show. Originally constructed as a stagecoach stop, the 19th-century inn features all sorts of set-ready accommodations: classic country furnishings, an elegant dining room, a casual pub and an enormous porch.

14 rooms. Pets accepted. Complimentary breakfast. Restaurant, bar. $61-150

QUECHEE
PARKER HOUSE INN

1792 Quechee Main St., Quechee, 802-295-6077; www.theparkerhouseinn.com

This chef-owned bed and breakfast has impressive Victorian credentials. Built in 1857, the grand brick house once served as a senator's residence. These days, it boasts French country-style furnishings. Best of all, though, is the food at the in-house restaurant—think brandy-spiked French onion soup and chicken breasts stuffed with local goat cheese.

7 rooms. Complimentary breakfast. Restaurant. $61-150

WAITSFIELD
TUCKER HILL INN

65 Marble Hill Road, Waitsfield, 802-496-3983, 800-543-7841; www.tuckerhill.com

A country inn with a variety of individually decorated rooms, the property has plenty of space to spread out in, including an in-house pub, a game room, a common living room and an outdoor patio. Don't miss the gourmet breakfast served daily in the sky-lit morning room.

18 rooms. Restaurant, bar. Pool. Tennis. $151-250

THE INN AT THE ROUND BARN

1661 E. Warren Road, Waitsfield, 802-496-2276; www.theroundbarn.com

Located on more than 200 acres of mountainside, ponds and meadows, this inn lives inside an unusual round barn. Check out the surrounding orchards and organic gardens—the chef sources many of his house-made meals right here. Cozy guest rooms feature rustic-style details like wood-beamed ceilings and fireplaces.

12 rooms. Complimentary breakfast. Pool. $151-250

WOODSTOCK

APPLEBUTTER INN

Happy Valley Road, Woodstock, 802-457-4158; www.applebutterinn.com

Built in 1846, this bed and breakfast first served as a stagecoach stop and a general store. Today, it features simple but plush rooms decorated with oriental rugs, antiques and floral prints. Morning means house-baked muffins and fresh fruit served in the sunny breakfast room. Afternoon means fresh-from-the-oven cookies and hot tea.

6 rooms. Complimentary breakfast. $61-150

THE LINCOLN INN AT THE COVERED BRIDGE

530 Woodstock Road, Woodstock, 802-457-3312; www.lincolninn.com

Sure, it's located within a renovated 1869 farmhouse, but this inn strives to offer the usual bed-and-breakfast comforts without all the stuffiness. Guest rooms are decorated in a variety of quirky themes, including "yin yang" and "passion." Common areas, meanwhile, are bright and spare, designed to favor the more beautiful scenes of the nearby Ottauquechee River and a classic covered bridge.

6 rooms. Complimentary breakfast. Restaurant. $61-150

WOODSTOCKER BED AND BREAKFAST

61 River St., Woodstock, 802-457-3896, 866-662-1439; www.woodstockervt.com

This quirky inn feels homier than the usual bed and breakfast. It features contemporary décor with pops of color, as well as the innkeeper's private selection of books (collected during her 25-year career in publishing). Guests love the 24-hour refreshment station stocked with serve-yourself goodies.

9 rooms. Complimentary breakfast. Pets accepted. $61-150

WHERE TO EAT

BARNARD

★★★BARNARD INN

5518 Highway 12, Barnard, 802-234-9961; www.barnardinnrestaurant.com

Situated in a 1796 colonial chateau, this inn exudes New England-style simplicity and charm. The restaurant serves dishes prepared with French technique, such as steamed mussels with saffron and garlic. Many of the ingredients come fresh from the restaurant's own garden.

French. Dinner. Bar. Children's menu. Closed Sunday-Monday. $151-250

KILLINGTON

★★★HEMINGWAY'S

4988 Highway 4, Killington, 802-422-3886; www.hemingwaysrestaurant.com

Housed in a charming 19th-century house, Hemingway's fuses classic comfort foods with contemporary fine dining, offering a six-course menu, a four-course vegetable menu and a three-course prix-fixe menu. Though it serves plenty of French dishes, the restaurant's American fare is its best regarded, including the pan-roasted pork with braised Brussels sprouts, corn cake and bacon.

International. Dinner. Bar. Closed Monday-Tuesday. $86 and up

MENDON

★★★RED CLOVER

7 Woodward Road, Mendon, 802-775-2290, 800-752-0571; www.redcloverinn.com

Check out this 19th-century farmhouse inn for sophisticated dining in four candlelit rooms. The menu changes frequently, though it always includes plenty of American classics prepared with European techniques and local ingredients. Try the oven-roasted quail, Tuscan bean salad or cider-marinated salmon.

American. Breakfast, dinner. Bar. Reservations recommended. Closed Monday-Wednesday. $36-85

QUECHEE

★★★QUECHEE INN AT MARSHLAND FARM

1119 Quechee Main St., Quechee, 802-295-3133, 800-235-3133; www.quecheeinn.com

Candlelight and Ottauquechee River views define this restaurant, which is situated in the main house of the 1793 Quechee Inn. The cuisine is served in a casual but sophisticated setting, with a carefully curated wine list to match. The cuisine incorporates fresh, New England ingredients, as in the maple stout-braised short ribs.

American. Breakfast, dinner. Bar. Children's menu. Reservations recommended. Outdoor seating. $16-35

★★★SIMON PEARCE

1761 Main St., Quechee, 802-295-1470; www.simonpearce.com

Yes, this restaurant is situated within the world-famous Simon Pearce glass-blowing and pottery complex, now an emblem of Vermont. As expected, the dining room is utterly artful—you won't believe the cantilevered deck that hovers above the falls in Quechee. The cuisine, meanwhile, is innovative American with Asian accents. Breads and soups are homemade.

American. Lunch, dinner. Bar. Reservations recommended. Outdoor seating. $36-85

SOUTH WOODSTOCK

★★★KEDRON VALLEY INN

Highway 106, South Woodstock, 802-457-1473, 800-836-1193; www.kedronvalleyinn.com

Located just outside the town of Woodstock, this inn boasts a dining room that's a local favorite thanks to its cheerful ambience and reasonable prices. The menu at the inn's restaurant features Vermont-raised produce and meat as well as gourmet takes on traditional tavern foods like onion rings and French fries.

American. Breakfast, dinner. Bar. Children's menu. Closed Tuesday-Wednesday, November-July, week of December 25. $16-35

WARREN

★★★THE COMMON MAN

3209 German Flats Road, Warren, 802-583-2800; www.commonmanrestaurant.com

A rough-hewn 1880s barn is the setting for this traditional New England restaurant, where the menu runs the gamut from traditional fish stew to more eclectic options like homemade gnocchi with lobster. A huge stone fireplace is the centerpiece of a cozy dining room with timbered interiors. Dinner is often served to the tune of live jazz.

American. Dinner. Bar. Children's menu. Reservations recommended. Closed Sunday-Monday, two-four weeks in spring and November. $16-35

WOODSTOCK

★★★PRINCE AND THE PAUPER

24 Elm St., Woodstock, 802-457-1818; www.princeandpauper.com

Chef-owner Chris Balcer offers a menu that changes seasonally, though the offerings always emphasize meat and fish. Past highlights have included Amish-raised veal and boneless rack of lamb in puff pastry with spinach and mushroom duxelles. For a simpler dinner, order off the bistro menu, which includes hickory-smoked ribs, Maine crab cakes and hearth-baked pizzas.

American. Dinner. Bar. Reservations recommended. $36-85

★★★WOODSTOCK INN

14 The Green, Woodstock, 802-457-1100, 800-448-7900; www.woodstockinn.com

Nightly piano entertainment perfectly suits the romantic atmosphere at this quaint restaurant. Back in the kitchen, though, the atmosphere is more compatible with local and seasonal produce. Don't miss the organic field greens with Vermont chevre, raspberries and maple mustard vinaigrette, or the char-grilled Black Angus filet mignon with a Vermont gorgonzola crust and a cider reduction.

American. Dinner, Sunday brunch. Bar. Children's menu. Reservations recommended. $36-85

SOUTHERN VERMONT

When it comes to history, Bennington boasts three significant areas: First, there are the Victorian and turn-of-the-century buildings that decorate downtown streets. Second, see the colonial houses, the church and the town commons in Old Bennington. Last, don't miss the three covered bridges of North Bennington. Once the home of Ethan Allen's famous Green Mountain Boys, Bennington is a haven for history buffs of all stripes. Notably, it's also home to Bennington College, one of the artiest (and spendiest) liberal arts schools in the nation.

For more than 100 years, the state's southernmost corridor has been the home of terrific year-round resorts. Luxury lovers shouldn't miss the Equinox, one of the state's most fashionable resorts with terrific farm-to-table food, abundant outdoor activities and a 13,000-square-foot pampering palace. When you've mustered up the strength, check out the nearby town of Manchester for a lineup of upscale outlet stores from Giorgio Armani, Coach, Escanda, Ralph Lauren and more.

HIGHLIGHTS

WHAT ARE THE TOP THINGS TO DO IN SOUTHERN VERMONT?

EXPLORE THE BENNINGTON MUSEUM
Check out the world's foremost public collection of paintings by Grandma Moses, the folk artist who took to painting late in life and became famous for her colorful renderings of rural life.

SET OUT ON THE EQUINOX SKY LINE DRIVE
For magnificent views of the regions' landscape, make the steep, five-mile trek (by car—not recommended on foot) along the paved road that leads to the tip of Mount Equinox.

WHAT TO SEE

BENNINGTON

BENNINGTON BATTLE MONUMENT
15 Monument Circle, Old Bennington,

Dedicated in 1891, this 306-foot monolith commemorates the Revolutionary War victory at Bennington in 1777. The towering monument comes complete with an observation deck and, thankfully, an elevator.

Mid-April-October, daily 9 a.m.-5 p.m.

BENNINGTON COLLEGE
Highway 67A and One College Drive, Bennington, 802-442-5401; www.bennington.edu

Founded as a women's college in 1932, this small liberal arts school went coeducational in 1969. The leafy campus features plenty of sights, especially the Usdan Gallery at the historic Visual and Performing Arts Center with its revolving exhibitions and lecture series.

BENNINGTON MUSEUM
75 Main St., Bennington, 802-447-1571; www.benningtonmuseum.org

Dedicated to commemorating Bennington's colonial past, especially the great Battle of Bennington in 1777, this museum contains early Vermont and New England historical artifacts—everything from American glass, paintings, and sculpture to decorative arts like silver and furniture. Notably, the organization possesses the world's largest public collection of Grandma Moses folk art and family memorabilia.

Thursday-Tuesday 10 a.m.-5 p.m. Genealogical library by appointment.

OLD BURYING GROUND

1 Veterans Memorial Drive, Bennington, 802-447-3311; www.bennington.com

The simple country cemetery is the final resting place of several soldiers killed in the Battle of Bennington, a handful of Vermont governors and the world-famous poet Robert Frost.

OLD FIRST CHURCH

One Monument Circle, Old Bennington, Vt. Route 9 and Monument Avenue, 802-447-1223; www.oldfirstchurchbenn.org

Built in 1805, the church was the first in Vermont to represent the separation of church and state—that is, the town would have nothing to do with its upkeep. Today, the church stands as a charming example of early colonial architecture with its white pine columns and steeple.

Guided tours: June, weekends; July-mid-October, Monday-Saturday 10 a.m.-noon, 1-4 p.m., Sunday 1-4 p.m.

PARK-MCCULLOUGH HOUSE MUSEUM

One Park and West Street, North Bennington, 802-442-5441; www.parkmccullough.org

Built in 1865 by a wealthy attorney and business owner, this 35-room Victorian mansion is filled with the finest period furnishings as well as immense collections of costumes, art and literature. Meanwhile, the estate's fabulous grounds feature lush Victorian gardens, a stable with antique carriages and an elaborate playhouse for children.

Mid-May-October, daily, tours 10 a.m.-4 p.m.; November-April, special events and group tours by appointment.

MANCHESTER

AMERICAN MUSEUM OF FLY FISHING

410 Main St., Manchester, 802-362-3300; www.amff.com

Founded in 1968 by a group of dedicated fishermen, this museum features a collection of vintage fly-fishing memorabilia as well as the tackle used by many famous persons, including Dwight D. Eisenhower, Ernest Hemingway, Andrew Carnegie, Winslow Homer, Bing Crosby and others.

Tuesday-Sunday 10 a.m.-4 p.m.

EQUINOX SKY LINE DRIVE

1A Street and Bruno Drive, Manchester and Manchester Center, 802-362-1114, 802-362-1115; www.equinoxmountain.com

This five-mile paved road rises from 600 to 3,835 feet to deliver spectacular views from the top of Mount Equinox. Fog and rain make for sketchy driving conditions, so drive carefully.

May-October, daily.

HISTORIC HILDENE

1005 Hildene Road, Manchester, 802-362-1788, 800-578-1788; www.hildene.org

This 412-acre estate was once home to Robert Todd Lincoln, chairman of the large Pullman Company and son of Abraham Lincoln. It includes a 24-room Georgian manor house, held by the family until 1975, as well as a carriage barn, formal gardens and nature trails.

Daily 9:30 a.m.-4:30 p.m.

MANCHESTER DESIGNER OUTLETS
Highways 11 and 30, Manchester Center, 802-362-3736; www.manchesterdesigneroutlets.com
From Betsy Johnson to Ben & Jerry's, there are dozens of outlet stores here, all housed in a concentrated shopping area along Highway 7.
Monday-Saturday 10 a.m.-7 p.m., Sunday 10 a.m.-6 p.m.

WEST DOVER
MOUNT SNOW SKI AREA
12 Pisgah Road, West Dover, 802-464-2151, 800-498-0479; www.mountsnow.com
The family-friendly ski area boasts three lodges, a summit house and 80 trails, everything from learning areas to cruisers. Other winter sports include tubing, snowshoeing, snowmobiling and cross-country skiing. Mount Snow also offers on-site childcare.
November-early May, daily.

WOODFORD
WOODFORD STATE PARK
142 State Park Road, Woodford, 802-447-7169; www.vtstateparks.com
At 2,400 feet, this 400-acre park has the highest elevation of any park in the state. Swimming, fishing, picnicking, camping and non-motorized boating are allowed. Since the park is located on a mountain plateau, it also features terrific views via its nature and hiking trails.
June-mid-October.

WHERE TO STAY

BENNINGTON
★★★FOUR CHIMNEYS INN
21 W. Road, Bennington, 802-447-3500; www.fourchimneys.com
This elegant 1783 inn blends modern amenities with old-world charms, including 11 acres of trees and rolling grass fields. Every morning, a complimentary breakfast is served in the sun-filled porch. The dining room opens again later in the day, this time with a dinner menu of gourmet New England classics like grilled salmon and lobster ravioli.
11 rooms. Complimentary breakfast. Restaurant, bar. $151-250

MANCHESTER
★★★RELUCTANT PANTHER INN AND RESTAURANT
39 W. Road, Manchester, 802-362-2568, 800-822-2331; www.reluctantpanther.com
Built in 1850 by a wealthy blacksmith, the Reluctant Panther boasts museum-quality furnishings and artwork, not to mention architectural features like original fireplaces. Guest rooms are decorated with shabby-chic floral prints and plaids. The dining experience is an epicurean one, whether you dine in the formal restaurant, the alfresco terrace or the ultra-casual pub.
21 rooms. No children under 14. Complimentary breakfast. Restaurant, bar. $151-250

MANCHESTER VILLAGE
★★★THE EQUINOX
3567 Main St., Manchester Village, 802-362-4700, 866-346-7625; www.equinoxresort.com
Open since 1769, this resort has seen centuries of notable visitors, from the

Lincolns to the Tafts and the Roosevelts. It stands to reason, then, that the resort features the utmost in swank accommodations: plush beds, marble bathrooms and Jacuzzi bathtubs. Tucked at the base of Mount Equinox, the Equinox also features loads of activities from putting at the Gleneagles golf course to the onsite Orvis fly-fishing and shooting schools and its very own falconry center. A full-service spa is located on the property, as are three restaurants, including the cozy and popular Marsh Tavern.

195 rooms. Restaurant, bar. Fitness center. Spa. Pool. Golf. Tennis. Ski in/ski out. Business center. $251-350

RECOMMENDED

INN AT MANCHESTER

3967 Main St., Manchester, 802-362-1793, 800-273-1793; www.innatmanchester.com

Housed in a 19th-century Victorian mansion, this country inn features cozy comforts like handmade quilts and in-suite fireplaces. Book a room in the main house or the private carriage house. Either way, you'll enjoy a morning meal of hearty, country-style breakfast foods, as well as an in-house pub with a terrific selection of wines and local beers.

18 rooms. No children under 8. Pool. $151-250

THE INN AT ORMSBY HILL

1842 Main St., Manchester, 802-362-1163, 800-670-2841; www.ormsbyhill.com

With panoramic views of the Green Mountains, this bed and breakfast makes a great romantic getaway. Housed in a 1764 Federal-style mansion, the inn boasts plenty of common areas filled with vintage china and unique fireplaces. Guest rooms are individually decorated with tapestry wallpapers, canopy beds and antiques. Your room rate comes with a home-cooked breakfast and a plate of freshly baked cookies.

10 rooms. Complimentary breakfast. $151-250

SPA

MANCHESTER VILLAGE

★★★THE SPA AT EQUINOX

The Equinox, 3567 Main St., Manchester Village, 802-362-4700; www.equinoxresort.com

Whether you want a facial or a massage, this 13,000-square-foot spa is famous for incorporating products from the Vermont countryside, including maple sugar, wildflowers and mineral clay. Signature treatments include the rejuvenating Gentle Rain body treatment, where a sea salt, maple or citrus scrub is followed with a warm waterfall shower and an application of a rich body cream. Once you've been fully pampered, retreat to the 75-foot heated indoor pool, the state-of-the-art fitness center, the sauna or the steam bath.

WELCOME TO QUEBEC

MONTRÉAL

Montréal is perhaps Canada's most romanticized city, and with good reason. It is, after all, the city that gave the world Oscar Peterson, Jackie Robinson and Leonard Cohen. Immortalized by the writings of Mordecai Richler, Michel Tremblay and Gabrielle Roy, Montréal's neighborhoods feature a vibrant blend of Old World bohemianism, immigrant verve and scrappy provincialism. The glue that holds this multifaceted city together is arguably the Montréal Canadiens hockey club, which

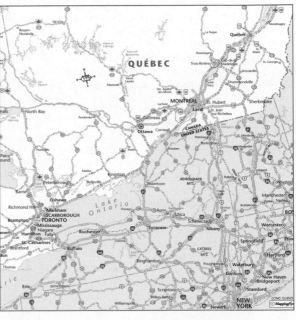

unites French, English and "allophone" (whose native tongue is neither French nor English) alike. Historic tensions between the French-speaking majority and economically powerful anglophone community persist, as does chatter of a new referendum on Quebec sovereignty. In recent years, however, the navel-gazing that defined Quebec politics since the 1970s has dissipated just enough to allow young Montréalers a glimpse of life beyond nationalist debates. With the growing number of allophone immigrants to the city, the old rivalries are giving way to a new wave of cosmopolitanism reminiscent of 1967, when Montréal hosted the future-forward international exposition Expo 67. Much like that famous Summer of Love, local heroes Cirque de Soleil, Yann Martel, Xavier Dolan, Arcade Fire and other homegrown talents are reinvigorating Montréal's international reputation as a cultural hothouse with global clout. The city's countless cafés, terraces and BYOB bistros are always buzzing, never more so than during the summer months when the city's streets welcome the Montréal International Jazz Festival, the Just For Laughs comedy festival and a mind-boggling array of other public spectacles.

WHAT TO SEE

MONTRÉAL

BIODOME DE MONTRÉAL

4777 Pierre-De Coubertin Ave., Montréal, 514-868-3000; www.biodome.qc.ca

The former Olympic Velodrome has been transformed into an environmental museum that combines elements of a botanical garden, aquarium, zoo and nature center. Four ecosystems—Laurentian Forest, Tropical Forest, Polar World and St. Laurent Marine—sustain thousands of plants and small animals. The Biodome also features a 1,640-foot nature path with text panels and maps.

Admission: adults $16.50, seniors and students $12.50, children 5-17 $8.25, children 2-4 $2.50, children 1 and under free. Mid-June-Labor Day, daily 9 a.m.-6 p.m.; Labor Day-September 30, December-early June, daily 9 a.m.-5 p.m.

CHÂTEAU RAMEZAY

280 rue Notre-Dame E., Montréal, 514-861-3708; www.chateauramezay.qc.ca

This historic building was constructed in the 18th century and was once the home to the governors of Montréal. Later, it housed the West Indies Company of France and the Governors General of British North America. It opened as a museum in 1895 and today is the oldest private museum in Québec. Collections include furniture, paintings, costumes, porcelain, manuscripts and art objects from the 17th through 19th centuries.

Admission: adults $10, seniors $8, students $7, children 5-17 $5, children 4 and under free. June-late-November, daily 10 a.m.-6 p.m.; late-November-May, Tuesday-Sunday 10 a.m.-4:30 p.m.

DORCHESTER SQUARE

1555 Peel St., Montréal

In the center of Montréal, this park is a popular meeting place. Check out Mary Queen of the World Cathedral, a one third-scale replica of St. Peter's in Rome, as well as the information center of Montréal and Tourisme Québec, located at 1255 Peel Street.

FLORALIES GARDENS

Île Notre-Dame, Montréal

This was the site of the original Les Floralies Internationales exhibition in 1980. Now installed as a permanent exhibit, it displays a collection of worldwide flowers and plants. There are walking trails, pedal boats and canoeing, as well as a picnic area and restaurant.

Third week in June-mid-September, daily.

FORT LENNOX NATIONAL HISTORIC SITE

Saint-Paul-de-l'île-aux-Noix, 450-291-5700; www.pc.gc.ca

Located 60 kilometers from Montréal on a small island in the middle of the Richelieu River, Fort Lennox was built between 1819 and 1829 to protect against an American invasion that never came. Costumed guides provide visitors with insight into the history of these fortifications. The island is accessible via a five-minute ferry ride.

HIGHLIGHTS

WHAT ARE MONTRÉAL'S CAN'T-MISS SIGHTS?

OLD (VIEUX) MONTRÉAL

The only fortified neighborhood in North America is very European in character, with narrow and winding cobblestone streets that lead visitors past many a shop, café and 17th-century building.

ST. JOSEPH'S ORATORY OF MONT ROYAL

Situated on the northern slope of Mont Royal, this gorgeous basilica was modeled after St. Peter's Basilica in Rome. Today, it looms above the Montréal cityscape with its expansive dome and luminous white façade. A popular destination for pilgrims, especially the sick who come in search of miracles, the interior wall features a display of crutches left by those who were supposedly cured.

POINTE-À-CALLIÈRE, THE MONTRÉAL MUSEUM OF ARCHAEOLOGY AND HISTORY

This remarkable building goes a step further than the typical history museum— this institution was built atop an actual archaeological dig, exposing the city's beginnings from more than 360 years ago.

LAFONTAINE PARK
Sherbrooke and Avenue du Parc Lafontaine, Montréal, 514-872-2644

LaFontaine Park is just as great for lazy afternoons as it is for recreation. Footpaths and bicycle trails wind their way around the park's central, artificial lake, which freezes over in the winter to form one of Montréal's best open-air skating rinks.

MAISON ST. GABRIEL
Pointe-Saint-Charles, 2146 place de Dublin, Montréal, 514-935-8136;
www.maisonsaint-gabriel.qc.ca

Built in the late 17th century as a farm, Maison St. Gabriel was later converted by Marguerite Bourgeoys, the founder of the Sisters of the Congregation de Notre-Dame, into a prep school for imported French girls (potential brides for the colony's many bachelors). The site includes vegetable, herb and flower gardens. The house itself has period furnishings, tools and artifacts of French-Canadian heritage, including woodcuts from ancient churches and chapels.

Admission: free. January 19-June 19 and September 7-December 19, Tuesday-Sunday 1-5 p.m.; June 20-September 5, Tuesday-Sunday 11 a.m.-6 p.m.

MONTRÉAL BOTANICAL GARDEN

4101 rue Sherbrooke East, Montréal, 514-872-1400; www.ville.Montréal.qc.ca

Within 180 acres of this botanical garden, there are more than 26,000 species and varieties of plants, with 30 specialized sections dedicated to roses, perennial plants, heath gardens, flowery brooks, bonsai, carnivorous plants and an arboretum. The garden has one of the world's largest orchid collections and seasonal flower shows. The bonsai and penjing collections are two of the most diversified in North America. There are also Chinese and Japanese gardens, a restaurant and a tearoom.

Admission: adults $16.50, seniors and students $12.50, children 5-17 $8.25, children 2-4 $2.50; rates are discounted in off-season from November-mid-May. Daily 9 a.m.-6 p.m.

MONTRÉAL MUSEUM OF FINE ARTS

1379-80 rue Sherbrooke Ouest, Montréal, 514-285-2000, 800-899-6873; www.mmfa.qc.ca

Canada's oldest art museum, founded in 1860, has a wide variety of displays ranging from Egyptian statues to 20th-century abstracts. A Canadian section features old Québec furniture, silver and paintings.

Admission: adults $15, seniors $10, students $7.50, children 12 and under free. Tuesday 11 a.m.-5 p.m., Wednesday-Friday 11 a.m.-9 p.m., Saturday-Sunday 10 a.m.-5 p.m.

MONTRÉAL PLANETARIUM

1000 rue Saint-Jacques Ouest, Montréal, 514-872-4530; www.ville.montreal.qc.ca

See the stars at the Montréal Planetarium, where a 385-seat theater holds multimedia astronomy shows with projectors that recreate the night sky. Just outside the theater are temporary and permanent exhibits on the solar system, meteorites, fossils and other astronomy-related topics.

Admission: adults $8, seniors and students $6, children 5-17 $4, children 4 and under free. Hours vary by season.

THE MONTRÉAL SCIENCE CENTRE

King-Edward Pier, 333 rue de la Commune Ouest, Montréal, 514-496-4724, 877-496-4724; www.centredessciencesdemontreal.com/en

Uncover the mysteries of science and technology through multimedia and hands-on exhibits, an IMAX theater and more.

Admission: adults $12, seniors and children 13-17 $11, children 4-12 $9. Monday-Friday 9 a.m.-4 p.m., Saturday-Sunday 9:30 a.m.-4 p.m.

MUSEÉ D'ART CONTEMPORAIN DE MONTRÉAL

185 rue Sainte-Catherine Ouest, Montréal, 514-847-6226; www.macm.org

This is Canada's only museum devoted exclusively to modern art. The collection emphasizes Canadian and Québécois artists, with the world's largest collection of Paul-Émile Borduas.

Admission: adults $8, seniors $6, students $4, children 12 and under free. Tuesday-Sunday 11 a.m.-6 p.m., Wednesday until 9 p.m.

NOTRE-DAME BASILICA

110 rue Notre-Dame Ouest, Montréal, 514-842-2925, 866-842-2925;
www.basiliquenddm.org

Completed in 1829, this church features Le Gros Bourdon, a bell cast in 1847 and weighing 24,780 pounds. Built of Montréal limestone, the basilica is neo-Gothic in design with a beautiful main altar and pulpit, and numerous statues, paintings and stained-glass windows.

Admission: adults $5, children 7-17 $4, children 6 and under free. Monday-Friday 8 a.m.-4:30 p.m., Saturday 8 a.m.-4 p.m., Sunday 12:30 p.m.-4 p.m.

NOTRE-DAME-DE-BON-SECOURS CHURCH

400 rue St. Paul E., Montréal, 514-282-8670

Founded in 1657 by teacher Marguerite Bourgeoys and rebuilt 115 years later, this is one of the oldest churches still standing in the city. With its location near the Port of Montréal, parishioners often prayed here for the safety of the community's sailors. In recognition of this, many fishermen and other mariners presented the church with miniature wooden ships, which hang from the vaulted ceiling to this day. The tower offers views of the river and city. Housed here is the Marguerite Bourgeois museum, which features objects pertaining to early settlers.

Museum: adults $8, seniors and students $5, children 6-12 $4. March-April and Canadian Thanksgiving-mid-January, Tuesday-Sunday 11 a.m.-3:30 p.m.; May-Canadian Thanksgiving, Tuesday-Sunday 10 a.m.-5:30 p.m.

THE OLD FORT

This is the oldest remaining fortification of Montréal, built between 1820 and 1824. Today, only the arsenal, powder magazine and barracks are still standing. Two military companies dating to the 18th century, La Compagnie Franche de la Marine and the 78th Fraser Highlanders, perform colorful military drills and parades.

Late June-August, Wednesday-Sunday.

OLD (VIEUX) MONTRÉAL

Bounded by McGill, Berri, Notre-Dame streets and the St. Lawrence River

The city of Montréal evolved from this tiny settlement, called Ville-Marie and founded by de Maisonneuve in 1642. The subsequent expansion of Ville-Marie led to what is now known as Old Montréal. The area roughly forms a 100-acre quadrangle, which corresponds approximately to the area enclosed within the original fortifications. The largest concentration of 19th-century buildings in North America is found here.

OLD PORT OF MONTRÉAL

333 Rue de la Commune St., Montréal, 514-496-7678, 800-971-7678;
www.oldportofMontréal.com

This Old Port is a departure point for boat cruises, as well as a recreational and tourist park hosting cultural exhibitions, special events and entertainment.

OLYMPIC PARK

4141 Pierre de Coubertin Ave., Montréal, 514-252-4141, 877-997-0919; www.rio.gouv.qc.ca

This stadium was the site of the 1976 Summer Olympic Games. It was also home to Major League Baseball's Montréal Expos until the team relocated to Washington in 2004. The world's tallest inclined tower (626 feet, leaning at a 45-degree angle) is found here. Tours of the stadium are given daily.

Admission to observatory: adults $15, seniors and students $11.25, children 5-17 $7.50, children 4 and under free. Mid-June-Labor day, daily 9 a.m.-7 p.m.; Labor Day-mid-June, daily 9 a.m.-5 p.m. Tours: adults $8, seniors and students $6, children 5-17 $4, children 4 and under free. Tours: mid-June-September, daily 10 a.m.-5 p.m. on the hour; mid-September-March, daily 11 a.m., noon, 1:30 p.m., 2:30 p.m., 3:30 p.m.

PARC DU MONT-ROYAL

Cote des Neiges and Remembrance roads, Montréal, 514-843-8240; www.lemontroyal.qc.ca

Designed by Frederick Law Olmsted, the creator of Central Park in New York City and the Emerald Necklace in Boston, Parc du Mont-Royal is a similarly large park located in the heart of a city. Popular with visitors and residents alike, it offers something for everyone, including cycling, hiking, cross-country skiing and snowshoeing. Bikes, skis and snowshoes may be rented at the park.

Daily 6 a.m.-midnight.

PARC JEAN-DRAPEAU

1 Circuit Gilles-Villeneuve, Montréal, 514-872-6120; www.parcjeandrapeau.com

This park consists of two islands in the middle of the St. Lawrence River. In order to access the park, visitors must take the Jacques-Cartier Bridge or Metro subway. St. Helen's Island was the main anchor site for the 1967 universal exposition, now better known as Expo 67. It is now a 342-acre multipurpose park with three swimming pools, picnicking areas, cross-country skiing and snowshoeing. Notre Dame Island, to the south, was built to accommodate the pavilions for Expo 67 from landfill excavated during the building of Montréal's subway. The former Pavilion of France is now the Montréal Casino. The Gilles-Villeneuve Formula 1 racetrack is located here along with a beach. You can rent paddleboats and go windsurfing and sailing as well.

PLACE D'ARMES

Rue St. Jacques, Montréal

Place d'Armes is one of Montréal's oldest public sites. Established in 1693 as Place de la Fabrique, it proved a popular site for military exercises and was given its current name in 1721. In the square's center is a statue of Paul Chomedey, Sieur de Maisonneuve, commemorating his defense of the young colony against an Iroquois attack in 1644. At one end is the St. Sulpice seminary of 1685, with its old wooden clock. At 119 St. Jacques Street is the Bank of Montréal. This magnificent building contains a museum (open Monday-Friday) with a collection of currency, mechanical savings banks and photographs, and a reproduction of an old-fashioned teller's cage. Some of the most important financial houses of the city are grouped around the square.

PLACE DES ARTS

260 Boulevard de Maisonneuve Oeste, 514-842-2112; www.pdarts.com

This four-theater complex opened in 1963 and remains the heart of Montréal's artistic life. L'Opera de Montréal, the Montréal Symphony Orchestra, les Grands Ballets Canadiens and La Compagnie Jean-Duceppe theatrical troupe have their permanent homes here. Additional programming includes chamber music, recitals, jazz, folk singers, variety shows, a music hall, theater, musicals, and modern and classical dance.

Check website for schedule and pricing.

PLACE JACQUES-CARTIER

Between rue Notre-Dame and rue de la Commune, Montréal

Named for the 16th Century French explorer who claimed Canada for France, this Old Montréal focal point was once a busy marketplace. Today restaurants, cafés, bars and street performers are found around the plaza, which is closed to traffic. The Nelson Column at the square's north end was erected in 1808 and predates its famous namesake in London, England, by 33 years.

POINTE-À-CALLIÈRE, THE MONTRÉAL MUSEUM OF ARCHAEOLOGY AND HISTORY

350 Place Royale, Montréal, 514-872-9150; www.pacmuseum.qc.ca

Built in 1992 over the site of Montréal's original foundations, the main museum building—the Eperon—actually rests on pillars built around ruins dating to the town's first cemetery and its earliest fortifications. Visitors can see the actual ruins in the building's basement. Two balconies overlook this archaeological site and a 16-minute multimedia show is presented using the architectural remnants as backdrop. From here visitors continue underground, amid still more remnants, to the Archaeological Crypt, a structure that allows access to many more artifacts and remains. Check out the architectural models that lay beneath a transparent floor, which illustrate five different periods in the history of Place Royale. The Old Customs House Ancienne-Douane houses thematic exhibits on Montréal in the 19th and 20th centuries.

Admission: adults $15, seniors $10, students $8, children 6-12 $6, children 5 and under free. Tuesday-Friday 10 a.m.-5 p.m., Saturday-Sunday 11 a.m.-5 p.m.

RUE SAINT-PAUL

This oldest street in Montréal, found in the Ville-Marie district, was once lined with mansions. Today, those have been replaced with commercial houses and office buildings.

ST. JOSEPH'S ORATORY OF MONT ROYAL

3800 Chemin Queen Mary, Montréal, 514-733-8211; www.saint-joseph.org

The chapel was built as a tribute to St. Joseph in 1904. A larger-crypt church was completed in 1917. Today, those buildings constitute a famous shrine that attracts more than two million pilgrims yearly. A basilica with a seating capacity of 2,200 was founded in 1924. It features an outstanding dome that towers over the city and a lovely 56-bell French carillon. The Oratory's museum features 200 nativity scenes from 100 different countries.

Admission: free (parking is $5). Daily 7:45 a.m.-9 p.m.

WHERE TO STAY

MONTRÉAL

★★★AUBERGE DU VIEUX-PORT

97 rue de la Commune E., Montréal, 514-876-0081, 888-660-7678;
www.aubergeduvieuxport.com

This historic landmark building served several functions before becoming a full-service inn. Guest rooms have contemporary furnishings, loft-like exposed beams and brick walls. Narcisse Bistro and bar serves up fine, French bistro cuisine and a rooftop terrace offers a panoramic view of the St. Lawrence River. What's more, the inn's guests are pampered with a full breakfast and afternoon wine and cheese.

27 rooms. Complimentary breakfast. Restaurant, bar. $151-250

★★★CHATEAU VERSAILLES HOTEL

1659 rue Sherbrooke Ouest, Montréal, 888-933-8111, 514-933-8111;
www.chateauversaillesMontréal.com

Located at the start of Montréal's Golden Square Mile historic district and at the foot of Mont-Royal, this hotel features unique guest rooms in four renovated Victorian townhouses. The property is also just minutes by metro to the Bell Centre and the Place des Arts.

65 rooms. Complimentary breakfast. Restaurant, bar. Pets accepted. Fitness center. Business center. $151-250

★★★FAIRMONT THE QUEEN ELIZABETH

900 Blvd. Rene Levesque Ouest, Montréal, 514-861-3511, 800-441-1414;
www.fairmont.com/queenelizabeth

This contemporary hotel is located in the city center, above the train station and linked to the underground system of shops and restaurants. The hotel's Beaver Club is a favorite for its gourmet meals, whereas the convivial Mediterranean-inspired Le Montréalais Bistrot-Bar-Restaurant is a more casual spot for dinner or drinks.

1,039 rooms. Restaurant, bar. Pets accepted. Fitness center. Pool. Business center. $151-250

★★★HILTON MONTRÉAL, BONAVENTURE

900 de la Gauchetiere Ouest, Montréal, 514-878-2332, 800-267-2575; www.hiltonMontréal.com

This hotel is perched on top of the Place Bonaventure Exhibition Hall. There are rooftop gardens to explore and a year-round outdoor pool. The central city location is perfect for sightseeing in Old Montréal, gambling at the casino or shopping the underground boutiques.

395 rooms. Restaurant, bar. Pets accepted. Fitness center. Pool. Business center. $151-250

★★★HOTEL DU FORT

1390 rue du Fort, Montréal, 514-938-8333, 800-565-6333; www.hoteldufort.com

Located steps from Sainte-Catherine Street and Concordia University's downtown campus, this boutique hotel is close to the city's top attractions, shops and restaurants. Understated guest rooms offer city views and traditional furnishings in neutral tones. Room service options include menus from area restaurants.

124 rooms. Complimentary breakfast. Restaurant, bar. Business center. $61-150

★★★HOTEL GAULT

449 rue Ste. Héléne, Montréal, 514-904-1616, 866-904-1616; www.hotelgault.com

Situated on a quiet side street in Old Montréal, this zen hotel blends concrete, brick, stone and oak with mod Pantonesque pop-art furnishings—their brightness provides a bit of grooviness to the serene, loft-like lobby and guest rooms. Each of the hotel's five floors has a color scheme inspired by a particular phase of the sun's daily journey through the sky: the first floor is morning; the second is noon; the sun sets on the third floor; it's evening on the fourth; and the fifth takes its hues from dreams. The Gault's 30 rooms are divided into eight different styles ranging from the more-than-adequate Essential rooms to the uber-deluxe Loft dwellings. All rooms feature heated bathroom floors, custom oak woodwork, deluxe linens, contemporary works by emerging Canadian artists and windows that open, often onto blooming flower boxes. A complimentary 5 à 7 cocktail takes place daily in the lobby restaurant and bar, where breakfast, lunch and a table d'hote dinner is also available.

30 rooms. Restaurant, bar. Fitness room. Business center. $251-350

★★★HOTEL INTERCONTINENTAL MONTRÉAL

360 rue Ste Antoine Ouest, Montréal, 514-987-9900; www.Montréal.intercontinental.com

This sophisticated, elegant and hip hotel is located across from the Convention Center in downtown Montréal, just a short walk from the popular Old Town. Popular features of this recently renovated hotel include its Victorian-style bistro-pub Chez Plume, the Provence-style bistro Osco! and a new absinthe bar called the Sarah B after Sarah Bernhardt who performed in the old Nordheimer building that is now part of the Intercontinental. Guest rooms are comfortable and traditional with plush bedding and ample workspaces. The hotel's building houses various shops and businesses, with lodgings starting on the 10th floor.

357 rooms. Pets accepted. Restaurant, bar. Fitness center. Pool. Business center. $61-150

★★★HOTEL LE GERMAIN

2050 rue Mansfield, Montréal, 514-849-2050, 877-333-2050; www.germainmontreal.com/en

Reputed as one of Montréal's best spots for making babies, Hotel Le Germain indeed exudes a romantic "je ne sais quoi" that couples will find hard to resist. It might have something to do with the signature glass wall between the shower and the bed (blinds are provided for the more discreet). Housed in a 1960s office building just steps away from McGill University and the shops of Ste-Catherine Street, Le Germain was fully renovated in 2009. Today, its black-and-white, streamlined aesthetic takes Art Deco into the 21st Century. Made-in-Quebec is a recurring theme throughout Le Germain, from its bedding accessories and staff uniforms by Montréal designer Marie St-Pierre to its locally made deluxe duvets, pillows and mattresses. The local focus is also central to Le Germain's restaurant, Laurie Raphaël Montréal. Chef Daniel Vézina takes diners on a dazzling, entrée-sized tour of Quebec that seems to assert that there's more to the province's cuisine than poutine.

101 rooms. Complimentary breakfast. Restaurant, bar. Pets accepted. Fitness center. $251-350

★★★★HOTEL LE ST. JAMES

355 Rue Saint Jacques, Montréal, 514-841-3111, 866-841-3111;
www.hotellestjames.com

Housed in a former bank built in 1870, the stately St-James' lobby is a symphony of polished marble floors, chandeliers, dark wood paneling and objets d'art from the owner's very own collection. Le St-James' 60 units are equally stunning, featuring antique furnishings and artwork thoughtfully appointed to each individual room. Guest rooms are united, however, by features like Frette linens and Molton Brown of London bath products. The hotel's luxurious Le Spa is housed in the old bank's former vault, whose stone walls were once part of Montréal's 17th Century fortifications. The hotel's elegant restaurant, XO, seamlessly blends the bank's original rococo with streamlined modernist touches, and emphasizes local, largely organic ingredients and a wine cellar worthy of the hotel's banking roots. Topping off Le St-James' charms is a young, affable staff that treats every guest like royalty.

60 rooms. Restaurant, bar. Spa. Pets accepted. Fitness center. Business center. $351 and up

★★★HOTEL NELLIGAN

106 Rue St-Paul West, Montréal, 514-788-2040, 877-788-2040; www.hotelnelligan.com

Named after celebrated Quebec poet Émile Nelligan, this boutique hotel wrings world-class comfort from the ancient stone and brickwork of Old Montréal. Located on Rue St. Paul, Hotel Nelligan is at once an ideal base for exploring Montréal's historic old port and a cozy reprieve from its crowded streets. Relax in the refined comfort of your brick-walled suite or enjoy complimentary afternoon wine and cheese in the sunlit atrium, whose 150-year old brick walls extend up five floors. The rooftop cocktail lounge, Verses Sky, is a popular hangout where hotel guests can mingle with local hipsters and enjoy an impressive view of Notre Dame Basilica and the old port skyline. Hotel Nelligan also features two top-notch restaurants: Verses specializes in contemporary French and Quebecois cuisine, whereas Méchant Boeuf is more of a brasserie and steakhouse. Guests in need of extra pampering can enjoy an in-room massage or schedule a treatment at the Rain Spa located at the Nelligan's nearby sister hotel, the Hotel Place d'Armes.

105 rooms. Complimentary breakfast. Restaurant, bar. Fitness center. Business center. $151-250

★★★HOTEL OMNI MONT-ROYAL

1050 rue Sherbrooke Ouest, Montréal, 514-284-1110, 800-843-6664;
www.omnihotels.com

This elegant property is centrally located in the historic Golden Square Mile, in the heart of downtown and at the foot of Mont-Royal. Shops, museums, nightlife and fine dining are within walking distance. McGill University is just across the street, too. Pets are not only welcome here—they also get their own specially designed treats.

299 rooms. Restaurant, bar. Spa. Pets accepted. Fitness center. Pool. Business center. $151-250

★★★HOTEL PLACE D'ARMES

55 Saint-Jacques Ouest, Montréal, 514-842-1887, 888-450-1887; www.hotelplacedarmes.com

Located just steps from Old Montréal's centuries-old charm, this hotel emphasizes new millennium modernism—a refreshing departure from the more traditional hotels in the area. Service is polished and professional. The onsite restaurant serves a full breakfast daily so you can start your day properly.

135 rooms. Complimentary breakfast. Restaurant, bar. Spa. $251-350

★★★HOTEL ST. PAUL

355 Rue McGill, Montréal, 514-380-2222, 866-380-2202; www.hotelstpaul.com

From the outside, the stately grandeur of the Beaux-Arts Hotel St. Paul suggests its past life as a bank and as offices for the Grand Trunk Railroad. Its facade, however, masks a stark interior design that can feel a bit bleak when the lobby's pièce de résistance fireplace isn't blazing away. A modern, minimalist vibe defines St Paul's rooms and suites, whose décor varies between the themes "Sky" and "Earth." In the Sky rooms, the cloud-like palette is accentuated by sunlight from the enormous windows. Bare white walls void of any artwork direct your focus to the furnishings, which are sleek and modernist with details in silk, faux-fur, stone and metal. In the Earth rooms, browns and reds nod to the natural hues of Canada's landscape. Just off the lobby is Vauvert, which features an eclectic menu framed around local produce. Thursday through Saturday local scenesters and DJs populate Vauvert's sleek black interior. Note: the lobby and bathrooms are to undergo renovations in 2011.

120 rooms. Complimentary breakfast. Restaurant, bar. Pets accepted. Fitness center. Business center. $251-350

★★★LE SAINT SULPICE HOTEL MONTRÉAL

414 rue Saint Sulpice, Montréal, 514-288-1000, 877-785-7423; www.lesaintsulpice.com

Step back in time at this luxury hotel, located in the historic section of Montréal, just steps from the Notre-Dame Basilica and the Old Port. Sample steaks and seafood as well as regional specialties in S Le Restaurant. The Essence Health Center features beautifying treatments in addition to modern exercise equipment.

108 rooms. Complimentary breakfast. Restaurant, bar. Spa. Fitness center. $251-350

★★★LOEWS HOTEL VOGUE

1425 rue de la Montagne, Montréal, 514-285-5555, 800-465-6654; www.loewshotels.com

The fresh spirit and chic modernity of the Loews Hotel Vogue breathes new life into old-world Montréal. The accommodations provide sleek shelter with silk upholstered furnishings while creature comforts like oversized bathrooms appeal to every guest. Stop in at L'Opéra Bar, a lively after-dark gathering spot.

142 rooms. Restaurant, bar. Pets accepted. Business center. $151-250

★★★MARRIOTT MONTRÉAL CHATEAU CHAMPLAIN

1050 de la Gauchetiere Ouest, Montréal, 514-878-9000, 800-200-5909; www.marriott.com

Charming Art Nouveau décor adorns these guest rooms, not to be outdone by the glorious views of the Cathedral, Parc Mont-Royal and Old Montréal. Hospitality rules at the Mediterranean-flavored Le Samuel de Champlain restaurant, while Le Senateur Bar satisfies discriminating tastes.

611 rooms. Restaurant, bar. Fitness center. Pool. $151-250

★★★SOFITEL MONTRÉAL

1155 Rue Sherbrooke Ouest, Montréal, 514-285-9000; www.sofitel.com

Modern and elegant, this hotel is set at the foot of Parc Mont-Royal on Sherbrooke Street. Best of all, it's convenient to the galleries, museums, boutiques and the historic center of the city. Enjoy morning croissants and evening cocktails in Le Bar or dine on Provençal-inspired cuisine in Renoir.

258 rooms. Restaurant, bar. Pets accepted. Business center. Fitness center. $251-350

WHERE TO EAT

MONTRÉAL

★★★AU PIED DE COCHON

536 Ave. Duluth E., Montréal, 514-281-1114; www.restaurantaupieddecochon.ca

The "Pig's Foot" serves hearty regional cuisine with an emphasis on beef, lamb, venison, duck and, of course, pork. There are several varieties of foie gras and fish, along with local favorites like poutine. Best of all, the cozy atmosphere and historic Montréal location make for an authentic dining experience.

French. Dinner. Closed Monday. Reservations recommended. $36-85

★★★CAFE FERREIRA

1446 rue Peel, Montréal, 514-848-0988; www.ferreiracafe.com

This restaurant is one of the most stylish dining rooms in Montréal. Here, the friendly staff serves up wonderful Portuguese cuisine, with an emphasis on fresh fish and a comprehensive selection of Portuguese wines and ports.

Portuguese. Dinner. Closed Sunday. Bar. Reservations recommended. Outdoor seating. $36-85

★★★CHEZ L'EPICIER

311 rue Saint-Paul East, Montréal, 514-878-2232; www.chezlepicier.com

This cozy and informal French restaurant is perfectly situated within a late 1800s building in Old Montréal. The food is sold in an neighborly, market-style setting, and the restaurant uses fresh, local produce for its daily menu.

French. Lunch, dinner. Closed two weeks in January. Reservations recommended. $36-85

★★★CHEZ LA MERE MICHEL

1209 rue Guy, Montréal, 514-934-0473; www.chezlameremichel.com

In a city with volumes of competition, this fine French restaurant has been succeeding in its historic downtown digs since 1965. The classic and well-prepared menu includes an unbeatable strawberry Napoleon for dessert.

French. Dinner. Closed Sunday. $36-85

★★★★L'EAU A LA BOUCHE

3003 Blvd. Sainte-Adèle, Sainte-Adele, 450- 229-2991; www.leaualabouche.com

Tucked into the forests that surround the Laurentian Mountains, near the village of Sainte-Adèle, you will find L'eau à la Bouche, a charming little restaurant located on the property of the Hotel L'eau à la Bouche. The gourmet menu is built around local produce, fish, meat and homegrown herbs and vegetables, woven together and dressed up with a perfect dose of French technique and modern flair. Attentive, thoughtful service and a vast wine list make this luxurious dining experience unforgettable.

French. Breakfast, dinner. Bar. $36-85

★★★LA MAREE

404 Place Jacques Cartier, Montréal, 514-861-9794; www.restaurant.ca

Situated in Old Montréal, this romantic dining room offers classic French cuisine in an ornate Louis XIII atmosphere. The historic 1808 building is just the place to enjoy old-fashioned, formal service and a great bottle of wine from the cellar.

French. Reservations recommended. Outdoor seating. $36-85

★★★LA RAPIERE

1155 rue Metcalfe, Montréal, 514-871-8920

Southwestern French cooking with a personal touch is the draw at this sophisticated restaurant in downtown Montréal. Cassoulet, foie gras and other specialties are served in a typical country-French setting.

French. Dinner. Jacket required. Closed Sunday; also mid-July-mid-August, 15 days in December. Reservations recommended. $36-85

★★★LALOUX

250 Pine Ave. E., Montréal, 514-287-9127; www.laloux.com

One of Montréal's most appealing Parisian-style bistros, this cozy spot delivers traditional bistro fare in a crisp, white-tablecloth environment. In addition to an excellent steak frites, you can sample hearty dishes like mushroom and herb casserole or seafood risotto with leeks and spinach. Polish it all off with a classic French dessert such as chocolate pot de crème.

French. Reservations recommended. Outdoor seating. $36-85

★★★LE MAS DES OLIVIERS

1216 rue Bishop, Montréal, 514-861-6733; www.lemasdesoliviers.ca

This small, traditional French restaurant has been offering rich cuisine in a Provençal setting for more than 30 years. First, settle into the rustic room, with its white tablecloths and exposed bricks. Then dig into classic dishes like frog's legs with garlic or rack of lamb with herbs de Provence and mustard sauce.

French. Dinner. Reservations recommended. $36-85

★★★LE PIÉMONTAIS

1145 Ave. de Bullion, Montréal, 514-861-8122; www.lepiemontais.com

Experience authentic Italian cuisine at this comfortable, elegant restaurant. Fresh pastas appear on the menu nightly, from linguine to gnocchi. The wine list features bottles from the Piedmont region of Italy. Meanwhile, guests find the service prompt and professional.

Italian. Lunch, dinner. Closed Sunday; mid-July-mid-August. Reservations recommended. $36-85

★★★LE PIMENT ROUGE

1170 Peel St., Montréal, 514-866-7816; www.lepimentrouge.com

This airy, contemporary restaurant in the Windsor Hotel serves up the spicy cuisine of China's Szechuan province. Signature dishes include spicy peanut butter dumplings, a recipe the restaurant is credited with inventing in Montréal. Le Piment Rouge also stocks more than 3,000 wines.

Chinese. Dinner. $16-35

★★★LES CAPRICES DE NICOLAS

2072 rue Drummond, Montréal, 514-282-9790; www.lescaprices.com

Perfect for special occasions, this restaurant features intimate candlelight and a romantic indoor-outdoor garden. Given the classic, formal service, it's a pleasant surprise to discover that the French menu has been refreshingly updated with light, vibrant flavors and seasonal market produce. A wine list of 500 labels adds to the excitement.

French. Dinner. Jacket required. Reservations recommended. $36-85

★★★MED BAR AND GRILL

3500 Blvd. St. Laurent, Montréal, 514-844-0027; www.medgrill.com

Rub elbows with Montréal's stylish set at this see-and-be-seen spot. Here, the food is upscale but remains lively and inviting. Classic Mediterranean dishes get a modern flourish, reflecting the seasons and incorporating the region's bountiful produce.

Mediterranean. Dinner. Closed Sunday-Monday. Reservations recommended. $36-85

★★★NUANCES

1 Ave. de Casino, Montréal, 514-392-2708, 800-665-2274; www.casinosduquebec.com

Nuances is located on the fifth floor of the Montréal Casino, which occupies the landmark Pavilion of France building by noted French modernist architect Jean Faugeron. Since acquiring Executive Chef Jean-Pierre Curtat in 2000, Nuances has achieved landmark status of its own. Today, the restaurant adds notes of elegance and subtle refinements to its blinking casino environment. Chef Laurent Saget's menu marries modern and classic French cuisine, with main courses like lobster meunière with roasted calamari, coral butter emulsion and avocado cream, and Quebec lamb chops flavored with Ethiopian spices accompanied by creamy quinoa with yellow beet juice. You can also choose a three- or five-course sampling menu with a flight of wines by glass. All of Nuances' waiters are professional, certified sommeliers who can help you pick the perfect pairing from an enormous list of almost 1,400 different bottles.

French. Lunch, dinner. Closed Monday-Tuesday. Jacket required. Reservations recommended. $36-85

★★★QUEUE DE CHEVAL

1221 Blvd. Rene-Levesque Ouest, Montréal, 514-390-0090; www.queuedecheval.com

Prime, dry-aged meats are the showstoppers at Queue de Cheval, a rustic, chateau-styled steakhouse accented with rich maple woodwork and tall, vaulted ceilings. In addition, the menu features a generous raw bar, a terrific selection of salads and vegetarian appetizers as well as a fresh fish market.

Steak. Lunch, dinner. Reservations recommended. Outdoor seating. $36-85

★★★RISTORANTE DA VINCI

1180, rue Bishop, Montréal, 514-874-2001; www.davinci.ca

This charming restaurant offers an authentic atmosphere, warm, attentive service and well-prepared traditional dishes made with fresh, local ingredients. The menu includes everything from freshly prepared pasta to grilled steaks.

Italian. Dinner. Closed Sunday. Reservations recommended. Outdoor seating. $36-85

★★★★TOQUÉ!

900 Jean-Paul Riopelle Place, Montréal, 514-499-2084; www.restaurant-toque.com

From its exclamation mark to its tastefully offbeat decor, Toqué! injects a sense of French-Canadian joie de vivre to haute cuisine. The brainchild of owners Christine Lamarche and Normand Reprise, Toqué! (pronounced Toe-kay!) represents the pair's quirky genius. Main courses are French-inspired and carnivore-inclined, from suckling pig cooked sous vide to duck magret, farm-raised veal in a bordelaise sauce and cavetelli with fois gras and white truffle oil. A seven-course tasting menu is available for $92 per person. You can add a five-glass selection of wines from Toqué's impeccable cellar for an extra $60-107. If you do opt for the tasting menu, allot yourselves a good three to four hours for the whole experience, and a good few days to digest.

French. Closed Sunday-Monday; also two weeks in late December-early January. Reservations recommended. $36-85

RECOMMENDED

DOMINION SQUARE TAVERN

1243 Metcalfe Street, Montréal, 514-564-5056, www.dominiontavern.com

Opened in early 2010, the Dominion Square Tavern is still one of Montréal's best-kept secrets. Step inside the tavern's vintage 1927 interior and you'll understand why the secret is starting to get out. Original ornamental tile flooring and carved wooden crests of Canada's provinces are just a few smart details of the tavern's decor. The menu, meanwhile, features upscale versions of traditional pub fare like the Ploughman's Lunch—duck ham, pig's head terrine, rosette, vegetables, old cheddar and deviled egg. The menu also includes familiar favorites like pan-seared salmon, grilled striploin and a pulled-pork sandwich. The Dominion is also making a name for its quality old-school cocktails.

French. Lunch (Monday-Friday), dinner. Reservations recommended. $36-85

L'EXPRESS

3927 St. Denis, Montréal, 514-845-5333

L'Express is a must-stop for visitors hoping to get a little Parisian flair from Montréal. Long and narrow with mirrored walls, high ceilings, marble-topped bistro tables and a long, zinc-topped bar, L'Express attracts the who's-who of Montréal (and Hollywood, on occasion) but it still makes everyone feel at home. Its scrumptious, buttery and surprisingly cheap breakfast menu features the best scrambled eggs in town.

French. Breakfast, lunch, dinner. Reservations recommended. $16-35

WHERE TO SHOP

MONTRÉAL

AMHERST STREET

Between Sherbrooke Street and De Maisonneuve Boulevard East, Montréal

Amherst Street is Montréal's mecca for fans of mid-century modern furniture and retro home décor. The three blocks between Sherbrooke Street and de Maisonneuve Blvd East contain a number of shops—including Jack's and Cité Décor—that deal almost exclusively in Scandinavian and Italian designs from the 1940s, '50s and '60s. (Cité Décor also deals in Art Deco). While you're at it, check with Antiquités A à Z at 1840 Amherst for a great selection of distinctly Montréal antiques.

BROWNS
1191 Ste-Catherine Street West, Montréal, 514-987-1206; www.brownsshoes.com

Brown's is one of Montréal's best bets for sneakers and fancy shoes. Brands run the gamut from Adidas to Stuart Weitzman, Costume National and Manolo Blahnik. Prices are just what you'd expect from these brands, though there are usually deals to be had.

Monday-Friday 10 a.m.-9 p.m., Saturday 10 a.m.-6 p.m., Sunday noon-5 p.m.

SIMONS
977 Ste-Catherine St. West, Montréal, 514-282-1840; www.simons.ca

Simons is a Quebec institution and the place to shop in Montréal for contemporary women's and men's fashions. From its affordably priced house lines to some of the biggest names in haute couture, Simon's has something for everyone. The popular spot gets especially chaotic on weekends, but shopping addicts will find Simons well worth the trouble, especially if you happen to catch one of their incredible end-of-season sales.

Monday-Wednesday 10 a.m.-6 p.m., Thursday-Friday 10 a.m.- 9 p.m., Saturday 9:30 a.m.-5 p.m., Sunday noon-5 p.m.

QUÉBEC CITY

Nestled on a historic rampart, the provincial capital is historic, medieval and lofty, a place of stone buildings and weathered cannons, horse-drawn coaches, ancient trees and narrow, steeply angled streets. Here the historic streets provide an easy clue as to what this city looked like in Colonial days. Once known as the "Gibraltar of the North," Québec's Upper Town is built high on a cliff and surrounded by fortress-like walls. From there one of the city's best-known landmarks, Le Chateau Frontenac, towers so high it's visible from ten miles away. Meanwhile, the Lower Town section of the city surrounds Cape Diamond and spreads up the valley of the St. Charles River, a tributary of the St. Lawrence. It's worth noting that the Upper and Lower sections of the town are divided by a funicular railway, which affords magnificent views of the harbor, river and hills beyond. The most ardently French of all Canadian cities, Québec City is a place where it's not uncommon to encounter folks who don't (or won't) speak English, and who proudly stick to their Gallic ways. Best of all, its plentiful cafés and shops deliver hours of old-world distractions.

WHAT TO SEE

QUÉBEC CITY
ARTILLERY PARK NATIONAL HISTORIC SITE
2 d'Auteuil St., Québec City, 418-648-4205; www.pc.qc.ca

In the 17th century, the French started using this four-acre site as a strategic

HIGHLIGHTS

WHAT ARE QUEBEC'S CAN'T-MISS SIGHTS?

LA CITADELLE
This unique, star-shaped structure is the largest British-built fortress in North America. Today, it houses the Royal 22e Régimen (the only Francophile infantry in Canada) and the governor general of Canada. A popular museum and British-inspired military rituals are the other site's other popular draws.

MUSÉE NATIONAL DES BEAUX-ARTS DU QUÉBEC
Located on the Plains of Abraham, a historic battleground-turned-public park, this museum offers a crash course on Québécois art, everything from early religious paintings to Inuit works.

PLACE-ROYALE
Step back in time with a visit to this gorgeous plaza. Known as the birthplace of French America, the neighborhood served as the longtime center of Québec City life. The plaza languished for several decades in the early 20th century, until a restoration initiative got underway in the 1960s. Today, the area is rich with restored 18th-century hotels, churches and cafés.

post in the defense of the St. Charles River. The French starting building military fortifications shortly thereafter. Until 1871, the park housed French and British soldiers, eventually becoming a large industrial complex. Today, it serves as a national park and historic landmark.

BASILICA OF STE. ANNE-DE-BEAUPRE
10018 Royale Ave., Québec City, 418-827-3781; www.ssadb.qc.ca
This basilica is noted as the oldest pilgrimage in North America. The first chapel was built on this site in 1658. The present basilica, built in 1923, is made of white Canadian granite and is regarded as a Romanesque masterpiece, with capitals that tell the story of Jesus' life in 88 scenes and vaults, each decorated with mosaics. Unusual techniques were used to create the 240 stained-glass windows that are outlined in concrete.

GASPÉ PENINSULA
357, route de la Mer Sainte-Flavie, Québec City, 418-775-2223, 800-463-0323; www.tourisme-gaspesie.com
Jutting out into the Gulf of St. Laurent, the Gaspé Peninsula is a region with varying landforms—mountains, plateaus, beaches and cliffs. It is blessed with abundant and rare wildlife and some unique flora, including 12-foot-tall,

centuries-old fir trees. The rivers teem with trout and flow to meet the salmon coming from the sea. Called "Gespeg" meaning "land's end" by the aborigines, the area was settled primarily by Basque, Breton and Norman fishermen, whose charming villages still cling to the shore beneath the gigantic cliffs. The French influence is strong, although English is spoken in a few villages.

GRAND THEATRE

269 Blvd. Rene-Levesque, Québec City, 418-643-8131; www.grandtheatre.qc.ca

This lobby of the ultramodern theater is adorned with a giant mural by sculptor Jordi Bonet. The theater is permanent home of the Québec Symphony Orchestra and Opera. The venue also features theatrical performances and concerts.

Check website for schedule.

ÎLE D'ORLÉANS

490, côte du Pont, Saint-Pierre-de-l'Île-d'Orléans, Québec City, 418-828-9411; www.iledorleans.com

This 23-mile-long island was visited by Samuel de Champlain in 1608 and colonized in 1648. Old stone farmhouses and churches of the 18th century remain. Here the farms grow an abundance of fruits and vegetables, especially strawberries, for which the island is famous.

JEANNE D'ARC GARDEN

835 Wilfrid Laurier, Québec City, 418-649-6159

This jewel of a flower garden was created in 1938 by landscape architect Louis Perron. It combines the French Classical style with British-style flowerbeds and features more than 150 species of annuals, bulbs and perennials.

LA CITADELLE

Côte de la Citadelle, Québec City, 418-694-2815; www.lacitadelle.qc.ca

Construction on the distinctly star-shaped La Citadelle began in 1820 and continued until 1850. Built by the British but spanning the French and Canadian periods, too, the fortress formed the eastern flank of the fortifications of Québec. Check out vestiges of the French regime, such as the Cap Diamant Redoubt and a powder magazine. The site also features panoramic views of the city and 50-minute guided tours. Be sure to catch the changing of the guard (late June-early September, daily 10 a.m.), a ritual inspired by the well-known traditions of Britain. Beating the Retreat, a recreation of a 16th-century French military ceremony, takes place late July through August on Friday and Saturday evenings.

Admission: adults $10, seniors and students $9, children 7-17 $5.50, children 7 and under free. April-October, hours vary.

LAURENTIDES WILDLIFE RESERVE

Québec City, 418-686-1717; www.sepaq.com

A variety of animals including moose, wolves, bears and numerous birds can be found here. Nature-lovers can also enjoy recreational opportunities like canoeing, fishing, hunting and camping, as well as boat, ski and snowshoe rental. The reserves features 140 cabins and 134 campsites.

Late May-early September, mid-December-mid-April.

MONT-SAINTE-ANNE PARK

2000 Blvd. Beau-Pré, Beaupré, 418-827-4561; www.mont-sainte-anne.com

Take the gondola to the mountaintop—standing at 2,625 feet, the summit affords beautiful views of the St. Lawrence River. Enjoy skiing and cross-country skiing here in winter. In spring and summer, there are two 18-hole golf courses, bicycle trails and campsites. The migration of 250,000 snow geese occurs in spring and fall at nearby wildlife reserve Cap Tourmente. *Daily.*

MUSÉE DE LA CIVILISATION

85, rue Dalhousie, Québec, 418-643-2158; www.mcq.org

The entrance of this museum is decorated by La Debacle, a massive sculpture that depicts the breaking up of the ice that happens every spring. Separate exhibition halls present four permanent and several changing exhibitions that deal with the history of Québec and the French-Canadian culture, as well as the cultures of other civilizations from around the world.

Admission: adults $12, seniors $11, students $9, children 12-16 $4, children 11 and under free. Labor day-mid-June, Tuesday-Sunday 10 a.m.-5 p.m.; mid-June-Labor Day, daily 9:30 a.m.-6:30 p.m.

MUSÉE NATIONAL DES BEAUX-ARTS DU QUÉBEC

Parc des Champs-de-Bataille, Québec city, 418-643-2150; www.mnba.qc.ca

This museum features collections of ancient, modern and contemporary Québec paintings, sculpture, photography, drawings and decorative arts.

Admission: adults $15, seniors $12, students $7, children 12-17 $4, children 12 and under free. June-August, daily 9 a.m.-6 p.m., Wednesday 9 a.m.-9 p.m.; September-May, Tuesday-Sunday 9 a.m.-5 p.m., Wednesday 9 a.m.-9 p.m.

MUSEUM OF THE ROYAL 22E REGIMENT

La Citadelle, Côte de la Citadelle, Québec City, 418-694-2815; www.lacitadelle.qc.ca

While at La Citadelle, be sure to check out this site. Located in a powder magazine from 1750, flanked on both sides by massive buttresses, this museum contains replicas of old uniforms of French regiments, war trophies, 17th to 20th-century weapons and a diorama of historic battles fought by Canadians under the French. The site also includes an old military prison that contains collections of antique rifles and bayonets.

Admission: adults $10, seniors and students $9, children 7-17 $5.50, children 7 and under free. April-October, daily. Changing of the guard: mid-June-August, daily 10 a.m.

NATIONAL ASSEMBLY OF QUÉBEC

Grande-Allee and Honore-Mercier Avenue, Québec City, 418-643-7239; www.assnat.qc.ca

Take a 30-minute guided tour of Québec's Parliament Building, constructed between 1877 and 1886. Guides provide an inside peek at the proceedings of the Québec National Assembly, while explaining the building's unique, Second Empire-style architectural features.

NATIONAL BATTLEFIELDS PARK

835 Wilfrid Laurier, Québec City, 418-648-4071

This magnificent park stretches for 250 acres along the edge of a bluff that overlooks the St. Lawrence River, from Citadel to Gilmour Hill. Also called the

Plains of Abraham, the park was the site of a 1759 battle between the armies of Wolfe and Montcalm. The next year, in 1760, it saw the battle of Sainte Foy between the armies of Murray and Levis. Today, the visitor center presents a history of the Plains of Abraham from the New France period to the present. The park also features two Martello towers and many statues and monuments, as well as the Jeanne d'Arc Garden.

NOTRE-DAME DE QUÉBEC BASILICA-CATHEDRAL

20 De Buade St., Québec City, 418-694-0665; www.patrimoine-religieux.com

Built in 1923, after the original 1647 basilica burned to the ground, this richly decorated Cathedral features all manner of architectural treasure—including a sculptural bishop's throne and a sanctuary lamp given by Louis XIV. What's more, its crypt is the final resting places of various governors and bishops of Québec.

Tours: $8. Guided tours: May-early November, daily.

PLACE-ROYALE

27 Notre Dame St., Québec City, 418-646-9072; www.mcq.org

This site encompasses the earliest vestiges of French civilization in North America. Once a marketplace and the city's social center, Place-Royale was recently restored to its original, historic appearance. Visitors come to enjoy the distinctly European feel of its stone buildings, winding and narrow streets, street performers, restaurants and retail stores.

QUÉBEC AQUARIUM

1675 Ave. des Hotels, Sainte-Foy, 418-659-5264; www.sepaq.com

Overlooking the St. Lawrence River, this aquarium features an extensive collection of tropical, fresh and saltwater fish as well as marine mammals and reptiles.

Admission: adults $15.50, seniors $14.50, children 6-17 $8.25, children 3-5 $5.50, children 2 and under free. June-August, daily 10 a.m.-5 p.m.; September-May, daily 10 a.m.-4 p.m.

QUÉBEC CITY WALLS AND GATES

Encompassing Old Québec, these eighteenth-century walls and gates encircle the only fortified city in North America. It includes the Governor's Promenade and provides a scenic view of The Citadel, St. Lawrence River and the city of Levis.

ST. ANDREW'S PRESBYTERIAN CHURCH

5 Cook St., Québec City, 418-694-1347; www.standrewsquebec.ca

Serving the oldest English-speaking congregation of Scottish origin in Canada, which traces its roots to 1759, this church was built in 1810. The interior is distinguished by a long front wall with a high center pulpit, not to mention its stained-glass windows and historic plaques. The original petition to King George III asking for a "small plot of waste ground" on which to build a Scottish church is on display in the Church Vestry. A spiral stairway leads to the century-old organ.

Worship services: Sunday 10:30 a.m.

WHERE TO STAY

QUÉBEC CITY

★★★AUBERGE SAINT-ANTOINE
8, rue Saint-Antoine, Québec City, 418-692-2211, 888-692-2211; www.saint-antoine.com

Explore historic Québec City from this sleek hotel housed in a building that has been occupied since the beginning of the French colony. A cannon battery runs through the lobby. Stonewalls and wooden beams enhance the décor in this small hotel, located in the middle of Old Québec's Port District on the St. Lawrence River.

95 rooms. Restaurant, bar. Business center. $251-350

★★★FAIRMONT LE CHÂTEAU FRONTENAC
1, Rue Des Carrieres, Québec City, 418-692-3861, 800-441-1414; www.fairmont.com

Reigning over this historic walled city from its perch along the roaring St. Lawrence River is the majestic Fairmont Le Château Frontenac. Built as a classic, sprawling railway hotel at the end of the 19th century, the hotel features guest rooms decorated in a classic European style. The cavernous, wood-clad lobby is presided over by the hotel's resident canine, though the lobby is also serviced by a friendly human staff.

618 rooms. Restaurant, bar. Pool. Business center. $251-350

★★★FAIRMONT LE MANOIR RICHELIEU
181, rue Richelieu, Charlevoix, 418-665-3703, 800-441-1414; www.fairmont.com

Located east of Québec City in the heart of Québec's scenic Charlevoix countryside, this majestic, castle-like hotel welcomes visitors with historic charm and world-class sophistication. Guest rooms and suites have a classic country appeal, but they're stocked with modern amenities like plush bed linens and marble bathrooms.

405 rooms. Restaurant, bar. Pool. Business center. $251-350

★★★HILTON QUÉBEC
1100 Rene Levesque East, Québec City, 418-647-2411; www.hilton.com

Located next to the Congress Centre, just a ten-minute walk from Old Town, the Hilton is extra convenient for business travelers and families. After a busy day of sightseeing, enjoy the cuisine and modern art at the hotel's Allegro Restaurant.

571 rooms. Restaurant, bar. Pets accepted. Pool. Business center. $151-250

★★★HÔTEL LE GERMAIN-DOMINION
126, rue Saint-Pierre, Québec City, 418-692-2224, 888-833-5253; www.hoteldominion.com

Old Québec is considered the cradle of French culture in North America, and the centrally located Hôtel Le Germain-Dominion is a wonderful base from which to explore it. This small, sleek hotel takes full advantage of the early 20th-century building's historic architectural features while providing updated, contemporary guest rooms with down-duvet topped beds.

60 rooms. Restaurant, bar. Fitness center. Pets accepted. $151-250

★★★LOEWS HÔTEL LE CONCORDE
1225 Cours du General De Montcalm, Québec City, 418-647-2222, 800-463-5256;
www.loewshotels.com

See a vision of Paris out the window from this hotel, which is perched along Québec City's version of the Champs-Elysees. Located just 15 minutes from the airport, the hotel features views of the St. Lawrence River, the city lights and the historic Plains of Abraham. No visit is complete without a peek, and hopefully a meal, at L'Astral, the revolving rooftop restaurant.

404 rooms. Restaurant, bar. Pets accepted. Pool. Business center. $61-150

RECOMMMENDED

CHATEAU LAURIER HOTEL
1220 Georges 5th Ouest, Québec City, 418-522-8108, 800-463-4453; www.old-quebec.com

Located in the heart of Old Quebec, this hotel is convenient to all manner of attractions, such as Grande Allée Street, and the Plains of Abraham. Choose between economical "European-style" rooms, the slightly more spacious standard rooms or the contemporary-styled superior rooms, located in the hotel's luxurious, new wing.

57 rooms. Restaurant, bar. $61-150

WHERE TO EAT

QUÉBEC CITY
★★★L'ASTRAL
Loews Hôtel Le Concorde, 1225 cours du General de Montcalm, Québec City, 418-647-2222;
www.loewshotels.com

Each turn of this rotating rooftop restaurant takes 90 minutes, which is plenty of time to enjoy its fine cuisine and the spectacular panoramic views of Québec City. The menu features an array of contemporary, seasonally driven recipes, including roasted Cornish hen with kalamata olives and grapes, and grilled salmon with sweet corn foam.

French. Breakfast, lunch, dinner. Reservations recommended. $36-85

★★★LAURIE RAPHAËL
117 Dalhousie St., Québec City, 418 692 4555; www.laurieraphael.com

Owners Daniel Vézina and Suzanne Gagnon named this popular restaurant for their children. Fittingly, they configured their friendly business to focus on simple, gourmet fusions like Jerusalem artichoke blinis with Abitibi sturgeon egg cream. The impressive wine cellar includes bottles from a broad range of countries.

French. Dinner. Reservations recommended. $36-85

★★★LE CONTINENTAL
26, rue Ste. Louis, Québec City, 418-694-9995; www.restaurantlecontinental.com

Deep colors and polished oak define the European atmosphere at this fine dining restaurant, located in Upper Québec. Order one of the flambé specialties for a unique tableside show. The remainder of the menu is filled with grilled steak and seafood options, and a solid list of French bottles makes up the wine list.

French. Dinner. $36-85

★★★LE SAINT-AMOUR

48, rue Ste. Ursule, Québec City, 418-694-0667; www.saint-amour.com

Family-owned and operated since opening in Old Québec in 1978, this charming restaurant is removed from the bustle of the tourist beat. Fresh, local ingredients are the highlight here. Meanwhile, the vast wine room houses more than 12,000 bottles.

French. Outdoor seating. $36-85

★★★MONTE CRISTO L'ORIGINAL

3400 Chemin Ste. Foy, Québec City, 418-653-5221; www.chateaubonneentente.com

At this relaxed yet modern restaurant, guests are treated to original Québec cooking that emphasizes local ingredients. Both the décor and the menu are contemporary, with dishes such as polenta with pea purée and duck tartare with wasabi.

French. Breakfast, lunch, dinner. $36-85

★★★★RESTAURANT INITIALE

54, rue Saint-Pierre, Québec City, 418-694-1818; www.restaurantinitiale.com

This modern French restaurant is located in a former bank, located just one block from the St. Lawrence River in the Old Port district. Country products from local producers give way to seasonal menus of fresh, pure flavors. Service is crisp and professional, and the staff can aptly recommend an appropriate wine from the lengthy list.

French. Lunch (Tuesday-Friday), dinner. Closed Sunday-Monday; also first two weeks in January. Reservations recommended. $36-85

INDEX

O

CONNECTICUT, MASSACHUSETTS AND

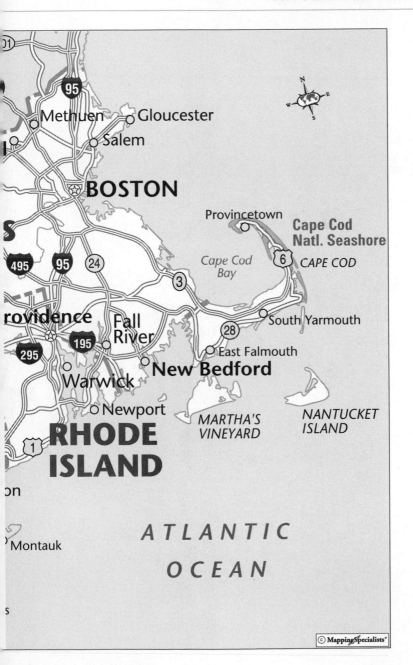

QUÉBEC

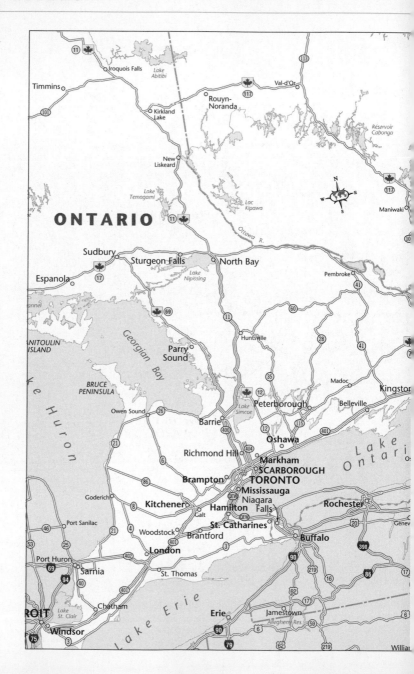

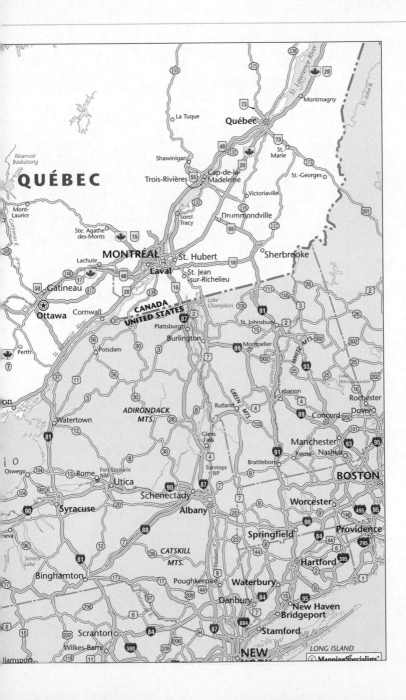

MAINE

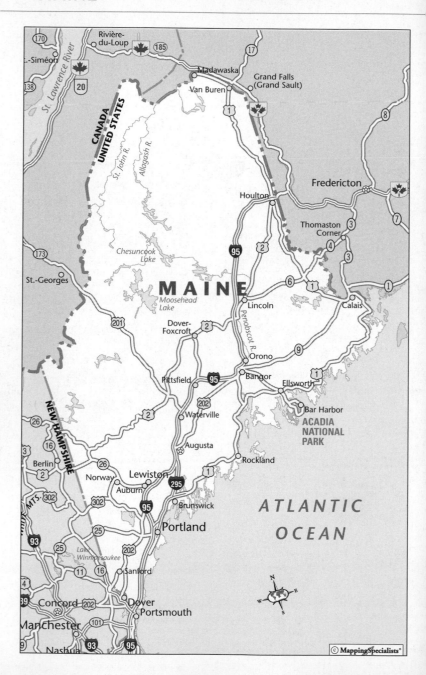

NEW HAMPSHIRE AND VERMONT

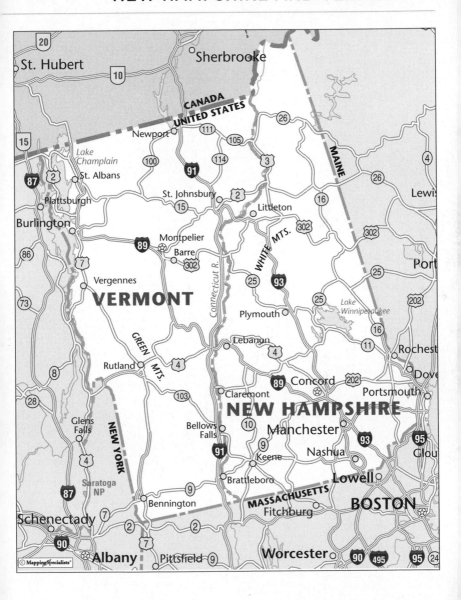

NOTES